Websters' First New
INTERGALACTIC
WICKEDARY
of the English Language

Websters' *Intergalactic Seal of Approval*

Websters' First New INTERGALACTIC WICKEDARY of the English Language

CONJURED BY MARY DALY

. . . IN CAHOOTS WITH JANE CAPUTI

BEACON PRESS · BOSTON

Beacon Press
25 Beacon Street
Boston, Massachusetts 02108

Beacon Press books
are published under the auspices of
the Unitarian Universalist Association of Congregations.

PRINTED IN THE UNITED STATES OF AMERICA

94 93 92 91 90 89 88 87   8 7 6 5 4 3 2 1

Text design by Ann Schroeder

Library of Congress Cataloging-in-Publication Data
Daly, Mary.
   Websters' first new intergalactic wickedary
of the English language.
   Bibliography: p.
   1. Feminism—Dictionaries.   2. Social ethics—
Dictionaries.   I. Caputi, Jane.   II. Title.
HQ1115.D34 1987   305.4'2'0321   87-1133
ISBN 0-8070-6706-7
ISBN 0-8070-6733-4 (pbk.)

In Metamemory of
Andrée Collard
true lover of the Wild

and
to the myriads
of Hopping Hoping women
and Other creatures
who continue to carry on

CONTENTS

THE FIRST PHASE

Preliminary Webs

WOVEN BY MARY DALY

THE SECOND PHASE

The Core of The Wickedary: Word-Webs

WOVEN BY MARY DALY
AND JANE CAPUTI

LIST OF ILLUSTRATIONS

PREFACE

The full title of this work is *Websters' First New Intergalactic Wickedary of the English Language*. The word *webster,* according to *Webster's Third New International Dictionary of the English Language,** is derived from the Old English *webbestre,* meaning female weaver.[1] The *Oxford English Dictionary* defines *webster* as "a weaver, as the designation of a woman." According to the *Wickedary, Webster* means "a woman whose occupation is to Weave, esp. a Weaver of Words and Word-Webs."

The word *Wickedary,* according to the Present work, is defined as *"Archaic:* Wicked/Wiccen dictionary; dictionary for Wicked/Wiccen women; Metamysterious Web-Work Spun by Websters." The adjective *wicked,* according to the *American Heritage Dictionary of the English Language,* can be traced to the same Indo-European root (*weik-*) as *wicce,* the Old English word meaning Witch. According to the *Wickedary, Wicked* means "beyond patriarchal 'good' and 'evil'; characterized by Original Integrity; Originally Sinful; actively participating in the Unfolding of Be-ing as Good."

The Weaving of the *Wickedary* is an Originally Sinful Act,[†] for it questions and challenges the old saws/laws of the Lecherous State. It springs from the Original be-ing of women, from which patriarchal religion attempts to "save" us, but which is inherently Untouchable, Inviolate, and Wild. The *Wickedary,* then, is a dictionary for Witches.

The *Wickedary* is a Metadictionary, that is, a "Metapatriarchal dictionary, written by and for Wicked/Wiccen Websters; dictionary that Gossips out the Elemental webs of words hidden in patriarchal diction-

---

* Hereafter, the *Wickedary* refers to that work simply as *Webster's.*
† See **Originally Sinful Acts** (*Word-Web One*). Readers are invited to look up this word and other Strange words in *The Second Phase* of the *Wickedary,* where they can be found in their appropriate Word-Webs.

WEBSTER: *Unwinding the bindings of mummified/numbified words*

aries and other re-sources." Thus the *Wickedary* is an entirely New Work. At the same Time, it is Ancient/Archaic.*

Many of the words contained in this book were Dis-covered in my earlier Word-Works.[2] Some of the Weaving was begun in my conversations with Cronies, especially during the past two decades, that is, since about 1968 A.F. (Archaic Future).[3]

The idea of the *Wickedary* itself first occurred to me in Leverett, Massachusetts in 1982, when I was immersed in the process of writing *Pure Lust*. Indeed, it began to appear in the pages of that work, as the astute reader has noticed. After I completed that book, I decided to bring the *Wickedary* into material existence and invited Jane Caputi to work on this Wicked project. In 1984 she joined me in Hammering out the general plan of this Work, and the adventurous Journey was well under way.

The creation of the Word-Webs in the Core of the *Wickedary* was an especially Strange and demanding task, impelling us to find peculiar solutions to the problems (metaproblems) that it posed. Many of the words had appeared in my Other books, but a large number of them were not simply defined but were explained at length in the context, or else by the context. The project of defining these words in *Wickedary* form, of Dis-covering many Other New Words, and of working out a system of classification was a strenuous and genuinely New creative endeavor. Since we were not unambitious, we added to a number of these definitions "Canny Comments," "Cockaludicrous Comments," and examples from various Sources. Many of these comments and examples were contributed by the Wild Hag Diana Beguine, who Searched them out in Weird places.

As I first wrote the Preliminary Webs and the Appendicular Webs, Jane and I brainstormed about the Wild Ideas contained therein and about the patterns of their flight. This Spinning/Working together was an inherent part of the *Wickedary*'s Journey.

Naturally, Animals and Other Wild Messengers joined us on this Intergalactic Journey. There were frequent visits from Divining Familiars,[†] including Gaggles of Wild geese, ducks, sea gulls, toads, squirrels, cardinals (the Elemental kind), and a special spider who said her Name was Sarah. These animals all appeared at Strange Times of synchronicity, urging the Work on. The trees, the moon, and the stars shining on Crystal Lake gave immeasurable inspiration. A constant com-

---

* For an explanation of the Archaic History of the *Wickedary*, see *Preliminary Web One*.
† For more on Divining Familiars, see *Preliminary Web Five*.

panion throughout the trip has been my Domestic Familiar, a Furry/ Grimalkin known as Ms. Wild Cat, who has sat faithfully on diction- aries, dipping her tail into cups of coffee, and Cat/atonically encourag- ing the work.

Emily Culpepper contributed Canny criticisms and comments as we carefully scrutinized the manuscript together prior to publication. Nancy Kelly Gossiped Out snoolish oldspaper clippings and Gooney News items as well; she also galley-slaved with Fanatic zeal. Nilah Mac- Donald Prudishly proofread and contributed many Shrewd sugges- tions. Charlotte Cecil Raymond acted as a Wise and Witch-Crafty *Wickedary* agent. The helpful and expert copy editor was Barbara Flanagan. Marge Roberson generously provided skillful assistance in the preparation of the manuscript. I wish to express my deep gratitude to all of these Wicked workers.

The Conjuring of the *Wickedary* was stunningly enhanced by the A-mazing illustrations by Sudie Rakusin, who understood the Spirit of this Work instantly and instinctively. She was able to bring many In- habitants of the Background vividly into Sight. These Muse, Race, Dance, and Hop off the pages, Acting as Wicked Guides that inspire us to Journey ever further.

The Scheme/Skein of the Wickedary

The design, or scheme, of the *Wickedary* can be Seen/Heard as a skein. As *Webster's* explains, *skein* means "a loosely coiled length of yarn or thread." It also means "something suggesting the twistings and contor- tions of a skein," and it means "a flock of wild fowl (as geese or ducks) in flight." The Labyrinthine design of the *Wickedary* may appear twisted and contorted to those accustomed only to linear patterns such as graphs and charts. In fact, its order is organic and purposeful, and it can be compared to a flock of Wild fowl in flight.

Websters Hear/Know words as birds—often in flight, sometimes at rest on the earth, in trees, or in the water (as geese in gaggles). Conse- quently, this is a Book of Augury. An Augur is a Soothsayer, "said to mean a diviner by the flight and cries of birds" (Walter W. Skeat, *A Concise Etymological Dictionary of the English Language*). The flight and cries of words/birds help us to Divine the way through the Labyrin- thine passages which are the true pathways of the Metapatriarchal Jour- ney of Exorcism and Ecstasy.[4] They also awaken the *Labyrinth* of the reader/hearer, that is, "the internal ear" (*Webster's*), which Websters understand to be the Elemental capacity for Hearing our way into and through these passages of the Background—the Wild reality hidden by the falsehoods of the patriarchal foreground.[5]

As Websters weave our ways on Labyrinthine Journeys, words come alive, and we weave and reweave their messages in Webs/Tapestries that depict their true context, their Background. In our weavings we follow the flights of words, which carry messages, hop, fly, soar, and sing. Like birds, words are winged. Moreover, they are ancestral spirits, awakening Memory. They can also be compared to Angels, messengers of the Goddess/es. The *Wickedary* is a Source Book of such messages.

The Phases of the Wickedary

The work of the *Wickedary* moves through three Phases. In *The First Phase* I have Woven special articles, or Preliminary Webs. These Strangely resemble and differ from the preliminary essays found in a normal patriarchal dictionary (dick-tionary). Thus the *Wickedary* has Preliminary Webs on the History/Metamystery of the work, Spelling, Grammar, Pronunciation, and Guides. All of these subjects, however, take on very different meanings in this context, for in the Tapestries of the *Wickedary* they come ALIVE. For example, Spelling is about the casting of Spells, and Guides are not mere banal guidelines, but, rather, vivacious spirited creatures. Thus elephants, cats, owls, Gnomes, Undines, and Sylphs guide the reader through Labyrinthine Wicked Ways.*

This Strange resemblance to and difference from the meanings of special article titles in ordinary dictionaries results from Dis-covering the magical powers of words as Labryses, or double axes wielded by Wild, Wicked women. While noting the banal definitions of such words as *pronunciation*, for example, Websters choose to Overlook† these and, forgoing the State of Boredom, to Re-member and wield deeper, more exciting meanings.

The Second Phase of this work conjures the Chorus of Wild Racing Words. The Race of Wild Words, like the Race of Wild Women, naturally gathers in tribes. Websters Dis-cover three major tribes of words, and consequently we find it appropriate to weave three large interconnecting Word-Webs, or Tapestries.‡ These constitute the Core or Center of the *Wickedary*.

---

* For example, Ways of thinking, Ways of sensing, Ways of traveling, Ways of connecting, Ways of daring, Ways of Re-membering.

† According to *Webster's*, one definition of *overlook* is "to look on with the evil eye: bewitch by looking on." Be-Witching Websters learn to Overlook the banal and/or negative definitions of words by Be-Speaking these words in ways that release their positive, Biophilic meanings.

‡ The parts of the Core, as well as all the parts of the *Wickedary*, can appropriately be Named "Webs" as well as "Tapestries." According to *Webster's*, the first meaning of *web* is "a fabric as it is being woven on a loom or as it appears when removed

Word-Web One of the Core consists of Elemental philosophical words and phrases and Other key words which are major clues to the Ways of the Labyrinthine Journey. These can help Websters make complex, ecstatic leaps further into the Background and exorcise the demon-wardens who try to prevent this Journeying. A *clue* (or *clew*) is "a ball of yarn or thread. . . . the ball of thread used by Theseus as a guide through the labyrinth of Minos on Crete" (*American Heritage*). The clues of *Word-Web One* are important balls of thread, i.e., words which, when snatched by Websters, enable us to weave our ways on many complex routes, Dis-covering other clues along the way. Indeed, our constant yet always startling experience is that one clue/word always leads to another.

It may not be possible to grasp all of these major clues immediately. Hence, excursions into the Other Word-Webs of the Core are advisable, for they can inspire renewed vitality for re-turning to *Word-Web One* as well as for moving on. Hence the jumping creatures, such as kangaroos and grasshoppers, join the rabbits, squirrels, and toads in urging such excursions. They point out that *Word-Webs Two* and *Three* of the Core also contain significant clues. "Catch a clue and swing!" advise the spiders. "Hop, skip, and jump!" croak the frogs.*

Following such arachnidian and amphibian advice, Journeyers through the *Wickedary* explore *Word-Web Two* and there Dis-cover the Inhabitants of the Background, such as Grimalkins and Gorgons, ob-serving and participating in their activities and characteristics. Swing-ing ahead into *Word-Web Three,* Travelers Realize that here we are view-ing the foreground from the perspective of the Background, that is, studying snools and their colleagues, their characteristics, behaviors, and products. Our observations in the various Word-Webs cause us sometimes to jump with joy, sometimes to wail with grief, often to howl with Rage, and even/ever more frequently to roar and roll around in spasms of uncontrollable Laughter.

Such Laughter is an expression of *exaltation,* which means "a flight of larks" (*American Heritage*). Larking women follow the flights and songs of melodious Archaic words/birds. Thus enspirited we join their

---

from a loom (a web of lace)." Thus the word *Web* can convey that this work is not completed/finished—that it is always in process. (Clearly, our Elemental associa-tion with spiders is also implied.) At the same Time, there is a certain sense of completion, and therefore the word *Tapestry* also applies. This tension between in-completion and completion, characteristic of a work which is truly *alive,* can be explained through the application of another Metaphor: "creative crystalizing." See Mary Daly, *Gyn/Ecology: The Metaethics of Radical Feminism* (Boston: Beacon Press, 1978), pp. 22–23.

* See *Preliminary Web Five.*

Chorus. The word *chorus,* derived from the Latin word meaning "ring dance, dance accompanied with singing, group of dancers and singers," carries messages concerning the activities of Wicked women. Our Original Chorusing is significantly Other than the wretched refrains and dull chorus lines of clonedom. Singing Websters Muse in harmony with the Music of the Spheres. Dancing Spinsters Prance, making the large and complex steps required for Macroevolution. The style of our Motion/E-motion is that of Nags who spring, caper, frisk, frolic, cavort, romp, gambol, and gallop into our own Original Time/Space.

Our Prancing sometimes becomes Soaring. Soaring beyond the Core, Journeyers reach *The Third Phase* of the *Wickedary.* Here I have woven four Deliberately Delirious essays designed to assist Wicked women to stray and stay off the tracks of trained responses and traditional expectations. These Delirious essays, or Wanton Webs, are essential to the Tapestry of the *Wickedary.* Unlike the Preliminary Webs of *The First Phase,* these weavings do not resemble/dissemble the format of normal patriarchal dictionaries in any respect. They simply Spin Off from the Core, in a Bio-logical manner. Thus they can be called appendices, or Appendicular Webs, since they are important appendages—derivative but not unessential parts of the *Wickedary's* Wicked design.

The first of these Wanton Webs is a complex exposé of snool-made terms and phrases, hereafter known as elementary terms and phrases. These are characterized by artificiality, lack of depth, of aura, of interconnectedness with living be-ing. Since elementary terms fall/fail into several classes, *Appendicular Web One* consists of several parts, or Weblets. The organic structure of these Weblets is due entirely to the Elemental knowledge of Websters, and not at all to any vital signs in these necrophilic terms themselves. These are inherently dead and therefore boring. However, the process of Seeing Through them is of great interest to Searchers, who find stimulation in exposing simulations. In particular this exercise stimulates/activates the Virtue of Disgust.

Appendicular Web Two, on the subject of Be-Laughing, is an exercise in Elemental Humor. Here Howling Hags practice the Virtue of Laughing Out Loud. After Nixing the drooling of fools and the droning of clones, we move on to Hexing and X-ing, Spinning the Stamina needed to reach *Appendicular Webs Three* and *Four.* Arriving at these, Wonderlusting Wanderers Spin beyond the compasses and jump off the clocks that have kept us in line, locked up in the prisons of fathered time. Encouraged by dolphins and whales, we learn to trust our own Sense of Direction and Timing.

Joined by the Guides who have brought us this far, we prepare for the awesome arrival of Others. Reaching the end of the *Wickedary* is arriving at the beginning, for the work of Wicked Schemers/Skeiners continues. Our Wording Spirals on. Indeed, our project is Intergalactic, for it is an expression of Star-Lust, of seeking and finding Astral dimensions, Cosmic connections.

For such an Astral Adventure, standard english is pathetically inadequate, and even Wicked English is far from sufficient. Websters therefore invite Wild women of other tribes and tongues to weave their own Wickedaries.* We conjoin in the Conjuring of these Other Weird works—not as copies or clones but as Sister Word-Works expressing the Rainbow-Radiant Diversity of Hags, Nags, Furies, Spinsters whose different Mother Tongues can speak of Wonders yet unNamed. May this book be a catalyst, then, for such Other Wicked Dreams.

Preface

Mary Daly
Newton Centre, Massachusetts
Summer Solstice, 1987

*Of course, these will not be called *Wickedaries,* but will have their own untranslatable titles. A superb example of how this can happen is the New Intergalactic German Word *Hexikon,* Dis-covered by Erika Wisselinck, literally meaning Witches' Lexicon. See her translation of *Pure Lust—Reine Lust: Elemental-feministische Philosophie* (Munich: Verlag Frauenoffensive, 1986).

EXPLANATORY NOTES

A few explanatory notes concerning matters of style are in order. These will be brief, for it is not in keeping with Wicked Style to go on and on about such things.

Capitalization

Capitalization of words and phrases defined in the *Wickedary* is capitally irregular, conforming to meaning rather than to standard usage.* Many entries Strangely begin with an uppercase letter. Words wear capital letters for a variety of reasons. First, this can indicate that they Name Background realities. Background-Naming Words are among those to be found in *Word-Web One* (for example, *Metamemory*), and all *Word-Web Two* words Name Background reality (for instance, *Hag; Third Eye*). Second, capitalization is sometimes intended to distinguish *Wickedary* words from standard english words and phrases. For example, *Boredom* (*Word-Web Three*) does not designate merely a feeling of ennui (boredom), but rather "the official/officious state produced by bores," that is, patriarchy. Again, *State of Depression* Names not merely a mood, but the society which generates this condition. Third, Websters sometimes even capitalize words Naming foreground fabrications simply for emphasis, for example, *Terrible Taboo; Trinity, Most Unholy* (*Word-Web One*). Fourth, words Naming inhabitants of the foreground

---

* Even this general rule is irregularly followed, for proper names (e.g., geographical names) and proper adjectives are usually capitalized according to convention. This apparent conventionality is due to the unconventional unwillingness of unruly Websters to bore ourSelves with unnecessary rule-making. It should be noted, however, that there are exceptions to such conventionality in the matter of proper names. See, for example, **tom, dick, and harry** (*Word-Web Three*).

and their products are sometimes capitalized to express Be-Laughing irony and humor. Some examples of this are *Bearded Brother No-it-alls; Yahweh & Son; Stag-nation* (*Word-Web Three*).

Many entries begin with a lowercase letter. Careful readers will note that most of these are in *Word-Web Three* of the Core, although some are found in *Word-Web One*.* Lowercase usually indicates that the words Name foreground inhabitants or their characteristics, activities, or products.

Explanatory NotesOne unique exception is the verb *be-ing*, meaning "actual participation in the Ultimate/Intimate Reality—Be-ing, the Verb." The verb *be-ing* clearly designates Background reality. The purpose of the lowercase is to distinguish such finite participation from the Reality designated by *Be-ing*, the constantly Unfolding Verb of Verbs—the Verb from whom, in whom, and with whom all true movements move.

Pronouns and Nouns

The pronoun *we* usually does not refer only to the Wickedarians whose Names appear on the title page. It is a Wicked *we*, including Other Inhabitants of the Background who have been Present to the Weaving of this work. Similarly such nouns as *Wickedarians, Websters, Journeyers, Be-Spellers* expand to include many, many Boon Companions who are the Network of Elemental Presences who make this sort of Qualitative Leaping possible.

The Meta-etymologies of the Wickedary

As a Metadictionary, the *Wickedary* Dis-covers webs of words that are hidden in patriarchal dictionaries and other re-sources. Websters per-

---

* As we have seen in the *Preface*, the Race of Wild Words naturally gathers in tribes. Some of those that weave their way into *Word-Web One* (which consists of key words) Name Background reality and some Name foreground counterfeits of that Wild reality, viewed from the perspective of the Background. Thus some of the words in *Word-Web One* are more closely allied to the words of *Word-Web Two* (which introduces Background Inhabitants), while others are more closely related to those inhabiting *Word-Web Three* (which Names foreground inhabitants). The fact that most *Wickedary* words are not in *Word-Web One* does not mean that they are second-class citizens. Such a foreground perspective is alien to their ways of be-ing. From a Wicked perspective it is clear that words flock together Crone-logically. All Wicked words are Guide Words, acting as Guides for Searchers on Wild word chases. All lead to Other words, opening doors to further magic meanings. They all have their own Ways, some of which can be glimpsed by word-chasing Searchers.

ceive that these derivative "sources," which are passed off in academentia as authoritative and original, contain fragments of and clues to our
own stolen heritage.

Given this situation, it is Crone-logical that our etymologies—the
bracketed material preceding some, but not all, definitions—must be
meta-etymologies. They are *meta-** in relation to ordinary etymologies
in the following senses: (1) They are being Dis-closed by Websters
after, or later than, patriarchal dictionary etymologies. That is, chrono-
logically speaking, they occur later.[†] (2) Meta-etymologies are situated
behind, or in the Background of, the ordinary etymologies. (3) They
transform the meanings of these etymologies, wrenching them out of
their old contexts and making them visible and audible in a New/Ar-
chaic context. Meta-etymologies move beyond and transcend the usual
etymologies.

The meta-etymologies of the *Wickedary* are of various types. The
first kind are those containing material that is presented in etymologies
in ordinary patriarchal dictionaries.[‡] In selecting such material, Websters strive for precision and accuracy, while carefully choosing information that is most enlightening. What makes such a selected etymology a meta-etymology is the illuminating Crone-logical context in
which it is presented in the *Wickedary*. An example is the meta-etymology of *fool* (in *Word-Web Three*), which is, in part: "[derived fr. L *follis*
bellows, bag, akin to Gk *phallos* penis (found at *blow*)—*Webster's* . . .]."
In order to Dis-cover the hidden connection between *fool* and *phallos*
Websters were obliged to seek and find the connection between the
Latin *follis* and the Greek *phallos* under the word *blow*. Both the *Wickedary* definition of *fool* and *Appendicular Web Two* (on Be-Laughing) pro-
vide a context in which this information can be appreciated.

The second type of meta-etymology is a common patriarchal dictionary's standard english definition taken as a re-source for a *Wickedary* definition. An example is the meta-etymology of *Glamour* (in *Word-
Web Two*), which is "['a magic spell: BEWITCHMENT'—*Webster's*]." This
information provides a context for Websters weaving Wild definitions
of *Glamour,* such as "an Archimagical Spell by which Nixing Nags dispel phallic pseudopresence/absence." A variation on the model of this

---

*The meanings of the prefix *meta-,* all applicable here, are, according to *Webster's,*
"occurring later," "situated behind," "change in, transformation of," and "beyond,
transcending."
†This chronological order pertains to time constricted by the barriers of patriarchal
limitations. Crone-logically speaking, and in the Realms of Archaic Time/Tidal
Time, meta-etymologies have priority.
‡Sometimes this etymological material is drawn from more than one dictionary. In
such cases all of the re-sources are carefully acknowledged.

second type occurs when a standard dictionary definition is taken over and awarded "*Websters'* Intergalactic Seal of Approval." For example, we find the Approved definition/meta-etymology of *Virago* taken from *Webster's:* "['a loud overbearing woman: SHREW, TERMAGANT . . .']." The words of *Webster's* definition, of course, take on New/Archaic meaning when Heard within the context of *Websters' First New Intergalactic Wickedary of the English Language.*

Explanatory Notes

The third type of meta-etymology is a combination of one or more patriarchal dictionary etymologies with one or more patriarchal dictionary definitions. See **Dragon** (*Word-Web Two*) or **bull, papal** (*Word-Web Three*).* Here it is the context provided by the *Wickedary* definitions as well as the general context of this Wicked Work that makes possible a transformation in the reader's understanding of this material.

The *Wickedary* contains a few meta-etymologies which have as their re-sources works which are not dictionaries. Two stunning examples of such re-sources are Thomas Aquinas, *Summa theologiae* (see **Passion, Pyrogenetic** in *Word-Web Two*), and Marabel Morgan, *The Total Woman* (see **totaled woman** in *Word-Web Three*).

In meta-etymologies, the *Wickedary* conforms to the style (abbreviations, capitalizations, punctuation, etc.) of the dictionaries or other works cited.

Throughout this work, the following abbreviations are used to refer to the most commonly cited dictionaries: *American Heritage,* for *The American Heritage Dictionary of the English Language; O.E.D.,* for *The Oxford English Dictionary; Skeat's,* for Walter W. Skeat, *A Concise Etymological Dictionary of the English Language; Webster's,* for *Webster's Third New International Dictionary of the English Language; Webster's Collegiate,* for *Webster's New Collegiate Dictionary.*

Cross-referencing

For purposes of cross-referencing within the Core, the abbreviations w-w 1, w-w 2, and w-w 3 are employed to refer to *Word-Web One, Word-Web Two,* and *Word-Web Three* of the Core. At the end of a definition, readers are often invited to "See" or "Compare" another *Wickedary* word. *See* generally refers the reader to synonyms or to words which give further relevant information. *Compare* refers the Searcher to ant-

---

*In these cases, the entire meta-etymology is contained within brackets. The part which is a citation of ordinary dictionary etymologies is contained within parentheses, in order to distinguish and separate this from the dictionary definition.

onyms. In cases where cross-referenced words are to be found in the same Word-Web, these are always noted first.

System of Symbols (●, ◑, ◐, ○)

The system of symbols employed in the Word-Webs to signify the works by Mary Daly in which *Wickedary* words first appeared is explained at the beginning of *Word-Web One*, pp. 59–60.

Explanatory Notes

Conclusion

Just about enough has been said now concerning matters of "style." Canny readers will be quick to comprehend the Crone-logical arrangement of the *Wickedary*. Weird Searchers of this work will find its Wicked system Sylph-explanatory.

THE FIRST PHASE | *Preliminary Webs*

WOVEN BY MARY DALY

PRELIMINARY WEB ONE

The Wickedary:
Its History/Metamystery

The work of the *Wickedary* is a process of freeing words from the cages and prisons of patriarchal patterns. Under the rule of snools, words are beaten down, banalized, reduced to serving the sentences of father time. They are made into ladies-in-waiting, wasted and worn in the service of thought-stopping grammar.

Websters unwind the bindings of mummified/numbified words. This process involves Hearing/Speaking through Other Time/Space. It implies unwinding the clocks of fathered time, which is tidy time. The Timing of the *Wickedary* deliberately counters the death march of patriarchal deadtime.

Websters Weave the *Wickedary* in the Thirteenth Hour. This Time is Moon-measured, Moon-Wise, beyond the reach of man-measured doomsday clocks,* the tedious timers and ticking time bombs of clockocracy. It is the Time of Crone-logical innovation/creation.

The *Wickedary* is a declaration that words and women have served the fathers' sentences long enough. Websters ride the rhythms of Tidal Time, freeing words. Like birds uncaged, these Soundings rush and soar, seeking sister-vibrations. *Wickedary* words, when Heard, sound the signal that Tidal Time has come.

* See **doomsday clock** (*Word-Web Three*).

The Archaic History of the Wickedary

In a Weird sense, these Wicked Weavings originated some immeasurable Time ago.[1] Indeed, the *Wickedary*'s origins are Archaic. They are whenever/wherever women first began/begin Be-Speaking. The *Wickedary*'s background is the Background.

PRELIMINARY
WEB ONE

Many of the *Wickedary*'s threads were Originally caught in ordinary patriarchal dictionaries such as the *Oxford English Dictionary, American Heritage Dictionary,* and, of course, *Webster's.* This has been possible and continues to be possible because such lexicons themselves contain countless hidden Webs. Websters/Wickedarians are familiar with the experience of "chasing through the dictionary," that is, of catching the thread of a word and following it (for example, by checking out synonyms, looking up words contained in the definition, following clues in the etymology, or simply lighting upon another word on the page, for instance, a Guide Word). This following and chasing of words is a process of tracing a hidden Web and then Webs of Webs, threading/treading the way/ways through the Labyrinth of words buried in dictionaries.

Websters are aided in the Dis-covering of Webs in dictionaries by the fact that these lexicons still contain "archaic" and "obsolete" words and definitions. Our Web-finding is aided also by the fact that there are deep resonances even in currently used words, which carry in their wake ancestral Memories of hidden Elemental meanings. Such words—in contrast to mere elementary terms—can be Deeply Heard by those whose Labyrinthine Sense has been awakened. That is, they can be Heard/Understood by the Internal Ear of a Wicked Webster—one who actively chooses her own Wildness. They can be Seen by a Spinster who chooses to Realize her Self and her own kind, that is, to See with Real Eyes.[2]

Wickedarians believe that one reason we can Dis-cover Webs of Wild Words in the ordinary dictionaries of patriarchy is that these were Archaically woven by Wild Women—by our own kind. Even when denied access to the written word and to the academented fraternities of Bearded Brother No-it-alls, women have always talked. Women have Be-Spoken logically, powerfully, magically, Elementally. The Race of Wild Women has always been a Race of Speakers, Spinners, Weavers. Weird Women have been Great Original Communicators, and with respect to these communications, the role of dictionary editors has essentially been merely to compile. The word *compile* is itself an A-mazing clue. Derived from the Latin *compilare,* meaning "to plunder," it means "to collect into a volume" and "to compose out of materials from other documents" (*Webster's Collegiate*). The dryasdust pedants of patriarchy have plundered and pillaged women's Word-Weavings. They have collected and twisted the Wise Words of Crones in their tedious tomes.

They have composed/decomposed documents from materials which are the Documents of Others' Lives.[3]

The *Wickedary*'s History, then, is interwoven with the History of the Race of Wild Women, and its Webs are comprised of Re-weavings as well as New Weavings of that History. Repairing and Dis-covering our own Archaic Webs, Websters create Archaic Futures. We Spin into Original Time and, from that perspective, wink at the pomposity of the "sacred" paternal pronouncement that "in the beginning was the word." Quite simply, "the word" of wasters/erasers of women's History is a colossal lie.

Websters Re-weaving our own Heritage howl at the "history" of wantwits and windbags. As Gossips, we Gossip out (divine and communicate) the secrets of our own History, which have been smoldering among the Embers of the Fires in which Fore-Crones/Fore-Websters were burned alive as Witches. These secrets—hidden by "history"— empower us to Gossip wisdom from the stars.

Wickedarians Dis-covering Webs hidden in dictionaries and Other Sources participate in the creation of Terrible Tapestries and Live in Crone-Time. We Weave in the Presence of Other Gossips, that is, Boon-Companions. Crone-logically and Super Naturally we Gossip out the true nature of the history of man, encountering and exposing The Mystery of Man.

The Mystery of Man

According to *Webster's,* the word *mystery* is derived from the Greek *myein,* meaning "to initiate into religious rites," and also meaning "to close (used of the eyes and lips)." It is said to be possibly akin to the Latin *mutus,* meaning "mute." These etymological clues can lead Websters a long way in the complex process of unraveling the mystery of the word *mystery.* In the process of unraveling, we should consider the fact that the Greek etymology itself is fraught with mystery. Why, we might ask, should initiation involve an injunction to close the eyes and the lips? A miasma of mystification and murkiness is attached to the very word *mystery.* If we look steadily at this word, Seeing it with Real Eyes, we understand that it functions within a patriarchal context as an archetypal elementary term, that is, as a mummy term.* It serves to mummify Crones, to confuse, ensnare, and tame Terrible Women, and ultimately to block Elemental Journeyers.[4]

Webster's serves up several definitions of *mystery,* each more unap-

---

* For an explanation and some examples of "mummy terms," see *Appendicular Web One.*

petizing than the next. Thus, for example, we read that it means "a religious truth revealed by God that man cannot know by reason alone and that once it has been revealed cannot be completely understood . . . *usu cap:* a Christian religious rite or sacrament: as (1) EUCHARIST (2) mysteries *pl:* HOLY MYSTERIES (3) any of the 15 meditations on the events of the life of Christ forming the major part of the rosary devotion." It is Crone-logical to point out that one possible reason why a "religious truth" said to be revealed by god continues to be unintelligible is simply that it makes no sense. Mystified believers are of course commanded to deny their own intellectual integrity and blindly believe the babbling of men to whom god purportedly has revealed the nonsensical mystery.

Wicked Women, who notice that the "religious mysteries" of men make no sense, are enabled to gain Pyromantic perspective on other activities of mysterious men. In sum: Their academented speech makes no sense; their military science makes no sense; their -ologies (classified information) make no sense; their politics make no sense; their laws make no sense; their medicine makes no sense. Of course, Seers are ordered to keep our eyes closed to all of this mysteriousness/nonsense and to say nothing. Such Crone-logical, unclassifiable information is taboo.

A Bitchy, Be-Witching woman—a Soothsayer—is compelled to Notice and Denounce the universal lack of sense masked by mysterious men.[5] Such Formal Denouncements by Furies could be grouped under several nonclassifications, such as "The Failure of Man"; "Flopocracy: A History of Man's Disasters"; "The Mysterical Man: A Critical Study in Male Psychology"; "The Eternal Mystery/Mistery/Misery of Man."

Many women, having frequently peeked behind the male veils and Gossiped out the facts, are able to Hear such Denouncements. Sensing and dreading the imminent possibility of such exposure, man cloaks himself in ever murkier mysteries.[6] He is constantly having mysterics/misterics. In his religious "revelations," especially, he mysterically reveals/re-veils himself. He withdraws into all-male clubs and secret societies—those manifold priesthoods of cockocracy marked by mumbo-jumbo, ridiculous rituals, and cockaludicrous costumes.[7] Hoping to distract from his own stupendous senselessness and to prevent women from Seeing through and Naming his illusions/delusions, he requires/prescribes female "mysteriousness," pompously proclaiming that women's eyes and lips must be sealed.

The Weaving of the *Wickedary* requires Opening our eyes, particularly our Third Eye, emitting Eye-Beams/I-Beams—Radiant Glances of the Eye/I. It demands the Opening of Augurs' lips to Name Reality. Under phallocratic rule, the Eyes and Lips of women have been forcibly sealed by the stupendously stupefying weight of the omnipresent mysteries of phallicism. Fired and empowered by Fury, Labrys-wielding Amazons and Viragos rip the veils of male mysteries, especially the "supernatural" ones. We Announce the Arrival of the Super Natural, the Supremely Natural. We unveil and release the Powerful Witch within our Selves—the Great Original Witch who is hidden by such man-made mysterious archetypes as the "eternal feminine."

Lacking Biophilic History, patriarchal males have needed to make up "mystery" to hide an abysmal absence of Presence. They have distracted Others from this ruse by projecting and fixing the label "mysterious" not only onto women but also upon all Wild be-ing, blocking Realization of Elemental Powers.[8] Countering this ruse, the *Wickedary* participates in the work of exposing the sordid mysteries of sadosociety's priesthoods, which are contrived to confound their victims, to mute the Wicked Words of Moon-Wise Weirds and Websters.

Wickedarians unfold the man-made blindfolds that are intended to block Visionary Powers and prevent the Unfolding of Be-ing. We tear away the gags intended to stop the Nagging of Nags and Hags. When we speak of such Unfolding/Ungagging as History we are saying that the Be-Speaking of our Selves as Seers is twined with the work of creation. Our task is nothing less than Dis-covering and creating Real History behind/beyond mystery, finding our Final Cause, participating in Realms of Metamystery.

Metamystery

The History that is Dis-covered and created by Websters is Metamystery, in dimensions that incorporate all of the senses of the prefix *meta-*. First, the breakthrough to Metamystery occurs only *after* a woman has refused to keep her eyes closed and remain silent about the Awesome Archaic Powers of her Self and all Elemental be-ing. Second, a woman rips open man's mystery by actualizing these Elemental Powers, thus Dis-covering what is *behind* the man-made veils that have clouded her Vision. She sees through the non-sense of phallocracy/fooldom and Touches her own Wild Reality, her Background.

The third dimension of Metamystery follows logically from such an experience—or series of experiences—of breakthrough to the Background. That is, there is a release of pent-up Gynergy which *transforms* a woman's ways of thinking, feeling, acting. The Fire of her Fury melts down the embedded man-made plastic passions and unpots the potted passions that marked/marred her former life as a patriarchally possessed "mysterious" woman. She sloughs off the pseudovirtues of victimhood that were enforced during long years in the State of Servitude and acquires the Volcanic Virtues/Vices of a Virago. Breaking out of bondage, she learns to bond with Others. Re-membering ancient connections, she enters Metamorphospheres.

This transformative activity brings a Metamorphosing woman to the fourth dimension of Metamystery, which is movement *beyond* the mysteries of man into Original Time, that is, Creative Time—the Time of Metamemory and of Archaic Futures. Moved by Wonder at the absolutely Natural workings of Elemental Reality, Creative Crones transcend the mummified state that is legitimized and sustained by dead faith in man's mysteries.

The Concealment of Elemental Communicating Powers

Female History/Metamystery actually happens when Wicked women refuse complicity in the patriarchs' concealment of our Powers, particularly our Metamysterious Elemental Powers of Communication. By labeling women and nature "mysterious," the paternal propagandists have committed a colossal crime of reversal, negating/denying the Powers of Seers and Soothsayers. There is a major clue in this strategy of the mindbinders, spookers, and wasters who rule the Phallic State. By attempting to hide Elemental Powers of Communication they have indicated how strong these Powers are.

Indeed, Elemental Powers of Communication are at the root of those abilities which are readily attributed to women in the State of Mystery/Misery, such as aptitudes for nurturing, healing, teaching, social facilitating, organizing. The very attribution of these capabilities to women conveniently functions to hide the depth and scope of Wicked Communicating Powers. The phallocrats have worked feverishly to reduce these Powers and then have fetishized their stunted derivatives, which are allowed expression only under male control. These "gifts of women" that are acknowledged within patriarchy have been rendered shallow and disconnected from women's own deep purposefulness. They have been fashioned to suit the masters' dead ends, to support the agendas of popocracy.

The sadosocietal system fixes and freezes women's Elemental Powers of Communication, confining their expression to "appropriate" stereotypic activities, such as those assigned to wives and mothers, nurses, schoolmarms, hostesses, and efficient do-gooders. Thus enslaved by the snoolish rules and rulers, women become complicit in the stunting and fragmentation of our Selves. A phallically fixed wife and mother keeps pop on his pedestal and nurtures future faithful followers of fa-

8

therland's rules/roles. A nurse whose loyalty is to physicians and patriarchal medicine is a servant of disease-causing agents.[9] A female teacher, whether she works in a nursery school or in a Ph.D. program, who uncritically transmits the dogmas of doublethink is an agent of maledom's mindbinding.

In order to free the Metamysterious Elemental Communicating Powers of women that have been tied down by the spiritbindings of sadospiritual fixers, it is essential to begin adequately to Name the complex and interwoven meanings and dimensions of these Powers. This brings us to the Strange and Sinister Subject of Mediumship.

The Wickedary:
Its History/
Metamystery

Metamystery and Mediumship

Dictionaries offer clues concerning Metamysterious Powers through the medium of definitions, for example, definitions of the word *medium*. Among the meanings of this word are "something intermediate in position" and "an intermediate agency, means, instrument, or channel" (*O.E.D.*). These definitions can aid Websters in the process of locating the Place/Time where/when we Touch and transmit Metamysterious Powers. This ever moving Labyrinthine Location is on the Boundary between the elementary/restored/plastic world which is the State of Possession and the Wild Realms of Metabeing.

As Journeyers become Wilder, the location of the Boundary shifts further away from the centers of patriarchal possession and deeper into the Otherworld. As this happens, the man-made "mysteries" lose their power to conceal from Journeyers the Realms of our own Reality. Be-Wildering Websters Unweave the veils designed to hide our Selves from ourSelves and Weave further into the Background. With Eye-Biting Powers, Be-Witching women snap the blinding/binding ties that have kept us from Seeing and Be-Speaking. Breaking these evil ties, we See with truly Wicked Eyes. The shimmering splendor of Sister-Voyagers is Realized, further revealing the foolishness of snools. Unveiled, these mysterical men evoke our Wholly Hysterical Laughter. With every Laugh, Lusty Leapers Leap further, bounding to Other Boundaries.

With each Leap and Bound, each shifting of Boundaries, more mindbindings/spiritbindings come undone. Our Mediumship springs, spirals, and soars. Our Space-Craft moves outside all hitherto known directions. We Spin beyond the compass of every compass.

Mediums are Sylph-satisfied with the clues provided in *Webster's* definition of *medium* as "something through or by which something is accomplished, conveyed, or carried on." A Metamysterious Medium experiences her Self as someone through or by whom something is accomplished and conveyed. As for carrying on, Happy Mediums do indeed carry on about the Wonders of our Mediumship, Announcing that a Sylph-identified Medium is, like the Air, a conveyer of Words, and that a Salamandrous Medium is, like Fire, a conveyer of Light and Warmth.

Also pleasing to Happy Mediums is *Webster's* definition of *medium* as "a condition, atmosphere, or environment in which something may function or flourish." We note that by choosing our Mediumship we participate in the creation of a condition, atmosphere, or environment—that is, a Gyn/Ecological environment—in which Biophilic being can function and flourish.

Sylph-affirming Mediums/Muses join in the chorus of Others, creating an atmosphere in which New Words can be spoken and sung, participating in the Cosmic Concento—the Crone-logically simultaneous sounding of the tones of Accord among all Biophilic beings. Moreover, New Words themselves are Mediums, carriers of messages, and their Soundings break through man's mysteries. They Weave together, forming magic tapestries/carpets, carrying Muses/Mediums further into Metamysterious Realms.

All Elemental beings are Mediums, conveyers of knowledge and power. Searchers can find countless affirmations of this fact in studies of folklore and magic. The following passage is a typical Eye-opening Example:

> Among the Celtic races we observe divination, or forecasting the future, by means of omens and auspices, through the media of the flight and motions of birds, by the casting of bones, or omen-sticks, the movements or direction taken by animals, by dreams and crystal-gazing, almost precisely as we find these several methods employed by many other races.[10]

As this passage illustrates, Mediumship implies participation in Tidal Time, movement into Archaic Future. It is therefore prophetic.

The Elements, as Metamysterious Mediums, communicate with Crones engaged in the work of prophecy/divination. This is suggested by such words as *Aeromancy, Geomancy, Hydromancy, Pyromancy.* The Air, Earth, Water, and Fire Be-Speak to those whose Senses are alive. It is evident also that the stars have been known as Mediums by astrologers for millennia, together with the moon, sun, and other planets. The word *Angel,* since it is derived from the Latin *angelus,* meaning "messenger," points to the fact that Elemental Spirits, too, are Mediums.

The Call of the Elemental Mediums

The Call of the Elemental Mediums is the Call of the Wild, summoning us beyond the foreground, the elementary world. It is an unremitting Howl, warning those muted and stranded in the State of Possession and mystified by its media to leave the land of the dead. Thus Elemental Mediums Scold mesmerized Seers who are glued to television sets, dead mind-sets, and dis-spiriting social sets, urgently urging them to break set and reclaim their Eyes/I's. They Nag tone-deafened Augurs who are trapped in babblespheres to close their ears to the mind-rapists' musak and creeds, and listen again to the Music of Birds and of Be-Witching Words.

The Wickedary: Its History/ Metamystery

Elemental Mediums Howl to silenced Soothsayers to shout down the lies of "authorities." They call to housebound/housebroken Gossips to get off the phone, get away from the phoneys, and once again Gossip Wisdom from the stars. They admonish those Sibyls who are trapped in the State of Appeasement to refuse "adultery of the brain."[11] They remind these compromised Sages that in the science of logic the meaning of *medium* is "middle term," or the connecting link that makes possible the drawing of a logical conclusion. They Plead with these muted Mediums to Re-call their Powers of Knowing and of Proclaiming the Crone-logical connecting links and conclusions that can make Sense for women's lives.

Wicked Women, who Hear this Call of the Wild, Re-call our Primal Powers and Finally reclaim for our Selves the word *Mysterious*. This word makes Sense when wrenched from its patriarchal context and Heard in a Metamysterious way. It Names a necessary attribute of Journeyers, who choose to close our eyes to the barrage of illusions intended by trickers and frauds to delude us and who refuse to recite the framers' party lines. When Heard and Be-Spoken in this Sense, *Mysterious* is a New Word and it describes the Creative Caution of Boundary-living women.

Metamysteriously Mysterious women are positively entrancing and entranced. Indeed, Websters sometimes experience be-ing in a *trance,* in the sense of "a state of profound abstraction or absorption accompanied by exaltation" (*Webster's*). Moreover, unshackled from the mind-bindings of snooldom, we are enabled to *trance,* meaning "to move briskly: PRANCE" (*Webster's*). Whereas the masters' media fix/attach women to all that is dead, dis-spirited, and deadly, the Mediumship of trancing, prancing Websters enables us to Con-Quest, Con-Question, Consort, and Cavort with the Living. Among our lively Boon-Companions are Fore-Familiars and Fore-Crones who Live in Archaic Time.

As a Work of Entrancement, the *Wickedary* is a multiwebbed record and map as well as a book of clues for those who choose to Prance. It is a Hope-full History of, by, and for Happy Mediums deciding that Mediumship is our vessel/vehicle. In Other Words, the *Wickedary* is a Word-Webbed Wonderbook for Boundary-Bounders, for Hopping/ Hoping Wonderers who are Leaving Boredom and Leaping toward Somewhere—the Time and Space of those who Spin and Weave.

PRELIMINARY WEB TWO

Spelling:
The Casting of Spells

Websters break the boring rules of spelling imposed by snoolish schoolmasters and move on to the casting of Spells. According to *Webster's*, one definition of the noun *spell* is "a spoken word or set of words believed to have magic power: CHARM, INCANTATION." It also means "a state of enchantment." The connection between Spells and spelling has been acknowledged by at least one dictionary editor, who wrote:

> The words of a living language are like creatures: they are alive. Each word has a physical character, a look and a personality, an ancestry, an expectation of life and death, a hope of posterity. Some words strike us as beautiful, some ugly, some evil. . . . There are magic words, spells to open gates and safes, summon spirits, put an end to the world. What are magic spells but magic spellings? [1]

The magic Spellings in the *Wickedary* open gateways, summon spirits, brew brainstorms, and Be-Speak Other worlds. There are several Ways in which such Spell-casting/Spell-speaking is done.

Ways of Spelling/Be-Spelling[2]

1. The Changing of Spelling

**PRELIMINARY
WEB TWO**

The first method of Spell-Weaving—a Way highly favored by Web-sters—is the changing of spelling. For example, when the "normal" word *bewitching* becomes *Be-Witching* the ultimate ontological powers of Haggard female be-ing are conjured. Such changing of spelling is Archimagical Shape-shifting. It is transforming the physical form of a word in order to convey Super Natural meanings that have been masked and muted by man's mysteries.

Lusty women often use our double axes, our Labryses, to carve such Spellings. Thus *Gyn/Ecology* is created by a slash in the old word *gyne-cology,* an oppressive word used to designate a gynocidal branch of mur-derous modern medicine. The capitalization signifies the capital im-portance of this New Word. The slash of the Labrys also empowers *Gyn/Ecology* to Name Gynocentric Ecology. In a double sense, then, the use of the double ax to create this word wrenches back Weird Word-power to cast Spells on the malignant medicine men and polluters who prey upon women and nature.

Such enchanting/changing of spelling is Spell-Craft. Spell-Crafty Websters, by Be-Spelling patriarchal words, Dis-cover and release onto-logical powers encased/encaged within them. This ontological Shape-shifting of words Be-Spells Speakers and Hearers as well, awakening latent powers of be-ing. We are thus enabled to Be-Speak with words in two senses: We communicate with the words themselves as Other Ele-mental creatures seeking to be freed, and we Be-Muse Archimagically with the help of such liberated/liberating words, creating New contexts. This brings us to the subject of the second method of Be-Spelling.

2. The Changing of Context

In the process of Be-Spelling, Websters are aided by such Guides as the wonderful Spelling Bees.* These apian accomplices, experts at un-conventional communication, suggest buzz words from their own lan-guage. They playfully hum slogans to inspire our emulation of their Ways, which can only be roughly translated, for example: "The Bees are Busy Bee-ing." Occasionally they even allow Weird women to observe their Bee-Spelling round dances and wagging dances. These contain coded messages concerning the direction and distances of nearby food supplies as well as information about the abundance and quality of pol-

---

* For an elaborated discussion of animal accomplices in the work of the *Wickedary,* see *Preliminary Web Five.*

BE-SPELLING: *Dis-covering and releasing the Archimagical powers of Words*

len and nectar. Bee-Spelled Websters, inspired by such performances, wax Busier, Spelling out directions for Wanderlusting/Wonderlusting Journeyers.

As the Bee Dancers demonstrate, Spelling for them involves rhythmic movement, Weaving around, conveying essential clues to their sisters in a Bee-identified context. Websters also acquire an Other method of Spelling—one that essentially implies the creation of a Woman-identified context. Weaving around rhythmically, breaking set, we alter the environment in which a word is Heard, thereby releasing its powers of incantation.*

PRELIMINARY WEB TWO

When the context is thus transformed, the material form of a word need not always be changed. The Realizing of a Metapatterning context awakens Metamemory, so that Archaic senses of a word can be Heard. *Hag,* for example, is commonly used disparagingly by snools to describe "an ugly or evil-looking old woman" (*Webster's*). Websters, considering the source and context of such disparagement, take this as a compliment, Re-calling the Archaic definition of *Hag* as "a female demon: FURY, HARPY" (*Webster's*). Thus Wickedarians keep this word intact (capitalizing it, to be sure), freeing it to Be-Speak once again, to Name the fierce beauty, courage, and wisdom of Crones. *Hag* is liberated to Spell New/Archaic idea-shapes, relation-shapes, action-shapes, passion-shapes.

Another example of a word whose shape is shifted in this way is *prude*. Under the rule of snoolish usage this word is doomed to designate "a person who is excessively or priggishly attentive to propriety or oversensitive to slight breaches of decorum" (*Webster's*). When freed from the patriarchal word-prisons, *Prude* reclaims its Archaic ancestry and Spells Female Pride. This word, in fact, has the same origins as its sister-word *proud* and is directly derived from the French *prudefemme,* meaning "a wise or good woman." Websters, therefore, can Re-call the word *Prude* and Spell it forth in a Gyn/Ecological environment.

It would be impossible to overexaggerate the importance of context for Be-Spelling. The word *context* itself, according to *Webster's,* has as its first and "obsolete" meaning "the weaving together of words in language." Be-Spelling Websters follow the cues of words, cooperating with them in the Weaving together of a Biophilic context/atmosphere. This requires wrenching ourSelves away from the necrophilic State of Possession and, with the indispensable aid of Guide Words, breathing forth Life-Lust.

All New Words *sound* different from old words, even when the spelling (in the traditional sense of *spelling*) is the same. Thus, for example, the New Word *New* does not sound like the old word *new,* for the context changes the vibrations when the New Word is spoken. *Be-Witching,* of course, does not sound like *bewitching.* See *Preliminary Web Four.*

This Life-Lusty atmosphere has several noteworthy qualities by which it can immediately be identified. It is marked by Haggard Humor—the Lusty Laughter of Leaping Women who Laugh Out Loud at cockaludicrous loutishness. It is characterized also by explosions of Righteous Rage on behalf of all Elemental sisters. This Metapatriarchal atmosphere vibrates with Virtuous Disgust at the dreariness of daddyland, with its deceptive dickspeak and dis-spiriting, dryasdust dogmas and daddygods.

Many Other distinguishing traits pervade the Crone-logical context in which Wild/Weird Words can be uttered/muttered. Word-chasers can detect the contagiously Contrary-Wise style of Crackpot Crones. Nag-noteworthy also is the Volcanic Prudence of Prudes, who choose words of Extreme Power and in so doing exercise extravagant Shrewdness and Wild Caution. Present also is the Regal Rationality of Word Witches, practitioners of Word-Magic whose Be-Spoken words are wands emitting vibrations that Transverse the archetypes of the State of Deadly Deception, overturning and reversing its reversals. Of crucial significance to this environment is the Presence of Nemesis, the Virtue beyond justice that is acquired by Inspired Acts of Righteous Fury and that makes possible Passionate Spinning/Spiraling of Archaic Threads of Gynergy.

Such qualities are essential to the context in which words are freed to Act as Mediums of exchange and of change, to Speak as Metamorphic Messengers of Musing Powers. Within such a Be-Speaking context, yet an Other Way of Be-Spelling can be Realized.

3. Spinning Off

The third method of Spelling/Spell-Casting is a Spin-off from the second Way. It involves Hearing words in a Gyn/Ecological context and Weaving around these, sometimes combining parts of words or entire words, thus Realizing Other words and phrases of a heretofore unknown character.

The Spelling of *Wickedary*, for example, first of all involves Hearing *Wicked* in a Hag-identified context and then combining this Be-Witching word with the suffix *-ary* (meaning "of or belonging to or connected with"). The word *Wickedary* instantly makes sense to Spell-Brewers when Heard in conjunction with the word *Websters'*, for this combination Conjures the idea of a dictionary that is of or belonging to or connected with Wicked women.* The very sound of *Wickedary* links

---

* To those familiar with Crone-logical contextual Spelling, it is also clear that since animals are essential Guides to the *Wickedary* and since Witches are known to have Familiars, the *Wickedary* is also a *Bestiary* (in the best sense of the word).

17

it inevitably with *dictionary*. The rhyme and rhythm of these words Announce their association with each other. The only remaining task is Spelling Out the definition.*

An Other example of this method of Spelling is the construction of the word *Nag-Gnostic*. According to *Webster's*, the verb *nag* means "make recurrently conscious of something." The adjective *gnostic*, according to the *Oxford English Dictionary*, means "believing in the reality of transcendental knowledge." Hearing both of these words in a Wicked context, Wickedarians can Weave them together—or, to be somewhat more accurate—participate in the process of these Wild Words' Weaving together. The result is the New Word *Nag-Gnostic*, which, as a noun, Names a Nag who Senses with certainty the Reality of transcendental knowledge and who therefore practices the Virtue of Nagging, combating the psychic numbing that is demanded by all the religions of the sadosociety, the State of Oblivion.

Spelling as Brewing of Brainstorms

Wicked Spellings open doors to Other Worlds where Words—like Other Wild creatures—are alive. In these Other Worlds, their Powers of revelation, both as nouns and as verbs, are ecstatically Realized. Spell-Speaking women Spelling the Ways into these Strange yet utterly Familiar Realms break the Great Silence imposed upon us by man's mysteries. Such Silence-breaking is Taboo-breaking. It is Archimagical expression of Spiritual Touching Powers, enabling Travelers to Break Out of the touchable caste.

By such Taboo-breaking/Spelling, Weird women raise tempests—a fact recognized by all who have been confronted with the Spelling Powers of Witches. It is Nag-noteworthy that the Witch persecutors who composed the "authoritative" work of demonology, the *Malleus Maleficarum*, included a chapter entitled "How They Raise and Stir up Hailstorms and Tempests, and Cause Lightning to Blast both Men and Beasts." The conclusion of these malefactors/male-factors is clear: "just as easily as they [witches] raise hailstorms, so can they cause lightning and storms at sea; and so no doubt at all remains on these points."[3] And indeed this is true.

Spell-Speakers know very well that the raising of hailstorms and tempests by Hags is related to brewing of brainstorms. The lightning that flashes in the sky and the Light that gleams from a Spell-Glancer's Eye Spark in cosmic concordance. Be-Spelling women can find even

* See **Wickedary** (*Word-Web One*).

18

in the writings of phalloscholars material that acknowledges Electrical Spelling Powers. Thus, for example, Julian Jaynes writes:

> The function of meter in poetry is to drive the electrical activity of the brain, and most certainly to relax the normal emotional inhibitions of both chanter and listener. A similar thing occurs when the voices of schizophrenics speak in scanning rhythms or rhyme.[4]

Though Spell-Casters scoff at the concept of "normal emotional inhibitions" and at such pat labels as "schizophrenic," we recognize here a dim perception of Augurs' Awesome Elemental Electrical Powers. Jaynes has lifted his male veil just enough to glimpse the Electrical Connection.

Pyromancers know that the word *electric* is related in its origins to the Sanskrit *ulkā,* meaning "fiery phenomenon in the sky, meteor" (*Webster's*). We know that the Musings of Muses are Meteoric and ecstatically Electromagnetic, Sparking Cosmic Connections. Brewsters' Brainstorms brighten skies/eyes.

Spell-Speaking, word-hurling/world-whirling women are kin to Fire-breathing Dragons, whom we join in the work of Distempering the man's world. The verb *distemper* means "to throw out of order or proper or smoothly working adjustment" (*Webster's*). It also means "to disturb or derange the condition of the air, elements, weather, climate, et cetera" (*O.E.D.*). Brainstorming, Be-Spelling women Distemper in both of these senses, throwing bore-ocracy out of its odious order and smoothly working adjustment by Raising Hailstorms and Tempests and Otherwise Exercising Disturbing Elemental Powers.

To Be-Spellers overthrowing dronedom/clonedom it is clear that such disturbance/derangement is absolutely necessary.[5] The Spelling of Soothsayers throws the old order out of order, Dis-covering New/Archaic Orders. In this Stormy atmosphere other women begin to Realize their own Ecstatic E-motional Disorder. Finding her Rage and Hope, a woman observes the melting away of plastic passions that had possessed her, blocking the flow of Elemental Communicating Powers. The old guilt, anxiety, depression, bitterness, resentment, frustration, boredom, resignation, and—worst of all—feminine full-fillment begin to disappear. Seeing these as pseudopassions injected into her soul by the fathers of fixocracy, she flushes them away. As she exorcises these plastic parasites she begins Be-Spelling. She finds it especially efficacious to begin Spelling/Be-Spelling Out Loud.

Spelling Out Loud

Spelling Out Loud is utterly relevant to the practical realities of women's lives, for it involves Spelling Out the situation of women, both as the universally oppressed caste and as Raging Race breaking free into Ecstatic Space.

Most women instinctively know the importance of "talking things over" with other women, but the force of this instinct/intuition is diminished by the inaccessibility of Living Words to express such "things." Imprisoned by patriarchal usage, words are forced into taking on the usual habits of prisoners. They become isolated and unimaginative, unable to bond with each other in creative ways. They appear and sound untrustworthy, hopeless, depressing. Their capacity to express Deep Memory and E-motion is muted. Women, then, are baffled/bamboozled in their victimization by the concomitant confinement of words under patriarchal rule.

PRELIMINARY WEB TWO

It is necessary, therefore, that words and women find and fight for each other, bonding in Mutually Magnetizing Meetings, Realizing our common cause. Only the meeting/conjoining of the Race of Wild Women with the Race of Wild Words can render possible Spelling Out the context of oppression and Spelling the Way Out. Moreover, with every act of Spelling a woman joins words in coming Alive. The emerging and bonding of Living Words provides an atmosphere in which Metamorphosing women can really breathe.[6]

This emergence of women and words requires Spelling Out Loud. Even the pedants of the ubiquitous elementary schools of snooldom recognize the importance of making their pupils spell out loud their spellings, their rules, their grammar—thereby inducing logorrhea, spreading/embedding their labels, their lies. When Spell-casting women Spell Out Loud in Original/Archaic Words the truths of our lives we counter and overcome these negative vibrations.

Spelling Out Loud means women Be-Speaking with each Other—privately and in groups. It means Speaking and Singing in private and public gatherings, producing works of art, books, journals, political actions. Spelling Out Loud is the Original Sounding of Original Women. In other words, Be-Witching women Spell Other Words. Witches Spell these into the Ether, where they continue sending vital vibrations, joining each Other in Metapatterning connections, changing Reality.[7]

Women engaged in Spelling Out Loud Spell Out also the problem of decoys that mimic this Primal activity. One of these decoys/distractions is the incessant droning of the mass media. Another snare that badly imitates Spelling Out Loud is academented sadoscholarship. This form of verbigeration repeats and defends in paralyzing detail the dogmas of

Boredom, which can sometimes be dressed up even as "feminist scholarship." It challenges nothing (while pretending defiance) and cannot Name Nothing. It has the aura of styrofoam and the texture of plastic. It is recognized by Be-Spelling women as manifesting presence of absence—as mental/spiritual bloat, a garbage heap of details without focus, a decentralized mass without organic purpose.

A particularly seductive substitute for and imitation of Spelling Out Loud is the psychobabble of the Therapeutic State. It is therefore important to Spell Out the differences between this elementary mirror image of Spelling and genuine Metamorphic Musing. First, this uninspiring unspelling is quiet. Even when its adherents indulge in "primal screams" it fails to be Loud, for its feeble vibrations cause no cracks in the sacred canopies of male myths that cover/smother women's be-ing. The therapeutic way-of-talk may smile, but it does not Roar. It may permit anger, but it does not Rage. It may show mild disapproval, but never Disgust. It has its own jargon, but it does not Electrically Name Out Loud. It does not Spell Out/Spell Away the man-made mystifications, but rather it mystifies further. It induces "serenity" but it does not give Gynergetic Furious Focus that reaches for the stars. Only Elemental Soundings have such scope/hope.

Be-Spelling and Elemental Sounding

Be-Spelling Websters Hear Elemental Power in the Sounds of the alphabet. Indeed, one ancient meaning of the word *element* is "the spoken letters of the alphabet."[8] Unnaturally, the deadmen of daddyland block the ears of women so that these Sounds will not be Heard, babbling obscenely: "In the beginning was the [phallic] word." Moreover, they strive to mute these Sounds by all their deadly distractions. Spell-Crafty women learn to unblock our Inner Ears, and by listening carefully we begin to Hear the Original tones and rhythms of Elemental Sounds. As Gyn/Ecological Shape-shifters we participate in the rearranging of these Sounds in Natural Orders, generating and regenerating New/Archaic vibrations, Be-Musing Musical Macromutations.

By so Hearing and Speaking, Augurs become Abecedarians. According to *Webster's,* an *abecedarian* is "one that is learning the alphabet," and the "archaic" meaning of this word is "one that teaches the alphabet and the rudiments of learning." Websters, Hearing this word in our own context, understand an *Abecedarian* to be an Augur who is learning and teaching the Archaic Alphabet: one who Dis-covers the Sounds of Rudimentary/Elemental learning. Since Websters clearly are Abecedarians, it follows that the *Wickedary* is an *Abecedarium*—not merely in the usual sense of "ALPHABET BOOK, PRIMER" (*Webster's*), but in an Archimagical sense. That is, it is an Archaic Alphabet Book, a Primal Primer of Elemental Philosophy.[9]

As Abecedarians, Spell-Weavers are agents of Nemesis, counter-Acting the babblers of babblespheres, Denouncing the dickspeak dicktated by the drones and dummies of dummydom. Spelling Websters intend and participate in Elemental disruption of patriarchal equilibrium.

As Abecedarians, Websters recall important knowledge that is partially recorded in the re-search of Robert Graves:

PRELIMINARY
WEB TWO

> There is evidence . . . that before the introduction of the modified Phoenician alphabet into Greece an alphabet had existed there as a religious secret held by the priestesses of the moon—Io, or the Three Fates: that it was closely linked with the calendar, and that its letters were represented not by written characters, but by twigs cut from different trees typical of the year's sequent months.[10]

Now is the Time for Re-membering the Primal Sounds of the Alphabet held secret by the priestesses of the Fates. Be-Spellers are beginning to sense the interconnectedness of these Sounds with our own Bio-rhythms, our consciousness of cosmic calendars. In tune with the moon and with trees, we Spell Archaic, Rudimentary Runes.

This Spelling/Spilling of Archaic Sounds into the Ether, by transforming vibrations, counterbalances and cancels out the negativity that prevails in archetypal deadtime. It spills the beans concerning the inanity/insanity of babblespheres, the place of sadospeak/pseudospeak.

Elemental Sounding cuts the dead lines of daddyspeak. It opens Musing Minds and Spins threads of spiraling communication. It sends out Musical Messages whose creative zinging/singing harmonizes with sounds of waters, winds, grasses, trees, thunder, and crackling fire. Cackling Crones brew veritable alphabet soups of sounds, stirring the worlds. The Spelling Bees hum "Sound Louder!"

This Sounding prepares the way for Nemesis to do her work—encouraging Acts of Righteous Rage, disrupting the patriarchal balance of terror/error, releasing Gyn/Ecological vibrations. Elemental creatures urge the work on, Sounding Out the alphabets of their own languages and concording in the chorus of be-ing (or, as some would hum, "bee-ing"). Seals bestow their Seal of Approval on the Whole Ecstatic Enterprise. Owls concede that the Idea of Cosmic Concordance seems Wise. Frogs croak that they like this Preposterous Joke. Most enthusiastic of all are the wondrous multicolored winged creatures who, mocking patriarchal pomposity, declare: "In the Beginning was the Bird." All seem to agree that they have the Last Word.

PRELIMINARY WEB THREE

Grammar:
Our Wicked Witches' Hammer *

J ust as the word *spell* immediately proclaims the connection between words and magic, so too does *grammar*. Be-Witching Grammarians therefore Spell out the magical meanings of *Grammar*.

These meanings are first suggested when Websters examine its etymological twin, *glamour*. The first meaning of the noun *glamour* given in *Webster's* is "a magic spell: BEWITCHMENT." The word itself was formed simply as an alteration of *grammar*, a development which *Webster's* explains as the result of "the popular association of erudition with occult practices." *Wickedary* Websters proclaim that the ignorant "erudition" of the patriarchs has deliberately hidden the essence of Grammar, forcibly rendering it boring and "occult."

The usual definitions of *grammar* in patriarchally constructed contexts are indeed boring, suggesting the rote drills of "elementary" or "grammar" schools. It is said to mean "a branch of linguistic study that deals with the classes of words . . . as employed according to estab-

---

*The most "authoritative" textbook for Witch-hunters and Witch-burners was the fifteenth-century work by the Dominican priests Heinrich Kramer and James Sprenger, entitled *Malleus Maleficarum—The Hammer of Witches*. The work was intended to be a hammer for destroying Witches and their heresy. In the *Wickedary*, Websters take up our own Hammer—the Labrys/double ax which is our Grammar, to Destroy the illusions (phalloglamour) propagated by patriarchs to destroy women.

lished usage . . . ," et cetera. *Glamour,* too, is reversed and banalized; it is lowered to the level of *Glamour Magazine.**

The Elemental meanings of *Glamour* and *Grammar* are perversely hidden by patriarchal "glamour" and "grammar." The latter are examples of "elementary" products, in the sense that Paracelsus wrote of "elementaries." That is, they are artificial man-made beings, resulting from degeneration of faculties and powers which should be actualized in Other Ways.

PRELIMINARY
WEB THREE Artificially separated from their Original, interconnected meanings and powers, these words are confined by "established usage." *Grammar* is reduced to the tidy arrangement of words in a sentence. *Glamour* is voided of life, made mindless and soulless as a made-up mannequin.

Seers See through these elementary usages to the Elemental powers they conceal. Sibyls Announce the resurgence of the Natural Order of Original Words, declaring that the word *Grammar,* freely and Wildly Spoken and Heard, suggests the Elemental Powers of Be-Witching.

One way of Be-Witching is Wording. The Wording of Websters twines meanings and rhythms, unleashing Original forces/sources. Arranging our words to convey their Archaic meanings, we release them from cells of conventional senses. Dis-covering their own natures, their Wildness, Words join in racing harmonies, breaking from patterns of flatness, combining in new and ancient ways, regrouping beyond paralyzing patterns, forming magical Metapatterns.

Releasing words to race together, Websters become Muses. We do not use words, we Muse words. Metapatterning women and words have magical powers, opening doorways of Memories, transforming spaces and times. Rhymes, alliterations, alterations of senses—all aid in the breaking of fatherland's fences. Thus liberation is the work of Wicked Grammar, which is our basic instrument, our Witches' Hammer.

Unfixing the fixations of phallogrammar

Under phallocracy, grammar is an instrument of social control. Consequently it must be controlled by the sadosociety's linguistic overseers. The author of the introductory essay in *Webster's New Collegiate Dictionary,* entitled "The English Language and Its History," wrote:

---

*Jane Caputi uncovered the etymological connections between *grammar* and *glamour* in her article "The Glamour of Grammar," *Chrysalis: A Magazine of Women's Culture,* no. 4 (1977), pp. 35–43. Caputi's analysis shows how the Original meaning of *glamour* has been reversed and how this word has been used, along with patriarchal *grammar,* to conceal the Presence of women.

Creating a GLAMOUR

The largest and most complicated vocabulary would be of little value without a grammar to control the ways in which words can be put together to make larger constructions.[1]

PRELIMINARY
WEB THREE

At first glance, this statement may seem innocent enough. The fact is, however, that the author chose the word *control* to describe the role of grammar in putting words together. This opens the door to the question: *Who*, exactly, presumes to have the right to control the ways in which words are put together? This question is not really answered by the dictionary schoolmen, of course. Yet the use of the word *control* implies that there is a politics of language. There are, in fact, rulers who make up and enforce the rules/roles.

Readers who have reflected upon the use of language as an instrument of oppression are aware of the problem of pseudogenerics, reflected in such obvious cases as the use of the pronoun *he* and the noun *man* when these are supposed to "include" women. On a more sophisticated level, this problem and many other issues of "syntactic exploitation" have been analyzed by feminist linguists, most notably by Julia Penelope.[2] The point here is to remind ourSelves that the fixers of women and nature have always known that it is in their interest to fix grammar, assuring for themselves the maintenance of control.

The eighteenth century, a period of insufferable boredom, saw many attempts by bores to standardize, refine, and fix the English language.[3] Jonathan Swift unselfconsciously revealed the true mentality and motivation of phallogrammatical fix-masters:

> What I have most at Heart, is, that some Method should be thought on for *ascertaining* and *fixing* our Language for ever, after such Alterations are made in it as shall be thought requisite. For I am of Opinion that it is better a Language should not be wholly perfect, than that it should be perpetually changing: and we must give over at one Time or another, or at length infallibly change for the worse.[4]

The stagnation (in a Stag-nation) desired by Swift was, of course, in the basest sense, self-serving. He would gladly mummify words in order to preserve his own scribblings for posterity. Elemental Grammarians will not fail to note his phallogrammatical agent-deleting use of the passive voice. Reading in the passage cited above, we note that he proposes that "Alterations" shall be made in language "as it be thought requisite." Left unstated is the answer to the suppressed question: "thought requisite" *by whom?* Websters know that no woman's thoughts on the subject would be considered "requisite" by Swift and his ilk.

Even the sanctimonious scribbler Samuel Johnson described Swift's

Proposal as "petty."[5] Johnson, however, was himself a fidgety fixer. In *The Plan of a Dictionary of the English Language* he droned:

> One great end of this undertaking is to fix the English language.[6]

Moreover, in his Preface to *A Dictionary of the English Language* (1755) Johnson intoned:

> Tongues, like governments, have a natural tendency to degeneration; we have long preserved our constitution, let us make some struggles for our language.[7]

Elemental Grammarians will not fail to notice the typically snoolish usage of the pronouns *we, our, us*. Recalling the fixed condition of women under the constitution in eighteenth-century England (and in twentieth-century America), Crone-logical thinkers will immediately grasp the implications of this linkage of "our constitution" with "our language." Clearly, this phallogrammarian was aware of the necessary connection between the repression of language and the oppression which was the foundation of his constitutional privilege, and he was determined to maintain the fixed state in both arenas.

Johnson was filled with foreboding, however, and even gloomily prognosticated the defeat of fixed grammar:

> The tropes of poetry will make hourly encroachments, and the metaphorical will become the current sense; pronunciation will be varied by levity or ignorance, and the pen must at length comply with the tongue; illiterate writers will at one time or another, by publick infatuation, rise into renown, who, not knowing the original import of words, will use them with colloquial licentiousness, confound distinction, and forget propriety.[8]

Hearing these words, Websters cheer on the hourly encroachments of the tropes/troops of poetry and herald with joy the onslaughts of Metapatriarchal Metaphor. Prudes Announce New/Archaic Pronunciations with Lusty Levity. Shrewd Shrews revel in Studied Ignorance, and Pixies proclaim that the pen must indeed comply with the tongue. Laughing Soothsayers reclaim colloquial licentiousness, confounding the false distinctions of drones, Furiously Forgetting propriety.

Wicked Grammarians, Unfixing words, revel in breaking the phallogrammatical taboos. Together with Virginia Woolf, Hags howl: "Words do not live in dictionaries; they live in minds."[9] Indeed, the minds of

Muses and Maenads are our Primary Sources. As a Mexican proverb states: "A woman is the best dictionary."[10] Of course, books are also sources, but these live only in interaction with Living Minds. Moreover, words living in women's minds are not isolated from each Other. As Woolf explained: "A word is not a single and separate entity. . . . Words belong to each other."[11]

It serves the interest of phallogrammarians to hinder such Be-Longing and Be-Friending of words and women. To achieve this end they employ phalloglamour. It is essential that Eye-Biting Grammarians examine this process.

The lies of the mysterical mediators and the Eyes of Elemental Mediums

Patriarchal grammar blocks/blunts the Elemental Powers of Mediumship of words and women. The mysterical mediators attempt to stop the flow of communication by means of elementary magic or trickery. The method of stoppage/blockage consists primarily in the manufacture of illusions, which is phalloglamour. These illusions are debased substitutes for and replications of genuine means of communication. Phalloglamour, then, is implied in phallogrammar.

These twin strategies render women passive, de-formed and re-formed. Made fashionable, women are fashioned and re-fashioned by the fascist phallocrats. Not only the physical appearance but also the opinions and words of fashionable women are distorted by the depraved shape-shifters of snooldom/fooldom.

By means of such bad magic women are passivized, reduced to seeing everything with passive eyes. A woman in this condition sees herself only as being seen. Regarding herself through men's eyes, she is a prisoner of the mirror.[12] Wearing invisible blindfolds, she is tricked into "seeing," but does not See with Glamour Eyes, Real Eyes.

Passivized women frantically peer into mirrors, their passive eyes checking out innumerable defects and flaws, marks of failure to conform to the norms designed to keep them in line. Nothing seems fine. Eye-shadowed, hookwinked women search their mirrors for signs of failed femininity. Too fat or too thin, encased in inevitably aging skin, mirror-peering women turn to bores for scores and for scores of directions. Thus, mummified made-up women forget their Original Selves.

Only our Witches' Hammer can crack the mirrors of phalloglamour.[13] As the cracks become greater, the Magnetizing Eyes of Crones, radiating Elemental attraction, can rouse women out of the State of Possession. Wild Eyes can Wildize, Untame, Uncivilize—awakening the capacities of captive women to Hear and follow the Call of the Wild.

28

In sum: The Eyes of Be-Witching Grammarians Overlook the mendacious mediators of women's experience, looking on and Naming their lies as evil. In the course of this process of exorcism, we evoke and employ our Shape-shifting Powers. Wielding these Wicked Powers, Grammarians turn to the topic of tactics.

Sin-Tactics: Wielding Our Witches' Hammer

The Grammar of Wicked Websters includes not only Metamorphosing Morphology (already Spelled Out in the preceding Web) but also Spinning/Sinning Syntax/Syntactics, hereafter Named Sin-Tactics.* The Sagacious Sin-Tactics of Terrible Women break the taboos against Be-Speaking that are imposed by the fathers of phallogrammar and phalloglamour. By such taboo-breaking we free words to Act Naturally in relation to each Other, forming their own Archaic arrangements without snoolish interruption and interference.

Wielding our Witches' Hammer, Websters Dis-close the Glamour of words, their magical/musical interplay as they Sound and Resound together in complex compositions. We Dis-cover connections, not only among words, but among the realities they Name.

Elemental Grammarians See with Glamour Eyes—the Eyes of Eye-biting Witches that dispel the delusions of Witch prickers, danglers, and other deadfellows. As we work for the liberation of our Selves and of words, we induce and communicate Glamourie, which has been described as "the state of mind in which witches beheld apparitions and visions of many kinds."[14]

Continuing the Haggard tradition of Glamourie requires the performance of brazen Sin-Tactical Acts. These include the feats of Gossips who Gossip Out Original meanings and arrangements of words, as well as the Singing of Sirens who Sound out such Metapatterning combinations for all to Hear. Our continuation/communication of Glamourie also demands the Scolding of Scolds and Shrews who, scoffing at the cult of the occult, opt for Shouting Out Loud—openly Naming and exorcising the deceptive demons of phallocracy, Be-Laughingly reversing the reversals of mirrordom.

---

*The word *sin* is derived from the Indo-European root *es-*, meaning "to be" (*American Heritage*). When Websters affirm who we truly *are*, we break the basic taboo of gynocidal patriarchy and all of its religions and thus Sin in the most Positively Revolting Way. Our Courage to Be/Sin enables us to reclaim our Witches' Hammer, our Grammar, and to wield this Sin-Tactically—that is, to affirm Be-ing Sinfully, over and against the lies of phallogrammar. Moreover, our tactics are tactile. Touching Spiritual Powers, the Grammar of Wicked Websters affirms our participation in Be-ing and invites Others to Be-Speak such Sinful Self-Realization.

To conventional grammarians such Sin-Tactics seem/sound like disorder. Indeed, such Sinister strategies, by Touching and awakening the Powers of Terrible Women, do wreak Dreadful Dis-order. For this is a work of Tidal Weaving and Re-weaving, of breaking through the tidy order/orders of Boredom. Sinister syntax implies Elemental disruption of tidydom's tyranny. It is musical Metapatterning that counters patriarchal patter by participating in the Natural Gossiping of words themSelves. As Gossip Gertrude Stein explained: "I like the feeling the everlasting feeling of sentences as they diagram themselves."[15]

Wicked Grammarians breaking fatherland's rules are committing the Sin of Creative Dis-ordering, effecting Metamorphosis. Grammar-Hammering Hags, releasing words from male-ordered boxes and cages, enable these to Spin about freely. Spinning, whirling words swirl Wildly, winding/wending their ways in New directions.

Like fairy dancers/prancers, Pixilated words enjoin Spinsters and Websters to join the dance/prance and practice Gyromancy. Gyrophobic phallogrammarians, feeling the force of these Wordstorms/Weirdstorms, whine their usual line: "Follow the rules or go back to [snool] school!" Refusing to be bullied into "order" by the gods/rods of these foolish fraternities, words and women Spin beyond the schoolmen's syntax, phrasing Primordial Questions, Spinning sentences that Transverse the trickers' traditional tracks. Such Sin-Tactics bring us in Touch with Other Words/Worlds. Grammar, then, is an essential and creative form of Elemental Mediumship.

To understand the wide implications of the creativity of Cronelogical Grammar we must Re-call the fact that the arrangement of words is not merely a matter of sterile "style" but of complex analysis— of Naming, that is, Truth-telling. This is the only adequate antidote for phallocracy's Biggest Lies. As Truth-telling Mediums, Wicked Grammarians break the brokenness of consciousness that is crushed under the rule/rules of the sadosociety.

Our Sin-Tactics, then, are designed to mend the broken connections within women's psyches, among our Selves, and between women and Other Wild creatures. As this healing progresses, as we experience ever more deeply the reality of our Natural connectedness in the Background, we develop our abilities to detect patterns in the foreground— the male-centered, monodimensional arena where fabrication, objectification, and alienation take place. We begin to See and Name connections among apparently disparate phenomena.* Such pattern-detecting is the basis of Gyn/Ecology, of Radical Feminist Metaethics,

* For examples of such Sin-Tactical analysis, see **deadly sins of the fathers; Sado-Ritual Syndrome; Sadospiritual Syndrome** (*Word-Web One*).

of Elemental Feminist Philosophy. It is also the basis of the work of the *Wickedary,* which is a Grammar of Elemental Communication.[16]

This detecting of connections is possible for Websters insofar as we are in Touch with our Final Cause, the indwelling, always unfolding goal or purpose, perceived as Good and attracting one to Act, to Realize her own participation in Be-ing.[17] In Other words, Wicked Grammar is possible because of the Glamour of the Good as Verb.

The Glamour of the Good as Verb

Wicked Websters proclaim that our Direction is toward the Good. This proclamation is a Paradox. According to *Webster's, paradox* means "a tenet or proposition contrary to received opinion." Since the opinions forcibly "received" by women under the control of phallogrammar are fabrications, the Propositions/Proclamations of Proud Prudes are indeed Paradoxical. They are entirely against the "going logic."[18]

According to that ill-logic, only evil is attractive and exciting, whereas the good is boring. This assumption/tenet is upheld not only by those who openly flaunt their practice of patriarchally defined "evil," but also—subliminally, at least—by those who pontificate and sermonize in support of the patriarchally defined "good." For their droning, grinding, mind-binding insistence upon "goodness" convincingly conveys that this is not very interesting. The good-peddlars are proficient propagandists for its opposite, and indeed they require this opposition of opposites to keep the snoolish sadosystem going. Such "good" and "evil" are essential contents in the phalloglamour boys' bags of dirty tricks.[19]

As Grammar of Elemental Communication, the *Wickedary* is designed for dispelling such tricks and enabling Websters to Dis-cover the potency of the Good as Verb. This Verb inspires us to Realize Be-Witching Powers, becoming ever more Wicked, free from the rules of sadosnools, Dis-closing Original Integrity.

Originally Sinful Websters/Grammarians actively participate in the Unfolding of Be-ing as Good. In Touch with our own Focusing, Spinning Powers, we communicate Glamour, most explicitly by our Grammar, which is marked by the prevailing influence of the Good as Verb.

This Verb is the attracting force that draws Wild women further into the vortex of Be-ing, inducing Vertigo. Derived from the Latin *vertigo,* this word, meaning "action of whirling" (*Webster's*), clearly has relevance for the Spinning/Spiraling of Spinsters.

Spinning and Weaving further into Vertigo, Spinsters/Websters enter Metamorphospheres, where Whirling Dervishes live and learn the

Grammar of the Good as Verb. Bidding good-bye to goody-good Boredom, Magnetized women voice New Senses of the Verbal Tenses. Present, Past, and Future are experienced Crone-logically, unfettered by the flatland's tidy tenses/fences. Our Past lives in the changing Present that is the swirling movement of the Good as Verb.

Wicked Grammarians Presentiate the Good by be-ing actively Present to ourSelves and Others, reclaiming our Past, Weaving our Future. In this Grammatical work we are aided by the Weird Sisters, the Fates, the Norns, as we Spin and Weave around and among the Tenses of our own Re-membering Time.

The Glamour of the Good invigorates, inviting Volcanic Dis-coverings. As these are Realized, Grammarians overcome the bad magic of phalloglamour. Scolds and Viragos counter the badland's bad news by Announcing News of the Good, practicing the Volcanic Virtue of Shouting Out Loud. This brings us to the subject of the following Web, which is Pronunciation.

PRELIMINARY WEB THREE

PRELIMINARY WEB FOUR

Pronunciation: Denouncing, Pronouncing, Announcing

According to the *Oxford English Dictionary, pronunciation* means "the action of pronouncing authoritatively or proclaiming." The *Wickedary* definition of this word is "the action of Denouncing, Pronouncing, or Announcing authentically, or Naming." These three modes of Pronunciation will be examined in this Web.

Preliminary to the Weaving of this Web, it is helpful to ponder an important question posed in an essay entitled "The Spelling and Pronunciation of English," in the *American Heritage Dictionary:*

> What is the nature and extent of the correlation, in English, between spelling and pronunciation? [1]

Hearing this question with our Labyrinthine Sense, our Third Ear, Websters Announce that there are many correlations between Spelling and Pronunciation. Witches cast Spells by means of Pronunciation, and we sometimes change spelling in order to Pronounce Spells. The threads of Spelling and Pronunciation are intricately intertwined. In this Web "the nature and extent of the correlation" will be Divined.

I. Denouncing

According to *Webster's*, the verb *denounce* means "to pronounce . . . to be blameworthy or evil." Websters Pronounce patriarchal ideologies, institutions, and practices to be blameworthy and evil. The power of our Denouncing is suggested by an "obsolete" definition of *denounce:* "to indicate by or as if by omen: PORTEND, AUGUR" (*Webster's*). Websters portend the end of phallocratic evil, Auguring Other realities.

The ideologies, institutions, and practices thus Denounced have as their common method *usage*. Websters Denounce the patriarchal usage of women and nature and of words. We Denounce both "good" usage and "bad" usage, proclaiming the termination of such usage.

The usual sense of *usage* is expressed in the following definition: "habitual use, established custom or practice" (*O.E.D.*). The patriarchs are perpetual users of women, nature, and words, according to "customs" and practices that are established, ruthlessly regulated, and legitimated by themselves, exclusively for their own benefit and much to the detriment of those whom they use.

Prudes note with Disgust that one definition of the noun *use* is "employment or maintenance for sexual purposes" and that the verb *use* can mean "to have sexual intercourse with" (*O.E.D.*). Moreover, Be-Witching women note that the same dictionary offers the following fascinating example of usage of the verb *use*, from a text published in 1584: "Manie are so bewitched that they cannot use their owne wives."

Clearly, Websters oppose phallic usage. So also do Wicked words, especially Originally Wild Words that have been bound, gagged, and distorted, rendered unable to prevent the usage of their sister-words and women. Among such words are *Amazon, Spinster, Virago, Angel, Archimage, Familiar, Fury, Muse*.* These words are freed when Websters summon the courage to Denounce their users/abusers.

It is by gagging Wild Women that the abusers stifle Wild words. The verb *gag* is derived from the Middle English *gaggen*, meaning "to strangle." One definition is "to stop the mouth of by thrusting something in it in order to hinder or prevent speaking or outcry" (*Webster's*). The gaggers strangle women by thrusting into their minds and mouths man-made seminal ideas, infecting their victims with such communicable diseases as logorrhea and verbigeration, culminating in logocide, verbicide, gynocide, biocide.

Yet Wild words continue to live in Musing women's Metamemory. From these depths they howl and yell inside the women who have been made into their prisons and prison guards. Re-membering women

* See *Word-Webs One* and *Two*.

hear these howls as Calls of the Wild within and join the gagged Hag-words/Nag-words who Nag us into Naming. Women and words free our Selves as we Denounce the gaggers and their usage/abusage.

Witches refuse the users' tricks and treats. Shrews shriek at their hoaxes and Prudes portend their end. Scolds scald the users with torrents of boiling words. Grimalkins grin with satisfaction at such Denouncing Action. Spinsters celebrate at Old Maids' Dances.

Denouncers Name the doublethink, doublespeak, doublefeel, and doubledream of gaggers/trickers/users. In this work we are aided by Animal Guides. The Wicked Wasps, for example, show how to be Waspish, winging their way from one target to another, stinging appropriately and accurately. Moreover, they remind Websters that the word *wasp* is akin to the Old English *wefan,* meaning "to weave" (*Webster's*).

Pronunciation: Denouncing, Pronouncing, Announcing

Other Spirited animals also Denounce. The formerly baited and "dancing" bears, for example, dance rings around rippers who have used them for atrocious a-Musement. Viragos dance with them, proclaiming the end of such tyranny. Sagacious Seals, Denouncing their "training" in prestigious aquariums—the degrading institutions where they learned to bounce balls in return for a fish—Bark Out Loud their Seals of Disapproval and Disdain. Bitches Bark with them, Outshouting the users of animals, women, and words.[2]

Daredevil dolphins, declaring an end to jumping through hoops, take Muses for Be-Musing rides. Mischievous monkeys mimic men of science. Denouncing the latter as "missing links to nothing," whose sadistic kinks require a final solution, they foment revolution. Encouraged by guinea pigs, rabbits, and mice, they "deconstruct" cages, mazes, treadmills, and other shocking tools employed by evil "experts"/fools.[3]

Elemental elephants, refusing to pose on stools for the puerile entertainment of little snools, elicit Memories of an Other Time, trumpeting Denouncements of dummydom. Unleashed dogs decry the "clever" tricks required of them by deadeyed dicks. Whinnying and neighing, high-spirited horses persist in inveighing against the abusers' usage. Breaking out of their traces they retire from "horse racing" to Act as Nagging Guides for the Race of animals, women, and words.

Lions and tigers rear scathing rebukes at hunters and hackers, offering to feed them "animal crackers." They chide and deride their trainers and tamers, declaring them "tasteless." "Not even good for a snack!" is a favorite furious crack of the tigers. "Nutritionally worthless!" roar the lions. "'All natural' junk food. They smack of toxins and smell like Big Macs."

Raging words and women join in this roaring, rebuking, reproaching, reproving—Re-proving our Untamed powers of Denouncing the users/abusers of the Necrophilic State.

II. Pronouncing

We have seen that Spelling and Pronunciation are intricately inter-related. The Pronouncing of *Wickedary* words is Elemental Sounding of the spoken letters of the alphabet, as these combine to form the Primal Race of Words. Websters Pronounce cosmic sounds, meanings, rhythms, vibrations, Naming forth creation.* This is possible when women Hear ourSelves and each other to speech.

PRELIMINARY WEB FOUR In her remarkable book *The Journey Is Home,* Nelle Morton describes the experience of a group of women hearing another woman to speech. She quotes one participant in such a gathering who had been heard to her own story:

> "I had no words. I paused. I stuttered. I could find no word in the English language that could express my emotion. But I had to speak. Old words came out with a different meaning. I *felt* words I could not express, but I was on the way to speaking—or the speaking was speaking me. I know that sounds weird."[4]

Indeed, it all Sounds *very* Weird—bordering on the Super Natural. A Prude might say that the woman was Pronouncing New/Archaic Words. She was Be-Speaking.

When women do this, we are speaking and Dis-covering the Lost Word.[5] By Be-Speaking, we are freeing words to issue from our mouths as Labryses/double-axes. Such Pronouncing is Speaking Out Loud. While it is possible to Speak Out Loud inside one's own mind, it is more effective to say the words aloud. Thus Searchers who read and/or

---

*The importance of rhythm and rhyme in the Pronunciation of Spells has long been recognized by Witches and even by the scholars of patriarchy. Robert Briffault gives numerous examples illustrating worldwide acknowledgment of these connections. Thus, he cites Sir John Rhys, who in 1901 wrote: "Verse-making appertained from the outset to magic, and it was magicians, medicine men [sic], or seers who for their own use first invented the aids of rhythm and meter." See Robert Briffault, *The Mothers: A Study of the Origins of Sentiments and Institutions,* 3 vols. (New York: Macmillan, 1927), I, 18. Moreover, Giuseppe Ferraro in 1886 explained: "Incantations do not consist in words pronounced in a low voice, but in formulas uttered with solemnity, like the responses of an oracle. The mind of the common people, and not theirs alone, is impressed by words pronounced with a certain rhythm, cadence and emphasis, whatever be their actual meaning; the ear, rather than the brain, so to speak, is impressed." To this, Briffault adds the following information: "The Hindus and Arabs have a simple means of depriving a sorceress of the power to do harm; they extract her front teeth, so that she is unable to sing or articulate distinctly." See *The Mothers,* I, 19.

write Weird Works—such as the *Wickedary*—are encouraged to Read Out Loud. Many Animal Guides not only concur but also inspire such Out Loudness. Not least among these inspirers are the birds. For example, gulls, crows, and parrots exhort us to this practice. So also do gaggles of geese and flocks of ducks. Not only birds, but also howling wolves and dogs, croaking frogs, meowing cats, hissing snakes, lowing cows, buzzing bees, chirping crickets, snarling camels, growling bears, and many, many Others urge us to Pronounce Out Loud.

This is particularly important because Pronouncing is rhythmic, emitting powerful vibrations. Unlike the flat, dummy speech of daddy-land, which is petrifying, Be-Speaking/Pronouncing is Electric/Electrifying, evoking changes. It is, as one Glamour Puss purrs, cat/alytic.

Pronunciation:
Denouncing,
Pronouncing,
Announcing

Moreover, individual Elemental words Sound different, and they Sound differently than the bland replacements/replicants which pervade Boredom. Thus, when the New Word *a-Musing* is Pronounced, it obviously is unlike the old word *amusing,* and the Pronouncing of *A-mazing* demonstrates that it is not reducible to *amazing.* Clearly, *Gyn/Ecology* does not sound like mere *gynecology,* nor does *Crone-ology* sound like *chronology,* for multileveled meanings are Heard and Said by Pronouncing Sibyls.[6]

New/Archaic Words may look exactly the same (except for their capitalization) as the replicants and dull derivatives imprisoned within a patriarchal context. However, when a Nag Pronounces a word such as *Nag* (the noun or the verb), we hear a ring of pride and defiance—in ringing contrast to the leering, accusatory tone of the patriarchally possessed word *nag* when this is spat at strong women by snools. This Metamorphic principle applies to countless other words, such as *Witch, Shrew, Dragon, Vixen.*

Clearly, entire sentences change when such Pronouncing occurs. These do not sound like the sentences of snooldom. When one Wild woman says of an Other, "She is a Revolting Hag," this Proud Pronouncement sounds not at all like the mouthings of a sneering snivel-ard who whines, "She's a revolting hag." When a Virago respectfully expresses her admiration of a peer, exclaiming, "What a Bitch!" this exclamation bears no resemblance to the droning of a dickspeaker, who complains, "What a bitch!" The statement, "She is Weird!" when Pronounced by a Prude, is not at all the derogatory declaration intended in snooldom by such comments as "She's weird." The phrase "Chairman of the Bored" sends out utterly Other vibrations, in no way sounding like the boring title which it so Strangely resembles.

Waves of Wild Words Pronounced Out Loud can counter and overpower the pedantic prattle of the processions of "the sons of educated men."[7] These patriarchal processors attempt to marshal the Race of

Wild Words into forced marches. The professional trickers—the oldest professionals—act as traffic police, regimenting words. As pimps they traffic in words as well as in women, using them as prostitutes. Dressed up ornately, women and words are made to serve.

Pronouncing women Name these games and thus release words to fly. As Be-Speakers we are nonprofessionals, refusing to join the processions of the sons of educated men, to be hangers-on and henchwomen for their heinous crimes. As Namers, we Pronounce in a Vernacular mode. One definition of *vernacular* is "language that is spoken or written naturally at a particular period: LIVING LANGUAGE" (*Webster's*). Pronouncing, then, is Natural Speaking of Living Words.

Women who Pronounce in the Vernacular are often labeled "fanatic." This can be Heard as a thought-provoking word. *Fanatic* is derived from the Latin *fanaticus,* meaning "inspired by a deity." Its "obsolete" definition is "possessed by or as if by a demon" (*Webster's*). Of course, the possessors choose to see inspired Pronouncing women as "possessed" by demons, while in reality Be-Speakers are escaping the State of Possession. Moreover, in addition to the negative sense of *demon,* *Webster's* gives as the *first* definition of this word "an attendant, ministering, or indwelling power or spirit: DAIMONION, GENIUS." One who Pronounces Living Words is in Touch with her Demon, her Genius, her Muse, her Self. This enables her to Name her own Real Presence. To such a woman, the negative definition of *demon* as "evil spirit" suggests the deceptive and ghostly presences of absence and absences of Presence that have been devised to divide her from her own Genius/Demon.

As she Pronounces, a woman experiences well-being, Happiness. In Greek this is called *eudaimonia,* which means "having a good attendant or indwelling spirit." Since such a woman is in Good company, she is enabled to release the Angelic powers of words—their powers to act as messengers. These release her in turn. Thus women and words Act as Guides for each other away from the possessors' processions.

Women who Pronounce Wild words are also sometimes called "enthusiasts." Since this word is derived from the Greek *enthousiazein,* meaning "to be inspired," this appellation need not be taken as an insult. Moreover, it is enspiriting to read the following "archaic" definition of *enthusiasm:* "a state of impassioned emotion: exaltation of feelings: TRANSPORT, ECSTASY" (*Webster's*). Since Pronouncing women are enthusiastic, our Wicked words fly in exaltation, like a flight of larks.

Naturally, those who speak Living Words are also called "eccentric." Since this means "deviating from conventional or accepted usage or conduct" and "being away or remote from a center" (*Webster's*), this word is also acceptable. Be-ing far away from the center of patriarchal convention and usage, we Be-Speak Out Loud on the Boundary.[8] Boundary Living and Speaking reinforces idiosyncracies that are incomprehensible to the processions of wantwits who attempt to control conduct and usage.

Fanatic, Enthusiastic, Eccentric, Idiosyncratic women, then, can take on the slander and labels of foreground fixers. Preferring Animal and Bird Guides to academented analysts, we laugh at such labels as "quack." Pronouncing in harmony with hilarious ducks, we Quack back and Quack away, finding Natural speech more inspiring than conventional clichés.

III. Announcing

According to *Webster's,* the verb *announce* means "to make known publicly." It also means "to give notice of the arrival, presence, or readiness of." Yet another definition is "to declare beforehand: FORETELL." The *Wickedary* Announces publicly the arrival, readiness, and Presence of women and words whose Time has come. It declares beforehand, foretelling triumphs of the Fates.

Announcing, then, is Oracular. The word *oracle* is derived from the Latin *orare,* meaning "to speak." One definition of *oracle* is "a medium by which a pagan god reveals hidden knowledge or makes known the divine purpose" (*Webster's*). The Announcements of Sibyls are Oracles which unveil the shamefully hidden ignorance of patriarchs and their gods and Divine publicly their deadly "divine" purposes. Such Announcements release women from mindbinding mystifications intended to stop our movement, to hide the Pixy-paths of our own Divining.

Announcing women make known publicly the fact that mysterious men and their gods have no power to Divine/Foretell the ways of Wild be-ing.[9] We point out that this is why they are obsessed with reducing the world to a laboratory under their control, where they "predict" the responses of their victims.[10] Announcing Mediums give notice of the Presence of unpredictable animals, words, and women, as well as Other Unpredictable Elements. These live in the Background, untamed and undomesticated.

Announcing women declare the end of mirrordom. In the preceding Web we have seen that Wicked Grammar cracks the mirrors of phalloglamour. Such mirror-cracking is most effectively achieved when Shrews Announce Out Loud the end of the Looking Glass Society—the society whose essential mechanics were eloquently Dis-closed by Virginia Woolf:

Women have served all these centuries as looking-glasses possessing the magic and delicious power of reflecting the figure of man at twice its natural size. . . . Whatever may be their use in civilised societies, mirrors are essential to all violent and heroic action. That is why Napoleon and Mussolini both insist so emphatically upon the inferiority of women, for if they were not inferior, they would cease to enlarge.[11]

**PRELIMINARY
WEB FOUR**

In order to Announce efficaciously the end of mirrordom it is absolutely essential that Oracular women be uncompromising Truth-Tellers/Soothsayers. As Woolf Explains:

> *For if she begins to tell the truth* the figure in the looking-glass shrinks; his fitness for life is diminished. How is he to go on giving judgement, civilising natives, making laws, writing books, dressing up and speechifying at banquets, unless he can see himself at breakfast and at dinner at least twice the size he really is? . . . The looking-glass vision is of supreme importance *because it charges the vitality: it stimulates the nervous system* [emphases all mine].[12]

Refusing to stimulate the nervous systems of Nothing-lovers whose nocturnal emissions are converting the earth into a junkyard and polluting even the heavens as far as they can reach, Nags Announce the Truth about tom, dick, and harry and their totaled world. Shrews smash the Mystery of Man—his secret need for mirrors. Crones crack his house of mirrors by cracking up with Lusty Laughter at his attempts to pronounce judgment, civilize Natives, make laws, write books, dress up, and speechify.

Leaping through the cracks, Racing women Roar publicly at the "announcements" of bore-ocracy—its birth announcements, death announcements, wedding announcements, graduation announcements, and all its other commercial announcements—the milestones of "memory" in Boredom. Nags Announce that these "announcements" erase Metamemory, reducing Memory to a set of answers to an elementary questionnaire.[13]

Sibyls Announce the Presence of Weird women whose Time is measured by the creation of Future Memories. In this Oracular work, Augurs are aided by the auspicious owls, those Wise Hags who Divine the secrets of the night.[14] The owls are joined by choruses of birds who Announce the coming of dawn and by groundhogs predicting the early arrival of spring. Packs of wolves and coyotes can also be Heard, as they Announce the Wonders of the Wild. Inspired by these sounds, Magpies and Muses harmonize, smiling with Wicked Eyes, proclaiming the Time for Magpiety.[15]

Elephants trumpet the triumph of Metamemory and Announce Gatherings of our Guides—Muses, Angels, Words, Fairies, Trees, Stars, Animals of all kinds. These are our companions on the Wicked Weaving Journey. They will be encountered again in the following Web.

PRELIMINARY WEB FIVE

Guides to the Wickedary

The Muses/Demons attending all Wild women are Writers'/ Readers' Guides to the *Wickedary*.* Moreover, the *Wickedary* itself is a Guide Book for the Otherworld Journey, and it is filled with Guide Words that lead the reader ahead/around. As the Old Wives say: "One word/world leads to another." Thus the words themselves, together with Websters who Hear them into speech/song, work to Spin threads and webs, and ultimately to Weave tapestries that represent the terrain of Realms Re-membered in this book.

Wild women recognize our Guide Words as they cry out within our psyches, trying to break patriarchally embedded Sound barriers— those walls of elementary "definitions" that limit/dull their senses and dull our senses, keeping us all prisoners. The Hearing of Hags releases jailed words, who, like jailbirds freed at last from the masters' cages, sing and soar.

As the freed words speak/sing, we learn to follow the skeins of their flight. Guided by these sisters, these ungagged Holy Crones, we tour the Realms of words, learning New meanings and connections. We see/hear that words fly together, sounding each other to freedom. They free each other as well as our Selves, breaking the patriarchal prison-keepers' patterns and soaring in Musing Metapatterns. Wise Women, who know that our Race is akin to the Race of Wild Words, find here

*According to the *Oxford English Dictionary,* one definition of the noun *guide* is "one who leads or shows the way, esp. to a traveller in a strange country." According to the *Wickedary,* a **Guide** is "an Otherworldly Helper who shows a Traveler the way into the Country of the Strange, her Homeland" (*Word-Web Two*).

clues to our own liberation. Words and women reclaim our own Nations, our tribes and formations. In this process, words and women aid each other. Our guiding is reciprocal, requited. United, we work to expel the bore-ocratic chairmen of the bored. We strive to make the world Weirder.

Elemental Mediums as Guides

The word *guide,* according to *Webster's,* is akin in its origins to the Old English *wītan,* meaning "to look after, depart," and to *witan,* meaning "to know." Websters exercise our wits to know the words that will guide us in our departure from the State of Possession. In this process we experience Guidance from many Sources.

These Sources/Springs of Guidance are channels between the world of patriarchal possession/deception and the Realms of Metabeing, that is, the Background. As we have seen in *Preliminary Web One,* all Wicked women and words are Mediums, as are all Other participants in Elemental Be-ing. In this Web we are considering these Mediums as Guides to the *Wickedary,* helping us to Weave its tapestries and Weave our way into the Realms which they reflect.

Websters ponder the question: How do these Guides guide us? What are their Mediumistic ways of helping us? There are clues in the fact that one synonym for the verb *guide* is *lead.* Viragos considering this word readily dismiss the idea of "leading" that implies ordering someone about, as in the case of a military officer who leads. We find it more enlightening to consider such a phrase as "leading question," and then Hear this in a New way. Such Questions do not push, shove, or command, like drill sergeants. Rather, the Leading Questions that act as Guides invite, attract, beckon, prompt, inspire, teach, warn.* Leading Questions are First Questions, inspiring us on the Quest of Be-ing.

One definition of the verb *lead* is "to guide by indicating the way: mark out or show the way to (*led* through the fog by the distant lights

---

*One example of such a question is: "What does it mean, on a day by day level, to live with integrity on the boundary of patriarchal institutions?" The process of asking Leading Questions is described by science fiction writer Alice Sheldon (alias James Tiptree, Jr.) in her story "The Psychologist Who Wouldn't Do Awful Things to Rats." The deviant psychologist ponders: "The privilege of knowing how, painfully, to frame answerable questions, answers which will lead him to more insights and better questions as far as his mind can manage and his own life lasts. It is what he wants more than anything in the world to do, always has." See James Tiptree, Jr., *Star Songs of an Old Primate* (New York: Ballantine Books, 1978), p. 236.

of the city)" (*Webster's*). Elemental Mediums lead/guide in this way, attracting attention in the right direction. Websters can understand this principle better by considering further the workings of the Final Cause, which causes by attraction, and which is the Cause of Causes, the Guide of Guides.

The Guide of Guides

The ultimate Guide of each Weaver/Journeyer is her Final Cause, her indwelling, unfolding Purpose. A woman is really "leading her own life" only when she is in harmony with her Final Cause.[1] That is, she is on her true course, and it is by *acting* in accord with this Sense of Direction * that she is enabled to Sense and understand the messages of the Mediums/Guides she encounters along the way.

Of course, there are obstacles and traps set by the rulers of snooldom, intended to distract and deafen each woman to the Call of her Final Cause, which is the Call of the Wild. Among the obstacles to clear Hearing is the continual white noise of the patriarchal Passive Voice—the noise/noose that keeps women passive. The Passive Voice—that ubiquitous patriarchal voice that subliminally spooks women, luring its victims into passivity, rendering them unable to recognize and Name the agents of oppression—calls from all sides. It is embedded in the voices of the secret agents, manipulators, possessors who attempt not only to disguise *who* are the agents of androcracy's atrocities but also to pacify/passivize their victims/patients.[2] Yet the Call of the Wild within—the call of the Active/Activizing Voice of the Final Cause—can be Heard by women who choose to be attentive to our own Sense of Direction, refusing to be distracted.

Listening to the Active Voice of the Final Cause actualizes the capacity for discernment.[3] The verb *discern* is derived from the Latin *dis-*, meaning "apart," and *cernere,* meaning "to sift." One meaning of this verb is "to recognize or identify as separate and distinct: DIFFERENTI-ATE, DISCRIMINATE (discern right from wrong) (discern the false from the genuine)" (*Webster's*). *Discern* not only means "to make out with the eyes" but also "to detect or discover with other senses than vision." Thus it means "to sense or come to know or recognize mentally, especially something that is hidden or obscure" (*Webster's*).

The Final Cause within, as this is Realized, guides Journeying women in our struggles to sift apart right from wrong, the false from the genuine—the fabrications of the foreground from the Reality of Back-

---

* For more on the Sense of Direction see *Appendicular Web Three.*

ground be-ing. This discerning is accomplished in multileveled ways, not only with the ordinary sense of sight, but also with Other Senses.

When Weaving women Presentiate the Final Cause within, this Presence actualizes also our abilities to communicate with other women who Realize this Inner Sense of Direction. Thus a Network is woven by and among such women. This Network makes possible intuitive connections with each Other, as well as quantum leaps of understanding and power. Wicked women, united in this way, break through the fathers' façades, sifting apart good and evil. Refusing to be confused by the Passive Voices of the patriarchs, such women discern, distinguish, differentiate. As Namers we Name such atrocities as pornography and the torture of animals as evil. We Name the foreground of the phallocrats as false.

Suspecting the essential power of the Final Cause, the fixers/framers attempt in every way to muffle its Voice and to distract from its Guidance. Their intent is to break our internal connection with deep purposefulness, which makes all other Elemental connections possible. Thus they create a State of Craziness by embedding mindbinding messages, manufacturing madness and fragmentation. Crazed by such messages, women who are not profoundly in Touch with their Sense of Purpose become the enemies of their own Wild Selves.

Just as phallocracy must manufacture craziness, it must create suffering in order to maintain itself. The production of suffering in women, animals, and all of nature is a major achievement of the sadosociety. While the Wild is being destroyed, millions of animals are forcibly bred only to suffer atrociously at the hands of "scientists."[4] In the necrophilic society, the state of enforced procreation, millions of children are born to die of hunger and deprivation of all kinds. The proliferation of senseless suffering is *intended** to block awareness of the Final Cause, that is, to stop deep Elemental purposefulness and break harmonious communication. For the deadly deadfellows know that they can be overthrown by the Forces of Life.

The Primal project of Wicked women is unblocking the flow of Final Causality. Hearing its Active Voice will enable women to communicate with each other and with Other Guides, Sounding out cosmic connections. "Let Consciousness be your Guide" is the Guideline of Sibyls and Soothsayers, and by this is meant both individual and shared Cronelogical Consciousness—the Elemental force that cannot be defeated.

---

*The word *intended* applies here. The question of whether the intent is "conscious" or "unconscious" is irrelevant, since the intent is inherent in the institutions and behaviors dictated by the sadosociety.

Mutual Attraction: Re-membering Connections

We have seen in *Preliminary Web Three* that the Good is that which attracts Wicked women to transcend the patriarchally defined/confined categories of "good" and "evil." Those who strive for participation in Be-ing experienced as Good and as the Source of true Originality are attracted to each other and to Other Elemental creatures. This attraction is not sentimental, nor does it imply monotonous, monodimensional sameness. Rather, since we are attracted precisely to the Source of each Other's Originality, this brings out the Diversity that is required for harmony and that is Gyn/Ecological. This Wicked Law of Attraction repels the forces of fragmentation.

Unblocking the flow of participation in the Good makes possible Wicked contemplation. *Contemplation* is derived from the Latin *com-*, meaning "with, together, jointly" plus *templum*, meaning "space for observation marked out by the augur." When Websters are united in purpose, we Act as Augurs, observing and contemplating from Spaces marked out by ourSelves. Moreover, *templum* is said probably to be akin to *tempus*, meaning "period of time" (*Webster's*). Websters/Augurs observe and contemplate in our own Time. In his *Etymological Dictionary* Skeat explains that the *templum* was "an *open* [emphasis mine] space for observation (by the augurs)." The Space/Time of contemplating Augurs is indeed open—to the Elements, to the possibility of Elemental Divination.

Insofar as our minds and imaginations are blunted by bore-ocracy, we may believe that such contemplation/communication is either impossible or "merely" metaphorical. Since phallocracy systematically works to seal off our consciousness of the Elemental world, our perfectly Natural abilities to communicate with Other Elemental beings seem unreliable, even unbelievable. Moreover, the Wonder-full communicative capacities of animals are hidden from us.

It is instructive to study the writings of patriarchal predators who claim to have knowledge of communication among animals. An author of fiction (who is also an avid hunter) describes through the words of one of his characters the communication between birds and rabbits in a bog:

> So hard is it for man to speak with man when separated by no more than a frontier, that it surprised me the first time that I saw twenty rabbits sent hurrying to safety by no more than a single remark from a passing rook, who had seen me stalking them though I was out of sight of the rabbits. And I learned that a rook does not merely say Caw, having, at least, one

note of warning that probably means Man, and another that certainly means "Man with a gun." I learned, too, that a small bird among trees would go on and on repeating a warning note until hundreds of hidden ears must have been thrilled with the menace; and, however quietly I went after that through the wood, I would see fewer rabbits, and those that I saw would be at once away.[5]

Such information—as far as it goes—rings true to Augurs. Of course, the rook would warn the rabbits, for they inhabit the same bog, unfairly invaded by man. Yet it is impossible to fail to note that the character speaking here is a hunter. A Leading Question is: Wouldn't his knowledge be limited and/or distorted by his invasive, violent behavior? The author himself unwittingly provides clues as the passage continues with further comments by the hunter:

And so by pitting myself against the rabbits I came to know a little about them, and about their other enemies; and I know no other way in which I could have learned as much. Nobody standing behind a chess-player and watching him play can learn half as much of chess as the man that is playing against him, for rivalry is the essence of the game, as it is of the woods.[6]

The comparison of a hunter pitted against a rabbit to two men engaged in a game of chess is, of course, ludicrous. The hunting and killing of the rabbit is not a fair game. The author attempts to veil this fact with the ill-logic of a false analogy. It is easy to discern the fallacy, however, for clearly no rabbit consents to play the deadly game, and no rabbit is a winner, although some are escapees.

The hunter/predator's knowledge of the communication between bird and rabbit is limited by his distorted purpose. He knows of certain habits and of warning signals concerning his own necrophilic presence and intent, but he lacks Other dimensions of sensitivity—including basic awareness of the fact that there is something profoundly wrong with hunting as a sport. His perspective is limited by the predator's preoccupation with "rivalry." His concern is primarily with dynamics of opposition/repulsion rather than with the Wicked Law of Attraction. He is able to sense and write about enmity and about warnings sent out by animals concerning the invasive presence of Man, but his vision does not extend to the possibility of friendly communication and interaction.

The knowledge of contemplating Augurs must be far Other-Wise

HOPPING HOPE

than this, for insofar as it is true knowledge it is rooted in Biophilia, which is Pure Lust for Life and which is a Source of Mutual Attraction. It is Biophilia that inspires Augurs to be open to messages from Wild Guides and to Re-member connections broken by the hunters and other killers of the necrophilic society.

Living according to the Wicked Law of Attraction requires the acquisition of New Habits/Virtues. Augurs/Websters struggle constantly to overcome the bad habits fostered in fatherland (which the patriarchs call "virtues") and to acquire Volcanic Virtues. These Wild Virtues are Realized through repeated Acts, and patriarchal "virtues" are exorcized by such Acts.[7]

In order to Hear the inspirations, advice, healing messages, and warnings of Guides, Wicked Websters need Volcanic Courage. Listening to such promptings requires defying the embedded voices in the head—the multitudinous stereotypical man-made echoes of the Passive Voice which are the warped words of phallocracy. Outrageous Courage enables Websters to Actively Voice such defiance and move on.

In addition, Pyrosophical Distemperance is needed to overcome the embedded plastic and potted passions and virtues that hinder Hearing.[8] Pyromantic Prudence is required to distinguish genuine Guides from the elementary/dummy "guides" provided by snools to misguide Musing women.* So also such Virtues as Fey Faith, Hopping Hope, Nemesis, Pure Lust, Disgust, and Laughing Out Loud are necessary.

As the foreground conditions become worse, as the snoolish destruction and poisoning of Earth and its inhabitants and surroundings escalates to a state that can appear irreversible, our Guides draw nearer and Call women with urgency. Particularly loud and pleading are the Voices of animals, whose victimization and suffering at the hands of the rakes and rippers of patriarchy are similar in many ways to the rape, battering, torture, and massacre of women. This brings us to the Strange subject of Familiars.

---

*Among blatant examples of these are "tour guides," which predigest knowledge, making Original experience of women's history almost impossible. Similarly deceptive are "museum guides." Any well-traveled Crone knows that these erase the clues that would make possible the awakening of Deep Memory. An important archaeological museum in Heraklion, Crete, for instance, is replete with such studied deletions and misrepresentations (although the clues are there for those who can look with Real Eyes). Among elementary guides are also TV "guides," which lure readers into fixation on TV screens, so that they become inured to the horror of Boredom and lose the capacity for dreams and visions. Other pseudoguides include scientific "experts," politicians, and priests of all kinds, including all the medical and psycho-logical bad counselors who attempt to prevent women from Hearing our Wild Guides.

Familiars as Guides

PRELIMINARY
WEB FIVE

According to *Webster's*, one definition of *familiar* is "a supernatural spirit often embodied in an animal and at the service of a person (the loathsome toad, the witches' familiar—Harvey Graham)" (*Webster's*). Be-Witching women can decode this to mean "a Super Natural Spirited Background animal, the Graceful friend of a Witch." The word *familiar* is derived from the Middle English *familier*, meaning "member of one's household, intimate associate." Weird women know that our animal familiars are intimate associates, although not all are members of our households in the narrow sense of this word. However, if we take the word *house* to Name our habitat, the Earth, which we share with the animals and all Elemental creatures, we can recognize as our familiars many animals who do not live under the same roof. Moreover, when we consider that the word *house* is akin in its origins to the Gothic *gudhūs*, meaning *temple* (*Webster's*), this brings our thinking full spiral to the idea that as Augurs we share our open Spaces and Times of contemplation with animals who are inhabitants of the Wild, the Background.

Websters are aware of the well-known distinction between Domestic Familiars and Divining Familiars. According to Margaret Murray, Domestic Familiars are often obtained by gift from a "fellow-witch" and by inheritance.[9] Divining Familiars often appear "accidentally" after the performance of certain magical ceremonies. Witches have been said to foretell the future with the aid of such animals. Murray writes:

> The method was probably such as obtained in other places where auguries by animals and birds were practised, i.e., by the direction and pace of the animal, by its actions, by its voice if it emitted any sound, and so on.[10]

Wicked women perform many "ceremonies," including the Weaving of Wickedaries and Other Wonders. Lustily Weaving, we are graced by visitations of Elemental Spirits and Elementally Spirited Animals—Boon Companions who arrive to ensure that we are following the right threads and to guide us further.

These Elemental friends are eager to speak with those who have powers of Hearing. They remind us of women's Archaic tradition of conversations and friendships with animals, trees, stars, the moon, flowers, lakes, winds—and many Other Life-forms. They also remind us of the unnatural silencing of Elemental Voices under patriarchy.

The animals who are Guides to the *Wickedary* point out that they are commonly called "dumb" by the wantwits and babblers who prevail in snooldom. Thus, although they Be-Speak very eloquently and in many languages, they are continually ignored, insulted, and harassed. Our brilliant Bird Guides remind us of the insulting expression "bird brain." The remarkably intelligent geese call attention to the expression "silly goose." The fantastically diverse and beautiful schools of fish demonstrate the foolishness of the adjective "fishy" when used to discredit a statement or story.

All of these Spirited creatures join in explaining that such belittlement, which may appear "harmless" to members of the "human species," is a surface manifestation of the sadosociety's ignorance and devaluation of animals and all of nature. They point to the torture, mutilation, and massacre of animals in the name of science, the senseless hunting down and killing of Wild beasts in the name of sport, the destruction of whole tribes of animals and of all remnants of ecological balance in the name of agribusiness. They declare that all of these horrors are interrelated parts of patriarchy's worldwide program of biocide. So also is the systematic desensitization of humans by phallocracy's religion, media, politics, and education—manifested by the fact that protests against this massacre of the Wild are met with colossal indifference and malice.

Guides to the Wickedary

Our Familiars further explain that all of the Elements are unheard in patriarchy. The Earth, the Air, the Fire, and the Water are not Heard in the necro-apocalyptic society that is bent on nuclear holocaust. They are silenced by the sadosociety's lethal military and "peaceful" industries whose tentacles stretch into outer and inner space.

Hearing Hags add to this account the fact that the Voices of Elemental Spirits have been ridiculed out of "existence" in the foreground world which is phallocracy/foolocracy, so that they are now beyond the range of "normal" hearing.

Paranormal, Super Natural Websters and our Familiars pledge our Great Refusal of this lethal silencing. Raging and Laughing Out Loud, we prepare together for our Journey further into Wicked Realms. Our assembly is colorful, bold, and cheering to behold. Our Spirits are High as we prepare for passage into the Core of the *Wickedary,* where we will Hear and Speak and Sing in the Chorus of Wild Racing Words.

The Animals' Parade

Websters preparing to Weave into the Core/Heart of the *Wickedary* decide to prepare ourSelves for this adventure by conjuring a celebration of Life. The Pixies suggest a picnic and so, Pixie-led, we Prance down Pixie-paths that lead us to the edge of the sea. As we Prance, we notice that we are joined by many Fore-Crones. Sojourner Truth and Joan of

S<small>PRITE</small> *and Friend: "Let's have a parade!"*

Arc are there. So also are Matilda Joslyn Gage, Mary Wollstonecraft, Hatshepsut, Hildegarde of Bingen, Sappho, Jiu Jin, Amelia Bloomer, Tituba, the Brontë sisters, Rachel Carson, and many, many Others.

We are joined also by many Elemental creatures. The Gnomes, Undines, Salamanders, and Sylphs are with us, as we pass through meadows and across streams, feeling the warm sun and breathing the fragrant air. As we Prance through the woods we meet Dryads and at brooks and waterfalls we encounter Naiads and Nixes. All of these friendly folk decide to come along. Oreads skip down from the nearby mountains, and as the whole gathering approaches the sea we are greeted by Oceanids and Mermaids swimming near the shore.

Setting our picnic baskets on the sand, the assembly/dissembly discusses how to prepare for the awesome Journey into and through the Core. One of our number—a true Wickedarian—suggests we examine the word *prepare*. A dutiful Dryad, perusing an etymological dictionary which she always has with her, opens to this word and finds that it comes from the Latin *parāre* and is akin in its roots to the word *parade* (*Skeat's*). "Let's have a parade!" shout three Shrews and a Prude. They are greeted with Roars of Approval.

At this moment a Muse cups her ear and tells all to be silent. She says that she Hears thundering of hooves, flapping of wings, splashing of flippers. "They're coming!" she cries. "Our parade Guides are here."

Suddenly animals appear out of Everywhere. They approach in a Prancing Parade. This Parade of Parades is a parody of pompous processions and marches—which Woolf called "the processions of the sons of educated men." Unlike the fathers and sons, the animals disdain the wearing of uniforms and refuse to walk in order. "We never goose step!" honk the geese. "We like to lumber," growl the bears. A laughing jackass Laughs Out Loud.

Instead of marching, the animals parade in different styles. They tumble, hop, leap, gallop, crawl, scamper. Some twirl widdershins as they walk. As the land animals parade on the edge of the sea, the sea animals swim alongside them. These dive and jump with joy. Dolphins offer rides to watching Websters. Seals bark invitations to Sirens to join their pods and paddle together. Birds and butterflies fly and flit above the traveling crowd.

Wondering Websters notice that these, our Guides, travel together but in different tribes. Consulting her conventional "animal guide," some schoolmarm proclaims that wolves and dogs move in "packs," whereas elk and buffalo go in "gangs." Further, she reads, the roe deer, larks, and quail gather and travel in "bevies," while hogs move in "drifts" and peacocks gather in "musters." A Prude proudly notes that a company of lions is called a "pride," and a Shrew remarks that a company of apes is called a "shrewdness."

53

"Called by whom?" croaks a parrot, flying from tree to tree. "Do you think we need your words in order to be? We deign to speak them to help you along." "Right!" roars the throng. The gathering of Websters laughs at the joke. A laughing hyena laughs with us.

"We're here to guide you into the Core," explains a Wild boar. "Listen to your animal friends when writing and reading your *Wickedary*," chirps a nearby canary. "Your Wicked work is an Archimagical Journey requiring our animating assistance," explains a shrewd ape. "And that's because we animals are always in the State of Metabeing, Be-Longing in the Background," a groundhog explains.

By this time Websters have found ourSelves following and joining the romping throng, listening eagerly for their advice. "When reading the Core of the *Wickedary,* you must feel at home on the road," explain the hermit crabs and turtles. "Read erratically," the butterflies advise. "And never let your Questing be domesticated," the Wild cows warn. "Allow the Words to lead you into deeper waters," sing the whales. "We're there already."

At this point Wicked women are aware of Other voices. The wise old trees, swishing their branches, say: "Re-member your roots." The Moon says: "Take your own Time when traveling these Word-paths." The stars call from afar: "Continue the Journey."

Our attention then is drawn to the sky. We see there the star Venus, sacred to Oshun, Goddess of love and beauty.[11] We hear the voices of many Sky Goddesses, including Chih Nu, the Weaving Woman of heaven,[12] who is engaged in cosmic conversation with Spider Grandmother. The latter, known also as Thought Woman, Spins/Thinks all the meanings and paths of Fate.[13]

While we listen in suspense to this Heavenly Gossip, one Sibyl points to a glorious sight: The Goddess Freya is riding through the sky in a chariot drawn by cats. Then suddenly, while all are watching, she leaps to the back of a huge golden-bristled boar.[14] A Nag recalls that this happens to be Friday the Thirteenth, Freya's sacred day combined with her sacred number. A Crone-ographer reminds us that this day was proclaimed "unlucky" by christian monks.[15] A Wild sow snorts. Six large cats growl. A Wise owl hoots.

A far-sighted Fury points to another wonder, crying that the Great Witch, Medea, rides the skies in a winged chariot drawn by serpents.[16] A hundred snakes hiss their approval.

When the hissing dies down, a little bear who has been riding on her mother's back drowsily points her paw toward the constellation of the Little Bear, which contains the Polestar. An old bear explains that this conspicuous star that at any period is nearest the north celestial pole is also called the North Star. All Websters know that *polestar,* according to

Webster's, generally refers to "a directing or controlling [sic] principle: GUIDE."

Guided by such signs and Wonders in the heavens, Wicked Weavers can follow our stars into and through the Core of the *Wickedary,* adventuring and Questing for the Lost Words. We are assured by the animals that we *can* find these and that when we Sound them, we will be Heard.

THE SECOND PHASE

The Core of the Wickedary: Word-Webs

WOVEN BY MARY DALY
AND JANE CAPUTI

WORD-WEB ONE

Elemental Philosophical Words and Phrases and Other Key Words

T his Word-Web consists of Elemental philosophical words and phrases and some Other key words. These are Original words Naming the Background and the foreground from the perspective of the Background. That is, they Name Wild Reality and its patriarchal counterfeits from the perspective of those who choose the Background as our Homeland, electing to be members of the Outsiders' Society, and Living on the Boundary between the worlds.

System of Symbols (●, ◕, ◑, ○)

The following symbols signify the works by Mary Daly in which *Wickedary* words first appeared:

● *The Church and the Second Sex.* The most recent edition (Boston: Beacon Press, 1985) contains the original text (New York: Harper and Row, 1968) and the "Autobiographical Preface" and "Feminist Postchristian Introduction by the Author" from the 1975 Harper Colophon edition, as well as the 1985 "New Archaic Afterwords." The edition in which the word first appears is indicated in the entry.

● *Beyond God the Father: Toward a Philosophy of Women's Liberation.* The most recent edition (Boston: Beacon Press, 1985) contains the original text (Boston: Beacon Press, 1973) and an "Original Reintroduction by the Author." All references are to the original edition unless otherwise indicated in the entry.

○ *Gyn/Ecology: The Metaethics of Radical Feminism* (Boston: Beacon Press, 1978).

○ *Pure Lust: Elemental Feminist Philosophy* (Boston: Beacon Press, 1984).

The absence of any symbol signifies that the word first appears in the *Wickedary*. Words invented by other women are indicated by the women's names at the entries.

WORD-WEB ONE *Cross-referencing*

Cross-referenced words, which appear at the end of some definitions, are grouped according to their respective Word-Webs. In cross-referencing, the indicators w-w 1, w-w 2, and w-w 3 refer to *Word-Web One, Word-Web Two,* and *Word-Web Three.* Cross-referenced words from the same Word-Web are always listed first.

Absence of absence ○ : ecstatic condition of Wild Women; state achieved by Crones who have succeeded in exorcising phallic pseudo-presence, i.e., ontological absence. *Compare* **absence of Presence; presence of absence** (w-w 1)

absence of Presence ○ : lack of content and purpose; the normal nothingness of bore-ocracy; the routinized rule in snooldom; absence of soul. *Examples:* negation of meaning in a conversation; lack of affection or of intelligence in a face; nonresponse to a question or to an act of love

Allocentric Perception ○ **1 :** a Be-Witching woman's encounter with the inexhaustible Other, in which her true Self and all other Others participate **2 :** knowledge of interconnectedness that transcends the conventional "subject-object" split of patriarchal categories and labels **3 :** the ever unfolding intuition of Original integrity which is the source of all Metapatriarchal creativity[1]

Anamnesia ○ (Louky Bersianik[2]) *n* **:** Unforgetting the Elemental connections of women; overcoming the "normal" condition of amnesia inflicted upon women in patriarchy, the State of Oblivion

Angel ○ *n* [derived fr. Gk *angelos* messenger—*Webster's*] **:** an Elemental Spirit of the universe whose duration and movement are outside the limitations of tidy time and whose principal activities are knowing and willing; bearer of Archaic knowledge and wisdom

ANGEL: *Elemental Spirit of the universe . . . bearer of Archaic Knowledge and Wisdom*

Animals *n* [derived fr. L *anima* soul—*Webster's*] : Elementally en-souled beings characterized by rich Diversity; instructors in the arts of Spinning, healing, communication, navigation; Helpers/Guides on the Journey beyond the State of Extinction into the Realms of Elemental Reality

Anno Feminarum (A.F.) ● (1975 ed.) : Feminist Postchristian Time/ Space, on the Boundary of patriarchal time and space. *Example:* 1989 A.F. *See* **Archaic Future (A.F.)** (w-w 1). *Compare* **archetypal dead-time (a.d.)** (w-w 1)

Antichurch, Sisterhood as ● : the Movement of Feminist Spirituality understood as bringing forth Archaic be-ing, annihilating the credibility of patriarchal religious myths that have been contrived to legitimate the man-made world

Archaic ○ *adj* : occurring in Tidal Time; Original, Primal, Primordial

Archaic Future (A.F.) ●(1985 ed.) **1** : direction of the movements of Archaic Time; *real* future, which transcends the stagnation/timelessness of archetypal deadtime **2** : reality created through successions of Original Acts/Actions. *Compare* **archetypal deadtime (a.d.)** (w-w 1)

Archaic Time ● (1985 ed.) : Original Creative Time, beyond the stifling grasp of archetypal molds and measures; the measure of Original Motion/E-motion/Movement. *See* **Tidal Time** (w-w 1)

Arche *pl* **Archai** ○ *n* ["something that was in the beginning: a first principle"—*Webster's*] : This definition has been awarded *Websters'* Intergalactic Seal of Approval.

Archelogy ○ *n* ["the science of first principles"—*Webster's*] **1** : the study of Elemental Origins **2** : Realizing Native Powers; Re-calling First Questions; Dis-covering the radiant sunrise of Archaic Be-ing

archetypal deadtime (a.d.) ● (1985 ed.) : the year of the lord—any year of any lord, a.d.; the perpetual bedtime of the comatose sleeping beauties and prince charmings who are fused into their roles in the frozen state of fatherland; Timeless time, lacking genuine movement, having no real past, present, or future. *See* **tidy time** (w-w 1)

archetype ○ *n* [derived fr. Gk *arche-* original + *typtein* to strike, beat; akin to L *stuprum* defilement, dishonor, Skt *tupati, tumpati* he hurts—

62

Webster's] : model/pattern designed to beat, defile, dishonor, and hurt Original Female Elemental Powers. *Examples:* the Great Whore of Babylon, the Eternal Feminine, the *vagina dentata*

Archespheres ○ *n* : the Realm of true beginnings, where Shrews shrink alienating archetypes and Unforget Archaic Origins, uncovering the Archimage, the Original Witch within

Archimage ○ \är kə māj\ (rhyming with *rage*) *n* [derived fr. Gk *archi*-original, primary + *magos* wizard—*Webster's*] **1** : the Original Witch within **2** : Power/Powers of Be-ing within all women and all Biophilic creatures **3** : Active Potency of Hags **4** : Metaphor pointing toward Metabeing, in which all Elemental Life participates

Elemental Philosophical Words and Phrases and Other Key Words

Arch-Image ○ \'ärch + 'im ij \ (rhyming with *march* + *image*) *n* : Mary: vestige of the Goddess symbol that has been preserved in christianity as a hook for the Heathen masses; tamed Goddess symbol which, although it is intended to conceal the Background Memory of the Archimage, functions at times to evoke Archaic Active Potency in women

Archimagical ○ *adj* : participating in the powers of the Archimage; Originally magical

Background ◗ (Denise D. Connors [3]) *n* : the Realm of Wild Reality; the Homeland of women's Selves and of all other Others; the Time/Space where auras of plants, planets, stars, animals and all Other animate beings connect. *Compare* **foreground** (w-w 1)

Be- ○ : prefix signifying ontological depth. *See* **Ontology, Elemental** (w-w 1)

Be-Dazzling [*dazzle* "*archaic:* eclipse with greater brilliance: OUT-SHINE"—*Webster's*] : eclipsing the foreground/elementary world by the brilliance of be-ing

Be-Falling [*befall* "to happen esp. as if by fate"—*Webster's Collegiate*] : the Original Ontological Sinning of Fallen Women who follow the Call of the Fates. *See* **Sin** (w-w 1); **Fates** (w-w 2)

Be-Friending ○ [*befriend* "to act as a friend to: show kindness, sympathy, and understanding to (befriend a helpless person)"—*Webster's*] : radically active transcending of the need for the belittling "befriending" bestowed upon women by their many "protectors" in the state of helplessness/Self-lessness which is patriarchy; overcoming the unnatural separation of women from our Selves and each Other imposed by phallocracy; weaving a context/atmosphere in which Acts/Leaps of Metamorphosis can take place; Realizing the Lust to share Happiness. *Example:* the Weaving of a context of Wild Otherworldliness and Genius by the Brontës

WORD-WEB ONE

Be-ing ● *v* **1 :** Ultimate/Intimate Reality, the constantly Unfolding Verb of Verbs which is intransitive, having no object that limits its dynamism **2 :** the Final Cause, the Good who is Self-communicating, who is the Verb from whom, in whom, and with whom all true movements move

be-ing ● *v* **:** actual participation in the Ultimate/Intimate Reality—Be-ing, the Verb

Be-Laughing : expression of Elemental humor, carrying Lusty Laughers into the Background: ontological Laughing; be-ing Silly together; Laughing that cracks man-made pseudo-reality; Laughing that breaks the Terrible Taboo, Touching the spirits of women, enlivening auras, awakening Hope. *See* **Metafooling; Terrible Taboo** (w-w I); **Laughing Out Loud, Virtue of; Silly** (w-w 2)

Be-Longing ○ [*belong* "to be suitable, appropriate, or advantageous. . . . to be in a proper, rightful, or fitting place, situation, or connection. . . . to be the property of a person or thing. . . . to become attached or bound (as to a person, group, or organization). . . . to be properly classified (whales belong among the mammals)"—*Webster's*] **:** transcending the patriarchally embedded need to belong; ontological yearning for participation in Metabeing; Realizing one's Lust for the intensely focused ontological activity which is Happiness

Be-Monstering [*monster* "*obs:* something unnaturally marvelous: PRODIGY"; also *bemonster* "to address or refer to as a monster"—*Webster's*] **:** be-ing a natural, marvelous Monster; Pronouncing oneSelf or an Other to be a Monster. *Example:*

> May we comprehend that we cannot be stopped.
>
> May I learn how to survive until my part is finished.
> May I realize that I
> > am a
> > monster. I am

64

a
monster.
I am a monster.

And I am proud.
—Robin Morgan[4]

Be-Musing [*bemuse* "to cause to dream or muse: induce a state of reverie in"—*Webster's*] **:** be-ing a Muse for oneSelf and for Other Muses; refusing Musing to a-Musing scribblers; Spinning great dreams and reveries of Female creations, of Lesbian nations.[5] *See* **Muse** (w-w 2). *Compare* **a-Musing** (w-w 3)

Be-Shrewing : be-ing a Shrewd Shrew; Pronouncing oneSelf or an Other to be Untamable, Intractable, Turbulent, and Wise. *See* **Shrew; Shrewish Shrewdness** (w-w 2)

Be-Speaking [*bespeak* "to tell of or betoken beforehand; to prognosticate, augur. . . . to speak (a person) into some state. *Obs.* 1604 'How a young fellow was even bespoke and jested to death by harlots.'"— *O.E.D.*] **1 :** Auguring, foretelling, Speaking of what will be **2 :** bringing about a psychic and/or material change by means of words; speaking into be-ing

Be-Spelling [*bespell* "to cast a spell on: ENCHANT"—*Webster's*] **:** Discovering and releasing the Archimagical powers of words; ontological Shape-Shifting of words which awakens latent powers of be-ing in the Spell-speaker, in the hearer, and in the words themselves. *Example:* concert performances by feminist musician Willie Tyson singing her own incantation "The Witching Hour":

> In the Witching Hour you come to your power
> You feel it deep inside you, it's rising, rising
> And you think it's a dream until you hear
>   yourself scream
> Power to the witch and to the woman in me
>   —Willie Tyson[6]

Be-Thinking [*bethink* "to recollect oneself, return to oneself. *Obs.*"— *O.E.D.;* also "*archaic:* to call to mind: REMEMBER"—*Webster's*] **:** Remembering the Original Self; Re-calling Original Questions; thinking the way ever deeper into the Wilderness, the Background

Be-Tiding 1 : moving in the flow of Tidal Time, in harmony with the Fates **2 :** having Tidal encounters; experiencing synchronicities

Be-Tidings *n* **:** ontological messages from the Fates, often taking the form of dreams, intuitions, visions, visitations, encounters, "coincidences": ANGELIC MESSAGES

Be-Wilder *v* [*bewilder* "to cause to lose one's way, as in a wild or unknown place; to lead or drive astray"—*O.E.D.*] **:** to lead the Self and Others on Pixie-paths that wind ever deeper into the Unknown; to hear and follow the Call of the Wild

Be-Wishing [*wish* "to influence in a magical or occult way by wishing; to bewitch by a desire or imprecation. *dial.*"—*O.E.D.*] **:** to influence in a Magical way by ontological Wishing; to Be-Witch by a desire or inspiration

Be-Witching ○ [*bewitch* "to attract or please to such a degree as to take away all power of resistance or considered reservation: ENCHANT, CHARM, FASCINATE (she bewitched King James no less than her first lover—*N.Y. Times*) (that time-honored privilege of saying foolish things in the grand manner which seems to have bewitched our gallant forefathers—Norman Douglas)"—*Webster's*] **1 :** breaking the rules/roles of boring bewitchingness; ontological Witching **2 :** leaping/hopping/flying inspired by Lust for Metamorphosis; Macromutational moments/movements of be-ing; Shape-shifting **3 :** the exercise of Labrys-like powers that ward off attacks and attract Elemental forces

Biggest Lies, use of ○ **:** fundamental strategy of the Cockocratic State for breaking minds/spirits/senses: DEADLY DECEPTION; dismemberment of consciousness through enormous and often flagrant deception, making acceptable and even invisible the smaller lies that prevail in patriarchy; deadening of deep intuitive powers over and over again, forcing the deceived repeatedly to reinvent the wheel. *Examples* **a:** the christian doctrine of "transubstantiation," according to which the substances of bread and wine are changed into the body and blood of Christ **b:** the pornographic lie that all women secretly desire to be humiliated, possessed, abused, raped, mutilated, and even murdered **c:** the psycho-logical insinuation that whatever misfortune befalls any individual is secretly desired or deserved by the victim, e.g., the accusation that Black poverty is due to laziness

biocide ○ (Anne Dellenbaugh[7]) *n* ["A substance, such as a pesticide or an antibiotic, that is capable of destroying living organisms"—*American Heritage*] **:** the attempted annihilation of all life, which is the lethal intent of the patriarchs. *Canny Comment:*

Can anyone believe it is possible to lay down such a barrage
of poisons on the surface of the earth without making it
unfit for all life? They should not be called "insecticides," but
"biocides."
  —Rachel Carson[8]

Biophilia [⁹] *n* : the Original Lust for Life that is at the core of all Elemental E-motion; Pure Lust, which is the Nemesis of patriarchy, the
Necrophilic State. *See* **Pure Lust; Nemesis** (w-w I). *Compare* **necrophilia** (w-w I). *N.B.: Biophilia* is not in ordinary dictionaries, although the word *necrophilia* is. Several years after the publication of
Gyn/Ecology, Biophilia was used as an elementary book title by Edward O.
Wilson to promote his views on the new/old field of sociobiology.

*Elemental
Philosophical
Words and
Phrases and
Other Key Words*

Biophilic Bonding [○] **1 :** the Lusty combining of Elemental forces
among Others **2 :** the uniting of Life-Loving women in Hopping/
Hoping harmony

Biophilic Communication [○] **1 :** the natural communication among
Elemental creatures—animals, plants, seas, the sun, the moon, the
stars **2 :** participation of Wild Women in the cosmic conversation

Boundary, the [◑] *n* : the location of New Time/Space; Time and
Space created by women Surviving and Spinning on the Boundaries of
patriarchal institutions; dimensions of be-ing experienced by Labrys-
wielding Amazons who choose not only to combat the phallocratic
order but also to wrench back our Archaic Heritage and Journey into
the Background. *See* **Surviving; Spinning** (w-w I)

Boundary Living [◑] **:** Realizing Power of Presence on the Boundaries
of patriarchal institutions; Presentiating the Background in the midst
of foreground conditions by communicating contagious Courage,
Pride, and Other Volcanic Virtues. *Examples* **a:** the Chinese marriage
resisters (nineteenth and twentieth centuries)[9] **b:** the Beguines of medieval Europe[10]

Burning Times, The [⁹] **:** a Crone-logical expression that refers not
only to the period of the European witchcraze (the fifteenth, sixteenth,
and seventeenth centuries) but to the perpetual and worldwide witchcraze perpetrated by patriarchy

castration, female [⁹] **:** the depriving of female vigor and vitality
under patriarchy; the systematic physical, emotional, and mental weak-
ening of women. *Examples* **a:** African genital mutilations (clitori-

67

BE-WITCHING: *leaping/hopping/flying inspired by Lust for Metamorphosis . . . the exercise of Labrys-like powers*

dectomies and infibulations) **b:** Western gynecological mutilations (clitoridectomies, unnecessary ovariectomies and hysterectomies) **c:** the mutilation of women by sex killers, rippers, and snuffers **d:** psychoanalysis (masked by the deceptive doctrine of "penis envy") **e:** the institutionalized starvation and discouragement of women's intellectual capacities. *See* **penis envy** (W-W 3)

Cause of causes ● : *See* **Final Cause; Feminism, Radical** (W-W 1)

Code, Elemental ○ **1** : the vast Virgin potential in every Elemental being **2** : the potential in each woman which she can choose to Discover and Realize; Elemental promise hidden by the phallocentric system/code of symbols that has been embedded in female psyches in order to block Self-Realization and to program women in man-made directions

Courage, Ontological ○ [*courage* derived fr. L *cor* heart— *Skeat's*] : the Courage to Be through and beyond the State of Negation which is patriarchy; participation in the Unfolding of Be-ing— continuing on the Journey always [11]

Courage, Outrageous ○ : [*outrageous* "not conventional or matter-of-fact: EXTRAVAGANT, FANTASTIC. . . . extremely offensive: showing a disregard for decency or good taste"—*Webster's*] : the Courage to be an Other; the Courage of Revolting Hags who reverse the reigning reversals, becoming ever more Offensive, more Tasteless

Courage to Leave ● (1985 ed.) : Virtue enabling women to depart from all patriarchal religions and other hopeless institutions; resolution springing from deep knowledge of the nucleus of nothingness which is at the core of these institutions. *N.B.:* An analysis of "norms for non-cooptation" can be found in Daly, *Beyond God the Father,* pp. 55–59.

Courage to Live ● (1985 ed.) : the Courage to refuse inclusion in the State of the Living Dead, to break out from the deadforms of archetypal deadtime, to take leap after leap of Living Faith; Fiercely Biophilic Courage

Courage to See ● : the Courage to become dis-illusioned, to See through male mysteries, to become a Seer, envisioning an Archaic Future

Courage to Sin ○ [*sin* derived fr. Indo-European root *es-* to be— *American Heritage*] : the Courage to commit Original Acts of participation in Be-ing; the Courage to be Elemental through and beyond the horrors of the Obscene Society; the Courage to be intellectual in the most direct and daring way, claiming and trusting the deep correspondence between the structures/processes of one's own mind and the structures/processes of reality; the Courage to trust and Act on one's own deepest intuitions. *See* **Originally Sinful Acts** (w-w 1)

Daughter [1] *n* : the Original Self; the Untouchable Integrity in every woman; the Wild Virgin within every woman who Lives beyond the confines of patriarchal rules and roles, reveling in be-ing Alone and fiercely bonding with her own kind

Daughter-Right [1] *n* : the Right of a woman to Re-member her Original Integrity; the Right of every Daughter to proclaim her Divinity, to Name her Self, to Act as Nemesis, to right the reversals of "divine sons," to reclaim her place in the sun. *See* **Nemesis** (w-w 1). *Compare* **daughter-blight** (w-w 3)

deadly sins of the fathers [1] : the primary manifestations of patriarchal evil, incarnated in phallo-institutions and in those who invent, control, and legitimate these institutions; biocidal blockages/obstructions to Wild Women's Otherworld Journeying. These are:

> **processions:** the basic sin of phallocracy: *deception;* the production of distorted mirror images of Spinning Process which corral/track Movement/Creativity into endless dead and deadening circles. *Example:* the ritual embedding of patriarchal fairy tales into the minds of little girls
>
> **professions:** the ultimate manifestation of empty male *"pride"* (vanity); assumption by males of self-legitimating control in every cultural activity deemed prestigious by themselves; the consequent condensation of the process of know-ing into inert and mystifying "bodies of knowledge." *Example:* male assumption of control over the sphere of healing, reducing this to the "field of medicine"—a reversal and caricature of genuine healing
>
> **possession:** androcratic *avarice;* demonic seizure and domination of Elemental energy sources accomplished through political, economic, and technological means and, most profoundly, through the manufacture and proliferation of male myth. *Example:* the "divine commands" in Genesis: "God blessed them, saying to them 'Be fruitful, multiply, fill the earth and conquer it. Be masters of the fish of the sea, the birds of heaven and all living animals on the earth.'"—Gen. 1:28 [J.B.]. Also: "To the woman he [god] said: 'I will multiply your pains in childbearing, you shall give birth to your children in pain. Your yearning shall be for your husband, yet he will lord it over you.'"—Gen. 3:16 [J.B.]

70

aggression: malevolent male violence, misnamed *anger;* the raping, killing, and leveling of all forms of life. *Examples* **a:** the nuclear arms race relentlessly marching to its ill-logical conclusion—nuclear holocaust **b:** the European witchcraze **c:** the holocaust of the Jews under the nazis

obsession: phallic *lust;* the deadly dis-passion that prevails in patriarchy; the life-hating lechery that seeks to penetrate, violate, and spoil all Elemental Integrity. *Examples* **a:** the incessant despoliation of women's bodies by the eight-billion-dollar pornography industry **b:** the colonization and conquest of America—the "Virgin Land"—its native inhabitants and its wilderness **c:** incestuous abuse of girls

assimilation: gynocidal/biocidal *gluttony* which expresses itself in vampirism/cannibalism, feeding upon the *living* flesh, blood, spirit of women and Others while tokenism disguises the devastation of the victims. *Examples* **a:** patriarchal marriages **b:** slavery **c:** zoos and circuses

elimination: necrophilic *envy* of Biophilic powers, which demands the eradication of ensouled matter and the fabrication of replacements, imitations, simulations of Life. *Example:* the invention of technological miracles such as television, urbanization, and Disneyland—"The Happiest Place on Earth"

fragmentation: patriarchally enforced *sloth* which enslaves women and other living creatures, severing them from their Original Capacities to Act, to Realize their potential to glimpse their Final Cause; the stunting and confining of Elemental growth, movement, and creativity by mandatory subservience assuming the forms of enforced passivity and/or ceaseless busyness. *Examples* **a:** S. Weir Mitchell's rest cure for women[12] **b:** the busy housewife syndrome **c:** the professional "rat race" and structural unemployment **d:** the usage of animals as "biomachines" in agribusiness[13] **e:** forest management by the lumber industry

demon-wardens ◗ *n* : personifications of the deadly sins of the fathers; wardens who block gateways to the Passages throughout the Otherworld Journey and who must be exorcised by Naming. *See* **Naming; Otherworld Journey** (W-W 1)

Demons, Tidal ○ [*demon* (derived fr. Gk *daimōn* spirit, deity; prob. akin to Gk *daiesthai* to distribute, divide): "an attendant, ministering, or indwelling power or spirit: DAIMONION, GENIUS"—*Webster's*] : Goddesses, Geniuses, Spirits; Sources and Mediums of Positively Wicked Inspiration; Guides who Presentiate their Selves to women who are coming into Touch with Tidal rhythms, enabling

Spinsters to separate our Selves from the fixations of tidy time. *See* **Tidal Time** (w-w I)

demons, tidy ○ : evil dis-spiriters; the deceptive and ghostly presences of absence and absences of Presence that have been devised to divide every woman from her own Genius, Demon, Muse; projections/ emanations of the tyrants who impose tidy order, fixing the flow of women's creativity, tying us down

Depth Hearing ᵒ : "hearing that takes place before the speaking—a hearing that is far more than acute listening. . . . engaged in by the whole body that evokes speech—a new speech—a new creation"— Nelle Morton.[14] *Example:*

> Held between wars
> my lifetime
>   among wars, the big hands of the world of death
> my lifetime
> listens to yours
>   —Muriel Rukeyser, "Käthe Kollwitz"[15]

Earthquake Phenomenon ᵒ **1** : the experience of cosmic shakiness, trembling, and dislocation, during which time Gyn/Ecologists share with our sister the Earth the agony of phallocratic attacks **2** : Ordeal experienced by Crones engaged in the Otherworld Journey beyond patriarchy, which involves confronting one's Aloneness as the ground splits open, and Spanning the chasm by Acts of Surviving, Spinning, and Weaving Cosmic Connections

Elemental ○ *adj* ["characterized by stark simplicity, naturalness, or unrestrained or undisciplined vigor or force . . . CRUDE, PRIMITIVE, FUNDAMENTAL, BASIC, EARTHY"—*Webster's*] : This definition has been awarded *Websters'* Intergalactic Seal of Approval.

Elemental Feminist Philosophy ○ : a form of be-ing/thinking that is rooted in Metapatriarchal consciousness; reason rooted in instinct, intuition, passion; philosophy having its Source in women breaking out of the tamed/tracked modes of phallocratic thinking and feeling; the philosophy of Wonderlusters returning to the Original Questions of childhood, listening to the promptings of Ancestral Memory. *See* **Philosophia** (w-w I)

Elemental Memory ○ : *See* **Memory, Elemental** (w-w I)

72

Elementals ○ *n* [*elemental* "SPIRIT, SPECTRE, WRAITH"—*Webster's*] : Spirits of the Elements: Gnomes (Earth), Undines or Nymphs (Water), Salamanders (Fire), Sylphs (Air) [16]

Elemental Sounding ○ **1** : the Speaking of all Elemental creatures in the chorus of be-ing. *Example:*

> Even more directly the tides address the sense of hearing, speaking a language of their own, distinct from the voice of the surf. . . . In the stillness of night the strong waveless surge of a rising tide creates a confused tumult of water sounds— swashings and swirlings and a continuous slapping against the rocky rim of the land.
> —Rachel Carson [17]

2 : Weird activity of Searchers who seek to fathom the depths of Elemental Memories and experiences

Elemental Spirits ○ : Spirits/Angels/Demons manifesting the essential intelligence of spirit/matter; Intelligences ensouling the stars, animating the processes of earth, air, fire, water, enspiriting the sounds that are the Elements of words, connecting words with the earth, air, fire, water, and with the sun, moon, planets, stars [18]

elementaries ○ *n* : simulations of and planned replacements for the Elemental, the Wild; fabrications which distort experience of the Elements and which are largely invisible by reason of being all-pervasive; incarnations of phallic myth that constitute the foreground; man-made phenomena lacking depth, radiance, resonance, harmonious interconnectedness with living be-ing. [19] *Examples* **a:** the poisonous fumes and radioactive emissions of phallotechnology **b:** the transmissions of popular media and the erudition of specialized fields **c:** traditional assumptions, spoken and unspoken **d:** shopping malls **e:** plastics

elementary ○ *adj* : characterized by artificiality, lack of depth, aura, and interconnectedness with living be-ing; marked by a derivative and parasitic relation to Elemental reality

Elements ○ *n* **1** : the spoken letters of the alphabet; the primal Race of Words—their cosmic sounds, meanings, rhythms, and connections **2** : fire, air, earth, water, constituting the deep Realms of Reality with which all sentient beings are naturally and Wildly connected **3** : the larger cosmos including the sun, moon, planets, and stars; the vast context within which the Primal Powers of Witches and all Wild beings must be understood   **4 :** Elemental Spirits/Angels/ Demons. *See* **Elemental Spirits** (w-w 1)

Elixir of Words ○ **:** the vital nature, the Elemental force in symbols and words; the capacity of words to Act as powerful natural agents; the quintessential transforming powers and Life-fostering force of words

E-motion ○ *n* [derived fr. L *exmovēre, emovēre* to move out, move away—*Webster's*] **:** Elemental Passion which moves women out/away from the fixed/framed State of Stagnation; Pyrogenetic Passion that fires deep knowing and willing, stirring Metamemory, propelling Wild Women on the Otherworld Journey. *Compare* **pseudopassions** (w-w 3)

endless *adj* **1 :** having no deep purpose, without Final Cause **2 :** incessant, interminable, tedious, boring—applied to phallic lechery and other phallocentric activities and their products. *Example:* the media's coverage and re-coverage of the explosion of the space shuttle *Challenger. Cockaludicrous Comment:* "The graphic details of tragedy are being played and replayed endlessly."—Mike Barnicle, *Boston Globe,* Jan. 29, 1986, p. 21

endlessness *n*   **1 :** purposelessness   **2 :** interminableness—the quintessential attribute of all patriarchal constructions (e.g., housework, committee work, a-Musing amusements, manufactured suffering, war, ad infinitum). *See* **phallic infinity** (w-w 3)

erasure ◗ *n* **:** the planned, self-serving obliteration throughout phallocracy of the lives, words, and achievements of women; the attempted annihilation of the Reality of all Others. *Example:* the attempted obliteration of Sappho's work and reputation. The erasers/obliterators did not fully succeed, however. In Oxyrhyncus, Egypt, between 1897 and 1906, an archaeological expedition uncovered papyrus mummy wrappings which had been used to stuff coffins and embalmed animals. In this ancient garbage dump, on wadded strips of papyrus, were the fragmented poems of Sappho.[20] *Canny Comment:*

> You may forget but
>
> Let me tell you
> this: someone in
> some future time
> will think of us
>   —Sappho[21]

Exorcism • (1968 ed.) *n* : series of A-mazing Acts of Dis-possession, expelling both internal and external manifestations of the godfather; Naming the demons who block each passage of the Otherworld Journey and thereby ousting these obstacles to the Ecstatic Process. *See* **Naming** (W-W 1)

Fall • *n* : women's Movement beyond patriarchy's "good" and "evil"; the Dreadful Biophilic Bounding of women from imposed ignorance and false guilt into Wicked Wisdom. *See* **Original Sin of Women; Prance of Life** (W-W 1)

fall, the • *n* : one of patriarchy's Biggest Lies; the biblical story of the "original sin" of Adam and Eve, which projects all guilt upon the woman, enshrining the myth of feminine evil as revealed by god

Elemental Philosophical Words and Phrases and Other Key Words

Feminism, Radical • **1** : the Cause of causes, which alone of all revolutionary causes exposes the basic model and source of all forms of oppression—patriarchy—and thus can open up consciousness to active participation in Movement, Transcendence, and Happiness **2** : be-ing *for* women and all Elemental Life, which implies going to the roots of the oppression of all Others **3** : way of be-ing characterized by (a) an Awesome and Ecstatic sense of Otherness from patriarchal norms and values (b) conscious awareness of the sadosociety's sanctions against Radical Feminists (c) moral outrage on behalf of women *as women*: WOMAN-IDENTIFICATION (d) commitment to the cause of women that persists, even against the current, when feminism is no longer "popular": CONSTANCY. *Canny Comment:*

> My friends, do we realize for what purpose we are convened? Do we fully understand that we aim at nothing less than an entire subversion of the present order of society, a dissolution of the whole existing social compact?
> —Elizabeth Oakes Smith (1852) [22]

Fey Faith ○ [*fey* "being in a wild or elated state of mind. . . . able to see fairies or to have intuitions about the future: possessing a sixth sense: CLAIRVOYANT"—*Webster's*] : the Faith of a woman who identifies with the Fates; Faith which implies the natural clairvoyance of those who reject master-minded mediation of sense experience; the source of the Hope that is characteristic of Hags. *Compare* **"Faith of Our Fathers"** (W-W 3). *N.B.*: Although the modern word *faith* can be traced back to the ME *fey*, there appears to be no etymological connection between *faith* and the modern word *fey*. Wickedarians, however, inspired by similarities in sound and by our own Wicked word sense, Bespeak hitherto unheard connections.

Final Cause • 1 : the indwelling, always unfolding goal or purpose, perceived as Good and attracting one to Act, to Realize her own participation in Be-ing; the beginning, not the end of becoming; the First Cause and Cause of causes, which gives an agent the motivation to Act **2 :** Radical Feminism, the Cause of causes. *See* **Feminism, Radical** (w-w 1)

First Philosophy ○ [*"Aristotelianism:* a study of being as being. . . . *Aristotelianism:* a study of supersensible immutable being"—*Webster's*] **1 :** *Elemental Feminist Philosophy:* a study of be-ing as be-ing **2 :** *Elemental Feminist Philosophy:* a study of Super Sensible Shape-shifting be-ing

First Questions ○ **:** fundamental ontological questions raised in the First Philosophy of the First Sex. *Examples* **a:** "Why is there so much Nothing, where there should be Something?" **b:** "What does it mean for a woman to *be* in the face of phallocracy's nothingness?"

foreground ⁹ *adj* **:** elementary, plastic, contrived, possessed. *See* **elementary** (w-w 1)

foreground ⁹ (Denise D. Connors [23]) *n* **:** male-centered and mono-dimensional arena where fabrication, objectification, and alienation take place; zone of fixed feelings, perceptions, behaviors; the elementary world: FLATLAND. *See* **elementaries** (w-w 1); **fix** (w-w 3). *Compare* **Background** (w-w 1)

Fury ⁹ *n* **:** Righteous Female Rage; focused Gynergetic will to break through the obstacles that block the flow of Female Force; Volcanic Dragonfire; Elemental breathing of those who love the Earth and her kind, who Rage against the erasure of our kind. *See* **Rage** (w-w 1); **Furies** (w-w 2)

Goddess *n* **:** *See* **Goddess the Verb; noun-goddess** (w-w 1)

Goddess the Verb ○ **:** Metaphor for Ultimate/Intimate Reality, the constantly Unfolding Verb of Verbs in which all be-ing participates; Metaphor of Metabeing. *See* **Be-ing; Metaphors, Metapatriarchal** (w-w 1)

Grammar *n* **1 :** harmonious interplay among the primal sounds of words; concordance of words Sounding and Resounding together in complex compositions, as they communicate manifold meanings; the agreeable agreement of words as spoken/written/sung by Metapatterning Muses **2 :** Original order in the rhythms of all Elemental be-ing; natural affinity among all living beings which makes possible communication, relationship, and concordance

Gyn/affection ° *n* [*affection* "a fond or tender feeling toward another. . . . feeling or emotion. . . . the act of influencing, affecting, or acting upon. . . . the state of being influenced or acted upon"—*American Heritage*] **:** "woman-to-woman attraction, influence, and movement. . . . female friendship. . . . a loving relationship between two or more women . . . a freely chosen bond which, when chosen, involves certain reciprocal assurances based on honor, loyalty, and affection"—Janice G. Raymond[24]

Gyn/Ecology ᵭ *n* **1 :** knowledge enabling Crones to expose connections among the institutions, ideologies, and atrocities of the foreground; habit of Dis-covering threads of connections hidden by man-made mazes and mysteries; practical wisdom concerning the complex web of relationships among Spinsters and all Elemental beings **2 :** the process of A-mazing any male-authored "science of womankind,"[25] of Dis-covering the real agents of women's dis-ease in the State of Dis-memberment; the ecstatic Realization of Female Powers of Healing/Re-membering. *See* **Metaethics** (W-W I)

Gynergy • *n* **:** "the female energy which both comprehends and creates who we are; that impulse in ourselves that has never been possessed by the patriarchy nor by any male; women-identified be-ing"—Emily Culpepper[26]

gynocide • *n* **:** the fundamental intent of global patriarchy: planned, institutionalized spiritual and bodily destruction of women; the use of deliberate systematic measures (such as killing, bodily or mental injury, unlivable conditions, prevention of births), which are calculated to bring about the destruction of women as a political and cultural force, the eradication of Female/Bio-logical religion and language, and ultimately the extermination of the Race of Women and all Elemental be-ing; the master model of genocide; paradigm for the systematic destruction of any racial, political, or cultural group

Elemental Philosophical Words and Phrases and Other Key Words

77

Gynophilia *n* : love for women; Original E-motion which inspires Nags to Nix the Static State, whirl Widdershins, and ride with the Race of Wild and Raging Women. *See* **Biophilia; Biophilic Bonding** (w-w 1)

Happiness ○ *n* : a life of activity/creativity governed by Wild, Woman-identified Wisdom; Realization of Be-Longing

hetero-relations ○ *n* : "the wide range of affective, social, political, and economic relations that are ordained between men and women by men"—Janice G. Raymond[27]

Hopping Hope ○ [*hope* derived fr. OE *hopian*; akin to . . . MHG *hoffen* to hope, and perh. to OE *hoppian* to hop—*Webster's*] : Hope that hops, leaps, jumps intuitively in harmony with the rhythms of the Elemental world. *Example:*

> Mama exhorted her children at every opportunity to "jump at de sun." We might not land on the sun, but at least we would get off the ground.
> —Zora Neale Hurston[28]

Incarnation, The ○ *n* : supremely sublimated male sexual fantasy promulgated as sublime christian dogma; mythic super-rape of the Virgin Mother, who represents all matter; symbolic legitimation of the rape of all women and all matter. *See* **Sadospiritual Syndrome** (w-w 1)

Journey ᴗ *n* : *See* **Otherworld Journey** (w-w 1)

Lesbian ᴗ *n* : a Woman-Loving woman; a woman who has broken the Terrible Taboo against Women-Touching women on *all* levels; Woman-identified woman: one who has rejected false loyalties to men in every sphere. *N.B.:* Websters point out that the terms *gay* or *female homosexual* more accurately describe women who, although they relate genitally to women, give their allegiance to men and male myths, ideologies, styles, practices, institutions, and professions. *Lesbian* is capitalized to indicate Woman-identification. The word *lesbian,* when it is used to refer to degraded caricatures of Lesbian reality, actually means *pseudo-Lesbian* or *sadolesbian*. Such perverted portrayals are commonly disseminated in the popular media, in pornography, and in pseudo-Lesbian books, magazines, graphics, films, and videos. *See* **Terrible Taboo** (w-w 1); **Amazon; Spinster; Woman-Touching woman** (w-w 2)

lust, phallic : *See* **pure lust** (w-w 1)

Lust, Pure : *See* **Pure Lust** (w-w 1)

Macroevolution ○ *n* ["evolutionary change involving relatively large and complex steps (as transformation from one species to another)"— *Webster's*] : consciously intended Self-transformation of Metapatriarchally Moving Crones who dismiss as ineffably accidental any connection with the species that has planned and executed witchcrazes, death camps, slavery, torture, racism, world famine, chemical contamination, animal experimentation, the nuclear arms race. *Canny Comment:*

> The more aware we become of our own evolutionary process, the more we are empowered to will and direct that process: an incredible evolutionary leap, a macro-mutation on a level with (and having similar dynamics to) the development of language.
>   —Barbara Starrett[29]

memories, elementary : standardized memories fabricated in fatherland which function to mask and stifle Deep Memory; mass-produced collective memories intended to obliterate the past and to control the present and future. *Canny Comment:*

> And if all others accepted the lie which the Party imposed—if all records told the same tale—then the lie passed into history and became the truth. "Who controls the past," ran the Party slogan, "controls the future: who controls the present controls the past."
>   —George Orwell, *1984* [30]

Memory ○ *n* : the power to Re-member; the power to transcend the categories of tidy time, to connect with the sources of instinctive, ecstatic knowledge. *Example:*

> Pretty soon all this will be gone . . . twenty years, ten. This house, me, you. But the river's still here, and the fields, and the trees, and the smell of the Gulf. I always got my strength from that. Not from houses and not from people.
>   —Geraldine Page as Mrs. Watts, in the film *The Trip to Bountiful* [31]

Memory, Elemental ○ : faculty that Re-members knowledge, emotions, and experiences beyond the fabricated elementary "recollections" of the foreground; Deep Memory, grounded in primal experience of the Elements; Memory of Archaic Time, where/when the commonplace brims with meaning, the trees and animals speak, and Crones *know* our connections with the moon and stars. *Example:*

> If life has a base that it stands upon, if it is a bowl that one fills and fills and fills—then my bowl without a doubt stands upon this memory. It is of lying half asleep, half awake, in bed in the nursery at St. Ives. It is of hearing the waves breaking, one, two, one, two, and sending a splash of water over the beach; and then breaking, one, two, one, two, behind a yellow blind. It is of hearing the blind draw its little acorn across the floor as the wind blew the blind out. It is of lying and hearing this splash and seeing this light, and feeling, it is almost impossible that I should be here; of feeling the purest ecstasy I can conceive.
> —Virginia Woolf [32]

See **Tidal Memory** (w-w 1)

Memory, E-motional ○ **:** Elemental Memory, stirring deep Passion, generating Movement out of the Fixed State. *Canny Comment:*

> I feel that strong emotion must leave its trace; and it is only a question of discovering how we can get ourselves again attached to it, so that we shall be able to live our lives through from the start.
> —Virginia Woolf [33]

Memory of the Future ○ **:** active participation in Tidal Time; action that affects/effects the Future. *See* **Tidal Time** (w-w 1); **Fateful Fore-making** (w-w 2)

Meta- ["occurring later . . . after; situated behind. . . . change in, transformation of. . . . beyond, transcending"—*Webster's*] **:** These definitions have been awarded *Websters'* Intergalactic Seal of Approval.

Metabeing ○ *n* **:** Realms of active participation in Powers of Be-ing; State of Ecstasy

Metadictionary *n* **:** Metapatriarchal dictionary, written by and for Wicked/Wiccen Websters; dictionary that Gossips out the Elemental webs of words hidden in patriarchal dictionaries and other re-sources: WICKEDARY. *See* **Wicked** (w-w 1)

Metaethics ◑ *n* **:** Gyn/Ecological ethics; Gynocentric study of Pyrogenetic Passions, Volcanic Virtues/Vices, Final Causality, and Happiness; the science of Journeying into the Background, beyond patriarchal "good" and "evil"

Metafooling [*fool* derived fr. L *follis* bellows, windbag; akin to Gk *phallos* penis (found at *blow*)—*Webster's*] **:** disdaining the fooling of snools; Seeing and Acting in ways that transcend the rules of fools; Outrageous, Contagious Departure from phallic fixations; effecting Rollicking, Riotous Transformations. *See* **Be-Laughing** (w-w 1); **fool** (w-w 3)

Metamemory ○ *n* **:** : Deep, Ecstatic Memory of participation in Being that eludes the categories and grids of patriarchal consciousness, Spiraling into the Past, carrying Vision forward; Memory that recalls Archaic Time, Re-calling it into our be-ing; Memory beyond civilization. *Example:*

> *What do you remember?*
> *What is it that you long for still? . . .*
>
> *Repeat the syllables*
> *each cell has unforgotten:*
> *There was the Word before their word.*
>   —Robin Morgan [34]

Metamorphic Movement ○ **:** Macroevolutionary leaps of women developing sensory/psychic powers that have been erased and repressed in the State of Patriarchal Paralysis

Metamorphosis ○ *n* ["a change of physical form or substance, especially such a change brought about by or as if by supernatural means (the metamorphosis of men into animals)"—*Webster's*] **:** changes of physical/spiritual form or substance, especially such a change brought about by Super Natural means (the Metapatriarchal Metamorphosis of tamed women into Wild Witches). *N.B.:* Even the *Oxford English Dictionary* defines *metamorphosis* as "the act or process of changing in form, shape, or substance, especially transformation by magic or witchcraft."

Metamorphospheres ○ (Denise D. Connors [35]) *n* **:** Realm of macromutational transformations, where Prudes explore the States of Grace (Be-Longing, Be-Friending, Be-Witching), where Websters see Stamina as its own reward, where Dragons are in our Elements, and where Muses Muse, Compose, Create

Metamystery *n* **:** depths/surfaces that are hidden by man's mysteries/ misteries; Wonders of Wild Reality that are behind/beyond the fathers'

façades; ever Unfolding reality glimpsed by Seers and announced by Be-Speakers: the Radiant Integrity of Be-ing. *Compare* **Mystery of Man, the** (w-w 1)

Metapatriarchal ⊘ *adj* : situated behind and beyond patriarchy; transformative of and transcending the Static State

Metapatterning ○ : process of breaking through paternal patterns of thinking, speaking, acting; Weaving the way through and out of male-ordered mazes; Metapatriarchal Erratic Movement. *See* **Erraticism, Feminist** (w-w 2)

Metaphors, Metapatriarchal ○ [*metaphor* derived fr. Gk *metapherein* to transfer, change, fr. *meta-* + *pherein* to bear—*Webster's*] : words that function to Name Metapatriarchal transformation and therefore to elicit such change; the language/vehicles of transcendent Spiraling; words that carry Journeyers into the Wild dimensions of Other-centered consciousness by jarring images, stirring memories, accentuating con-tradictions, upsetting unconscious traditional assumptions, eliciting Gynaesthetic sensing of connections, brewing Strange Ideas.[36] *N.B.:* Metapatriarchal Metaphors are by no means to be confused with the mere "figures of speech" that are described in textbooks on composi-tion. Rather, they are bearers of complex multiple meanings which re-flect the complexity and diversity of Life itself.

Methodicide ● *n* : a form of deicide; deliberate murder by Maenads of the patriarchal god Method—the god of academia; deicide by means of asking Nonquestions and Dis-covering, reporting, and ana-lyzing Nondata. *See* **Nondata; Nonquestions** (w-w 1); **Studied Un-learning** (w-w 2)

methodolatry ● *n* : common form of academic idolatry: glorification of the god Method; boxing of knowledge into prefabricated fields, thereby hiding threads of connectedness, hindering New discoveries, preventing the raising of New Questions, erasing ideas that do not fit into Respectable Categories of Questions and Answers

mysteries/misteries, man's : *See* **Mystery of Man, the** (w-w 1)

Mystery of Man, the : [*mystery* derived fr. Gk *myein* to close (used of the eyes and lips), close the eyes—*Webster's*] **1** : irrationality of the patriarchal male, projected onto women and nature, whom he arche-typically brands as "mysterious"; the non-sense and purposelessness of the phallic male, which is hidden from women by means of the twofold

82

injunction against Seeing and Naming Female Elemental Powers. *Cocka-ludicrous Comment:*

> A woman of mystery is one who also has a certain maturity and whose actions speak louder than words. Any woman can be one, if she keeps those two points in mind. She should grow up—and shut up.
> —Alfred Hitchcock[37]

2 : the ontological lack which is the *raison d'être* of all patriarchal religions and institutions **3 :** the male veil of pomp and circumstance designed to conceal snoolish ineptness, vacuousness, inanity, and malignancy. *Example:* the mystifying ritualism and authoritarianism of the roman catholic church, illustrated in the following statement concerning the "extraordinary" synod of bishops held in Rome in 1985:

> Among the prominent issues raised by conservatives were the need for ending abuses in liturgy and theology, infusing a greater sense of "mystery" into the church and restoring authority in the highest levels of church hierarchy centering in the Pope.[38]

Compare **Metamystery** (W-W 1)

Nag-Gnosticism ○ *n* [*nag* + *gnostic* "believing in the reality of transcendental knowledge"—*O.E.D.*] : the philosophy of those who Sense with certainty the reality of transcendental knowledge and at the same time never cease to Nag our Selves and Others with recurrent awareness of questions and uncertainties; the philosophy of those who overcome the pseudodichotomy between transcendence and immanence, between otherworldliness and worldliness. *See* **Nag** (W-W 2)

Naming ● : Original summoning of words for the Self, the world, and ultimate reality; liberation by Wicked Women of words from confinement in the sentences of the fathers; Truth-telling: the only adequate antidote for phallocracy's Biggest Lies; exorcism of patriarchal labels by invoking Other reality and by conjuring the Spirits of women and of all Wild natures; Re-calling the Race of Radiant Words

necrophilia ◗ *n* ["fascination with the dead; *specif:* obsession with and usu. erotic attraction toward and stimulation by corpses typically evidenced by overt acts (as copulation with a corpse)"—*Webster's*] : the most fundamental characteristic and first principle of patriarchy: hatred for and envy of Life; the universal message of all patriarchal religion: death worship. *Examples:*

Set your minds on things that are above, not on things that are on earth. For you have died and your life is hid with Christ in God.
 —saint Paul (Col. 3:2–3 [R.S.V.])

I suspect that all really higher intelligences will be machines. Unless they're beyond machines. But biological intelligence is a lower form of intelligence, almost inevitably. We're in an early stage in the evolution of intelligence but a late stage in the evolution of life. Real intelligence won't be living.
 —Arthur C. Clarke[39]

Canny Comment:

The male likes death—it excites him sexually and, already dead inside, he wants to die.
 —Valerie Solanas[40]

Nemesis ○ *n* [derived fr. L *Nemesis,* goddess of divine retribution—*Webster's*] **1 :** Virtue beyond justice, acquired by Inspired Acts of Righteous Fury; Virtue enabling Seers to unblindfold captive Justice **2 :** participation in the powers of the Goddess Nemesis; Elemental disruption of the patriarchal balance of terror; Passionate Spinning/Spiraling of Archaic threads of Gynergy

New *adj* **1 :** Truly Original. *Example: Three Guineas,* by Virginia Woolf **2 :** recognized or experienced by any Wonderlusting woman for the first time, although known before by Sister Hags. *Example:* the Dis-covering of the primal creative powers of women by Matilda Joslyn Gage in the nineteenth century, Dis-covered again by Elizabeth Gould Davis in the mid-twentieth century and discussed in her groundbreaking book *The First Sex.*[41]

New Space ◉ **:** Space on the Boundary of patriarchal institutions; Space created by women which provides real alternatives to the archetypal roles of fatherland; Space in which women Realize Power of Presence. *See* **Boundary, the** (w-w 1); **Fairy Space** (w-w 2)

New Time ◉ **:** Time on the Boundary of patriarchal time; women's Life-Time; Time in which the past is changed and Archaic Futures are Realized. *See* **Fairy Time** (w-w 2)

New Words ◉ **:** words Heard in a new semantic context and arising from qualitatively Other experience; words of Gynocentric communi-

NEMESIS: *participation in the powers of the Goddess Nemesis;*
Elemental disruption of the patriarchal balance of terror

cation—many of which are not "new" in the old sense (materially) but New in a New sense, having different meanings because they are Heard and Spoken in New ways

Nondata ● *n* : information that is disruptive and disturbing to pedants and therefore banned from the categories and classifications of academented re-search, theory, and method

Nonquestions ● *n* : genuinely Questing Questions; Canny Questions frequently raised by women and erased by men and their henchwomen in the elementary schools of snooldom. *See* **elementary school** (w-w 3)

noun-goddess ● (1985 ed.) *n* : static symbol derived from the noun-god, who is a reified reversal of the Archaic Verb-Goddess, the Triple Goddess of many names; malfunctioning/male-functioning symbol which inevitably works to baffle Metapatriarchal Journeyers. *Example:* "The Great Mother" used by Erich Neumann and other jungians to symbolize the archetypal feminine. *Compare* **Verb-Goddess.** *N.B.:* To Dis-cover how "Goddess" (singular or plural) is functioning for women, it is useful to observe how this affects be-ing in the world. Insofar as the image inspires passivity, self-absorption, the plastic passion of full-fillment, and in general the therapeutic syndrome of rage-less returning, there is ample indication that it is functioning only as a noun.

O-logy ○ *n* : holistic process of knowing that encircles all of the *-ologies,* Spinning around and through them, unmasking their emptiness, reducing their pretentious façades to Zero, freeing the flow of their "courses" through Spiraling creation: Gyn/Ecology. *Compare* **-ologies** (w-w 3)

Ontology, Elemental ○ : the philosophical quest for Be-ing; philosophy rooted in the intuition that Powers of Be-ing are constantly Unfolding, creating, communicating; philosophy grounded in the experience of active potency to move beyond the foreground of fixed questions and answers and enter the Radiant Realms of Metabeing

Ontophany, Creative Political ● : manifestation of Be-ing in the living of Radical Feminism; Realization of Final Causality in successions of creative political Acts. *See* **Be-ing; Final Cause; Feminism, Radical** (w-w 1)

Originally Sinful Acts ○ : Natural Acts proceeding from a Prude's Self-centering Lust; Acts of questioning and challenging the old saws/

86

laws of the Lecherous State. *Example:* Rosa Parks' defiance of Southern segregation laws, Montgomery, Alabama, 1955 [42]

Original Sin of Women ○ [*sin* derived fr. Indo-European root *es-* to be—*American Heritage*] : the Original be-ing of women, from which patriarchal religion attempts to "save" us, but which is inherently Untouchable, Inviolable, and Wild

original sin of women ◉ : state of complicity in patriarchal oppression that is inherited by women through socialization processes; socially transmitted dis-ease involving psychological paralysis, low Self-esteem, hatred of Self, emotional dependence, horizontal violence, and a never ending conviction of one's own guilt

Elemental Philosophical Words and Phrases and Other Key Words

Other ○ *adj* : outside the parameters of patriarchal predictability; Wicked, Wild, Strange

Other ○ *n* : one who participates in the Realms of Otherness

Otherness ○ *n* : the Super Natural State of Original Women and all Other Others

Otherworld ◑ *n* : Realms of Metamorphosis; true Homeland of all Hags, Crones, Furies, Furries, and their Friends; Country of the Strange; Naturally Wild State of the Elemental World; the Real World

Otherworld Journey ◑ : Metapatriarchal Labyrinthine Journey of Exorcism and Ecstasy, in the course of which patriarchal demons are dispelled by Voyagers; discovery of a world Other than patriarchy

otherworld, patriarchal : more of the same; boring non-alternative to the State of Boredom; place of "reward" for sameness/tameness, for doing Nothing

particularization ◉ *n* : strategy used to avoid Naming gynocide by deceitfully limiting the recognition of women's oppression to particular times, places, or institutions or to specific areas of activity

patriarchy ◉ *n* **1** : society manufactured and controlled by males: FATHERLAND; society in which every legitimated institution is entirely in the hands of males and a few selected henchwomen; society characterized by oppression, repression, depression, narcissism, cruelty, racism, classism, ageism, objectification, sadomasochism, necrophilia; joyless society, ruled by Godfather, Son, and Company; society fixated on proliferation, propagation, procreation, and bent on the destruction of all Life **2** : the prevailing religion of the entire planet, whose essential message is necrophilia

Physical Ultimacy ○ : actualization of relations that are fired/inspired by Pure Lust; Realization of connections with Others as well as with one's Self that are far-reaching, demanding the stretching of physical, imaginative, psychic powers beyond "normal" limitations; mode of connection among Elemental Women, the rhythms of whose bodies/minds are—like those of the tides—in harmony with the moon, the sun, and the farthest stars

Postchristian ● (1975 ed.) *adj* : occurring after definitive departure from christianity in all its religious and secular forms and simultaneously with entry into New Time/Space

Power of Absence ● : Power of women's Presence to each Other, experienced as Absence by those who have adopted a parasitic mode of existence and who habitually sap female energy; shielding power that protects women against stratagems and maneuvers intended to siphon off Gynergy. *Examples* **a:** refusal to attend oppressive meetings, social gatherings, etc. **b:** noncooperation (Acting Strangely/Weirdly) at such functions **c:** active resistance. *See* **Power of Presence** (w-w i)

Power of Presence ● : flow of healing energy experienced by women who are Present to each Other in New Time/Space; Power of woman-identified women that radiates outward, attracting Others. *Example:*

> I never knew a person who possessed so much of that subtle controlling power called presence as Sojourner.
> —Harriet Beecher Stowe, speaking of Sojourner Truth [43]

Powers of Be-ing ○ : Be-ing the Verb, understood in multiple and diverse manifestations, e.g., Knowing, Creating, Loving, Unfolding—and through diverse Metaphors—e.g., the Fates, Changing Woman (Estsan Atlehi, Creatrix of the Navaho People), Shekhina (female divine Presence in Hebrew lore)

Prance of Life ○ : style of Original Motion/E-motion of Muses/Prudes/Nags and Other Wild Creatures who make the large and complex steps required for Macroevolution; the springing, capering, frisking, frolicking, cavorting, romping, gamboling of Journeyers into Archaic Time/Space. *See* **Race of Elemental be-ing** (w-w i)

88

presence of absence ○ : meaninglessness of male-centered myths and ideologies, experienced as mental/spiritual bloat; expansion of emptiness that fills the mind and makes the victim absent to her Self— the glut of non-sense experienced watching television, reading news-papers, or attending an ordinary university. *See* **absence of Presence** (w-w 1). *Compare* **Absence of absence** (w-w 1)

Presence of Presence ○ : Self-Realizing Presence of Prudes and Vir-agos who communicate Gynergetic Ecstasy

Presentiate ○ *v* ["to make or render present in place or time; to cause to be perceived or realized as present"—*O.E.D.*] : to Realize as Present the past and future; to Conjure the Presence of Fore-Crones, Fore-Familiars and Other Background beings

Primordial *adj* [derived fr. L *primus* first + *ordiri* to begin, begin a web—*Webster's*] : Primal, Archaic—applied esp. to the Original Acts of Websters

Principalities and Powers ○ : classes of Elemental Spirits, or Angels, recognized by saint Paul as inimical to christianity; Elemental Spirits hated and feared by Paul and his ilk

Prudish Prudence ○ : practical wisdom of Prudes; Volcanic Virtue enabling Shrewd Shrews to question taken-for-granted, traditionally implanted ends/purposes and to ask Wild Whys in the light of which radically Other ways and means can be considered. *Canny Comment:* "A woman has to listen to her own voice."—Response of the wise old woman to a younger friend's request for advice in the film *Wildrose.*[44] *See* **Prude** (w-w 2)

Pure Lust ○ [*lust* "VIGOR, FERTILITY. . . . an intense longing: CRAV-ING. . . . EAGERNESS, ENTHUSIASM"—*Webster's*] : the high humor, hope, and cosmic accord/harmony of those women who choose to es-cape, to follow our hearts' deepest desire and bound out of the State of Bondage, Wanderlusting and Wonderlusting with the Elements, con-necting with auras of animals and plants, moving in planetary com-munion with the farthest stars; pure Passion: unadulterated, absolute, simple, sheer striving for abundance of be-ing; unlimited, unlimiting desire/fire

pure lust ○ : the deadly dis-passion that prevails in patriarchy; the life-hating lechery that rapes and kills the objects of its obsession/aggression;

Elemental Philosophical Words and Phrases and Other Key Words

violent, self-indulgent desire to level all life, dismember spirit/matter, attempt annihilation; ontologically evil vice, having as its end the breaking/braking of female be-ing, the obliteration of natural knowing and willing and of the deep purposefulness which philosophers have called *final causality. Example:*

> Whatever may be the future economic repercussions of the atom bomb . . . the fact remains that in laying hands on the very core of matter we have disclosed to human existence a supreme purpose: the purpose of pursuing even further, to the very end, the forces of Life.
> —Pierre Teilhard de Chardin [45]

Pyrosophical Temperance ○ : Fiery Temper, Distemper, Distemperance of Dragon-identified women who cause derangement, disturbance, and disorder in the sadostate. *See* **Tempering; Distemper; Distemperance** (w-w 2)

Pyrospheres ○ *n* [*pyrosphere* "a hypothetical spherical zone of molten magma that is held to intervene between the crust of the earth and a solid nucleus and to supply lava to volcanoes"—*Webster's*] **:** Spiraling zones of molten Passions that permit passage between the surfaces of Elemental female be-ing and the inner cauldron/core and that supply E-motional energy to Brewsters

Race of Elemental be-ing ○ [*race* "the act of rushing onward: RUN; a strong or rapid current of water that flows through a narrow channel; a heavy or choppy sea, *esp:* one produced by the meeting of two tides"—*Webster's*] **1 :** the Wild onward rushing movement of all Lusty Life **2 :** the Elemental kinship of all Biophilic creatures, of all who participate in the Prance of Life

Race of Radiant Words ○ : skein of Wild words/birds in flight; soaring movement of words which awakens Websters to Exaltation, inspiring Ecstatic Imagination. *See* **Exaltation** (w-w 2)

Race of Women ○ **1 :** the Metapatriarchal Movement of Wayfaring Wayward Women **2 :** the Sisterhood of Racy, Raging Women who experience Archaic memories and Tidal encounters and who participate in the Race of Elemental be-ing, bonding/bounding with our own kind. *Canny Comment:*

> We are a race of women that of old knew no fear and feared no death, and lived great lives and hoped great hopes; and if

today some of us have fallen on evil and degenerate times, there moves in us yet the throb of the old blood.
    —Olive Schreiner [46]

Rage ○ *n* ["violent action of the elements (as wind or sea). . . . a furious storm: TEMPEST. . . . extreme force of feeling: PASSION, FRENZY"—*Webster's*] **:** transformative focusing force that awakens transcendent E-motion; Passion that unpots the potted passions and melts down the potted ones; Passion which, when unleashed, enables Furies to sever our Selves from the State of Severance, breathe Fire, and fly into freedom. *Examples:* **a:** the Righteous Rage of Celie, expressed just before leaving Mr. _____ in Alice Walker's *The Color Purple:*

Elemental Philosophical Words and Phrases and Other Key Words

> I curse you, I say. . . .
> I say, Until you do right by me, everything you touch will crumble. . . .
> Until you do right by me, I say, everything you even dream about will fail. I give it to him straight, just like it come to me. And it seem to come to me from the trees. . . .
> Every lick you hit me you will suffer twice, I say. Then I say, You better stop talking because all I'm telling you ain't coming just from me. Look like when I open my mouth the air rush in and shape words. . . .
> The jail you plan for me is the one in which you will rot, I say. . . .
> A dust devil flew up on the porch between us, fill my mouth with dirt. The dirt say, Anything you do to me, already done to you. . . .
> I'm pore, I'm black, I may be ugly and can't cook, a voice say to everything listening. But, I'm here.
> Amen, say Shug. Amen, amen. [47]

b: the Righteous Rage of dolphins against rippers who massacred their sisters at Iki Island, Japan in 1980:

> About 4000 dolphins massed around this island today, forcing fishing boats back to port, a day after fishermen from the island slashed and stabbed about 200 dolphins to death after trapping them in nets. [48]

rapism ◉ *n* **:** the fundamental ideology and practice of patriarchy, characterized by invasion, violation, degradation, objectification, and destruction of women and nature; the fundamental paradigm of racism, classism, and all other oppressive -isms.

Real Eyes ○ (Denise D. Connors[49]) : the Authentic, Elemental, Wild Capacity to Realize. *Example:*

> I looked at my hands to see if I was the same person now I was free. There was such a glory over everything. The sun came like gold through the trees, and over the fields, and I felt like I was in heaven.
> —Harriet Tubman[50]

Realize ○ *v* ["to make real . . . bring into concrete existence: ACCOMPLISH . . . to bring from potentiality into actuality: ACTUALIZE. . . . to conceive vividly as real: be fully aware of"—*Webster's*] : These definitions have been awarded *Websters'* Intergalactic Seal of Approval.

Real Presence ○ : Female Elemental participation in Powers of Be-ing, which implies Realizing as Present our past and future Selves

real presence ["the doctrine that Christ is actually present in the Eucharist"—*Webster's*] **1** : the real absence of christ in the eucharist **2** : the vacuum created by the appearance of V.I.P.'s on television and in the flesh **3** : the "presence" of power, brains, beauty, charm, etc. in the consumer products of the phallotechnic establishment: presence of absence. *Canny Comment:* "If Nixon is alone in a room, is anybody there?"[51]

Re-calling ◗ **1** : persistent/insistent Calling of the Wild; recurring invitation to Realms of Deep Memory **2** : Active Unforgetting of participation in Be-ing; Re-membering and giving voice to Original powers, intuitions, memories

Re-considering ◗ [*consider* derived fr. L *considerare* lit., to observe the stars—*Webster's*] : transcending paternally prescribed choices and conclusions; daring to See and to reach for the stars; reclaiming Prehistoric Questing Power. *See* **Prehistory** (w-w 2)

Re-fusing ◗ : Self-Realizing by Positively Revolting Hags who, by re-fusing unreal loyalties, reunite/re-fuse powers (e.g., thinking, feeling, sensing) that have been artificially split/splintered in the State of Severance[52]

Re-membering ◗ **1** : Re-calling the Original intuition of integrity; healing the dismembered Self—the Goddess within women; Re-calling the Primordial connections/conversations among women, animals, and

92

Other Elemental beings **2** : Realizing the power to See and to Spell out connections among apparently disparate phenomena: Spinning, Creating

reversal ⦿ *n* : fundamental mechanism employed in the world-construction and world-maintenance of patriarchy; basic method employed in the making of patriarchal myths, ideologies, institutions, policies, and strategies; mad, master-minded maneuver characteristic of mirrordom: INVERSION—turning everything inside out and upside down. *Examples* **a:** the absurd story of Eve's birth from Adam **b:** the belief that man is superior to animals **c:** the worship of male divinity **d:** the belief that the Radical Feminist world view is "narrow" and/or "dated"

Rhythms, Elemental ○ **1** : rhythms displaying the infinite interplay of unity and diversity characteristic of Elemental phenomena such as tides, seasons, phases of the moon: TIDAL RHYTHMS **2** : cadences and vibrations of the wordings of Websters, which are Be-Spoken in cosmic concordance

sado-asceticism ○ *n* : a primary aspect of sadospirituality; flight from phallic lust/lechery into sadomasochistic self-abuse—a pattern which only reinforces the obsessions from which the ascetic is trying to escape. *Examples* **a:** the pathetic behavior of saint Jerome (342–420), who described his experience in the following words:

> I sat alone, the companion of scorpions and wild beasts, and yet was in the midst of dancing girls. My face was white with fasting, but the mind in my cold body was hot with desires. The fires of lust burnt up a body that was already dead.[53]

b: the view of life expressed by Robert Oppenheimer:

> Therefore I think that all things which evoke discipline: study, and our duties to men and to the commonwealth, war, and personal hardship, and even the need for subsistence, ought to be greeted by us with profound gratitude; for only through them can we attain to the least detachment; and only so can we know peace.[54]

N.B.: In the sadosociety asceticism is *imposed* upon all of the oppressed, taking such forms as war, racism, economic poverty and famine, environmentally caused ill-health, the subtly spreading drabness, banality, ugliness of the man-made environment, the all-pervasive lies that deaden minds under the reign of the sadostate.

sado-rituals ⁰ *n* : rituals which recreate and reinforce the primordial patriarchal mythic event—the murder/dismemberment of the Goddess within women and all be-ing; rituals devised to accomplish and legitimate the dis-spiriting and devastation of the Wild; rituals designed to destroy the integrity of Life and creative divine powers in women. *Examples* **a:** Chinese footbinding **b:** hindu suttee and dowry murders **c:** the systematic rape of Black female slaves in america **d:** the ongoing murder and mutilation of women by sex killers (e.g., "the Boston Strangler," "the Hillside Strangler," "the Yorkshire Ripper") throughout the United States and the world[55] **e:** the normalized/routinized use of "pesticides" (biocides) in agriculture. *See* **biocide; gynocide** (W-W I)

Sado-Ritual Syndrome ⁰ : a set of interconnected components of sado-rituals which, when Dis-covered, can be seen by Searchers as links among seemingly unrelated atrocities, such as witchburnings, gynecological practices, lynchings, pogroms, nuclear arms buildup, the exploitation and torture of animals. *See* **sado-rituals** (w-w I). *N.B.:* The essential components of the Sado-Ritual Syndrome are (1) obsession with purity; (2) total erasure of male responsibility; (3) inherent tendency to "catch on" and spread; (4) use of women as scapegoats and token torturers; (5) compulsive orderliness, obsessive repetitiveness, and fixation upon minute details, which divert attention from the horror; (6) readjustment of consciousness, so that previously unacceptable behavior becomes accepted, acceptable, and even normative; (7) legitimation of the ritual by the rituals of patriarchal scholarship[56]

sadosociety ⁰ *n* : society spawned by phallic lust; the sum of places/times where the beliefs and practices of sadomasochism are The Rule; Torture Cross Society: PATRIARCHY, SNOOLDOM

sadospirituality ⁰ *n* : pseudospirituality characterized by obsessive and imposed asceticism and by refined and disguised lechery. *See* **sadoasceticism** (w-w I)

Sadospiritual Syndrome ⁰ : sick/sickening syndrome assuming two aspects: **a:** phallic flight from lust into phallic asceticism **b:** phallic flight from lust into refined lechery manifesting itself in three interconnected ways:

> **the sado-sublime** [*sublime* "to cause to pass from the solid to the vapor state by the action of heat and again condense to solid form (many chemicals . . . are *sublimed* to rid them of impurities)"— *Webster's*] : warped ideas/images which are products of the pa-

triarchs' attempts to rid themselves of consciousness of their impurities by subliming themselves into "God" and his supporting cast of symbolic characters; a system of symbols which allows believers to indulge self-righteously in refined, perfected, heightened lechery. *Examples:* the christian symbol of the crucifix; the fundamentalist symbol of "the Rapture"

sado-sublimation [*sublimate* "to direct the energy of (an impulse) from a primitive aim to one that is higher in the cultural scale . . ."; also *sublimation* "discharge of instinctual energy . . . through socially approved activities"—*Webster's*]: discharge of phallic lust through rapist activities, resulting in the production of a culture of warped ideas/images/words *made "flesh"*; manufacture of an increasingly artificial environment which blocks Elemental/Wild sensing, knowing, and creation; the incarnation of phallic lust (legitimated by the christian dogma of "The Incarnation"), taking such forms as nuclearism, chemical contamination, racial oppression, obscene medical experimentation, and endless manufacture of gross consumer products. *See* **restorationist syndrome** (w-w 3)

sado-sublimination [*subliminal* "existing or functioning outside the area of conscious awareness: influencing thought, feeling, or behavior in a manner unperceived by personal or subjective consciousness"—*Webster's*]: mental manipulation characteristic of the sado-sublimated society, involving deliberate perversion of the natural phenomenon of subliminal perception so that it becomes a tool of the sadostate; the embedding of phallocentric messages into every product of the patriarchal state: the warped "flesh" of the sado-sublimated society refined/re-sublimed into an endless proliferation of warped "words," e.g., the messages in advertising, films, liberal and secular theologies, and all the other -ologies

Elemental Philosophical Words and Phrases and Other Key Words

sadostate ○ *n* : *See* **sadosociety** (w-w 1)

Second Coming of Women ● : New arrival of Archaic Female Presence; spiritual awakening beyond christolatry and all patriarchal religions

Self ᕮ *n* : the Original core of one's be-ing that cannot be contained within the State of Possession; living spirit/matter: the psyche that participates in Be-ing

self ᕮ *n* : any of the many false identities inflicted upon women under patriarchy; the internalized possessor that covers and re-covers the Original Self

Separatism, Radical Feminist ○ : theory and actions of Radical Feminists who choose separation from the Dissociated State of patriarchy in order to release the flow of elemental energy and Gynophilic communication; radical withdrawal of energy from warring patriarchy and transferral of this energy to women's Selves. *Compare:* **Dissociated State; separatism, phallic** (w-w 3)

Shape-shifting ○ : transcendent transformation of symbol-shapes, idea-shapes, relation-shapes, emotion-shapes, word-shapes, action-shapes; Moon-Wise Metamorphosis

Sin *n* : *See* **Originally Sinful Acts; Original Sin of Women** (w-w 1)

Sisterhood • *n* : authentic bonding of women who Biophilically affirm individual freedom and Originality, refuse tokenism, and actively give primal loyalty to women. *Compare* **brotherhood** (w-w 3)

Spinning ◑ **1** : Gyn/Ecological creation; Dis-covering the lost thread of connectedness within the cosmos and repairing this thread in the process; whirling and twirling the threads of Life on the axis of Spinsters' own be-ing **2** : turning quickly on one's heel; moving Counterclockwise; whirling away in all directions from the death march of patriarchy

spiritualization • *n* : strategy used to distract from present oppression by deceitfully projecting all "happiness" onto future full-fillment either in this world or in some cockocratic otherworld. *See* **otherworld, patriarchal** (w-w 1); **full-fillment** (w-w 3)

States of Grace ○ : Realms of Metapatriarchal Metamorphosis: Be-Longing, Be-Friending, Be-Witching

Super Natural ○ [*supernatural* "transcending nature in degree and in kind or concerned with what transcends nature (a divine order which directs history from outside and keeps man in touch with the eternal world through the Church and the sacraments—*Times Lit. Supp.*)"— *Webster's*] : Unfolding Nature or concerned with what Unfolds Nature (an Elemental order which directs History from inside and keeps women and all Biophilic creatures in Touch with the real world through the senses—*Tidal Times*): SUPREMELY NATURAL, PERFECTLY NATURAL

Surviving ◑ [derived fr. L *super-* beyond + *vivere* to live—*Webster's*] : the process of Spinsters living beyond, above, through, around the perpetual witchcraze of patriarchy; Metaliving, be-ing. *Canny Comment:*

> If anyone should ask a Negro woman what is her greatest
> achievement, her honest answer would be: "I survived!"
> —Pauli Murray [57]

Telic Focusing Principle ○ **1** : all-pervasive principle within an organism, entirely present in all parts of the organism; Source of deep purposefulness, which makes possible growth, adaptation, creation **2** : Re-membering and Metapatterning principle in Metamorphosing women

Terrible Taboo ○ : the universal, unnatural patriarchal taboo against women Intimately/Ultimately Touching each Other; prohibition stemming from male terror of women who exercise Elemental Touching Powers. *See* **Total Taboo** (w-w I). *Compare* **Physical Ultimacy** (w-w I)

Tidal ○ *adj* : characterized by cosmic interconnections and rhythms; Elemental; Wild

Tidal Memory ○ : Memory of the Deep Background, characterized by Tidal Rhythms of Re-membering: ELEMENTAL MEMORY

Tidal Time ○ [*tide* derived fr. ME *tyde, tide* time, fr. OE *tīd;* akin to Gk. *daiesthai* to distribute, divide—*Webster's*] : Elemental Time, beyond the clocking/clacking of clonedom; Wild Time; Time that cannot be grasped by the tidily man-dated world; Time of Wicked Inspiration/Genius. *See* **Demons, Tidal** (w-w I). *Compare* **tidy time** (w-w I)

tidy ○ *adj* ["free from irregularity or slovenliness and often from any marked individuality: PRECISE (a tidy handwriting) (tidy thinking) (a tidy mind)"—*Webster's*] : tracked, tamed, sanitized, routinized, tied down, fixed up—esp. applied to women held captive in the State of Feminitude

tidy ○ *v* : to "correct" Life and natural activities, killing and destroying Wildness, manufacturing lifeless substitutes. *Example:*

> He [Constantine] did not formally become a Christian until
> near the end of his life. Then, having tidied the Empire of
> subterranean lunar cults, he tidied his own life: after murder-
> ing his wife and son he took baptism.
> —James Vogh [58]

tidy time ○ **:** fathered time; measurements/divisions that cut women's Lifetimes/Lifelines into tidy tid-bits; dismembered time, surgically sewn back together to mimic and replace Tidal Time; tedious time spent under the tyranny of tidy demons. *Examples* **a:** the twelve-month year **b:** the 9–5 workday **c:** the weekend **d:** the christmas season (snooltide) **e:** sunday/sonday. *See* **archetypal deadtime; demons, tidy** (W-W I). *Compare* **Tidal Time** (W-W I)

Torture Cross Syndrome ◑ **:** *See* **Sado-Ritual Syndrome** (W-W I)

Total Taboo ○ **:** prohibition against the Terrible Totality of female bonding—against direct physical and emotional contact and especially against the exercise of the Spiritual Touching Powers of women. *See* **Terrible Taboo** (W-W I)

touchable caste ○ [*touch* "to have sexual intercourse with. . . . to lay violent hands on. . . . to rob by swindling: CHEAT. . . . to reach the heart or secret of. . . . to hurt the feelings of: WOUND, STING"—*Webster's*] **:** fixed status imposed upon women and all of nature; condition of those condemned by phallocrats to be touched—physically, emotionally, intellectually, spiritually—by those in possession of a penis; condition of those systematically subjected to phallic violation, e.g., by rape, battering, medical experimentation, and butchery

Touching Powers ○ **:** Pyrogenetic Powers of Communication, actualized by women who break the Terrible Taboo and thus break out of the touchable caste

Trinity, Most Unholy ● **:** rape, genocide, and war—the logical expression of phallocentric power; interconnected manifestations of phallic lust that are self-perpetuating, eternally breeding further destruction. *Example:* the trinitarian syndrome of multiple rapes, massacres, and unjust wars against the American Indians committed by the white invaders/killers/plunderers/polluters/plug-uglies whose victories are celebrated each year on "Thanksgiving Day," when patriotic americans thank god for this glorious heritage. *See* **Sadospiritual Syndrome: sado-sublimation** (W-W I)

Unfolding ● **1 :** continuing process of Be-ing **2 :** evolving, actualizing, Realizing

universalization ● **:** false generalization used to avoid confronting the specific problems engendered by phallocracy/foolocracy. *Examples*

a: the tiresome argument that the "real issue" is "human liberation," not women's liberation **b:** the deceptive expression "family incest" **c:** the misleading phrase "spouse battering." *Cockaludicrous Comment:*

> Rape is not an issue of women's rights. It's a question of human rights.
> —Herman Snool, D.D., author of *The New Right: The Right to Rape* (Predatory State Press, 1990 a.d.), p. 1

verbicide ○ *n* : the gagging and enforced servitude of Wild Words; interruption of the Race of Radiant Words; distorted simulation of Wicked Words especially by the fabrication and proliferation of elementary terms

Verb, Intransitive ● : Be-ing, the Verb of Verbs which need not have an object to block its dynamism

Vice ○ *n* **1** : a good operative habit of Wicked women; Virgin Virtue **2** : WICKEDNESS

Virtues/Vices, Volcanic ○ : Fiery, Impassioned Virtues exploding out of the deeply buried cauldrons of women's experience; Virtues born in flames, which empower Virgins/Viragos to break the Terrible Taboo, depart from Stag-nation, and continue the Wonderlusting Voyage. *See* **Biophilic Bonding; Courage, Ontological; Fey Faith; Hopping Hope; Nemesis; Prudish Prudence; Pure Lust; Pyrosophical Temperance** (w-w 1); **Creative Caution; Disgust, Virtue of; Laughing Out Loud, Virtue of; Shrewish Shrewdness** (w-w 2)

Virtues, Virgin ○ [*virgin* "never captured: UNSUBDUED"—*Webster's*] : Life-affirming habits of Uncaptured/Unsubdued women; Virtues of Virgins/Viragos

virtues, virile ○ [*virtue* derived fr. L *virtut-, virtus* strength, manliness, virtue, fr. *vir* man—*Webster's*] : "good" habits conforming to the standards of the State of Reversal; habits legitimated by the code of phallic morality

Wanderlust ○ *n* : strong and unconquerable longing for Journeying. *See* **Wonderlust** (w-w 1)

Weaving ● **1** : Original activity of Websters: creating tapestries of Crone-centered creation; constructing a context which sustains Sisters on the Otherworld Journey **2** : mode of Traveling: wending one's way through and around the baffles of blockocracy; crisscrossing and connecting with other Voyagers. *Canny Comment:*

> All mother goddesses spin and weave. . . . Everything that is comes out of them: they weave the world tapestry out of genesis and demise, "threads appearing and disappearing rhythmically."
> —Helen Diner[59]

WORD-WEB ONE

See **Spinning** (W-W 1); **Unweaving; Webster** (W-W 2)

Wicked ○ *adj* [akin to OE *wicce* witch—*American Heritage,* Appendix on Indo-European Roots] **:** beyond patriarchal "good" and "evil"; characterized by Original Integrity; Originally Sinful; actively participating in the Unfolding of Be-ing as Good

Wickedary ○ *n* **:** *Archaic:* Wicked/Wiccen dictionary; dictionary for Wicked/Wiccen Women; Metamysterious Web-Work Spun by Websters; Guidebook for the Intergalactic Galloping of Nag-Gnostic Voyagers; Book of Guide Words for Wayward, Weirdward Wanderers. *See* **Metadictionary** (W-W 1)

Wild ⁹ *adj* ["living in a state of nature . . . not tamed or domesticated. . . . growing or produced without the aid and care of man . . . NATIVE. . . . not living near or associated with man. . . . not amenable to control, restraint, or domestication: UNRULY, UNGOVERNABLE, RECKLESS. . . . exceeding normal or conventional bounds in thought, design, conception, execution, or nature: EXTRAVAGANT, FANTASTIC, VISIONARY. . . . RUDE, UNCIVILIZED, BARBARIC. . . . SAVAGE, INTRACTABLE, REBELLIOUS. . . . ERRATIC. . . . not accounted for by any known theories. . . . EXTREME, PRODIGIOUS"—*Webster's*] **:** These definitions have been awarded *Websters'* Intergalactic Seal of Approval. *Canny Comment:*

> You better change your ways
> And get really wild.
> I want to tell you something
> I wouldn't tell you no lie.
> Wild women are the only kind
> That really get by,
> 'Cause Wild Women don't worry
> Wild Women don't get the blues.
> —Ida Cox[60]

Wild [◑] *n* **:** the vast Realm of Reality outside of the pinoramic world view constructed by the bores and necrophiliacs of patriarchy; true Homeland of all Elemental be-ing, characterized by diversity, wonder, joy, beauty, Metamorphic Movement and Spirit

Wild, Call of the [◑] **1 :** the recurring invitation to bound out of the State of Bondage **2 :** the Elemental Sounds of Otherness which awaken Be-Longing, summoning women to embark upon Journeys of Exorcism and Ecstasy. *Canny Comment:*

> I am like the she-wolf
> I broke with the pack
> I fled to the mountains
> Growing tired of the flatlands.
> —Alfonsina Storni[61]

Women's Space [◉] **:** Space created by women who choose to separate our Selves from the State of Servitude: FREE SPACE; Space in which women actualize Archimagical Powers, releasing the flow of Gynergy; Space in which women Spin and Weave, creating cosmic tapestries; Space in which women find Rooms, Looms, Brooms of our Own. *See* **New Space** (W-W I)

Wonderlust [○] *n* **:** strong and unconquerable longing for Elemental adventure and knowledge: Call of the Metamysterious. *Canny Comment:*

> If I had influence with the good fairy . . . I should ask that
> her gift to each child in the world be a sense of wonder so
> indestructible that it would last throughout life, as an unfail-
> ing antidote against the boredom and disenchantments of
> later years, the sterile preoccupation with things that are ar-
> tificial, the alienation from the sources of our strength.
> —Rachel Carson[62]

See **Metamystery; Wanderlust** (W-W I)

WORD-WEB TWO

The Inhabitants of the Background, Their Activities and Characteristics

I
n this Word-Web,* Journeyers Dis-cover the inhabitants of the Background, observing and participating in their activities and characteristics. The words and phrases of this Web Name the Wild Reality of Hags and Nags, Gorgons and Grimalkins, together with Other Friends and Familiars. This Web can be read as a Guidebook for travelers into the Background. It introduces the reader to the Natives, their world view and customs, describes places of interest, and provides words and phrases necessary for communication in the Country of the Strange.

Abecedarian *n* ["one that is learning the alphabet. . . . *archaic:* one that teaches the alphabet and the rudiments of learning"—*Webster's*] : a Be-Spelling woman who combines and recombines the Elements of words in New ways, Hearing New Words into be-ing; a Webster who Re-calls her Original connection with the rudiments and characters of Lusty Language: Wickedarian. *Examples* **a:** Hildegarde of Bingen (1098–1179), the Abbess of Rupertsberg, a Gynergetic Genius who created a language of her own and an alphabet consisting of 23 letters **b:** Alix Dobkin, Lesbian Feminist musician, composer of "Amazon ABC":

---

*The system of symbols (●, ◐, ◑, ○) used to identify the sources of words and phrases and the system of cross-referencing are explained at the beginning of *Word-Web One*, pp. 59–60.

A—you're an Amazon
B—coming so Brave and strong
Clearly and Consciously I see [C]
D—you're so Dyke-y
E—how you Excite me
how Fortunate a Female Faculty . . .

This song is described on the album notes as "A saucy romp through the Lesbo-alphabet."[1]

Abecedarium *n* ["ALPHABET BOOK, PRIMER"—*Webster's*] **:** an Archaic Alphabet book; Primer of Elemental Feminist Philosophy; Alphabetical, Theoretical, Her-etical Word-Work/Web-Work: Wickedary. *See* **Wickedary** (W-W 1)

Active Eyes : Eyes which scintillate, emitting Eye-Beams that crack mirrors meant to fix female Eyes/I's; Wicked Eyes

Activize *v* **:** to actualize the Archimagical powers of Active Eyes; to Beam through the archetypal images that block Vision

Aeroglyphic ○ *adj* **:** written in, constituted by, or belonging to that form of Archaic Elemental writing in which the characters are for the most part recognizable breathings/breezes of Aeromantic Musing Thought

Aeromancy ○ *n* ["divination from the state of the air or from atmospheric substances"—*Webster's*] **:** This definition has been awarded *Websters'* Intergalactic Seal of Approval.

After-Death of Daddydom ○ **:** Life beyond the perpetual "afterlife" which is the State of Boredom

A-mazing ◑ **:** essential process in the Journey of women becoming: breaking through the male-ordered mazes of the State of Reversal, springing into free space. *See* **maze** (W-W 3)

A-mazing Female Mind ◑ **:** the Labrys that cuts through the double binds and doublebinding words that block our breakthrough to understanding Radical Feminist Friendship and Sisterhood

Amazon ◑ *n* **:** a Wild Woman Warrior who fights for her Self and other women; Woman-Loving Woman; Terrible Woman; Lesbian. *Canny Comments:*

Aᴇʀᴏᴍᴀɴᴄᴇʀ: *one who Divines from the state of the Air or from Other atmospheric substances*

We *are* the myths. We are the Amazons, the Furies, the
witches. We have never not been here. . . .
 There is something utterly familiar about us.
 We have been ourselves before.
 —Robin Morgan[2]

Amazons of Dahomey
Amazons of Dahomey
I am haunted and sexed with your image
What need What memory
Do you awaken?
 —Brenda Walcott[3]

*The Inhabitants
of the
Background,
Their Activities
and
Characteristics*

In the beginning, if there ever was such a time, all the
companion lovers called themselves amazons. Living together,
loving, celebrating one another, playing, in a time when work
was still a game, the companion lovers in the terrestrial
garden continued to call themselves amazons throughout the
entire Golden Age.
 —Monique Wittig and Sande Zeig[4]

I am a warrior in the time of women warriors; the longing
for justice is the sword I carry, the love of womankind my
shield.
 —Sonia Johnson[5]

Amazon, A-mazing ⁹ **:** Labrys-wielding Female Warrior who Sees
and Names phallic deception, cutting through the layers of lies intended to baffle Journeyers

Amazon Argosy ⁹ **:** a fleet of vessels sailed by Con-questing/Con-
questioning Amazonian Argonauts

Archaic Smile ["an expression that resembles a smile and is characteristic of early Greek sculpture"—*Webster's Collegiate*] **:** characteristic expression of a Gorgon regarding a snool. *See* **snool** (w-w 3)

Archelogian ○ *n* **:** a practitioner of Archelogy; one who augurs pasts
and futures veiled by archetypes. *See* **Archelogy** (w-w 1)

Argonaut ⁹ *n* **:** Questing/Questioning Amazon who sails by her own
Power; Voyager who seeks the seemingly unattainable. *N.B.:* The *argo-
nauta* is the "paper nautilus," an animal related to the octopus "and like
it having eight arms two of which [only] in the female are expanded at
the tips to clasp the thin fragile unchambered shell" (*Webster's*). According to Elmer G. Suhr: "The male is smaller than the female; he devel-

ops no shell and hence was not so important in the ancient view. The female, it was assumed, raised a pair of arms into the air and expanded them into a shell to be used as a sail, while the two appendages in the water functioned as oars—hence the picture of the argonaut as a sailor."[6] The phallic myth writers stole this Originally Female-identified word, using it for Jason and his misnamed "argonauts" in their quest for the "Golden Fleece."

Augur ○ *n* ["a soothsayer; said to mean a diviner by the flight and cries of birds"—*Skeat's*] : Soothsayer; a Diviner by the flight and cries of birds/words

Banshee *n* **1** : a woman of Fairyland who foretells death, comforting and welcoming those whom she loves, portending doom to those who have been evil-doers **2** : a woman who participates in the power of the Banshee, encouraging Lusty Women on the Otherworld Journey and Pronouncing the doom of patriarchy

Battle-ax *n* ["*slang:* a quarrelsome, irritable, domineering woman"—*Webster's*] **1** : a Raging, Dreadless, Unconquerable Crone. *Example:* Carry Nation **2** : double-edged weapon of a Woman Warrior; Labrys wielded by an A-mazing Amazon

Batty *adj* : having the qualities of a bat—Self-directed, Uncanny, Eccentric, and Active by night, applied esp. to Crackpot Crones and Old Bats. *Examples:* Ruth Gordon, Old Batte Davis, Calamity Jane. *Canny Comment:*

> I can go into the Sioux and Cheyenne camps where a man couldn't go without being killed. They think I'm plain batty so I go unmolested. They all call me Calamity Jane.
> —Martha Jane Cannary Hickok (1852–1903)[7]

Bearish *adj* : having the characteristics of a bear—fierce, gruff, resourceful, intractable, adroit in the art of Self-defense, strong. *Examples:* Gertrude Stein, Willie Mae "Big Mama" Thornton. *Canny Comment:*

> It was always the dream of my childhood to sit upon an iceberg with a bear.
> —Jane Ellen Harrison[8]

Bee-Spelling : the casting of stinging/winging Word-spells. *Canny Comment:*

AUGUR: *Soothsayer, a Diviner by the flight and cries of birds/ words*

There are some bees under my bonnet, badly wanting to swarm. Each one of them has a small label attached to it, and on that label is written a WORD; sometimes several words; sometimes only a mark of punctuation. Allow me to let them out, one by one, not at all after the nature of a true swarm which may comprise some ten thousand bees, as my bee-keeping friends tell me, in a great black lump; but singly, each with a sting.

—Vita Sackville-West (1949)[9]

WORD-WEB TWO

Beldam, -dame *n* [[(derived fr. ME *beldam*, fr. MF *bel* fair, beautiful + ME *dam, dame* lady, mother—*Webster's*): "a grandmother *Obs.* . . . great-grandmother, or still more remote ancestress . . . a woman who has lived to see five generations of female descendents. . . . With depreciative sense: A loathsome old woman, a hag; a witch; a furious raging woman (without the notion of age), a virago"—*O.E.D.*] **:** Archaic Ancestress; Foresister/Hag who is Presentiated by Re-membering Hags, Witches, and Viragos. *N.B.: Beldam* is a Great-Great-Great Grandmother Word, a Guide Word whose aura contains Deep Memories of connections between the Race of Women and the Race of Radiant Words. The apparent depreciation of the meanings of this word illustrates the futility of patriarchy's persistent struggle to undermine the powers of women and words. Wickedarians note with glee that as the patriarchal debasers become more disparaging, the hidden powers of words become more explosive. Thus, as *beldam* has progressed from "grandmother" to "hag," its Volcanic capacity for Naming Be-Witching Powers has become more evident to Websters.

Bevy *n* ["used of a company of girls, roe deer, larks, or quail" (under synonyms at *flock*)—*American Heritage*] **:** This application has been awarded *Websters'* Intergalactic Seal of Approval.

Bio-logical ○ *adj* **:** "characterized by Life-loving wisdom and logic" —Wild Cat (Ms.)[10]

Biomancy *n* [*necromancy* "the art or practice of magically revealing the future, of magically influencing the course of natural events, or of magically attaining other purposes, esp. through communication with and the intervention of the dead"—*Webster's*] **:** the art or practice of magically attaining other purposes through communication/cooperation with the Living (e.g. Angels, Spirits of Fore-Crones, Animals, and Other sentient beings)

Bitchy *adj* **:** having the threatening characteristics of a female canine (a wolf, dingo, coyote, wild dog, fox) applied esp. to a woman who is

108

active, direct, blunt, obnoxious, competent, loud-mouthed, independent, stubborn, demanding, achieving, overwhelming, Lusty, strong-minded, scary, ambitious, tough, brassy, boisterous, turbulent, sprawling, strident, striding, and large (physically and/or psychically). *Canny Comment:*

> Bitches are good examples of how women can be strong enough to survive even the rigid, punitive socialization of our society. As young girls it never quite penetrated their consciousness that women were supposed to be inferior to men in any but the mother/helpmate role. They asserted themselves as children and never really internalized the slave style of wheedling and cajolery which is called feminine. . . . All Bitches refused, in mind and spirit, to conform to the idea that there were limits on what they could be and do.
> —Joreen, "The Bitch Manifesto" [11]

Boon Companion [*boon n* "an often timely and gratuitous benefit received and enjoyed: BLESSING"; also *boon adj* "MERRY, JOVIAL, CONVIVIAL, INTIMATE"—*Webster's*] : an intimate friend; one who arrives in Tidal Time; a companionate blessing. *Examples* **a:** Helen Keller and Annie Sullivan **b:** Rebecca Jackson (nineteenth-century Black spiritual leader and visionary) and Rebecca Perot:

> After breaking with her husband and brother [Rebecca Jackson] . . . lived and traveled throughout the rest of her life in close relationship with a single cherished, intimate woman friend [Rebecca Perot] who shared her religious ideas.
> —Jean McMahon Humez [12]

c: Charlotte Brontë and Ellen Nussey:

> We were contrasts—still we suited—affection was first a germ, then a sapling, then a strong tree.
> —Charlotte Brontë [13]

d: H.D. (Hilda Doolittle) and Bryher:

> Through poetry, Bryher escaped at last from surroundings that were her despair. Then she met Hilda Doolittle, who was to become her lifelong friend, and, through H.D., entered her own world, that of writers.
> —Sylvia Beach [14]

See **Chum; Crony** (W-W 2)

Brewster ° *n* [*brew* "to bring about (something troublesome or woeful) as if by brewing magical potions or spells (brewing mischief)"—

BREWSTER: *a Witch who Brews Archimagical Potions and Spells*

Webster's] : a Witch who Brews Archimagical potions and Spells, stirring up trouble for the trickers and torturers of women; a Wise Woman
who stirs female Passions and Imagination, conjuring Metamorphic
Dreams and Visions. *Example:* Sojourner Truth, who said in 1867:

> I am above eighty years old. . . . I suppose I am about the
> only colored woman that goes about to speak for the rights of
> the colored women. I want to keep the thing stirring, now
> that the ice is cracked. [15]

*The Inhabitants
of the
Background,
Their Activities
and
Characteristics*

Broom ° *n* : Hag-ridden vehicle propelled by Rage, Transporting
Dreadful/Dreadless Women out of the State of Bondage

Canny Moment ° ["moment of childbirth. *Scottish archaic*"—
O.E.D.] : Moment of Realizing Archimagical potency/creativity

Canny/Uncanny °*adj* [*canny* "skillful, clever, 'cunning' (in the old
sense). . . . supernaturally wise, endowed with occult or magical power
Scottish Obs."—O.E.D.; also *uncanny* "arousing feelings of dread or
of inexplicable strangeness: seeming to have a supernatural character,
cause, or origin: EERIE, MYSTERIOUS, WEIRD"—*Webster's*] : Elementally Cunning, Super Naturally Wise, Archimagically Powerful; Strange,
Eerie, Metamysterious, Weird

Canny Wives/Weirds ° [*canny wife* "'wise woman,' midwife (French
femme sage)"—O.E.D.] : Woman-identified creators of unfathered/
unfettered works. *See* **Parthenogenetic Creation** (w-w 2)

Cat/alyst ° *n* : Feline Agent of Elemental Intelligence who provokes
or inspires Shape-shifting; member of the Elemental Intelligence
Agency. *See* **Shape-shifting** (w-w 1)

Cat/astrophe ° *n* [*catastrophe* "an event producing a subversion of the
order or system of things"—O.E.D.] : an event precipitated by Catty
Conspirators that subverts the patriarchal order or system of things. *See*
Catty (w-w 2)

Cat/atonic ° *n* : healing exhilaration achieved through the companionship of Felicitous Felines. *Canny Comment:*

> I live with my few friends and my many cats.
> —Leonor Fini [16]

Cat/egorical Imperative ° : the Call of the Wild, the Summons of
the Weird, conveyed through the Mediumship of a Feline Familiar

Cat/egory ° *n* : an allegory written by and for cats and their friends

Catty *adj* : Self-reliant, independent, resilient; having the Wild, Witchy, and Wicked characteristics of a cat, applied esp. to Gossips. *Example:* Carrie Chapman Catt

Chaircrone ⁰ *n* : any Hag who occupies a chair. *Example:* Dame Edith Sitwell

Charmer *n* [[(derived fr. ME *charme,* chant, magic spell): "one who charms or has the power to charm, especially a girl or woman"— *American Heritage*] : Spell-Brewing Hag, esp. one who heals by means of charms and incantations. *Canny Comment:*

> The fairy doctors are generally females. Old women, espe-
> cially, are considered to have peculiar mystic and supernatural
> power. They cure chiefly by charms and incantations, trans-
> mitted by tradition through many generations; and by herbs,
> of which they have a surprising knowledge.
> —Jane Frances Lady Wilde (1826–1896) [17]

Chum *n* ["archaic: ROOMMATE . . . an habitual intimate companion: a close friend"— *Webster's*] : This definition has been awarded *Webster's* Intergalactic Seal of Approval. *Canny Comment:*

> My mother always told me I would never get married because
> I liked being with my chums too much.
> —Dorothy Balmer, a Crone living in Newton, Mass. [18]

See **Boon Companion; Crony** (w-w 2)

Clue (Clew) *n* [*clew* "a ball of thread which in various mythological or legendary narratives . . . is mentioned as the means of 'threading' a way through a labyrinth or maze"—*O.E.D.*] **1** : ball of thread, i.e., a word, which, when snatched by Websters, enables us to thread our way through Labyrinthine Passages, continually Dis-covering other clues/words along the way **2** : word or idea which leads Searchers to the solution/dissolution of the Mystery of Man

Con-Questing ⁰ : the Questing together of Amazon Argonauts, adventuring into Uncharted/Unchartable Realms. *Example:*

> "Good! I am happy. Now is the time for us to start." I held
> I Chin's head in my arms and kissed her madly. I Chin, too,
> was shedding tears of joy. "Now we are free!" . . .

"Good-bye, good-bye Changsha!" When the red disc of the sun began to appear above the water in the east, I held I Chin's hand as we sat on the deck and welcomed the coming of the dawn and the beginning of our new life.
—Hsieh Ping-ying [19]

Con-Questioning ◗ : Questioning together: proclivity/activity of Nag-Gnostic Searchers

Consent ○ *n* [derived fr. L *consentire* to feel together, agree, consent— *Webster's*] : the radical agreement of Crones Feeling/Sensing together, overcoming the divide and conquer tactics of patriarchy

Contrariwise *adv* : in a Different way: Weirdward

Contrary Whys [*contrary* "different, other *Obs.*"—O.E.D.] : Different, Other Questions; inappropriate, impertinent, and well-placed Questions which puncture the pomposity of wantwits and windbags. *Example:*

> What are these ceremonies and why should we take part in them? What are these professions and why should we make money out of them? Where in short is it leading us, the procession of the sons of educated men?
> —Virginia Woolf [20]

Contrary-Wise *adj* : Pixie-led, Wandering, Erratic, Weird—said of a Shrewd Prude who cannot be tamed, having learned to Sin Wisely. *Canny Comment:*

> We are contrary to men because they are contrary to that which is good.
> —Jane Anger (1589) [21]

See **Courage to Sin** (W-W 1)

Cosmic Concento ○ [*concento* "the simultaneous sounding of the tones of a chord"—*Webster's*] : Crone-logically simultaneous sounding of the tones of Accord among all Biophilic beings

Cosmic Coven ◗ [*coven* "a congregation or assembly of witches; *specif:* a band of 13 witches"—*Webster's*] : an Intergalactic Gaggle of Witches, Gossips, and Grimalkins who gather in a Time/Space that is beyond the reach of clockocracy and is evoked by the number Thirteen. *See* **Thirteen** (W-W 2)

Cosmic Covenant [*covenant* "agreement"—*Skeat's*] : the deep agreement/accord that is present within the Self and among Selves who are living out our own promise and therefore Surviving in harmony with the Elemental environment: Sisterhood

Cosmosis (Linda Barufaldi and Emily Culpepper[22]) : an intermingling of insights originating in women's discovery of our participation together in the rhythms of the cosmos

WORD-WEB TWO **Counterclock Whys** (1985 ed.) : Questions which whirl the Questioners beyond the boundaries of clockocracy and into the flow of Tidal Time. *See* **Tidal Time** (w-w 1)

Counterclockwise (1985 ed.) *adv* : in a direction contrary to the limitations imposed by the clocks and watches of father time. *See* **Widdershins** (w-w 2)

Counterclock-Wise (1985 ed.) *adj* : knowing how to Live, Move, Act in Fairy Time/Tidal Time

Crabby *adj* : having the characteristics of a crab—active, pugnacious, tenacious, Self-sufficient, able to move in all directions. *Example:* Susan B. Anthony

Crackpot Crone (1985 ed.) : an Outrageous, Be-Laughing woman; one whose laughter melts down the plastic passions and unpots the potted ones. *See* **plastic passion; potted passion** (w-w 3)

Creative Caution ○ : one of the parts (aspects) of Prudish Prudence: habit enabling Prudes to be wary of the patriarchal distortions of good and evil and to decide for our Selves what is a good and righteous act. *See* **Prudish Prudence** (w-w 1)

Crone *n* : Great Hag of History, long-lasting one; Survivor of the perpetual witchcraze of patriarchy, whose status is determined not merely by chronological age, but by Crone-logical considerations; one who has Survived early stages of the Otherworld Journey and who therefore has Dis-covered depths of Courage, Strength, and Wisdom in her Self. *Examples* **a:** Harriet Tubman, rescuer of slaves, psychically/physically fearless Foresister **b:** Ding Ling, twentieth-century feminist activist and author, Survivor of multiple political purges, one of China's best-known and most prolific female writers

CRONE: *Great Hag of History, who has Dis-covered depths of Courage, Strength, and Wisdom in her Self*

Crone-logical [9] *adj* : be-ing in accordance with the clarifying logic of Crones; able to see through man's mysteries/misteries; marked by a refusal to be side-tracked by the tedious, tidy, tiny, and ill-logical steps of male methodology/methodolatry

Crone-ography [9] *n* : work that records women's history from a Crone-identified perspective; work that chronicles the lives and deeds of the Great Crones, Foresisters of our present and future Selves; study that unmasks the deceptions of patriarchal history, foiling the erasers of women's lives. *Example: Woman, Church and State,* by Matilda Joslyn Gage[23]

Crone-ology [9] *n* : Radical Feminist chronology; an oral or written expression of Crone-logically understood connections between and among events normally erased in patriarchal chronologies/histories. *Example: Woman and Nature: The Roaring Inside Her,* by Susan Griffin[24]

Crone-Power [9] *n* : Amazon Energy: the most effective antidote to chemical and nuclear poison/power

Crone-Time [9] *n* : Time reclaimed by Crones and Cronies: Crone-logical Time; Time of qualitative leaping: Creative Time. *Canny Comment:*

> Oh Sisters,
> We will thrive in the soil
> Of our own making
> Taking the time to be
> The kind of woman
> We always wanted to be
> Womankindly
> Womankindly
> Womankindly.
> —Teddy Holtz[25]

See **Fairy Time** (w-w 2); **New Time** (w-w 1)

Crony *n* ["an intimate companion esp. of long standing: a familiar friend: an old chum"—*Webster's*] : This definition has been awarded *Websters'* Intergalactic Seal of Approval. *See* **Boon Companion; Chum** (w-w 2)

Cunning *adj* ["*obs:* possessed of or marked by knowledge, learning, or lore . . . possessing occult or magical knowledge"—*Webster's*] : This definition has been awarded *Websters'* Intergalactic Seal of Approval.

Cunning *n* ["*obs:* KNOWLEDGE, LEARNING . . . ART; *esp:* magic art"— *Webster's*] : the Magical Knowledge, Learning, and Art of Canny Wives/Weirds

Cute *adj* ["(short for *acute*) marked by acuteness and shrewdness: IN-GENIOUS, CLEVER, SHARP"—*Webster's*] : possessing an A-mazing Fe-male Mind: INGENIOUS, SHARP, SHREWD

Deliberate Delirium ○ [*delirium* derived fr. *de* from, off plus *lira* fur-row, track—*Webster's*] : a wont of Wanton Women: freely chosen habit of straying/staying off the tracks of tamed responses and traditional ex-pectations: Straying Power. *See* **Studied Unlearning** (W-W 2)

Denouncing [*denounce* "to pronounce . . . to be blameworthy or evil. . . . *obs:* to indicate by or as if by omen: PORTEND, AUGUR"— *Webster's*] : Pronouncing snools and snooldom to be foolish, blame-worthy, evil: Be-Speaking which portends the end of patriarchal evil, Auguring an Other Reality. *Example:*

> We are going to stop
> all confinement of women.
> WITCH calls down destruction
> on Babylon.
> Oppressors:
> the curse of women is on you.
> DEATH TO MALE CHAUVINISM.
>   —WITCH Documents (1969)[26]

See **Rage** (W-W 1)

De-terming : exposing/expelling elementary terms which contami-nate thought and emotion; unmasking nonwords/pseudowords that lack Archaic Radiance/Resonance. *See* **elementaries** (W-W 1); **dummy** (W-W 3)

Deviant Docility ○ [*docile* derived fr. *docēre* to teach—*Webster's*] : one of the parts (aspects) of Prudish Prudence: habit enabling Prudes to be taught by Wise Women, by experience, and by anyone who has any truth to teach. *See* **Prudish Prudence** (W-W 1)

Dike (Dyke) ○ *n* ["a barrier preventing passage, especially protecting against or excluding something undesirable"—*Webster's*] : This defini-tion has been awarded *Websters'* Intergalactic Seal of Approval.

Dis-closing ❯ **:** an essential activity of Metamysterious Seekers: opening eyes and lips that have been forcibly sealed by the keepers of man's mysteries/misteries; the process of Journeyers opening doorway after doorway into Other Reality

Dis-covering ❯ **:** uncovering the Elemental Reality hidden by the hucksters, frauds, and framers of phallocracy; finding the treasures of women's Memory, Knowledge, History that have been buried by the grave diggers of patriarchal re-search

Disgust, Virtue of ● (1985 ed.) **:** profound revulsion experienced and expressed by women who are overcoming psychic numbing and coming to our Senses; habit of Discerning Women whose honest loathing is aroused by the behavior of snools/fools/drools in the State of Lechery

Dis-ordering ❯ [*order* derived fr. L *ordo* akin to L *ordiri* to lay the warp, begin to weave, begin—*Webster's*] **:** Tidal Weaving and Reweaving; breaking through the tidy order/orders of Boredom. *See* **Tidal; tidy** (w-w 1)

Dis-possession ❯ *n* **:** Exorcism by Be-Witching Women: Act of driving away the priests/predators who fix, drain, and sap women in the State of Possession. *See* **priest** (w-w 3)

Dissembly ❯ *n* **:** an Intergalactic Un-Convention of Nag-Gnostic Archelogians, their Familiars, and Other Friends. *Canny Comment:*

> Went out last night
> With a crowd of my friends
> They must have been women
> 'Cause I don't like no men . . .
> —"Ma" Rainey (1928) [27]

Dis-Spelling ❯ **1 :** a form of Be-Spelling: the casting of Spells to dispel the demons who block the Passages of women's Otherworld Journeying **2 :** unspelling/respelling the possessed words of phallocentric language, releasing the Original Magical Powers of Words. *Examples: Gyn/Ecology, Be-Longing. See* **Be-Spelling** (w-w 1)

Distemper ○ *n* [*distemper v* "to disturb or derange the condition of the air, elements, weather, climate, et cetera"—*O.E.D.*] **:** one of the parts (aspects) of Pyrosophical Temperance: habit enabling Hags to healthily disturb the condition of the air and other Elements, releasing pent-up powers, dismantling the temples of pseudotemperance. *Cockaludicrous Comment:*

> The day dreams in which you habitually indulge are likely to induce a distempered state of mind.
> —Robert Southey (a nobody) in a letter attempting to dis-courage the Genius Charlotte Brontë from continuing to write [28]

See **Pyrosophical Temperance** (w-w 1)

Distemperance ○ *n* ["improper proportioning or mingling (of elements)"—*O.E.D.*] **:** one of the parts (aspects) of Pyrosophical Temperance: habit of Dragon-identified women whose mingling with the Elements is Highly Improper and involves such activities as breathing Fire, raising tempests, brewing brainstorms

Distemperate ○ *adj* ["out of order, not functioning normally"—*Webster's*] **:** utterly out of order; not at all normal; truly Haggard. *See* **Haggard** (w-w 2)

Diversity, Feminist ○ [*diverse* derived fr. L *divertere* to turn aside, go different ways, differ—*Webster's*] **1 :** the rich, complex variations among women and within each individual woman, understood within a context of Cosmic Commonality. *Canny Comment:*

> Harmony exists in difference no less than in likeness.
> —Margaret Fuller [29]

2 : convergence/community of Nag-Gnostic scholars who turn away from the base deception of uniform, unified, unilateral universities, electing Ecstatic Spinning Process over the accumulation of dead bodies of knowledge

Dragon ○ *n* [(derived fr. Gk *drakōn*, serpent, dragon "monster with the evil eye," fr. Indo-European root *derk-* to see): "A fabulous monster. . . . A fiercely vigilant or intractable woman . . ."—*American Heritage*] **1 :** Primordial Female Foe of patriarchy whom the gods, heroes, and saints of snooldom attempt to slay over and over again; Metamysterious Monster, Original Knower and Guardian of the Powers of Life **2 :** a woman who participates in the Powers of the Dragon, who sees through the mysteries of man and breathes forth Words of Fire

Dragon Eyes : Eyes that See through the male veils and into the Background; Eyes that Watch over the treasures of women and nature

Dragon-identified ° *adj* : Fiery, Gynergetic, Courageous, Vigilant, Intractable. *Examples* **a:** Mo-O-Inanea ("Self-Reliant Dragon")—Hawaiian Goddess[30] **b:** Jiu Jin—feminist, revolutionary activist, poet, teacher who fought the institution of footbinding[31]

WORD-WEB TWO

Dragonize *v* : to awaken the slumbering Dragonish Powers of women

Dreadful/Dreadless Woman ⁾ *n* : Terrible Woman/Fearless Woman, who is ineffably frightening to the ruling fools. *Example:* Bessie Smith (1894–1937), who was threatened by members of the ku klux klan during one of her shows (Concord, North Carolina, July 1927). Bessie asked some stagemen to help her get rid of the hooded hoods, but the stagemen were terrified and fled:

> Not Bessie. She ran toward the intruders, stopped within ten feet of them, placed one hand on her hip, and shook a clenched fist at the Klansmen. "What the fuck you think you're doin'?" she shouted above the sound of the band. "I'll get the whole damn tent out here if I have to. You just pick up them sheets and run!"
> The Klansmen, apparently too surprised to move, just stood there and gawked. Bessie hurled obscenities at them until they finally turned and disappeared quietly into the darkness.[32]

Dryad ° *n* : Spirit ensouling a tree, who communicates with those who participate in Biophilic Be-ing; Tree Spirit who listens, teaches, inspires, encourages. *Canny Comment:*

> She [Shug] say, My first step from the old white man was trees. Then air. Then birds. Then other people. But one day when I was sitting quiet and feeling like a motherless child, which I was, it come to me: that feeling of being part of everything, not separate at all. I knew that if I cut a tree my arm would bleed.
> —Alice Walker[33]

Ducky *adj* ["very satisfactory: FINE, PLEASANT"—*Webster's*] : This definition has been awarded *Websters*' Intergalactic Seal of Approval. *Canny Comment:*

120

DRYAD: *Tree Spirit who listens, teaches, inspires, encourages*

There are also for my delight a baker's dozen of coal-black ducks, arching their preened slick necks like serpents, and waddling about the garden like a Nonconformist congress all in dark grey galoshes.
  —Sylvia Townsend Warner [34]

Dyke *n* : *See* **Dike** (w-w 2)

Errata ○ **1** : Defiant/Deviant women **2** : the works of such women, for example their books, which from the patriarchal perspective are quite simply and entirely Mistakes

Erraticism, Feminist ○ [*erratic* "having no fixed course: WANDERING. . . . deviating from what is ordinary or standard (as in nature, behavior, or opinion): ODD, ECCENTRIC"—*Webster's*] : the Wanderlusting propensities of Untidy/Eccentric Women

Ethnic *n* [derived fr. LL *ethnicus*, heathen, foreign, fr. Gk *ethnikos*, fr. *ethnos*, band of people living together, nation ("people of one's own kind")—*American Heritage* (also its Appendix on Indo-European Roots)] : a Wholly Her-etical Heathen Hag; one characterized by Pure Lust; one who is Furiously Foreign to patriarchy; one who bonds with her own kind. *Canny Comment:*

  As a woman, I have no country. As a woman I want no country. As a woman my country is the whole world.
    —Virginia Woolf [35]

See **Heathen; Her-etical** (w-w 2)

Ethnic Background [*ethnic adj* "pertaining to a people not Christian or Jewish; heathen; pagan: 'These are ancient ethnic revels, Of a faith long since forsaken' (Longfellow)"—*American Heritage;* also *ethnic adj* "pertaining to race; peculiar to a race or nation"—*O.E.D.*] : Realm of the Race of Lusty Heathen Women, who revel in the Fey Faith never forsaken by Furies. *Compare* **"Faith of Our Fathers"** (w-w 3)

Exaltation *n* ["*British* a flight of larks"—*American Heritage*] : the joyous flight and song of melodious Archaic Words/Birds

Eye-Beam/I-Beam ○ *n* [*eye-beam* "*archaic:* a radiant glance of the eye"—*Webster's*] : *Archaic:* a radiant glance of the Eye/I

Eyebite/I-Bite ○ *v* [*eyebite* "Obsolete, rare: To bewitch with the eye." —*O.E.D.*] : to Be-Witch with the Eye/I. *Example:*

In Ireland it was supposed that certain witches could cast a
spell at a glance, and they were commonly called "eye-biting
witches."
—reverend Montague Summers [36]

Fairy *n* [derived fr. L *Fata* Fates, plural of *fatum* fate—*American Heritage*] **1 :** member of a Race of Super Natural creatures inhabiting a
middle Realm between women and Angels; Messenger and Medium
who guides women into Fairy Space   **2 :** a Wise One who participates in the Realm of the Fairies   **3 :** member of a Heathen nation
who is feared, hated, and oppressed by christians but Survives in the
Realm of the Wild.[37] *See* **Fates; Heathen** (w-w 2)

*The Inhabitants
of the
Background,
Their Activities
and
Characteristics*

Fairy Goddess-mother : an Archaic agent; an Angelic helper and
messenger sent by the Triple Goddess, the Fates

Fairy Space ° **:** Space Dis-covered by Fey Women who Spiral beyond
Stag-nation; Space where Weird Women gather and Gossip with Fairies. *See* **New Space; Women's Space** (w-w 1)

Fairy Tale : an Archaic story that transports the Hearer into Fairy
Time. *Examples* **a:** *Wuthering Heights*, by Emily Brontë **b:** *The Color
Purple*, by Alice Walker **c:** *Daughters of Copper Woman*, by Anne Cam-
eron **d:** *Grimalkins' Furry Tails*, by Ms. Wild Cat

Fairy Time ° **:** Time that is off the clocks of father time; Time that
measures intensity of experience and therefore can be stretched or
condensed; Time that moves Counterclockwise and is accessible to
those who ask Counterclock Whys; Time symbolized by the number
Thirteen

Familiar ° *n* ["a supernatural spirit often embodied in an animal and
at the service of a person (the loathsome toad, the witches' familiar—
Harvey Graham)"—*Webster's*] **:** a Super Natural Spirited Background
Animal, the Graceful Friend of a Witch. *Catty Comment:*

I am a Familiar in this sense—not a loathsome toad, to be
sure—but a stunning Feline.
—Ms. Wild Cat

See **Toad** (w-w 2)

Familiar Eyes : Canny/Uncanny Eyes of Furries and other Familiars;
Eyes that See across Boundaries into Fairy Space/Furry Space; Win-
dows of the Strange

Familiarize *v* ["to make known through experience or repetition: remove strangeness from"—*Webster's*] : to become familiar with the Strange, especially through contact with Familiar Eyes

Familiar Spirit : Angelic Spirit who guides and guards Weird Women

Fanatic *n* [derived fr. L *fanaticus* inspired by a deity—*Webster's*] : a Fey Woman inspired by the Fates; a Life-Time member of the Lunatic Fringe. *See* **Lunatic Fringe** (w-w 2)

WORD-WEB
TWO

Fascinate *v* ["*obs:* to cast a spell over: BEWITCH, ENCHANT . . . to transfix and hold spellbound by or as if by an irresistible power"—*Webster's*] : to cast a Spell over; to transfix fixers; to Spellbind mind-binders. *See* **Gorgonize** (w-w 2). *Compare* **fix** (w-w 3)

Fateful Fore-making ° : Fateful/Faithful Acting out of ever deepening Foresight; active participation in the Unfolding of one's Fate. *Canny Comment:*

> O from the summit of Olympus high,
> The three extremest heights of Heaven,
> Where dwell the Dealers-out of Destinies,
> O may my own Fate hear me,
> And, hearing, come unto me!
> —Greek folk song [38]

See **Foresight** (w-w 2)

Fates ° *n* [derived fr. L *fatum* prophetic declaration, oracle . . . destiny, fate, fr. *fari* to speak—*Webster's*] : the Norns, the Weird Sisters, the three Goddesses who determine the course of events; Moon Goddesses, Be-Speakers, Weavers, Spinners of Stamina—the Thread of Life; the Forces who can save the world

Fey Woman ° : Sibyl, Soothsayer, esp. one who foretells the death of patriarchy; a woman of Fey Faith; Clairvoyant Crone gifted with many Other senses

Fireground ° *n* : the purifying Realm of Fire through which all Otherworld Journeyers must pass: Pyrospheres

Fire-Works *n* : Daring Deeds of Dragonish Women; works that set fire to the old hypocrisies, the old rules, the old schools, the old masters, the old boys' toys; Acts that light/ignite the Fires of Female Fury. *Example: Three Guineas,* by Virginia Woolf, in which she writes:

> Take this guinea and with it burn the college to the ground. Set fire to the old hypocrisies. . . . And let the daughters of educated men dance round the fire and heap armful upon armful of dead leaves upon the flames. And let their mothers lean from the upper windows and cry, "Let it blaze! Let it blaze! For we have done with this 'education'!"
> —Virginia Woolf [39]

Flight of Ideas ["a rambling from subject to subject with only superficial associative connections, esp. in the manic phase of manic-depressive psychosis"—*Webster's*] **:** a Wandering from subject to subject, Dis-covering deep Elemental connections, esp. in the Magic Phase of Metapatriarchal Gnosis

Fore-Bear *n* **:** Foresister of Great Bears and Little Bears, honored by all Bearish Women. *Canny Comment:*

> I was turning over the fragments in the Acropolis Museum, then little more than a lumber-room. In a rubbish pile in the corner, to my great happiness, I lighted on the small stone figure of a bear. The furry hind paw was sticking out and caught my eye. I immediately had her—it was manifestly a she-bear—brought out and honourably placed. She must have been set up originally in the precinct of Artemis Brauronia.
> —Jane Ellen Harrison [40]

Fore-Crone ⁹ *n* **:** Crone who has blazed the trails of the Metapatriarchal Journey; Foresister who inspires those who Crone-logically follow her. *Canny Comment:*

> The women of today are the thoughts of their mothers and grandmothers, embodied, and made alive. They are active, capable, determined and bound to win. They have one thousand generations back of them. . . . Millions of women, dead and gone, are speaking through us today.
> —Matilda Joslyn Gage [41]

Fore-Familiar *n* **:** a Super Natural Spirited Background Animal who has gone before; a Graceful friend of a Fore-Crone. *Examples:* Basket, canine friend of Gertrude Stein, and Zelda, canine friend of Nancy Kelly

Fore-Gnome ○ *n* : Earthy Foresister. *Examples* **a:** the female potters of all ancient cultures[42] **b:** the women builders of the ancient Anasazi culture[43]

Foresight ○ *n* : one of the parts (aspects) of Prudish Prudence: habit of Seeing beyond the limitations of phallotemporality and consciously participating in the Tidal Timing of Biophilic Creation; habit strengthening a Prude's power to Realize the future

Foresister ◑ *n* : Great Hag whom the institutionally powerful but privately impotent patriarchs found too threatening for coexistence and whom historians erase. *Canny Comment:*

> Trammeled as woman might have been by might and custom, there are still many shining examples, which serve as beacon lights to show what might be attained by genius, labor, energy, and perseverance combined.
> —Matilda Joslyn Gage[44]

Foxy *adj* : having the characteristics of a fox—wily, quick, clever, and cunning. *Example:* Joan of Arc

Fumerist *n* : "a feminist humorist [who] makes light. . . . a sparking incendiary with blazes of light and insight. . . . [who] makes whys cracks"—Kate Clinton[45]

Furies ◑ *n* : ["*Greek and Roman Mythology.* The three terrible winged goddesses with serpentine hair . . . who pursue and punish doers of unavenged crimes"—*Webster's*] : This definition has been awarded *Websters'* Intergalactic Seal of Approval. *N.B.:* Often Radical Feminists have identified as Furies, for example, The Furies Collective, Washington, D.C. (1971–74), a group committed to Lesbian Feminism in theory and action.

Furry *n* **1** : Feline companion and friend of a Fury: Purry **2** : any Furry Familiar

Fury ◑ *n* **1** : Weird woman who acts as an agent for the Divine Furies; Wild woman who flies with the wings of Righteous Rage. *Example:* Jane Anger, who wrote (1589):

> Our tongues are light because earnest in reproving men's filthy vices. . . . and our fury dangerous, because it will not bear with their knavish behaviors.[46]

2 : female friend and companion of a Furry

Gabble *v* ["to utter inarticulate or animal sounds (a skein of duck . . . *gabbling* softly to themselves—Naomi Mitchison)"—*Webster's Collegiate*] **:** to utter utterly articulate sounds in Canny Conversations with Animals, Augurs, and Other Wise Ones; to mutter messages utterly unintelligible to snools

Gabblespheres *n* **:** the Background, considered specifically as a Realm of articulate communication, of Elemental Sounding. *Compare* **babblespheres** (w-w 3)

The Inhabitants of the Background, Their Activities and Characteristics

Gaggle *n* ["a flock of geese esp. when on the water"—*Webster's;* also "a flock of geese or, informally, a company of women" (under synonyms at *flock*)—*American Heritage*] **:** These definitions have been awarded *Websters'* Intergalactic Seal of Approval. *See* **Skein** (w-w 2)

Gale *n* [perhaps derived fr. Norwegian *galen,* bad, probably fr. Old Norse *galinn,* bewitched, enchanted, from *gala,* to sing, enchant, bewitch—*American Heritage*] **:** Be-Witching, Enchanting force released by the Laughing Out Loud of Lusty crowds of women and animals, including laughing frogs, laughing geese, laughing gulls, laughing hyenas, laughing jackasses, and laughing owls

Gammer *n* ["(prob. contr. of *godmother*): an old woman"—*Webster's*] **:** Fairy Goddess-mother. *See* **Gossip** (w-w 2)

Genius ○ *n* ["an attendant spirit of a person or place: tutelary deity. . . . a nature spirit or an elemental spirit: GENIE, DEMON. . . . extraordinary native intellectual power esp. as manifested in unusual capacity for creative activity of any kind"—*Webster's*] **1 :** an attendant Spirit of a Musing woman **2 :** a woman in Touch with Tutelary Deities, Elemental Spirits, Demons; a woman of extraordinary native intellectual power and capacity for creative activity; a Dangerous Woman, whom the patriarchs attempt to stifle, thwart, destroy, erase. *Canny Comment:*

> Did you have a genius of a great-great-grandmother who
> died under some ignorant and depraved white overseer's lash?
> Or was she required to bake biscuits for a lazy backwater
> tramp, when she cried out in her soul to paint watercolors of
> sunsets, or the rain falling on the green and peaceful pas-
> turelands? Or was her body broken and forced to bear chil-
> dren (who were more often than not sold away from her)—

eight, ten, fifteen, twenty children—when her one joy was the thought of modeling heroic figures of rebellion, in stone or clay?
  —Alice Walker[47]

Geoglyphic ° *adj* : written in, constituted by, or belonging to that form of Archaic Elemental writing in which the characters are for the most part recognizable carvings/markings of Geomantic Earthy Thought

Geomancy ° *n* ["the art of divination by means of signs derived from the Earth"—*O.E.D.*] : This definition has been awarded *Websters'* Intergalactic Seal of Approval. *See* **Gnomic Writing** (w-w 2)

Giving Heart ° : Communicating Outrageous Courage. *See* **Taking Heart** (w-w 2); **Courage, Outrageous** (w-w 1)

Glamour ° *n* ["a magic spell: BEWITCHMENT"—*Webster's*] **1** : an Archimagical Spell by which Nixing Nags dispel phallic pseudopresence/absence. *Cockaludicrous Comment:*

> We have already shown that they [Witches] can take away the
> male organ, not indeed by actually despoiling the human
> body of it, but by concealing it with some glamour.
>   —Heinrich Kramer and James Sprenger,
>   *Malleus Maleficarum*[48]

2 : the Attracting/Magnetizing Powers of Hags **3** : Word Magic: the Grammer of Wicked Websters. *N.B.:* According to Walter W. Skeat: "The word *glamour* is a mere corruption of *gramarye* or *grammar*, meaning (1) grammar, (2) magic."

Glamour Eyes : Eyes of Eye-Biting Witches: Eyes that dispel the delusions of Witch prickers, danglers, and other deadfellows. *Cockaludicrous Comment:*

> For, according to S. Isidore . . . a glamour is nothing but a
> certain delusion of the senses, and especially of the eyes.
>   —Heinrich Kramer and James Sprenger,
>   *Malleus Maleficarum*[49]

Glamourize *v* : to exercise the powers of Glamour Eyes: to exorcise the deceptive demons of phallocracy, reversing the reversals of mirrordom

Geomancer: *Diviner by means of signs derived from the Earth*

Glamour Puss : term of endearment, applied especially to an attractive Feline

¹Gnome ° *n* **1** : one of the four Elementals: Earth Spirit who lives in the Earth and guards precious ore and treasure   **2** : a Gyn/Ecological woman: one who understands, respects, and bonds with the Earth as her Sister. *Canny Comment:*

> The Zuñi Indians in New Mexico consider clay to be the flesh of a female supernatural, and all work in clay, including brick-making, is done by women.
> —Lucy Lippard[50]

²Gnome ° *n* ["a brief reflection or maxim: APHORISM, PROVERB"— *Webster's*] : an Earthy, Gyn/Ecological aphorism or proverb. *Examples:*

> Everything that IS is connected with everything else that IS.[51]

> Despite all the evils they wished to crush me with / I remain as steady as the three-legged cauldron.
> —Monique Wittig[52]

Gnomic ° *adj* : Earthy, Elemental

Gnomic plug ° : habit of restraint characteristic of a Prudent Prude, enabling her to practice Elemental Volcanic Timing for the venting of her Passions, e.g., rage, daring, sorrow, joy, love. *See* **Volcanoes, Women as** (w-w 2). *N.B.:* Gnomic plugs are comparable to those natural plugs of the Earth's volcanoes which hold back columns of molten rock from exploding until the volcano is ready to resume activity

Gnomic Present ° : the Present as lived by Gnomic women; a time in which the Presences of Foresisters and Fore-Gnomes are experienced

Gnomic writing ° **1** : writing by Crones, who live in the Gnomic Present; writing that expresses Earthy Reality   **2** : messages or signs emitted by the Earth, found in mountain chains, crevices, trees, sands, leaves, rocks. *See* **Geomancy** (w-w 2)

Gnomology ° *n* : the study of Gnomes and Gnomic phenomena by and for Gnomes and Fore-Gnomes

Gooney *n* **1** : an albatross: much maligned Weird bird who possesses an impeccable sense of humor and direction and who habitually

GNOME: *Earth Spirit who lives in the Earth and guards precious ore and treasure*

wanders on long, tireless flights **2 :** a woman who participates in the qualities of a Gooney [53]

Gorgon ° *n* ["one of three sisters in Greek mythology having snake-entwined hair and glaring eyes capable of turning the beholder to stone . . . one resembling a gorgon; *esp.:* an ugly, repulsive, or terrifying woman"—*Webster's*] **1 :** one of the three Moon Goddesses who petrify patriarchs **2 :** a Revolting Hag whose Glaring Eyes and Frightening Face can stop the doomers and their doomsday clocks. *Example:* Emily Erwin Culpepper (*see Appendicular Web Two*). See **doomsday clock** (w-w 3)

Gorgon Eyes : Staring Eyes that stop the processions of patriarchal predators; Glaring Eyes that turn the phallic fixers into stone

Gorgonize *v* ["to have a paralyzing or mesmerizing effect on: STUPEFY, PETRIFY"—*Webster's*] **1 :** to exercise the Petrifying Powers of Gorgon Eyes: FASCINATE, SPELLBIND **2 :** to organize Gorgonish Gatherings; to bond with the express purpose of stopping the doomsday cocks' clocks

Gorilla/Girlilla *n* [*gorilla* derived fr. Gk *Gorillai,* an African tribe of hairy women—*Webster's*] **:** member of an Intergalactic Tribe of Hairy Hags. *Canny Comment:*

> Under the male definition of femininity there is the notion of female "hairlessness." The feminine woman has no facial hair, no hair on arms or legs or underarms, and women who wish to conform to this definition of femininity will constantly present themselves to males without a hint of hair.
> —Dale Spender [54]

N.B.: It should be Nag-noted that a group of Radical Feminist musicians Be-Laughingly call themselves "The Girlillas." [55]

Gossip *n* ["A familiar acquaintance, friend, chum. Formerly applied to both sexes now only (somewhat *archaic*) to women. . . . *esp.* Applied to a woman's female friends invited to be present at a birth."—*O.E.D.*] **:** a Female Friend and/or Familiar, esp. applied to the Fates, Fairies, Familiars, and Friends who invite themselves to be Present at any Female Act of Creation

Gossip *v* ["To be a gossip or sponsor to; to give a name to. *Obs.* . . . To act as a gossip, or a familiar acquaintance; to take part (in a feast), be a boon-companion; to make oneself at home. . . . To tell like a gossip: to communicate. Also with *out*. **1650** 'The secret lay not long in the Embers, being gossiped out by a woman.' . . . **1827** 'And wisdom, gossip'd from the stars.'"—*O.E.D.*] **1 :** to exercise the Elemental Female Power of Naming, especially in the Presence of other Gossips **2 :** to take part in the festivity of wordplay among Boon-Companions **3 :** to tell like a Gossip; to divine and communicate the secrets of the Elements, the wisdom of the stars

Gossipdom *n* ["The class of gossips as a whole; the realm of gossip"—*O.E.D.*] **:** This definition has been awarded *Websters'* Intergalactic Seal of Approval.

Gossiphood *n* ["Now *rare* . . . Spiritual relationship. . . . A body of gossips"—*O.E.D.*] **:** These definitions have been awarded *Websters'* Intergalactic Seal of Approval. *Example:*

> BAND OF INTERGALACTIC GORILLAS (GIRLILLAS)
> WILDLY WELCOMED BY THE GOSSIPHOOD OF GNOMETOWN,
> U.S.A.
> —headline, *Tidal Times,* Dec. 5, 1990 A.F., p. 1

Gossipship *n* ["*Obs.* . . . The mutual relation of gossips. Also, the personality of a gossip or sponsor. . . . **1651** 'To the end that this Goshipship [sic] shold [sic] no way be a bar or impediment among the Gentlewomen in matter of Mariage [sic].'"—*O.E.D.*] **1 :** the mutual relation and Gyn/affection of Gossips, which in every way is a bar to the Self-loss of marriage **2 :** the Prudish personality of a Gossip **3 :** means of transportation favored by Gossips

Grace ○ *n* ["a free gift of God to man for his regeneration or sanctification"—*Webster's*] **:** a free shift away from the vicious circle of god and man's "regeneration or sanctification"; a Spiraling, Metamorphic Leap of Be-Witching. *Canny Comment:*

> A-mazing Grace
> How sweet the sound
> That saved a Witch like me
> I once was lost
> My Self I found
> Was bound
> But now I'm free
> —Diana Beguine[56]

Graceful/graceless ○ *adj* **1 :** agile, nimble, quick; adept at bounding into New Space **2 :** marked by constant refusal of the infusions

133

of "supernatural grace" that are pushed by the ubiquitous priestly predators of junkocracy. *See* **junkocracy** (w-w 3)

Graceful State ○ : the Wild and Super Natural State of Originally Sinning/Spinning Women and Other Others: State of Sin

Gramarye *n* [(derived fr. ME *gramarye, gramarie,* modif. of MF *gramaire* grammar, grammar book, book of sorcery) : "NECROMANCY, MAGIC, ENCHANTMENT"—*Webster's*] **1** : Book of Word-Magic; Handbook for Word-Witches: Wickedary **2** : BIOMANCY, MAGIC, ENCHANTMENT. *See* **Biomancy** (w-w 2)

Grammarian *n* **1** : one who participates in the harmonious interplay of the primal sounds of words; one who Realizes the Sounding of words: MUSE **2** : any Gyn/Ecologist who Dis-covers and listens attentively to the Grammar/Rhythms of Wild Reality and whose work is to communicate the messages she receives. *See* **Happy Medium** (w-w 2); **Grammar** (w-w 1)

Grimalkin *n* ["A name given to a cat; hence, a cat, *esp.* an old she-cat; *contemptuously* applied to a jealous or imperious old woman"—*O.E.D.*] : Name given to a cat, especially a Wise Old She-Cat, honorifically applied to a generous and powerful Old Woman

Grimalkined *adj* ["vexed by a 'grimalkin'"—*O.E.D.*] : Graciously Hexed by a Grimalkin

Guide *n* ["one who leads or shows the way, esp. to a traveller in a strange country"—*O.E.D.*] : an Otherworldly Helper who shows a Traveler the way into the Country of the Strange, her Homeland. *Example:*

> As you surmont those peaks
> among the stars, go south, until you reach
> the Amazons, who husbands hate. . . .
> To guide
> a girl will Amazons be more than glad . . .
> —Aeschylus [57]

Guide Word ["either of the terms at the head of a page of an alphabetical reference work (as a dictionary) . . ."—*Webster's Collegiate*] : Word acting as a Guide for Searchers on Wild Word chases, leading to Other Words, opening doors to further magic meanings

GRIMALKIN: *Name given to a cat, especially a Wise Old She-Cat, honorifically applied to a generous, powerful Old Woman*

Gynaesthesia [°] *n* [*synaesthesia* "a concomitant sensation; *esp:* a subjective sensation or image of a sense (as of color) other than the one (as of sound) being stimulated"—*Webster's*] : the synaesthesia of Wild Women who have awakened from the State of Anaesthesia; the vivid, complex interplay and expansion of senses that is experienced by Muses and Mediums who are overcoming the State of Amnesia, regaining our Sense of Direction, Unforgetting our Psychic Sensory Powers. *Example:* a Feminist Searcher, in tune with her work, finds that the books she needs seem to be virtually "jumping off the shelves" to her.

¹Gynaesthetic [°] *adj* : characterized by Gynaesthesia.

²Gynaesthetic *adj* [*aesthetic* "appreciative of, responsive to, or zealous about the beautiful"—*Webster's*] : having a woman-identified appreciation of and zeal for Elemental Beauty. *Examples:*

> I notice that it is only when my mother is working in her flowers that she is radiant, almost to the point of being invisible—except as Creator: hand and eye. She is involved in work her soul must have. Ordering the universe in the image of her personal conception of Beauty.
> —Alice Walker[58]

> I think it pisses God off if you walk by the color purple in a field somewhere and don't notice it.
> —Shug, in Alice Walker's *The Color Purple*[59]

Gyn/Ecologist [°] *n* : a practitioner of the science of Gyn/Ecology; a participant in the process of Gyn/Ecology. *See* **Gyn/Ecology** (w-w 1)

Gynergenesis *n* : the creation of Gynergy. *See* **Gynergy** (w-w 1)

Gynocentric Memory [°] **1** : Memory of a Gynocratic world that pre-existed patriarchy **2** : Crone-logical Memory: history that records/Re-calls events of central importance to women. *Example: The First Sex,* by Elizabeth Gould Davis, who wrote:

> This work is the result of the convergence of two streams of thought: the first, that the earliest civilization we know was but a renewal of a then dimly remembered and now utterly forgotten older one; and the second, that the impelling and revivifying agent in what we know as civilization was woman.[60]

Gynocentric Method [°] **:** Woman-centered Method, requiring not only the murder of misogynistic methods (intellectual and affective exorcism), but also ecstasy, i.e., Ludic Cerebration. *See* **Ludic Cerebration** (w-w 2); **Methodicide** (w-w 1). *Compare* **Methodolatry** (w-w 1)

Gynography [°] *n* **:** writings, pictures, or other forms of communication intended to confirm the Original integrity of all women; graphic communications which excite Pure Lust. *Canny Comment:*

> I am trying with all my skill to do a painting that is all of
> women, as well as all of me.
> —Georgia O'Keeffe[61]

*The Inhabitants
of the
Background,
Their Activities
and
Characteristics*

Gynomorphic Resonance : sequence of Gynergetic vibrations emitted by Shape-shifting Sibyls, inspiring concomitant Qualitative Leaping by Others

Gyromancy *n* ["divination in which one walking in or around a circle falls from dizziness and prognosticates from the place of the fall"—*Webster's*] **:** divination by Spiraling Spinsters

Hag [°] *n* [(derived fr. ME *hagge, hegge* . . . akin to MD *haghetisse* witch, OHG *hagzissa, hagazussa* harpy, witch; all fr. a prehistoric WGmc compound whose components are akin respectively to OE *haga* hedge and to G dialect (Westphalia) *dūs* devil): "*archaic:* a female demon: FURY, HARPY . . . an evil or frightening spirit . . . NIGHTMARE. . . . an ugly or evil-looking old woman"—*Webster's*] **:** Archaic: a Witch, Fury, Harpy who haunts the Hedges/Boundaries of patriarchy, frightening fools and summoning Weird Wandering Women into the Wild. *Canny Comment:*

> Where Hags are, will be Spells.
> Where Women are, will be Spells.
> —Gaelic proverb[62]

Haggard [°] *adj* **:** ["*obs:* INTRACTABLE, WILLFUL, WANTON. . . . wild in appearance: as **a** *of the eyes:* wild and staring **b** *of a person:* WILD-EYED"—*Webster's*] **:** These definitions have been awarded *Websters'* Intergalactic Seal of Approval.

Haggard [°] *n* ["*obs:* an intractable person; *esp:* a woman reluctant to yield to wooing"—*Webster's*] **:** This definition has been awarded *Websters'* Intergalactic Seal of Approval. *See* **Old Maid; Spinster** (w-w 2)

137

Haggard Woman ⁹ : one who refuses to assume the woes of wooed women, who casts off these woes as unworthy of Hags, of Harpies; one who is not man-wooed; one who rejects the curse of compromise

Hagged *adj* ["*dial Brit* BEWITCHED: ENCHANTED . . . resembling a witch or a hag"—*Webster's*] : BE-WITCHED; having an Uncanny resemblance to a Witch or a Hag

Hag-ocracy ⁹ *n* : the Background into which Feminist Journeying Spins; the Wild Realm of Hags and Crones

Hag-ographer ⁹ *n* : a specialist in Hag-ography; a Dis-coverer and biographer of Great Hags; a Searcher who uncovers clues, pieces together fragments, Weaves and Reweaves Haggard History. *Example:* Anne Cameron [63]

Hag-ography ⁹ *n* : the history of women who are on the Journey of radical be-ing; the lives of Witches, of Great Hags (past and present), which are deeply intertwined; history uncovered and created by women as we live/write our own stories. *Example:* Sojourner Truth's *Book of Life* [64]

Hag-ology ⁹ *n* : theoretical work of Haggard Wisdom

Hagstone *n* ["a naturally perforated stone used as an amulet against witchcraft"—*Webster's*] **1** : a Super Natural stone (any stone) or Other object used by Witches to ward off patriarchal evil **2** : any stone that speaks to a Hag. *Canny Comment:*

> Rocks do indeed make a sound. All things that the Great Spirit has put here continually cry to be heard. The problem is, there are few who listen. I remember the first time I ever heard the rocks crying. . . .
> There was so much pain inside of me that day. I believed a part of me was screaming. . . . When I let this feeling come into me, I was suddenly aware that the rocks sensed my pain and were crying with me. Don't imagine that I heard this sound by my ears alone—I heard it by my whole awareness.
> —Agnes Whistling Elk [65]

Happy Medium *n* **1** : a Hag or any Spirited creature who is in Touch with her primal Powers of Communication and who therefore Touches Others **2** : the Gyn/Ecological atmosphere in which Biophilic be-ing can flourish. *N.B.:* For a philosophical discussion of Mediums and Mediumship see *Preliminary Web One.*

Harridan *n* [(perh. modif. of F *haridelle* worn-out horse, tall lean ugly woman): "a haggard old woman: HAG"—*Webster's*] **:** tall, athletic, stunning Virago; Haggard Crone; Hag; Nag

Harpy ⁹ *n* ["a shrewish or depraved woman"—*Webster's*] **:** a Shrewish and Enraged woman, one who harps on Haggard themes. *Example:* Susan B. Anthony, who said:

> So while I do not pray for anybody or any party to commit outrages, still I do pray, and that earnestly and constantly, for some terrific shock to startle the women of this nation into a self-respect which will compel them to see the abject degradation of their present position. . . . The fact is, women are in chains, and their servitude is all the more debasing because they do not realize it. O, to compel them to see and feel, and to give them the courage and conscience to speak and act for their own freedom, though they face the scorn and contempt of all the world for doing it![66]

Heathen *n* [derived fr. Gk *heiden,* a heathen; Goth. *haithnō,* a heathen woman. Lit. a dweller on a heath, orig. "wild"—*Skeat's*) **:** "an unconverted member of a people or nation that does not acknowledge the God of the Bible: PAGAN"—*Webster's*] **:** a Wild, Uncivilized, Unconvertible, Pagan Woman. *See* **Pagan** (W-W 2)

Her-Ethical ○ *adj* **:** "in harmony with Gyn/Ecological standards of conduct"—Ms. Wild Cat.[67] *Canny Comment:*

> The freedom of women from sex oppression either matters or it does not; it is either essential or it is not. Decide one more time.
> —Andrea Dworkin[68]

Her-etical ○ *adj* **:** Weird Beyond Belief

Hex *n* ["SPELL, ENCHANTMENT. . . . a person who practices witchcraft: WITCH"—*Webster's*] **:** These definitions have been awarded *Websters'* Intergalactic Seal of Approval. *N.B.:* For the etymology of *Hex,* see **Hag** (W-W 2)

Hexing [*hex* "to practice witchcraft upon: put a hex on"—*Webster's*] : Spell-casting by Hags/Hexes who practice Witch-Craft on the Boundaries of patriarchy, the State of Atrocity; Positively Revolting Willing by Hags. *See* **Be-Wishing** (w-w 1)

Horsey *adj* : High-spirited; characterized by Horse Sense; applied esp. to Prancing, Racing, Galloping, Horselaughing Nags. *See* **Nag** (w-w 2)

WORD-WEB
TWO

Hydroglyphic ° *adj* : written in, constituted by, or belonging to that form of Archaic Elemental writing in which the characters are for the most part recognizable reflections of Hydromantic Tidal Thought

Hydromancy ° *n* ["divination by means of signs derived from water, its tides and ebbs, or the . . . appearance of sprites therein"—*O.E.D.*] : This definition has been awarded *Websters'* Intergalactic Seal of Approval.

Incommunication • (Jan Raymond[69]) *n* : process by which the community of Sisterhood expands: attraction into New Space/New Time. *N.B.:* Since this community—unlike such an institution as the catholic church—has no hierarchy and no dogmas, it cannot "excommunicate" its members for unorthodoxy. Rather, it invites the Unorthodoxy of women finding their Selves in New Haggard Harmony.

Influence ° *n* ["an ethereal fluid thought to flow from the stars and to affect the actions of men. . . . the exercise of a power like the supposed power of the stars: an emanation of spiritual or moral force"—*Webster's*] : a flow from the stars that affects the actions of Star-Lusty women, enabling us to participate in Archaic Angelic Powers, in emanations of Elemental, Astral Force

Journeyer ◗ : one who whirls through Other worlds, Spinning/Spiraling on multidimensional Voyages through Realms of the Wild, which involve Quests, adventurous Travel, the Dispelling of demons, cosmic encounters, participation in Paradise. *See* **Otherworld Journey** (w-w 1)

Knotting ◗ **1** : Mystical metaphor for Journeying, implying bonding in union with the Self and Other Journeyers **2** : Archimagical Act of Spellbinding. *Canny Comments:*

> The "slip knot" is a determinative sign in the Egyptian language, entering into the composition of words such as . . .

HYDROMANCER: *Diviner by means of signs derived from Water*

journey. The meaning must have originated in the idea of keeping in touch with someone who is far away.
　　　—J. E. Cirlot [70]

The woman is the possessor of the most secret arts of knotting which is practiced by almost all nations even today as magic against sickness and any kind of misfortune.
　　　—Helen Diner [71]

WORD-WEB TWO

Labrys ⁰ *n* ["an ancient Cretan sacred double ax"—*Webster's*] **1 :** "the double ax, 'the sign of Imperial might' . . . the symbol of gynocratic power in Crete as it was among the Lycians, the Lydians, the Amazons, the Etruscans, and even the Romans. . . . found in the graves of Paleolithic women of Europe, buried 50,000 years ago"— Elizabeth Gould Davis [72] **2 :** the A-mazing Female Mind that cuts through the double binds and doublebinding words of patriarchy; the double ax of Wild wisdom and wit that breaks through the mazes of man-made mystification, cutting the mindbindings of master-minded doublethink; Power of Discernment which divines the difference between Reality and unreality, between the Natural Wild and elementary fabrications **3 :** any double-edged word or phrase that exposes the evil of phallocracy, Dis-covering its corruption and evoking the Presence of the Background. *Example: Pure Lust—pure lust. See* **Background** (w-w 1)

Labyrinth ⁰ *n* [(derived fr. Gk *labyrinthos* . . . akin to Gk *labrys* double ax): "a structure full of intricate passageways. . . . the internal ear"— *Webster's*] **1 :** true pathway of the Metapatriarchal Journey of Exorcism and Ecstasy, leading into and through the Background **2 :** an Elemental capacity for Hearing the way into the Otherworld

Labyrinthine Journey ⁰ **:** *See* **Otherworld Journey** (w-w 1)

Labyrinthine Sense ⁰ ["a complex sense concerned with the perception of bodily position and motion . . ."—*Webster's*] **1 :** complex sense of Crones regaining a Sense of Direction, moving into and through Metapatriarchal Time/Space **2 :** the faculty of Hearing the difference between Real, Elemental Words and mere elementary terms. *See* **Labyrinth; Third Ear** (w-w 2)

Laughing Out Loud, Virtue of • (1985 ed.) **:** Lusty habit of boisterous Be-Laughing women: habit of cracking the hypocritical hierarchs' houses of mirrors, defusing their power of deluding Others;

cackling that cracks the man-made universe, creating a crack through which Cacklers can slip into the Realms of the Wild; Virtue of Crackpot Crones whose peals of laughter peel away the plastic passions and unpot the potted ones. *Canny Comment:*

> Firm in reliance, laugh a defiance,
> (Laugh in hope, for sure is the end).
> March, March many as one
> Shoulder to shoulder and friend to friend!
> —Cicely Hamilton and Ethyl Smyth [73]

Lesbian : *See* **Lesbian** (W-W 1)

Life-Time [•] *n* : New Time, on the Boundary of patriarchal time; women's *own* Time which *is* whenever we are living out of our own Sense of Reality, refusing to be possessed, conquered, and alienated by the linear, measured-out, quantitative time of the patriarchal system

Ludic Cerebration [•] (1975 ed.) : thinking out of the experience of being: the free play of intuition in New Space, giving rise to thinking that is vigorous, informed, multidimensional, independent, creative, tough

Lunatic *n* [[derived fr. L *luna* moon): ". . . one who is wildly eccentric: one capable of crazy actions or extravagances: CRACKPOT"— *Webster's*] : This definition has been awarded *Websters'* Intergalactic Seal of Approval. *See* **Crackpot Crone; Maenad; Weird** (W-W 2)

Lunatic Fringe ["the members of a group (as a political or social movement) espousing extreme, eccentric, or fanatical views: an extreme or wild group on the periphery of a larger group or of a movement"—*Webster's*] **1** : Crackpot Crones in tune with the moon, propelled by Pure Lust, who dare to Spin Wildly, always **2** : the truly moving center of the women's movement, comprising those who choose always to Survive/Thrive on the Boundaries, refusing compromise

¹**Luster** [○] *n* : a woman incited to rebellion by Pure Lust. *See* **Pure Lust** (W-W 1)

²**Luster** [○] *n* : [". . . a glow of light from within: LUMINOSITY, SHINE (luster of the stars) . . . an inner beauty: RADIANCE"—*Webster's*] : This definition has been awarded *Websters'* Intergalactic Seal of Approval.

Lusty ° *adj* : Fired/Inspired by Pure Lust: Wanton, Gynergetic, Biophilic, joyous, merry, robust, flourishing, strong, powerful, vigorous: having an unrestrained inclination for enjoyment

Lusty Leaper ° : a Wild Woman who carries threads of connectedness beyond already Realized limits. *Canny Comment:*

> And when she walks
> Upon the ground
> You'd never know
> How she can bound
> Upon the tree-tops, for she creeps
> With a snail's slow silver pace;
> Her milky silky wrinkled face
> Shows no sign of her disgrace.
> But walking on each
> Leafy tree-top—
> Those old witches,
> See them hop!
>   —Edith Sitwell[74]

Lusty Mover ° *n* : a Labrys-wielding Amazonian activist; one who refuses to settle down, to settle for cockocratic settlements; an instigator of rebellion; one who keeps the women's movement on the move

M.A.D. ° [*M.A.D.* (*Mutual Assured Destruction*) "a concept of reciprocal deterrence which rests on the ability of the two nuclear superpowers to inflict unacceptable damage on one another after surviving a nuclear first strike"—*A Glossary of Arms Control Terms*[75]] : a concept of Self-deduction/separation from the State of Boredom, which rests upon the ability of two or more enraged Female Powers to refuse further damage to our Selves and Sisters, after surviving innumerable phallic touches and strikes. *Compare* **m.a.d.** (w-w 3)

Maenad ° [derived fr. Gk *mainad-, mainas,* lit., madwoman—*Webster's*] : Mad, Furiously Fey, Wild Woman; Lunatic; Weird; Contrary-Wise Crackpot Crone

Magnet Eyes   1 : Eyes that attract Elemental Forces/Powers/Demons **2 :** Beckoning Eyes; Alluring Eyes that Be-Speak the lure/lore of the Strange. *Example:*

> I couldn't keep my eyes off Bryher's: they were so blue—
> bluer than the sea or the sky or even the Blue Grotto in

144

Capri. More beautiful still was the expression in Bryher's eyes. I'm afraid that to this day I stare at her eyes.
    —Sylvia Beach[76]

Magnetism, Animal [*magnetism* "an ability to attract: a power to charm"; also *animal magnetism* "a spiritlike force alleged by the Austrian physician Franz Anton Mesmer (1734–1815) to reside within himself and to be active in his use of therapeutical hypnosis"— *Webster's*] **1 :** an Animal's ability to attract: the Charm of an attractive Familiar **2 :** a Spiritlike force residing within and emanating from Animals, which is absolutely antithetical to the "therapeutical" activities of psycho-ologists and other professional snools

The Inhabitants of the Background, Their Activities and Characteristics

Magnetism, Elemental : the reciprocal and energizing attraction among all Elemental beings. *Canny Comments:*

> There is no drop of water in the ocean, not even in the deepest parts of the abyss, that does not know and respond to the mysterious forces that create the tide.
>   —Rachel Carson[77]

> Nowhere on the shore is the relation of a creature to its surroundings a matter of a single cause and effect; each living thing is bound to its world by many threads, weaving the intricate design of the fabric of life.
>   —Rachel Carson[78]

Magnetize *v* **:** to Realize the power of Magnet Eyes; to radiate Elemental attraction

Magnifi-Cat *n* **:** a magnificent, illustrious Cat; an imposing Feline

Magpiety *n* ["**1845** 'Not pious in its proper sense, But chattring like a bird'"—*O.E.D.*] **:** the impious impropriety of Prudes; irreverence for sir-reverence; Nagpiety; Hagpiety. *See* **sir-reverence** (w-w 3)

Mediumship *n* **1 :** the creative activity of Happy Mediums **2 :** the vessel/vehicle chosen by Happy Mediums for our Otherworld Journey. *See* **Happy Medium** (w-w 2)

Mermaid ○ *n* **:** member of an all-female tribe of water inhabitants (usually the sea, but also rivers, lakes, and streams): Sea Virgin. *Canny Comment:*

Because the mermaids' realm is not invaded by men, it can represent a place where there is female freedom and self-sufficiency. Living in water . . . physically conveys the idea of a different world, different from the patriarchal land in which we find ourselves struggling for female liberation.
—Emily Erwin Culpepper[79]

Cockaludicrous Comment:

I have heard the mermaids singing,
     each to each.
I do not think that they will sing to me.
   —T. S. Eliot[80]

Mister-ectomy *ᵓ n* : guaranteed solution to The Contraceptive Problem; tried and true and therefore taboo birth control method, recommended by Gyn/Ecologists, insisted upon by Spinsters. *Canny Comment:* "O, Come let us ignore him . . ." (unpopular holiday song)—Discourtesy of Diana Beguine[81]

Moments/Movements of be-ing ○ : Acts that propel Journeyers into Realms of Metabeing, especially A-mazing Acts of courage and imagination; Metamorphic Moments of contact with one's Genius/Demon/Muse

Moon-Wise *adj* : in tune with lunar rhythms; Touched by the moon. *Canny Comment:*

In my sensory education I include my physical awareness of the *word*. Of a certain word, that is; the connection it has with what it stands for. At around age six, perhaps, I was standing by myself in our front yard waiting for supper, just at that hour in a late summer day when the sun is already below the horizon and the risen full moon in the visible sky stops being chalky and begins to take on light. There comes the moment, and I saw it then, when the moon goes from flat to round. For the first time it met my eyes as a globe. The word "moon" came into my mouth as though fed to me out of a silver spoon. Held in my mouth the moon became a word.
   —Eudora Welty[82]

Multibious be-ing *ᵓ* : living/moving with Amazonian agility; transcending flatland; Surviving/Thriving in multiple dimensions

Muse ○ *n* [derived fr. L *Musa,* fr. Gk *Mousa;* prob. akin to Gk *mnasthai* to remember—*Webster's*] : the guiding Genius/Demon of a Musing woman; a woman in Touch with her Creative Spirit, her Self; one who Re-members/releases harmonious waves of meanings, so that New Archaic Words can be heard, spoken, and sung. *See* **Genius** (w-w 2); **Demon** (w-w 1)

Music of the Spheres ○ ["an ethereal harmony supposed by the Pythagoreans to be produced by the vibration of the celestial spheres upon which the stars and planets were thought to move"—*Webster's*] : an Earthy/Ethereal harmony Heard by Muses, and inspiring Journeyers as we move through Archespheres, Pyrospheres, and Metamorphospheres

The Inhabitants of the Background, Their Activities and Characteristics

Musing ○ [*muse v* "*archaic:* to become astonished: WONDER, MARVEL"—*Webster's*] : Marveling and Be-Laughing with astonishment at man's mysteries/misteries; Wonderlusting: participating in the Unfolding of Metamysterious Creation

Nag ○ *n* : a Scold with Horse Sense; a Biting Critic of cockocracy; one who has acquired the Virtue of Nagging. *See* **Horsey** (w-w 2)

Nag ○ *v* ["to affect with recurrent awareness, uncertainty, need for consideration or concern: make recurrently conscious of something (as a problem, solution, situation)"—*Webster's*] : This definition has been awarded *Websters'* Intergalactic Seal of Approval.

Nagging, Virtue of : Haggard habit of resisting and combating the psychic numbing demanded by the sadosociety, the State of Oblivion

Nag-Gnostic ○ *n* : a practitioner of Nag-Gnosticism; Elemental Feminist Philosopher. *See* **Nag-Gnosticism** (w-w 1)

Nag-Nation ○ *n* : worldwide Network of Nags; loose aggregation of loose women[83]

Nag-noted ○ *adj* : well-known to Nag-Gnostics; eminent among and celebrated by Nags

Nag-noteworthy ○ *adj* : deemed notable by Nags, especially applied to events of great significance that are invisible to and erased by the schoolmen of snooldom. *Example:*

147

MUSE: *a Woman in Touch with her Creative Spirit, her Self*

"Chloe liked Olivia," I read. And then it struck me how immense a change was there. Chloe liked Olivia perhaps for the first time in literature.
—Virginia Woolf[84]

Nagster ○ *n* : member of the Sisterhood of Nagging Women

Naiad ○ *n* : nymph who inhabits and enspirits the waters of lakes, rivers, springs, fountains; a species of Water Witch: NIX. *Example:* "Nessie," the Loch Ness Monster

The Inhabitants of the Background, Their Activities and Characteristics

Network, The ◑ *n* : the Gyn/Ecological context: tapestry of connections woven and re-woven by Spinsters and Websters; the Net which breaks the fall of Journeyers experiencing the Earthquake Phenomenon and springing us into New Space. *See* **Earthquake Phenomenon; New Space** (W-W I)

Nightmare ◑ *n* [(derived fr. ME *night* + *mare* (spirit)—*Webster's*): "a female spirit or monster supposed to beset people and animals by night, settling upon them when they are asleep and producing a feeling of suffocation by its weight"—*O.E.D.*] : a Female Spirit or Monster who visits women and animals by night, helping us to travel while sleeping, and producing a feeling of exaltation and light; Hag who gives protection, warnings, advice and consolation to Wanderlusters during sleep

Nix ○ *n* ["a supernatural creature orig. in Germanic folklore and conceived of in many forms but usu. as having the form of a woman or as half human and half fish, dwelling in fresh water usu. in a beautiful palace, and usu. unfriendly to man . . . called also *nixie*"—*Webster's*] **1** : This definition has been awarded *Websters'* Intergalactic Seal of Approval **2** : a woman who participates in the powers and activities of Elemental Nixes; a woman usu. unfriendly to man (called also *Nixie*)

Nix *adv* ["*slang:* NO—used to express disagreement or the withholding of permission"—*Webster's*] : This definition has been awarded *Websters'* Intergalactic Seal of Approval. *Canny Comment:*

Have Courage young girls to say No
Have Courage young girls to say No
Have Courage young girls,
Have Courage young girls
Have Courage young girls to say No!
—Georgia Sea Islands folk song[85]

Nixing [*nix "slang:* VETO, FORBID, PROHIBIT, BAN, REJECT, CAN-CEL"—*Webster's*] **:** Spell-casting by Nixes: Denouncing the drooling of fools, the droning of clones, the mindless devastations wrought by Stag-nations; the Nilling by Nixes of Nothing-lovers. *See* **Nothing-lovers** (w-w 3)

Nixnames *n* **:** words conjured by Nixes to ridicule and expose cockocrats, banning the butchery/botchery of prickers, rakes, fakes, and rippers. *Examples: papal bully, presbot, Uncle Sham*

Norn ○ *n* ["*Norse Mythology.* One of the Fates, Skuld (the Future), Verdaude (the Present), and Urd (the Past)."—*American Heritage*] **:** This definition has been awarded *Websters'* Intergalactic Seal of Approval. *Canny Comment:*

> Northern peoples said [a] chain held the cosmic doomsday-wolf Fenrir, who would be released by the Norns (triple Fate-goddess) to devour the heavenly father at the end of the world; this would signal the destruction of all the gods.
> —Barbara G. Walker[86]

See **Fates** (w-w 2). *N.B.:* Websters note with interest that the Norns have been called "Die Schreiberinnen" (women who write).[87]

Novice Nag ○ *n* **:** an apprentice Nag; one Newly Dis-covering the ways of Nag-Gnosticism

Nymph ○ *n* **:** guardian spirit, usually found in groves, forests, fountains, springs, meadows, and mountains

Oceanid ○ *n* **:** salt water nymph who inhabits oceans and seas. *See* **Mermaid; Siren; Undine** (w-w 2)

Ogre ○ *n* **:** Shrieking Shrew feared by frauds; Soothsayer, wholly Monstrous to flashers who dread her Eye-biting powers of total exposure; Sibyl who shrivels phallic erections

Old Maid *n* **:** a Crone who has steadfastly resisted imprisonment in the Comatose State of matrimony: SURVIVOR, SPINSTER. *Canny Comments:*

> They gossip that I'm not married, but I'm happier than they are. They have husbands but they are forced to beg. . . .
> While their husbands break the boards of the shack, I and my

Oceanid: *salt water Nymph who inhabits oceans and seas*

children sleep peacefully. I don't envy the married women of the favelas who lead lives like Indian slaves.

I never got married and I'm not unhappy. Those who wanted to marry me were mean and the conditions they imposed on me were horrible.
—Carolina Maria de Jesus [88]

Single girl,
Single girl
goes anywhere she please
Oh, oh, goes anywhere she please . . .
—Traditional Southern ballad, U.S.A.

Old Maid of Honor : any Old Maid

Oneiromancy *n* ["divination by means of dreams"—*Webster's*] **:** This definition has been awarded *Websters'* Intergalactic Seal of Approval. *Canny Comment:*

I've dreamt in my life dreams that have stayed with me ever after, and changed my ideas; they've gone through and through me, like wine through water, and altered the colour of my mind.
—Emily Brontë, *Wuthering Heights* [89]

Oread ° *n* **1 :** a Nymph who inhabits and enspirits mountains and hills **2 :** a woman who is at home in the hills and who participates in the powers of Oreads. *Canny Comment:*

I have dreamed on this mountain
Since first I was my mother's daughter
And you can't just take my dreams away
Not with me watching.

You may drive a big machine
But I was born a great big woman
And you can't just take my dreams away
Without me fighting. . . .

No you can't just take my dreams away.
—Holly Near [90]

Original Movement ⁹ **:** any movement (as a Passion, thought, word, action) that proceeds from one's Original Self, that is in harmony with one's Final Cause; primal tendency toward the Good

Original Race ○ : kinship of those who Re-member Archaic Time. *See* **Archaic Time; Race of Elemental be-ing** (w-w 1)

Original Woman : one who "charts her own beginnings from the deepest recesses of her Self and other women . . . [who] stands throughout history as the antithesis to the man-made females of patriarchal creation. . . . [who] seizes the power to originate"—Janice G. Raymond[91]

Other Whys ● (1985 ed.) : Whys that are uttered by Other-Wise women: NONQUESTIONS. *Example:*

> Mama, Mama, do you understand
> Why I've not bound myself to a man?
> Is there something buried in your
>   old widow's mind
> That blesses my choice of our own kind?
> Oh Mama, Mama.
>   —Meg Christian[92]

Otherwise *adv* : in a Weird way, in a Deviant direction: Widdershins

Other-Wise ● (1985 ed.) *adj* **1 :** possessing Otherworldly/Earthy Wisdom **2 :** having the Prudence of Prudes

Outsiders' Society : the company of women who recognize no allegiance to fatherland and its institutions and who strive to create a New world.[93] *See* **New** (w-w 1)

Overlook *v* ["to look on with the evil eye: bewitch by looking on"— *Webster's*] **1 :** to look on with Wicked Eyes; to Be-Witch by looking on **2 :** to see through the banal and/or negative meanings of words and to Be-Speak these words in ways that release their positive, Biophilic meanings. *See* **Eyebite/I-Bite** (w-w 2)

O-Zone ◐ (Denise D. Connors[94]) *n* : the anti-pollutant, purifying moving aura of Gynocentric consciousness; the enriching Gynergetic Presence of Spinning/Spiraling women which can make nonbe-ing sink back into itself

Pagan *n* [derived fr. Late L *paganus*, civilian (i.e., not a "soldier of Christ"), fr. L *paganus*, country-dweller, fr. *pagus*, village, country— *American Heritage*] **:** a Background dweller: Heathen, Wholly Her-etical Hag. *N.B.:* Skeat explains that *paganus* means (1) a villager, (2) a pagan, because the rustic people remained longest unconverted.

Paradise ⁹ [derived fr. Gk *paradeisos* enclosed park . . . akin to Iranian *pairi* around + *daēza* wall—*Webster's*] : Time/Space of Spinning which is not containable within the walls/hedges/boundaries of patriarchal parks, whose inhabitants are perpetually parked, locked into the parking lots of the past; Metapatriarchal movement that Weaves around and past the prison walls of the State of Fixation/Restoration: ECSTASY. *Compare* **paradise, patriarchal** (w-w 3)

Parthenogenesis ○ (Anne Dellenbaugh⁹⁵) *n* [derived fr. Gk *parthenos* virgin + Gk *genesis* birth—*American Heritage*] **1 :** process of a woman creating her Self **2 :** process by which a Virgin brings forth Daughters by herSelf without the interference or input of any male **3 :** process by which a Spinster creates unfathered works: SPINNING. *See* **Virgin** (w-w 2)

Parthenogenetic Creation ○ **1:** work of feminist creation produced by women alone; woman-made work which may use males as re-sources but never as progenitors, spiritual fathers, mentors, or models. *Examples: Les Guérillères,* by Monique Wittig; *Mooncircles,* by Kay Gardner; *Websters' First New Intergalactic Wickedary of the English Language* **2:** "method of Philosophia: method which seeks to construct a female train of thought, working with primary and secondary sources *only* by women; method which focuses more on actions of women for our liberation from patriarchy than on dissection and critique of patriarchy"—Emily Erwin Culpepper⁹⁶

Passion, Pyrogenetic ○ [*passion* "a movement of the sensitive appetite"—Thomas Aquinas, *Summa theologiae* I–II, q. 22, a. 3] : Fierce, Contagious Passion; Movement of the Sensitive Appetite of any Lusty being: Elemental E-motion. *See* **Sensitive Appetite** (w-w 2); **E-motion** (w-w 1). *Compare* **pseudopassion** (w-w 3)

Philosophia *n* : "the wisdom formulated by women; love for the wisdom of women; desire and passion for understanding: an intellectual urge toward love of life"—Emily Erwin Culpepper.⁹⁷ *See* **Parthenogenetic Creation** (w-w 2)

Phoenix ○ *n* : the Pyrogenetic Female Self/Spirit that rises from the ashes of all witchburnings, Outliving patriarchy; Metaphor of Metamorphosis. *Canny Comment:*

Herr God, Herr Lucifer,
Beware
Beware.

Out of the ash
I rise with my red hair
And I eat men like air.
—Sylvia Plath[98]

Pigheaded *adj* ["stupidly perverse: STUBBORN, WILLFUL: refusing to yield"—*Webster's*] **:** Prudently perverse: STUBBORN, WILLFUL: refusing to yield, applied esp. to Viragos and to Positively Revolting Hogs

Pixie (Pixy) ○ *n* ["FAIRY; *specif:* a cheerful sprite like an elf typically conceived of as . . . dancing in the moonlight to the sound of crickets or frogs"—*Webster's*] **:** This definition has been awarded *Websters'* Intergalactic Seal of Approval. *N.B.:* Katharine Briggs points out that in the West Country of England Pixies are commonly believed to be the souls of Druids or of Heathen people.[99] *See* **Heathen** (W-W 2)

Pixilated ○ *adj* ["mentally somewhat unbalanced: TOUCHED, DAFFY. . . . under or seeming to be under a magic spell: ENCHANTED, BE-WITCHED"—*Webster's*] **1 :** highly creative; Wandering far afield from the disciplines of pedants and schoolmen; intellectually rigorous; combining careful logic and Spinning Metaphor **2 :** Touched by the Fairies: Pixy-led

Pixy-led ○ *adj* ["Led astray by Pixies"—*O.E.D.*] **:** led by Pixies and Other Guides into Weird Labyrinthine ways; beckoned by Pixies into Wanderlust and Other Erratic behavior; awakened by Sprites to follow the Call of the Wild: BE-WILDERED

Pixy-path ○ ["a path by which those who follow it are bewildered and lost"—*O.E.D.*] **1 :** trail into the Background where Journeyers are Be-Wildered and forever lost to patriarchy **2 :** pathway that leads between the left and right hemispheres of the brain; path that leads off the map and into the Third Hemisphere. *See* **Third Hemisphere** (W-W 2)

Positive Paranoia ⊙ **:** Pyromantic Virtue: habit of psychic Self-defense; Virtue of anticipating, detecting, and breaking destructive patriarchal patterns; Angelic agility, essential ability of Positively Revolting Hags

Positively Revolting Hag ⁰ : a stunning, beauteous Crone; one who inspires positive revulsion from phallic institutions and morality, inciting Others to Acts of Pure Lust

Prehistory ⁰ *n* **1** : account of Pre-patriarchal Time **2** : account that Names Metapatriarchal events and dimensions of women's lives; Crone-logical account. *See* **Crone-ography; Crone-ology** (w-w 2)

priest-Ridder *n* : Elemental Exorcist: broomstick-riding Wicked Woman who sweeps out the priestly presence of absence, sweeping across the priest-ridden foreground, flying off into the Wild. *Canny Comment:*

> The greatest enemy of any enlightened society, and especially of women, is the organized clergy.
> —Shulamit Aloni[100]

Compare **priest-ridden** (w-w 3)

Pride, Virtue of ᵒ *n* [derived fr. ME *pride, prude* "a sense of one's own proper dignity or value; self-respect. . . . a company of lions"—*American Heritage*] **1** : Virtue of Self-respect, characteristic of Prudes **2** : a troop of Lion-identified Prudes. *Canny Comment:*

> The pride of women will never be laid in the dust.
> —Gaelic proverb[101]

Prime Matter ᵒ : Original Matter that is alive and that is also Spirit of the finest corporeality. *Examples:* rocks, trees, stars, butterflies, the readers of this book

Privacy *n* [derived fr. L *privatus* apart from the state, deprived of office, of or belonging to oneself, private—*Webster's*] : quality of being apart from the patriarchal State of Privation; condition of those who spurn the odious offices of officialdom, preferring the Company of Crones

Pro-Life ● (1985 ed.) *adj* : characterized by a commitment to *quality* of Life and to freedom of choice to ensure that quality in all dimensions: BIOPHILIC. *See* **Biophilia; reversal** (w-w 1). N.B.: This word has been stolen by anti-abortion crusaders who characteristically employ the patriarchal strategy of reversal.

Pro-Lifer ● (1985 ed.) *n* : one who puts her Life on the line in the struggle against the necro-apocalyptic nobodies who are running/ruining the world. *Example:* the women of Greenham Common and all peace encampments. *See* **necro-apocalyptic** (w-w 3)

Pronunciation *n* ["the action of pronouncing authoritatively or proclaiming"—*O.E.D.*] : the action of Denouncing, Pronouncing, or Announcing authentically, or Naming

Prude ° *n* [derived fr. F *prudefemme* wise or good woman, fr. OF *prode* good, capable, brave + *femme* woman—*Webster's*] : Good, capable, brave woman endowed with Practical/Passionate Wisdom; one who has acquired the E-motional habit of Wild Wisdom, enabling her to perform Acts which, by the standards of phallicism, are Extreme; Lusty Woman who insists upon the Integrity, Self-esteem, and Pride of her sex; Shrewd woman who sees through the patriarchal norms of "good" and "evil," constantly Re-membering the Good. *See* **Prudish Prudence** (w-w 1). *N.B.:* Prudes note with Pride that the word *proud* is etymologically akin to *prude*. Both are derived from OF *prode*.

The Inhabitants of the Background, Their Activities and Characteristics

Pyrogenesis ° *n* : the birthing/flaming of Female Fire; the Sparking of Radical Feminist consciousness

Pyroglyphic ° *adj* : written in, constituted by, or belonging to that form of Archaic Elemental writing in which the characters are for the most part recognizable pictures/portrayals of Pyromantic Passionate Thought

Pyrognomic ° *adj* : marked by deep Earthy knowledge, which arises from the fiery core of Volcanic experience

Pyrognostic ° *adj* : blazing with Passionate knowledge, applied to individuals, books, works of art, etc. *Example: Sula*, by Toni Morrison [102]

Pyrography ° *n* : Fiery/Passionate writing and/or painting. *Example:* Artemesia Gentileschi's painting *Judith Decapitating Holofernes* (c. 1620)

Pyrologian ° *n* : a Crone who pursues the Wisdom of Fire; a Hag who stirs the cauldrons of Kali, conjuring Elemental Electrical Powers

Pyromachy ° *n* ["*Obs.* fighting with fire"—*O.E.D.*] : Fighting with Fire/Desire: characteristic activity of Fuming Furies

Pyromagnetism ° *n* : mutual Archimagical attraction of Fire-Breathing, Dragon-identified women; the charisma of Crones

PRUDE: *Good, capable, brave woman endowed with Practical/ Passionate Wisdom . . . woman who insists upon the Integrity, Self-esteem, and Pride of her sex*

Pyromancy ○ *n* ["divination by means of fire or flames"—*Webster's*] : This definition has been awarded *Websters'* Intergalactic Seal of Approval.

Pyromantic/Pyrometric Prudence ○ : Queen of the Immoral Virtues/Vices of Prudes: E-motional habit of Outrageous reason. *See* **Prudish Prudence** (w-w 1)

Pyromantic Virtues ○ *n* : habits arduously acquired by Pyrosophical Journeyers, enabling Weird Wanderers to divine and actively work out ways of Surviving/Thriving beyond thralldom. *See* **Virtues/Vices, Volcanic** (w-w 1)

Pyrometry ○ *n* **1** : intuitive assessment of Pyrospheric conditions; psychic weather forecasting **2** : measurement of degrees of Gynergetic Fire **3** : knowledge enabling a Fury to measure her own psychic "temperature" and to assess the emotional climate in any given situation. *See* **Pyrospheres** (w-w 1)

Pyro-ontology ○ *n* : study of the burning/be-ing of Wicked Crones; Searing Science of Seers who have acquired the Courage to Sin

Pyrophile ○ *n* : a Lusty lover of Fire; a Crone who connects with the Element of Fire, generating Fire-Works

Pyrosophy ○ *n* : Salamandrous Wisdom, acquired by living in Fire; Wisdom that burns away the mindbindings of psychic numbing; Deep Knowing that springs from repeated Acts of Exorcism and Ecstasy, enabling women to rise like Phoenixes from the ashes of the Atrocious State

Pyrotechnics ᵔ *n* ["the art of making . . . fireworks"—*Webster's*] : the Archaic Art of making Fire-Works. *See* **Fire-Works** (w-w 2)

Pyrotic ○ *adj* **1** : able to Live in Pyrospheres **2** : capable of burning away plastic and potted passions and virtues; devoted to the burning down of bore-ocracy

Quack *n* : a quick, queenly utterance; the quintessential Elemental cry of a duck

Quack-pot Crone [akin to *Crackpot Crone*] : a wise old She-Duck; a Laughing Duck

The Inhabitants of the Background, Their Activities and Characteristics

Robbin Hagges' Merrie Band : "a Gaggle of Hags who give to the Witch and rob from the bore"—Diana Beguine [103]

Roboticide ° *n* **:** process of shedding the false selves manufactured in the State of Robotitude, releasing the Wild within. *Canny Comment:*

> What was wrong with my doll-babies? Why couldn't I sit still and make my dolls some clothes?
> I never did. Dolls caught the devil around me. They got into fights and leaked sawdust before New Year's. They jumped off the barn and tried to drown themselves in the lake. Perhaps, the dolls bought for me looked too different from the ones I made up myself. The dolls I made up in my mind, did everything. Those store-bought things had to be toted and helped around. Without knowing it, I wanted action.
> So I was driven inward. I lived an exciting life unseen.
> —Zora Neale Hurston [104]

Compare **robotitude** (w-w 3)

Salamander ° *n* **1 :** one of the four Elementals: Fire Spirit having the power to endure Fire without harm **2 :** a Pyrosophical, Dragon-identified woman. *See* **Pyrosophy** (w-w 2)

Salamandrous ° *adj* ["Living as it were in fire; fiery, hot, passionate"—*O.E.D.*] **:** This definition has been awarded *Websters'* Intergalactic Seal of Approval.

Scold ° *n* [derived fr. ME *scald, scold* . . . akin to ON *skald* poet . . . Icelandic *skālda* to make scurrilous or libelous verse; perh. akin to OIr *scēl* story—*Webster's*] **1 :** a Nag with a scalding tongue; abusive, abrasive, loud-mouthed Bitch **2 :** a scalding satirist/poet who tells the true story of women's experience under patriarchy and exposes the pretensions of fops and fools. *Example:* Aphra Behn (1640–1680), who wrote of the "coxcombs" who tried to silence women writers:

> As for you half wits, you unthinking tribe,
> We'll let you see, what e'er besides we do,
> How artfully we copy some of you:
> And if you're drawn to the life, pray tell me then,
> Why women should not write as well as men. [105]

Searcher ° *n* [derived fr. ME *cerchen* fr. MF *cerchier* to travel through, traverse, survey, search—*Webster's*] **:** one who traverses and surveys

SALAMANDER: *Fire Spirit having the power to endure Fire without harm . . . a Pyrosophical, Dragon-identified woman*

dangerous terrain, seeking the Knowledge buried and continually re-covered by the re-searchers of the State of Reversal. *Canny Comments:*

> If you are squeamish, don't prod the beach rubble . . .
> —Sappho, c. 625 B.C.

> If you are dreamish, prod the beach rubble . . .
> —Diana Beguine, 1981 A.F.

WORD-WEB TWO

See **re-cover; re-search** (W-W 3)

Seer ○ *n* : one who sees visions and dreams dreams; one whose Third Eye is open. *Example:* Zora Neale Hurston [106]

Self-centering ◑ : Selfish/Elfish Self-centered focusing on one's own Final Cause

Self-Lust ○ *n* : quintessential quality of all Questing women; Passion propelling women to break out of the Touchable Caste and join the Elemental Race

Self-Realizing ○ : Actualizing one's deepest potentiality. *Canny Comment:*

> Women, if you want to realize yourselves (for you are on the brink of a devastating psychological upheaval) all your pet illusions must be unmasked. The lies of centuries have got to be discarded. Are you prepared for the WRENCH?
> —Mina Loy (1914) [107]

Sensitive Appetite : a power of the soul which tends toward the Good and shrinks from the evil as perceived by the Senses. *N.B.:* Nag-Gnostic philosophers note that the medieval expression *sensitive appetite* (developed in depth by Thomas Aquinas) [108] becomes a New expression when Heard with the New ears of women Re-membering our Archaic Senses, such as our Crone-identified Sense of Direction, Depth Hearing, and Gynaesthesia.

Shrew ○ *n* ["a person, esp. (now only) a woman, given to railing or scolding or other perverse or malignant behavior"—*O.E.D.*] : an Untamed and Untamable Turbulent Termagant

Shrewd ○ *adj* [(derived fr. ME *shrewe* . . . scolding woman—*Webster's*): "depraved, wicked. . . . coming 'dangerously' near to the truth of the matter"—*O.E.D.*] : This definition has been awarded *Websters'* Intergalactic Seal of Approval.

Shrewish Shrewdness ° : one of the parts (aspects) of Pyromantic Prudence: habit of Dangerous Women who are quick to See Cronelogical connections and adept at sidestepping the traps of foreground rulers/foolers

Shrewdom [*"Obs.* wickedness"—*O.E.D.*] : the Queendom of Wicked Women

Sibyl ° *n* : Seer and Soothsayer; one who writes prophetic books; a Metamysterious Medium. *Canny Comment:*

> Foremost among the ladies of sovereign dignity are the wise sibyls, most filled with wisdom. . . . They were born in different countries of the world and not all at one time, and all foretold a great many things to come.
> —Christine de Pisan (Pizan) [109]

Silly *adj* [derived fr. ME *sely, silly* happy, blessed . . . fr. OE *sǣlig,* fr. *sǣl* happiness—*Webster's*] : Happy, Blessed, Graceful—applied esp. to giggling Gaggles of Geese and Gossips

Sin-articulate *v* : to Pronounce Wicked Words; to Be-Speak Sinful Spells

Sin-cantation *n* : Wicked incantation of Sinning/Spinning Spell-Speakers

Sin-capacitate *v* : to embolden an Other to Realize her natural capacity to Sin

Sin-conceivable *adj* : capable of being Wickedly conceived, imagined, or understood (frequently used to describe Terrible Taboo-breaking Acts)

Sin-discretion *n* : an act, procedure, or remark marked by Wicked discretion

Sinister *adj* ["situated on the left side"—*Webster's*] : associated with the female: Witch-like, Wicked; relating to movement that is Counter-clockwise, Moonwise, or Widdershins

Sin-Tactics *n* : Sinister Strategies, esp. tactics of Wicked Grammarians whose syntax Touches and awakens the Powers of Terrible Women

The Inhabitants of the Background, Their Activities and Characteristics

Sin-thesis *n* **1 :** a Wicked proposition or argument **2 :** the transcendence of patriarchal false opposites by Crone-logical Naming of Truth. *Example:*

> In male culture, police are heroic and so are outlaws. . . . the conflicts between these groups embody the male commitment to violence. . . . It is a mistake to view the warring factions of male culture as genuinely distinct from one another: in fact, these warring factions operate in near-perfect harmony to keep women at their mercy, one way or another.
> —Andrea Dworkin [110]

Siren ○ *n* **:** Bird-Woman/Fish-Woman whose songs guide Wayfaring Wenches into the Realms of Deep Memory. *Canny Comment:*

> Sirens presage the downfall of temporal powers, princes and lords, religious sects and creeds, and political parties.
> —Paracelsus [111]

Sisterhood of Man ＊ **:** transitional expression giving a generic weight to the word *sisterhood* while at the same time emasculating the pseudo-generic term *man*. N.B.: This phrase is marked by built-in obsolescence, for, once the expression is understood, the culturally entrenched assumptions it reflects can be discarded. *Man* can no longer pass as a functioning generic and *sisterhood* is freed of the burden of association with this pseudogeneric context.

Skein *n* ["a loosely coiled length of yarn or thread. . . . something suggesting the twistings and contortions of a skein. . . . a flock of wild fowl (as geese or ducks) in flight"—*Webster's*] **:** the organic purposeful design of any Spinning/Spiraling creation; the Metapatterning/Soaring which is characteristic of the Race of Wild Women and the Race of Wild Words/Birds in flight

Sloth *n* ["disinclination to action or labor. . . . a pack of bears"—*Webster's*] **1 :** Virtue/Vice of refusing to bear the unbearable burdens inflicted on women and animals in the State of Boredom; spurning the endless tidy tasks imposed by bore-ocrats **2 :** a pack of strong, active She-Bears. *Compare* **deadly sins of the fathers: fragmentation** (W-W I)

Snakey (Snaky) *adj* **:** having the characteristics of a snake: Wise, Wicked, Earthy, Archaic, Dangerous

164

Snap-Dragon *n* : a Dragon-identified woman with snapping jaws. *Example:* Flo Kennedy, who said: "If men could get pregnant, abortion would be a sacrament."[112]

Soothsayer ° *n* [derived fr. ME *soth, sooth* truth + *seyer, sayer* sayer—*Webster's*] : a woman who Dares to counter the partriarchal deadly sin of deception: Courageous Truth-sayer. *Example:* Rachel Carson, especially in her Bio-logical book of Augury, *Silent Spring* (1962)

Space-Craft *n* : the art of Spinning beyond the compass; Uncanny knack for mapping the dimensions of Metapatriarchal Space/Time; skill in walking/talking the Wrong Way, moving in Wicked directions, opening doors to Other dimensions, Other spatial perceptions

¹**Spanning** ⁹ [*span* "to grasp firmly: SEIZE"—*Webster's*] : grasping the fabricated opposites of patriarchal consciousness (e.g., *masculine–feminine*), comprehending that these are mindbinding traps, and breaking the hold of resultant deceptive combinations, such as the term *androgyny,* which is based on the assumption that two distorted halves can make a whole

²**Spanning** ⁹ *n* [*span* "to swim along rising to the surface to breathe at more or less regular intervals—used of a whale"—*Webster's*] **1** : Elemental movement of whales **2** : complex rhythmic mode of Journeying within the Elements of Air and Water characteristic of Wayward Wayfarers

Sparking ⁹ : speaking with tongues of Fire; igniting the divine Spark in women; lighting the Fires of Female Friendship; encouraging women to become sister Pyrotechnists; building the Fire that is fueled by Fury—the Fire that warms and lights the place where we can Spin and Weave tapestries of Crone-centered creation

Spell *n* **1** : a spoken, sung, or written word or set of words known by Crones to have Be-Speaking power: CHARM, INCANTATION **2** : any Archimagical thought, glance, or gesture

Spell-Brewer *n* : one who Brews brainstorms, stirring winds Widdershins, Re-calling the words of Weirdsome Incantations. *See* **Brewster** (W-W 2)

Spell-Craft *n* : the art/craft of Be-Spelling Witches. *See* **Be-Spelling** (W-W 1)

SOOTHSAYER: *a woman who Dares to counter the patriarchal deadly sin of deception; Courageous Truth-sayer*

Spell-Glance *n* **:** an Eye-Beam/Gleam that casts a Sparking Spell

Spell-Muttering : the mad mumbling/grumbling of Furious Crackpot Crones. *Example:* the mutterings of "Trudy," character created by Lily Tomlin and Jane Wagner for Tomlin's one-woman show, *The Search for Signs of Intelligent Life in the Universe* (1985)

Spell-Weaver *n* **:** Creative Crone who weaves contexts in which Wonders can happen: WEBSTER. *Canny Comment:*

> Inanna spoke:
> "What I tell you
> Let the singer weave into song.
> What I tell you
> Let it flow from ear to mouth
> Let it pass from old to young"[113]

Spinster ° *n* **:** a woman whose occupation is to Spin, to participate in the whirling movement of creation; one who has chosen her Self, who defines her Self by choice neither in relation to children nor to men; one who is Self-identified; a whirling dervish, Spiraling in New Time/Space. *See* **Spinning** (W-W 1)

Spiraling ° **:** Metamorphic movement that leaps off the confining circular paths/grooves of archetypal deadtime; swirling movement that is in harmony with the rhythms of whirlwinds, whirlpools, and spiraling galaxies of Other worlds. *Canny Comment:*

> The Eye-Goddess . . . becomes simply a double spiral representing her cosmic, magic eyes. This Eye-Goddess design is found on pottery, on statues, on clay and bone implements all over the Near East and Europe.
> —Monica Sjöö and Barbara Mor[114]

Spiration ° *n* ["*obs:* the action of breathing as a creative or life-giving function of the Deity"—*Webster's*] **:** Creation inspired by the Archimage: the breathing forth of Musings by Muses; Be-Speaking Original words, transversing the verbicide of the ages

Spooking ° **:** Re-membering Witches' powers to cast Glamours; Recalling our powers to detect and exorcise patriarchal patterns that spook women; Dis-possessing women's Selves of the demons of the Predatory State. *Example:*

SPARKING: *Igniting the divine Spark in women; lighting the Fires of Female Friendship; encouraging women to become sister Pyrotechnists*

Sometimes my mother felt longings to be free,
but then a bitter wave rose to her eyes
and in the shadows she wept.
And all this—caustic, betrayed, chastised
all this that in her soul she tightly kept,
I think that—without knowing—I have set it free.
　　—Alfonsina Storni [115]

Compare **spooking** (w-w 3)

Spring of be-ing ◗ **1 :** Original Integrity which is the inexhaustible Source of all true movement: the wellspring of Spinning **2 :** Source of Biophilic communication and healing, suffusing all Elemental be-ing

Sprite ○ *n* [derived fr. L *spiritus* spirit, breath—*Webster's*] **:** an Elemental Presence or Spirit: Fairy, Pixie

Stamina ○ *n* [(derived fr. L, pl. of *stamen* warp, thread of life spun by the fates): ". . . strength or courage of conviction: staying power: PER-SEVERANCE"—*Webster's*] **:** threads of Life Spun by the Fates; Staying Power/Straying Power of women who participate in the Spinning of the Fates, e.g., by creating Elemental philosophy and other Biophilic works. *See* **Straying Power** (w-w 2)

Starchase ○ *n* **:** a Nag-Gnostic Intergalactic Gallop; an Amazonian Astral Voyage

Star-Lust ○ *n* **:** Wanderlust/Wonderlust; longing for knowledge of Astral connections; Passion for scintillating cosmic conversation. *See* **Sparking** (w-w 2)

Strange ◗ *adj* [derived fr. L *extraneus* external, foreign . . . fr. *extra* outside—*Webster's*] **:** foreign to phallocracy; outside the parameters of predictability: ECCENTRIC, ERRATIC, ODD, QUEER, QUAINT, OUT-LANDISH, WEIRD. *Catty Comment:*

To be a Familiar you must first be very Strange.
　　—Ms. Wild Cat [116]

Straying Power ○ **:** ability to stray/stay off the tracks of traditions that betray women and nature

Studied Unlearning ○ **:** the intellectual project/process of a Nag-Gnostic Crone who studies a traditional discipline to the point of knowing it backwards and forwards, shifts her angle of vision, opens her Third Eye, and analyzes the field from a Crone-logical perspective; true truancy, requiring study/training and untiring untraining; unnarrowing, harrowing process of Feminist Searchers

Sylph ° *n* **1** : one of the four Elementals: one of a Race of Spirits who inhabit the Air **2** : a Tempestuous, Distempering woman; one who clears the Air of phallic pseudopresence, creating free space

Sylph-identified ° *adj* : a woman who identifies with Sylphs—their powers and their work; a Windy woman who stirs stagnant spaces with Life. *N.B.: Sylph-* can be used in many combined forms to create New Words, e.g., *Sylph-affirmation, Sylph-conscious, Sylph-help, Sylph-knowledge, Sylph-respect, Sylph-satisfied, Sylph-seeking, Sylph-taught.*

Syn-Crone-icities ° *n* : "coincidences" experienced and recognized by Crones as Strangely significant. *Examples:* too numerous to be Nag-noted here. Crones reading this book are invited to draw from their own experiences to illustrate this definition.[117]

Tabby *n* ["a domestic cat; *esp:* a female cat. . . . a prying woman: BUSYBODY, GOSSIP . . . SPINSTER"—*Webster's*] : These definitions have been awarded *Websters'* Intergalactic Seal of Approval.

Taking Heart ° : reclaiming Female Courage as the core of women's movement; the Courageous acting that reunites passion and intellect in the process of Realizing female powers. *Canny Comment:*

> Better, far, suffer occasional insults or die outright, than live the life of a *coward,* or never move without a protector. The best protector any woman can have, one that will serve her at all times and in all places, is *courage;* this she must get by her own experience, and experience comes by exposure.
> —Elizabeth Cady Stanton [118]

Tempering ° : process of a woman acquiring Pyrosophical Temperance: regaining Original strength and resiliency; becoming attuned to Elemental forces

Termagant *n* [[(derived fr. Italian *Trivigante* . . . the moon wandering under the three names of *Selene* in heaven, *Artemis* on earth, *Persephone* in the lower world—*Skeat's*): "an overbearing, quarrelsome, scolding, or nagging woman: SHREW, VIRAGO"—*Webster's*] : a Shrew who em-

SYLPH: *one of a Race of Spirits who inhabit the Air . . . a Tempestuous, Distempering Woman*

bodies the Rage of the Triple Goddess, who wanders among the Elements, Scolding and Nagging others into awareness of phallocracy's devastations

Terrible Woman ○ : a Be-Friending woman who breaks the Terrible Taboo, thus becoming herSelf Terrible, Taboo; one who consistently performs Natural Acts, giving allegiance to her own kind; an Outrageously Courageous woman who Touches Original Wholeness in her Self and in other women, who themSelves awaken to Touch others into Otherness. *See* **Terrible Taboo** (w-w 1)

Third Ear ○ : Super Sensory power that is attuned to Angelic messages and Hears the ways into the Third Hemisphere; power of Depth Hearing; the capacity to Hear New/Archaic words. *See* **Labyrinthine Sense** (w-w 2)

Third Eye ○ : Super Sensory power of transcendent vision; Elemental capacity of Nag-Gnostics to envision Other Whys, Other ways, and Other worlds. *Canny Comments:*

> She [Rebecca Jackson] was able to capture states of consciousness in which waking personality . . . drops away. Laws of nature are violated with ease, particularly in her accounts of visionary dreams. She soars, lifts, leaps easily into the sky, flies through the air, looks down from a great height, and can see things never visible from such a perspective before. She is given sudden, integrating flashes of understanding about the nature of the physical universe in visual form. She can leave the physical body behind, hold conversations with the angels, tour symbolic landscapes, and re-enter the body again.
> —Jean McMahon Humez[119]

> I saw all that I held forth—that is, with my spirit eye.
> —Rebecca Jackson[120]

Third Hemisphere : zone Dis-covered and explored by Contrary-Wise Crones who Spin beyond the compass and off the map; uncharted Zone: Fairy Space

Thirteen *n* : Positively Wicked Number. *See Appendicular Web Four*

Thirteenth Hour, the : the Other hour, beyond the direction of disaster; Time of jumping off the doomsday clocks of doomdom; Hour of Hope: Time beyond the parameters of patriarchal predictability; the Be-Witching Hour. *See* **clockocracy; doomsday clock** (w-w 3)

Tiger *n* **1 :** Ferocious, Fighting Feline **2 :** a Fierce, Catty Woman. *Example:* A tribe of Ferocious women, known among themselves as "The Tigers," began growling together in Boston in the early 1970s and has continued to stir up Trouble throughout the world. *Canny Comments:*

> Tyger! Tyger! burning bright,
> In the forests of the night:
> What immortal hand or eye,
> Dare frame thy fearful symmetry?
> —William Blake [121]

> . . . once, when I was a young lady and on a night express . . .
> I was awakened by a man coming in from the corridor and
> taking hold of my leg. . . . Quite as much to my own as-
> tonishment as his, I uttered the most appalling growl that
> ever came out of a tigress. He fled, poor man, without a
> word: and I lay there, trembling slightly, not at my escape
> but at my potentialities.
> —Sylvia Townsend Warner [122]

The Inhabitants of the Background, Their Activities and Characteristics

Time/Spaceship [○] *n* **:** vehicle of Memory, Divination, and Archaic/ Astral Travel; vessel steered/governed by the Witch within all Weirdsome women

Toad *n* **:** a Witch's Familiar; a *Wickedary* Guide who invites readers to hop from word to word. *Toady Comment:*

> I am a Familiar in an Other sense—not a "stunning Feline"
> to be sure, but a Lovely, Lunar, Lusty Leaper.
> —Luna, a Wise Old Toad

See **Familiar** (W-W 2)

Toadal Time : the Time of the Toad; Toadally experienced Time; Time of Toadal encounters: eventide; Hopping Time, outside the totaled time of clockocracy

Transversing [○] [¹*transverse* "to lie or pass across. . . . OVERTURN, RE-VERSE. . . . *obs:* ALTER, TRANSFORM"; also ⁵*transverse* "to turn or render into verse: VERSIFY"—*Webster's*] **:** transversing/passing across the fathers' territories, reversing their reversals, overturning their archetypes; transmitting Metaphoric words that awaken the Active Potency of the Archimage within women; emitting Word-waves/Wand-waves, chanting new and ancient rhythms that traverse/transform present, past, and future

Tree of Life ⁾ **1** : Cosmic Tree: the Goddess, inexhaustible Source of Wisdom and Life **2** : any Tree, Elemental being of extraordinary beauty and grace who communicates, heals, inspires; Weird Sister, rooted in the Earth and reaching toward the sky, Be-Speaking Elemental connectedness. *Canny Comment:*

> The Ethnics do still repute all great trees to be divine.
> —Evelyn, *Silva,* 1664
> (cited in *O.E.D.* under *ethnic*)

N.B.: The words *tree* and *true* are sister words; both are derived from the Indo-European root *deru,* which means "to be firm, solid, steadfast" (*American Heritage,* Appendix on Indo-European Roots).

Trivia ⁾ : [[(derived fr. L *trivium* crossroads): "unimportant matters: TRIFLES"—*Webster's*] : Name of the Triple Goddess, who is commonly encountered at crossroads; Name which conveys the commonplace character of meetings with the Goddess; Name which raises Counterclock Whys, countering the classic patriarchal hierarchical reversal/supposition that sacredness and great value imply scarcity and secrecy, i.e., "mystery." *N.B.:* The classical figure of Hecate, Goddess of Witches, was often built upon a triangle, with faces turned in three directions. The Hecate statues were set up at the crossing of three roads; hence the name Trivia.[123] Throughout the Middle Ages and even today, crossroads, specifically the places where three roads converge, were/are recognized as loci of Natural visions and happenings.

A Nag-noteworthy Radical Feminist journal is Named *Trivia: A Journal of Ideas.* As its founding editors explain: "TRIVIA . . . describes the matrix of our creative power, the gatherings of wise women in which our ideas originate and continue to live. . . . As we conceive it, TRIVIA is the place where our friendships and our ideas assume their original power and significance."[124]

Un-Convention ⁾ *n* : a Wild and unconventional gathering of Crones. *See* **Dissembly** (w-w 2)

Un-Creation ⁾ *n* **1** : inevitable by-product of Crone-logical Creation: the dissolution of patriarchy and all its works and pomps **2** : the revising of words and works which, though they have been necessary phases in the process of creation, can be seen in retrospect as transitional, containing built-in obsolescence and demanding the Unweaving and Reweaving of threads that are understood in a New context. *See* **Unweaving** (w-w 2)

Undine ○ *n* **1** : one of the four Elementals: Water Spirit; Wicked Nymph, dangerous and unfriendly to the predators who plunder and pollute rivers, lakes, and seas **2** : a Tidal woman; an Elementally Sounding woman who experiences Water as her Element. *See* **Mermaid** (w-w 2); **Elemental Sounding; Tidal** (w-w 1)

Unfield ᕯ *n* : an Outfield that confronts old molds/models of question-asking by be-ing itself an Other way of thinking/speaking; an Ourfield of Spinsters which Spins around, past, and through the established fields, opening the coffers/coffins in which "knowledge" has been stored, re-stored, re-covered. *Example:* Gyn/Ecology

Unknotting ᕯ : Mystical Metaphor for Journeying, implying the process of centering one's Self on the Labyrinthine Journey of Ecstasy. *See* **Knotting; Labyrinth** (w-w 2). *N.B.:* According to J. E. Cirlot in *A Dictionary of Symbols:* "To undo the knot was equivalent to finding the 'Centre' which forms such an important part of all mystic thought."[125]

Unpainting ᕯ : shucking off the shells of made-up femininity in which women are encased in the State of Animated Death. *See* **Painted Bird** (w-w 3)

Unstabled State ○ : blissful condition of Nags who have broken loose from the stable-world of phallo-institutions, such as prostitution, holy wedlock/deadlock

Unweaving ᕯ **1** : undoing our conditioning in femininity; unraveling the hoods of patriarchal woman-hood and pseudosister-hood— learning to distinguish tokens from Hags, to separate token selves from the Hag Self within **2** : revising/re-visioning earlier works of creation

Vertigo ᕯ *n* [derived fr. L *vertigo* the action of whirling—*Webster's*] : Spinning of Spinsters; Whirling of Websters; Distempering activity of Dizzy Dames. *See* **Gyromancy** (w-w 2)

Virago ○ *n* ["a loud overbearing woman: SHREW, TERMAGANT. . . . a woman of great stature, strength, and courage: one possessing supposedly masculine qualities of body and mind"—*Webster's*] : These definitions have been awarded *Websters'* Intergalactic Seal of Approval. *Canny Comment:*

> Now you have touched the women,
> you have struck a rock,

you have dislodged a boulder,
you will be crushed.
—South African Women's Freedom Song, Aug. 9, 1956 [126]

Virgin ○ *n* [*virgin adj* "never captured: UNSUBDUED"—*Webster's*] :
Wild, Lusty, Never captured, Unsubdued Old Maid; Marriage Resister

Vital Eyes 1 : Eyes that beam with radiant inner Life **2 :** the capacity to See through deceptive deadforms and to detect the Presence of Elemental Life. *Compare* **deadeye** (w-w 3)

Vitalize *v* **:** to activate the potential to See with Vital Eyes; to Gynergize the Eyes/I's of Others

Vixen ○ *n* ["a female fox. . . . a shrewish ill-tempered woman"—*Webster's*] **:** These definitions have been awarded *Websters'* Intergalactic Seal of Approval. *See* **Foxy** (w-w 2)

Volcanic Dis-coverings ○ **:** eruptions of E-motional Memory that Activize Archaic insights, enabling women to Act in Other-dimensional ways

Volcanic Wisdom : Pyrosophical habit enabling Furies to hold back and to release the molten rock, the steam and ashes of our Passion for the right moments of be-ing. *See* **Gnomic plug** (w-w 2)

Volcanoes, Women as ○ **:** all women under patriarchy, understood as containing deep Memories and Passions which always have the potential to rise explosively to the surface, making possible Self-Realization and Macromutational leaps of consciousness. *Canny Comment:*

> So what we have in effect, each of us, is miles and miles of underground corridors full of filing cabinets in which we busily file away mountains of data every day.
>
> Somewhere in these endless subterranean storage cabinets, women have a unique file entitled "What it means to be female in a male world." . . .
>
> The miraculous part of an epiphany is that when the file bursts, and all the file data flood into the conscious mind, they are perfectly organized; they present one with conclusions. I knew instantly what the women's movement was all about; I knew it in my very bones.
> —Sonia Johnson [127]

VIRGIN: *Wild, Lusty, Never-captured, Unsubdued Old Maid;*
Marriage Resister

Voyager *n* : Amazon Argonaut; Otherworld Journeyer. *See* **Journeyer** (W-W 2)

Wanton *n* [*wanton adj* "*archaic:* lacking discipline: not susceptible to control: UNRULY . . . excessively merry or gay: FROLICSOME. . . . LUSTFUL"—*Webster's*] : a Lusty, Uncontrollable, Unruly woman; one who, by the standards of Stag-nation, is excessively merry, gay, and frolicsome: PIXILATED WOMAN

Wanton Virgin : Gay, Frolicsome Old Maid

Water Witch *n* ["a witch reputed to live in or haunt a body of water" —*Webster's*] : This definition has been awarded *Websters'* Intergalactic Seal of Approval.

Webster *n* [(derived fr. OE *webbestre* female weaver—*Webster's*): "A weaver . . . as the designation of a woman"—*O.E.D.*] : a woman whose occupation is to Weave, esp. a Weaver of Words and Word-Webs. *See* **Unweaving** (W-W 2); **Weaving** (W-W 1). *N.B.:* The word *Webster* was Dis-covered by Judy Grahn, who has written:

> Webster is a word that formerly meant "female weaver," the "ster" ending indicating a female ancestor, or female possession of the word.
>   The word-weavers of recent centuries who have given us the oration of Daniel Webster and the dictionary listings of Merriam-Webster stem from English family names that once descended through the female line. Some great-great-grandmother gave them her last name, *Webster,* she-who-weaves.[128]

Weird *n* ["FATE, NORN . . . SOOTHSAYER . . . SPELL, CHARM . . . a supernatural tale . . . PROPHECY, PREDICTION"—*Webster's; also pl.* "the Fates, the three goddesses supposed to determine the course of human life"—*O.E.D.*] : These definitions have been awarded *Websters'* Intergalactic Seal of Approval.

Weird *adj* ["UNEARTHLY, MYSTERIOUS"—*Webster's*] : Earthy, Metamysterious, Uncanny

Weirddom *n* ["the supernatural world"—*O.E.D.*] : the Super Natural World; Country of the Strange: Familiar Territory

Weirdie (Weirdy) *n* ["one that is extraordinarily strange, eccentric, or unnatural"—*Webster's*] : one who is extraordinarily Strange, Eccentric: a Natural Woman

Weirdly *adj* ["*Scottish* Favored by fate, happy, prosperous"—*O.E.D.*] : Graceful: said of one who hears the Word of the Weird and follows the Call of the Wild

Weird Sister ["FATE, NORN"—*Webster's*] **1** : Fate, Norn **2** : Gossip, Boon-Companion, Chum

Weirdward ° *adj* ["bordering upon or approaching the supernatural. 1866 J. B. Ross tr. Ovid's *Metamorphosis* XIII. 697 'Unnumbered sisterhood of weirdward birth'"—*O.E.D.*] : on the Boundary of the Wild: Hag-identified. *Canny Comment:*

> Everywhere today, an Unnumbered Sisterhood of Weirdward birth are Be-Wishing Metapatriarchal Metamorphosis and Announcing the end of fooldom.
> —Robbin Hagge (May Day speech to the Merrie Band, May 1, 1991, A.F.)

See **Robbin Hagges' Merrie Band** (w-w 2)

Wicked/Wiccen Woman [*wicked* akin to OE *wicce* witch—*American Heritage*, Appendix on Indo-European Roots] : a woman who steadfastly Sees through patriarchal "good" and "evil," reversing the inherent reversals of phallic morality; a Good woman: Prude. *See* **Wicked** (w-w 1)

Widdershins (Withershins) *adv* [(derived fr. MHG *widersinnen* to go back, go against, fr. *wider* back, against + *sinnen* to travel, go . . . akin to OHG *sind* journey, road): "in a left-handed or contrary direction: CONTRARILY, COUNTERCLOCKWISE—used esp. of ritual circumambulation"—*Webster's*; also "in a direction opposite to the usual; the wrong way"—*O.E.D.*] : in a direction that counters the processions or clockocracy/cockocracy; in a manner that grinds the doomsday clocks to a halt, that turns back the clocks of father time: Contrariwise: the Wrong Way. *See* **doomsday clock** (w-w 3)

Wild Cat ° *n* ["The European wild species of cat, *Felis catus* . . . also applied to other wild animals of the cat tribe. . . . *fig.* applied to a savage, ill-tempered, or spiteful person, esp. a woman. . . . *fig.* one who forms a rash project or engages in a risky or unsafe enterprise"—*O.E.D.*] **1** : a

The Inhabitants of the Background, Their Activities and Characteristics

179

Savage, Tempered, or Spriteful Cat, esp. one who engages in a risky or unsafe enterprise; a Radical Cat   **2 :** a woman who participates in the qualities of a Radical Cat   **3 :** member of a worldwide Wild tribe composed of Witches and their Familiars

Wild Eyes [9] **:** Inner Eyes, which ask the deepest Whys; the capacity to See the Wildness of women's Selves and of all Elemental be-ing; Eyes that are Wild and staring: Eyes that are frightening to man

Wild-Goose Chase ["a pursuit after something unattainable: a futile pursuit or chase"—*Webster's*] **:** a Be-Laughing lark; a fruitful, hopeful, ecstatic Quest

Wildize [9] *v* **:** to Untame, Uncivilize, Uncultivate; to Unleash the Force of women who have been forced into servitude in the Domesticated State

Wild Whys : rude, uncivilized, barbaric questions; extravagant, fantastic, visionary questions; the Reckless Questions of Unruly Women

Wildwise *adv* **:** in a Strange direction: away from flatland, toward the Wild

Wild-Wise *adj* **:** knowing how to Survive in the Wilderness; able to See with Wild Eyes; gifted with a Strange Sense of Direction

Wiles, Female [*wile* akin to OE *wigle* divination, sorcery—*Webster's*] **:** female powers of Divination and Witchcraft; Glamorous/Magnetizing powers of Hags and Glamour Pusses. *See* **Glamour** (w-w 2)

Witch [9] *n* [derived fr. A.S. *wicce*. Allied to M.Du. *wicker,* 'a soothsayer.' . . . Cf. Norw *vikja,* (1) to turn aside, (2) to conjure away. . . . Thus *witch* perhaps = 'averter.'—*Skeat's*] **:** an Elemental Soothsayer; one who is in harmony with the rhythms of the universe: Wise Woman, Healer; one who exercises transformative powers: Shape-shifter; one who wields Labrys-like powers of aversion and attraction—averting disaster, warding off attacks of demons and Magnetizing Elemental Spiritual Forces. *Canny Comment:*

> The superior learning of witches was recognized in the widely extended belief of their ability to work miracles. The witch was in reality the profoundest thinker, the most advanced scientist of those ages.
> —Matilda Joslyn Gage [129]

Cockaludicrous Comments:

> Rebellion is as the sin of witchcraft.
> —I Sam. 15:23

> And what, then, is to be thought of those witches who in
> this way sometimes collect male organs in great numbers, as
> many as twenty or thirty members together, and put them in
> a bird's nest, or shut them up in a box, where they move
> themselves like living members, and eat oats and corn, as has
> been seen by many and is a matter of common report?
> —Heinrich Kramer and James Sprenger, *Malleus
> Maleficarum* [130]

*The Inhabitants
of the
Background,
Their Activities
and
Characteristics*

See **Heathen; Pagan** (w-w 2)

W.I.T.C.H. : acronym for numberless Radical Feminist groups. *Examples* **a**: Women's International Terrorist Conspiracy from Hell (New York Covens, 1969) **b**: Women's Inspirational Terrorist Conspiracy from Harvard (Cambridge, Mass., 1972–74) **c**: Wild Independent Thinking Crones and Hags (Cambridge, Mass., 1985–)

Witch-Crafty *adj* [*crafty* (derived fr. OE *cræftig* strong, skillful): "*dial chiefly Brit:* SKILLFUL, CLEVER, INGENIOUS. . . . CUNNING, WILY"— *Webster's*] : Wickedly strong, skillful, wily; endowed with the Cunning of Canny Wives/Weirds. *See* **Wiles, Female** (w-w 2)

Witch Way, Every [*every which way* "in every direction. . . . in a disorderly manner: IRREGULARLY"—*Webster's*] : in every Weird direction: Erratically; in any Sparking/Spooking way that Dis-orders boreocracy. *See* **Labyrinth; Pixy-path** (w-w 2)

Wolfish *adj* : having the characteristics of a wolf—strong, beautiful, agile, fierce, Cunning, Wild. *Examples:* Virginia Woolf, Christa Wolf. *Canny Comment:*

> She [the old, grim Goddess] is the one we most need to
> understand: not the pretty Virgin; not the fecund Mother;
> but the wise, willful, wolfish Crone.
> —Barbara G. Walker [131]

Woman-Touching Woman ○ : an Elementally Touching Woman; one who communicates Be-Witching Powers; one who has broken the Terrible Taboo, Touching Original Integrity in her Self and other women. *See* **Lesbian; Physical Ultimacy** (w-w 1); **Terrible Woman** (w-w 2)

Wording ○ : Original activity of Word Witches; practicing the art of Word-Magic: Word-Weaving; Be-Spelling; communicating with the Race of Radiant Words

Word-Magic *n* ["magic involving the use of words in a manner determined by a belief that the very act of uttering a word summons or directly affects the person or thing that the word refers to"—*Webster's*] : This definition has been awarded *Websters'* Intergalactic Seal of Approval. *See* **Be-Speaking** (w-w 1). *Compare* **logorrhea; verbigeration** (w-w 3)

Word-waves/Wand-waves ○ : vibrations emitted by Be-Spoken words, which are the wands of Word Witches; waves of Word-power which transverse the archetypes of the State of Deadly Deception, overturning and reversing its reversals

Word Witch *n*   **1 :** one who practices the craft of Word-Magic   **2 :** a Witch who haunts libraries and bookstores, beckoning Searchers to the best books, guiding us to the right pages, to needed knowledge

X-factor *n* : the Spring of be-ing; the unpredictable, unpossessable Nature of the Wild, which forever escapes the technocrats, medical and scientific re-searchers, "developers," and other demonic destroyers of living creatures

X-ing : the Qualitative Leaping of Contrary-Wise Crones who are experiencing Syn-Crone-icities and Other "inexplicable" phenomena

WORD-WEB THREE

The inhabitants of the foreground, their activities and characteristics

In this Word-Web,* Journeyers Name the inhabitants of the fore-ground, their activities, and characteristics, from the perspective of the Background. Here, Nag-Gnostic Voyagers momentarily fold our wings, perch on the fences of fatherland, and observe its fatuous "reality" with Eyes wide open.

The words and phrases of this Web Name the fathers' games and Reverse their reversals. They expose the conventional cockocratic labels as mere terms intended to fix Elemental reality into phallocentric categories, to block the flow of be-ing.

Here, Nags break the Terrible Taboo against Women Touching the Spirits of Women by Naming Out Loud the fathers' farces—the foolish acts of fops and flops, lackeys and leeches, dicks and deadfellows. Scolds tickle the minds of Lusty Leapers with Daring definitions of flying fetuses, male menstruation, penis envy, and other phallic phenomena. Shrews encourage Others to practice the Virtue of Disgust and the Virtue of Laughing Out Loud. Our gales of Rage and Laughter clear the air and send us flying further on our Ecstatic and Exhilarating Quest.

abominable snowmen of androcratic academia ◑ : freezers and packagers of learning; chilling throng of frigid fellows, specialists in verbigeration and refrigeration of knowledge

*The system of symbols (●, ◕, ◑, ○) used to identify the sources of words and phrases and the system of cross-referencing are explained at the beginning of *Word-Web One*, pp. 59–60.

Absent State ○ : the present state of "consciousness" under the reign of Boredom

academentia (Diana Beguine[1]) *n* : normal state of persons in academia, marked by varying and progressive degrees; irreversible deterioration of faculties of intellectuals

WORD-WEB THREE

adultery of the brain : "brain prostitution"—Virginia Woolf[2]

a-motional *adj* : deficient in active properties; lacking the capacity to feel, move, Spin: INERT, BORING

a-Musing ○ [*amuse* "*archaic:* to divert the attention of . . . DECEIVE, DELUDE, BEMUSE"—*Webster's*] **1** : patriarchal habit of deceiving and deluding women by means of alienating amusements **2** : androcratic murder of female Genius and evisceration of the Muse which is a woman's Self. *Example:* Ted Hughes's marriage to Sylvia Plath.[3]

Androcratic Assumers ○ [*assume* "to take as one's right or possession: ARROGATE, SEIZE, USURP. . . . to take in appearance only: pretend to have or be: FEIGN"—*Webster's*] : usurpers of women's rights; impotent fakes who feign possession of Elemental powers; frauds who use man-made myths and symbols to perpetuate their false assumption/appearance of Original Creative powers. *Examples:* all fabricators and hucksters of patriarchal creation myths; all the "geniuses" of jockocracy who have depended upon these myths to legitimate their status as "creators"

androlatry ○ *n* : the worship of maleness, which is the fundamental dogma and commandment of all patriarchal religions. *Example:* "One hundred women are not worth a single testicle."—Confucian proverb.[4] *See* **phallicism** (w-w 3)

archetypical *adj* : having typical characteristics of archetypal deadtime (a.d.); perfectly conforming to patriarchal party lines, exactly mouthing daddyland's dead lines. *Examples:* prince charming and sleeping beauty; ronald reagan and nancy reagan; Donald Duck and Daisy Duck

babblespheres ○ *n* : the foreground, considered specifically as a place of babble/verbigeration. *See* **bubblespheres** (w-w 3). *Compare* **Gabblespheres** (w-w 2)

Bearded Brother No-it-alls ○ **1 :** the archetypal naysayers of patriarchy. *Examples:* Moses, "Thou shalt not . . ."; Hammurabi, "blah, blah, blah . . ." **2 :** common fellows in the academented fraternity, characterized by beard-stroking, pipe-puffing, know-nothing behavior

Beatific Vision ◑ **:** the "face to face" vision of god in patriarchal heaven promised as a reward to good christians; an afterlife of perpetual Boredom: union/copulation with the "Divine Essence"; the final consummate union of the Happy Dead Ones with the Supreme Dead One

The inhabitants of the foreground, their activities and characteristics

bibliolater *n* **:** a hot air type who attempts to contain the universe within the confines of one bible/bubble. *See* **bubble** (w-w 3)

bibliomaniac *n* **:** a bibliolater whose grandiose obsessions are too big for his own bible/babble/bubble and compel him to continually spread the bible/babble/bubble

Big Brothers of Boredom ○ **:** the all-male corporate caste in the perpetual 1984 of Boredom; the ruling/snooling class

birthwrong ○ *n* **:** the absence of rights, privileges and possessions that is socially inherited by women in the State of Possession, that is, patriarchy

blob ○ *n* **1 :** common, hideous product of modern architecture—windowless, airless, lifeless structure which reflects the intellectual and moral gravity/depravity of its designers and owners. *Examples:* the laboratories and offices of phallotechnocracy; hospitals; state universities **2 :** a lump in inner space: plastic passion **3 :** a dull, heavy lout. *See* **lob; plastic passion** (w-w 3)

blobber *n* **:** an engineer, fabricator, or user of blobs, one who prefers and finally requires an artificial environment

blobular *adj* **:** having the characteristics of a blob; bloblike and liking blobs *Example:* Blob Hope

blockocracy *n* **:** rule by blockers, cocks, and jocks; world made to the image of its makers, a chip off the old blocks/cocks: THE CONSTIPATED STATE

bootlicker *n* : a servile flatterer; one willing to prostrate himself before any authority; one determined to succeed (suckseed), following the usual route to success in snooldom. *Cockaludicrous Comment:*

> Pope John Paul II named seven bishops today. . . . About
> 10,000 people watched as the seven candidates prostrated
> themselves on the floor of St. Peter's Basilica before John Paul.
> —*New York Times*, Jan. 7, 1986, p. A4

bore ○ *n* : one who drills, penetrates, fills with ennui and depression, creating the State of Boredom. *Canny Comment:*

> Life in a "society" made by and for creatures who, when they
> are not grim and depressing are utter bores, can only be,
> when not grim and depressing, an utter bore.
> —Valerie Solanas[5]

Boredom ○ : the official/officious state produced by bores

bored, chairman of the ○ : any bore-ocratically appointed bore who occupies a chair—a position which enables him to bore others all the more

bore-ocracy ○ [*bureaucracy* "a system of administration marked by officialism, red tape, and proliferation"—*Webster's Collegiate*] : a system of bad-ministration marked by officialism, red tape, and the proliferation of bores

bore-ophilia ○ *n* **1** : love of bores **2** : romantic love

bore's-eye-view ○ : a pinoramic world view: reduction of the range of reality to the head of a pin

botcher ○ *n* : one who painstakingly and methodically spoils, ruins, and bungles any given task: archetypical technocrat

brotherhood ⁹ *n* : transitory and shallow substitute for Friendship; condition dependent upon emergencies, violence, and the existence of The Enemy; male merging in the communal "ecstasy" of self-loss; bonding of those who are malfunctioning/male-functioning as cells in a military organism: necrophilic comradeship.[6] *Cockaludicrous Comment:*

> Woman is inadequate for the last merging. So the next step
> is the merging of man-for-man love. And this is on the brink
> of death. It slides over into death.
> —D. H. Lawrence[7]

Canny Comment:

> The common erotic project of men destroying women makes
> it possible for men to unite into a brotherhood; this project is
> the only firm and trustworthy groundwork for cooperation
> among males and all male bonding is based on it.
> —Andrea Dworkin [8]

bubble *n* : an artificial total environment (material or mental) which distances, destroys, and replaces the physical/spiritual Elemental world: an Eye-sore/I-sore. *Examples:* disneyworld; the bible

bubblespheres *n* : the foreground considered specifically as an expanding bubble complex. *See* **bubble** (w-w 3)

bubble-omaniac *n* : one who is obsessed with building bubbles

bull *n* ["(short for bullshit) *slang:* empty boastful talk"—*Webster's Collegiate*] : the most solemn and respected form of discourse under patriarchy. *Examples:* the apostles creed; the hippocratic oath; the gettysburg address, which states:

> Fourscore and seven years ago our fathers brought forth on
> this continent a new nation, conceived in liberty, and dedi-
> cated to the proposition that all men are created equal.
> —"Honest Abe" Lincoln

bull, papal [*bull* (derived fr. L. *bulla* bubble, amulet): "a solemn papal letter sealed with a bulla or with a red-ink imprint of the device on the bulla"—*Webster's Collegiate*] : the most sacred form of bull; Wholly, Holey, Holy Baloney. *Example:* the papal bull of Innocent VIII, *Summis desiderantes affectibus* (1484), giving the support of Rome to "Our dear sons," the dominican inquisitors, Kramer and Sprenger, the authors of the *Malleus Maleficarum*

bully *n* : characteristic type in the rapist society: one who uses institutionalized privilege, phallic appendages, and technological extensions thereof to intimidate and destroy Others. *Examples* **a:** Teddy Roosevelt, who intoned the bully old adage, "Speak softly and carry a big stick" **b:** James Ferrands, imperial wizard of the ku klux klan, who sniveled, "The Pope is startin' to get too damn liberal for my way of thinking" (Reported in Boston's *Gay Community News*, January 4–10, 1987, p. 2)

bully, papal : the supreme sacred bully. *Example:* pope John Paul II, who told an audience of 4,000 women from around the world who

The inhabitants of the foreground, their activities and characteristics

work as maids for priests that they can never thank the Lord enough for letting them serve the clergy. The pontiff pontificated:

> Be happy that you can keep the residence of the priest clean and so free him from these material duties that would absorb part of his time that is necessary for apostolic work.
> You could never thank the Lord enough for giving you the gift of choosing to serve the clergy.[9]

WORD-WEB THREE

N.B.: During his November 1986 visit to Australia, pope John Paul II, traveling through inner city streets of Sydney in his bullet-proof pope-mobile, was confronted at every turn by gay males garbed as nuns. "Mother Inferior," "red lesbian Cardinal Titi," "Sister Mary-Mary Quite Contrary," and others displayed pink triangle flags before the pope-mobile. Pope-FREE Zone Posters were strategically placed in the area. When the pope spoke at Sydney University two gay men unfurled white flags with pink triangles and shouted, "Anti-woman, anti-gay, fascist pope, go away!" Sister Mary-Mary was strip-searched by police and taken to Catholic Psych Hospital for evaluation. He was pronounced sane and released. (Reported in Boston's *Gay Community News*, January 4–10, 1987, p. 2)

butcher ○ *n* ["one that kills ruthlessly or brutally or bloodily"—*Webster's*] : a bloody operator, esp. one who receives professional recognition and prestige for his "successes." *Examples* **a:** Egas Moniz, Portuguese neurologist who devised the operation which came to be known as "lobotomy," for which he was awarded the Nobel Prize in Medicine in 1949 **b:** Walter Freeman, an American psycho-surgeon, called the "dean of lobotomists," who popularized the operation. Freeman is known among feminists for his view that lobotomized women make good housekeepers.[10]

cardinals *n* : foppish popocrats; pontifically chosen members of the Sacred Men's Club; colorless pretenders to the beauty and status of colorful songbirds; favored sons of the papal bully; pompous hypocrites who unflaggingly lobby in favor of the most flagrant abuses and atrocities, under the aegis of their respective national flags. *Examples* **a:** the war-mongering prelate Francis cardinal Spellman, who ceaselessly agitated for the escalation of the United States' genocidal/biocidal devastation of Vietnam **b:** Terrence cardinal Cooke, who blathered in 1981:

> Nuclear deterrence can be morally tolerated if a nation is sincerely trying to come up with a rational alternative[11]

cardinal vices and sins/sons : *See* **deadly sins of the fathers** (w-w 1). *N.B.:* Sons of these vices/sins include: vanity, frivolity, weakness, back-biting, tale-bearing, cheating, cruelty, idolatry, usury, hypocrisy, boasting, flattery, meanness, pusillanimity

christotechnology *n* : technology subliminally modeled upon the myths, dogmas, and cherished obsessions of the christian tradition. *Examples* **a:** television as temporal substitute for the "Beatific Vision" **b:** woman-erasing reproductive technologies as materializations of mythic male motherhood **c:** nuclearism as the ultimate manifestation of christian warfare against the Elemental world, as expressed in 2 Pet. 3:10:

> But the day of the Lord will come like a thief, and then the heavens will pass away with a loud noise, and the elements will be dissolved with fire, and the earth and the works that are upon it will be burned up.

Cockaludicrous Comment:

> The bombing of Hiroshima was the greatest event in world history since the birth of Jesus Christ.
> —Senator Brien "Mr. Atom" McMahon, 1952 [12]

christmas spirit **1** : dis-spirited mood induced by the pious propaganda and grim greed of christotechnological society; rip-off and reversal of the Original Spirit of Winter Solstice **2** : miserable mood induced by the lyrics of omnipresent crushing christmas carols, e.g.: "O come let us adore him . . ."; "Fall on your knees. . . ." *Canny Comment:*

> "Ho, Ho, Ho." Ho hum.
> —Nellie Nag

christmas trees ○ : ritually murdered and dismembered trees which are subliminally symbolic of the massacred and dismembered Goddess; the cut down, dragged indoors, dolled-up trees which serve as disguised symbols and tokens for the cut down, dolled-up women who are victims of the State of Atrocity

christolatry ◉ *n* : the worship of christ as divine sacrificial victim whose sacrifice was followed by resurrection and triumphal ascent into heaven; form of idolatry that functions to mandate and legitimate intolerance, self-hatred, hatred and scapegoating of others, inquisitions,

The inhabitants of the foreground, their activities and characteristics

sadomasochism, pornography. *Example:* theologian Paul Tillich's pornographic exploits, described by his wife:

> There was the familiar cross shooting up the wall. . . . A naked girl hung on it, hands tied in front of her private parts. . . . More and more crosses appeared, all with women tied and exposed in various positions. Some were exposed from the front, some from the side, some from behind, some crouched in fetal position, some head down, or legs apart, or legs crossed—and always whips, crosses, whips.
> —Hannah Tillich [13]

cipherdom *n* ["the state of being a nonentity"—*Webster's*] **1** : the self-loss promised to adherents of patriarchal religion: STATE OF THE GRATEFUL DEAD **2** : normal condition of any clone, drone, or bore

clockocracy ° *n* : society dead set by the clocks and watches of fathered time; the tidily Man-Dated World characterized by male-ordered monotony that breaks biorhythms, preparing the way for the fullness of tidy time, i.e., doomsday

clonedom ° *n* : the domain of clones: the world of fashion, mass production, mechanical reproduction, standardized tests and texts, chain stores and restaurants, and the endless processions of uniformed snools

cock ° *n* [³*cock v* "to act big, arrogant, or menacing: STRUT, SWAGGER"; also ⁵*cock n* (derived fr. ME, influenced by *cok* cock, male fowl): "*obs* GOD—used in oaths"—*Webster's*] : arrogant, menacing, strutting, swaggering fool; one who worships and swears by his god/rod. *See* **fool; god/rod** (W-W 3)

cockalorum *n* ["a self-important little man"—*Webster's Collegiate*] : a self-important little cock. *Examples:* Napoleon, Andy Warhol, Fiorello La Guardia, Mickey Mouse

cockaludicrous *adj* : snoolishly foolish, laughably loutish; epitomizing androcratic authoritativeness: perfectly, pompously *wrong*

cock and bull story **1** : patriarchal history **2** : any highly respected account of the exploits of cocks and bullies which effectively erases the existence and history of women and all Others. *Example:* [Cock and] *Bulfinch's Mythology*

cock art : penile, puerile art: PATRIARCHAL ART. *Example:* the paintings of Auguste Renoir, who reportedly said that he "painted his paintings with his prick." [14]

cock-eyed *adj* **1 :** having the limited sensory awareness of a cock **2 :** having the characteristic expression of an eyeballer **3 :** marked by the propensity to see glory, heroism, and excitement only in cruelty, carnage, and catastrophe. *Cock-eyed Comment:*

> Part of the love of war stems from its being an experience of great intensity; its lure is the fundamental human [sic] passion to witness, to see things, what the Bible calls the lust of the eye and Marines in Vietnam called eye fucking.
> —William Broyles, Jr. [15]

The inhabitants of the foreground, their activities and characteristics

cockfighting *n* ["the sport of matching gamecocks in a cockfight; *also:* the patronizing of such matches esp. for the purpose of betting on the outcome"—*Webster's*] **:** the sport/game of matching missiles/munitions in multinational cockfights; *also:* the patronizing of such matches esp. for the purpose of betting, speculation, investment, and capital gain

cockocracy ○ *n* **:** the state of supranational, supernatural erections; the place/time where the air is filled with the crowing of cocks, the joking of jocks, the droning of clones, the sniveling of snookers and snudges, the noisy parades and processions of prickers: pecker order

Comatose State [*comatose* derived fr. Gk *kōma* deep sleep—*Webster's*] **:** full-fillment (brain death) promoted and produced by patriarchal professions and institutions. *See* **home, patriarchal** (w-w 3)

consciousness razing ○ **:** the normal feminine socialization/terrorization process, meant to inhibit, thwart, and destroy the spark of Self-Realization. *Examples:* the propagation of fairy tales and romance novels; the sexual abuse of female children

consumer *n* [*consume* "to destroy or do away with completely . . . cause to waste away utterly"—*Webster's*] **:** a consummate snool; an extremely proficient destroyer/waster; member of the priesthood of the consumer society, one devoted to bringing that society to its logical conclusion—absolute annihilation. *Example:* Edward Teller, "father of the hydrogen bomb" and zealous proponent of the Strategic Defense Initiative ("Star Wars")

consumer society : patriarchy, the State of Annihilation; the State of Reversal, in which the consumed are misnamed/blamed as "consumers" and the true consumers are honored as prolific producers/creators

covert *adj* ["*of a woman:* married and under cover, authority, or protection of the husband"—*Webster's*] : *of a man:* operating under cover of patriarchal law and "divine" authority to push the protection racket of holy matrimony

coxcomb *n* ["a vain conceited foolish usu. male person that is falsely proud of his achievements and foppish or finical about his dress"—*Webster's*] : This definition has been awarded *Websters'* Intergalactic Seal of Approval. *Examples:* all of the signers of the "Declaration of Independence"

daddydreams ° *n* : man-made daydreams—his romances, his theories, his religions, his soap operas. *Cockaludicrous Comment:*

> Such are the dreams of the everyday housewife
> Who gave up the good life for me.
> —From the popular song "Dreams of the Everyday House-
> wife," recorded by Glen Campbell, 1968

dangler ° *n* ["one who dangles: one who hangs or hovers about a woman; a dallying follower. . . . a dangling appendage or part"—*O.E.D.*; also fr. *dangle* "to hang loosely esp. with a swinging or jerking motion"—*Webster's*] : a patriarchal parasite; one who is forever hanging on/hanging around; a sapper who is dependent upon his fetal fettering of the female

Daughter-blight *n* **1** : negation of Daughter-Right: systematic undermining of women's capacity to Re-member Original Integrity, to proclaim our Divinity, to Name our Selves, to reclaim our place in the sun **2** : the common, everyday patriarchal devastation of daughters, taking such forms as female infanticide, sexual abuse, the institutionalized stunting of female bodies and minds **3** : the projection of phallic nothingness onto all women. *Example:*

> It is a universal custom among the Rajputs for neighbors and friends to assemble to congratulate the father upon the birth of a child. If a boy is born, his birth is announced with music, glad songs and by distributing sweetmeats. If a daughter, the father coolly announces that "nothing" has been born into his family, by which expression it is understood that the

child is a girl, and that she is very likely to be nothing in this world, and the friends go home grave and quiet.
　　—Pandita Ramabai Sarasvati[16]

deadeye *n* : any leering, jeering goon who eyeballs, harasses and objectifies women, e.g., pornographic photographers, peeping toms, and "the boys on the corner"

deadfellows *n* : strange bedfellows and common allies in the Necrophilic State, e.g., agribusinessmen and pesticide manufacturers

deadly de-vicers ○ : phallomoralists who attempt to purify women of Wild Virtues/Wickedness, by misnaming and condemning these as "vices." *See* **Virtues, Virgin** (W-W 1)

deadly dis-passion ○ **1** : patriarchal objectivity **2** : the a-motional absence of passion that characterizes phallic lusters **3** : the grinding machine-like inertia of the automatic killers and spoilers who run—and run amok in—the State of Robotitude

de-light ❾ *v* : to dim/drain the aura of an Other, while pretending to entertain, educate, or inspire

de-partment, academic ❾ : territorial division of academia from which Spinning Spinsters depart, escaping academentia

Depressing State ❾ : patriarchy: the Necrophilic State, which requires depression in its inhabitants/victims to perpetuate its cruel rule; the Aggressing State which regularly schedules wars to lift itself out of its depressions

Deprived State ○ : patriarchy: the state of extreme sensory, physical, emotional, intellectual, and spiritual impoverishment, often disguised as abundance

dick ○ *n* ["PENIS—usu. considered vulgar"—*Webster's*] **1** : the second person (member) of the vulgar trinity—tom, dick, and harry **2** : a common member of the thrusting throng. *Examples:* tricky dick nixon, dick tracy. *See* **tom, dick, and harry** (W-W 3)

dickspeak *n* **1** : deadly diction of dicks, esp. applied to official military, technological, and pornographic terminology. *Examples: nuke, fuck, fallout, meltdown, gang bang, gook, scumbag* **2** : seminal emis-

The inhabitants of the foreground, their activities and characteristics

sions of phallic lusters, ranging from comic strips to literature, from pornography to theological treatises, addresses and dick-tionaries of philosophy. *Examples:*

> License my roving hands, and let them go,
> Before, behind, between, above, below.
> O my America! my new-found land.
> —John Donne[17]

WORD-WEB THREE

> The church by means of the Council did not wish to shut herself up within herself, or to refer to herself alone. On the contrary, she wanted to open herself up more widely.
> —pope John Paul II, addressing extraordinary Synod of Bishops[18]

dickspeaker *n* : one who dickspeaks; one who speaks for dicks. *Example:* any "Speaker of the House"

dick-tionary *n* : any patriarchal dictionary: a derivative, tamed, muted lexicon compiled by dicks, which, despite its distortions, contains clues for Word-Weaving Websters/Wickedarians. *Examples: Webster's, Oxford English Dictionary,* Cirlot's *Dictionary of Symbols. Compare* **Wickedary** (W-W I)

dis-couraging ⁹ : a base activity of snools: tearing out the heart; attempting to annihilate courage, joy, creativity, and Lust for be-ing in women. *Examples:*

> Literature cannot be the business of a woman's life, and it ought not to be. The more she is engaged in her proper duties, the less leisure will she have for it, even as an accomplishment and a recreation.
> —Robert Southey to Charlotte Brontë[19]

> Nut book of the year. . . . Bitter, brainless absurdity pervades every page. . . ."
> —John Greenway, in his "review" of Elizabeth Gould Davis, *The First Sex*[20]

dis-ease ⁹ *n* : sickening complex of plastic passions, e.g., guilt, anxiety, depression, and frustration, which are embedded into women in the State of Possession

Dissociated State ○ **1** : condition of low-grade multiple-personality disorder common among women under patriarchy; the state of a woman who is severed from her Original Self and splintered into myriad false selves   **2 :** patriarchy, the state of separation from Biophilic purposefulness. *See* **separatism, phallic** (w-w 3)

dis-spiriting ⦿ **:** necrophilic process of denying and attempting to negate the ensoulment and intelligence of all Elemental be-ing: process logically culminating in nuclear holocaust and even in a dis-passionate craven craving for this

The inhabitants of the foreground, their activities and characteristics

doomsday clock   1 : instrument for measuring archetypal dead-time: any clock of clockocracy, Crone-logically recognized as marking out the beat of the patriarchal death march   **2 :** symbol for the measurement of time in the State of Possession; symbol for possessed time, tidy time, nuclear time, doomed time. *N.B.:* Since 1947 the *Bulletin of the Atomic Scientists* has displayed a "doomsday clock" which represents the degree of nuclear peril as perceived by the editors. "Midnight" represents the hour of nuclear holocaust. Twice the hands of the clock have been moved as close as three minutes to midnight.[21] *See Appendicular Web Four.*

doublethink *n* **:** nonthought process by which patriarchal reversals are generated and which makes belief in these absurdities possible. *N.B.:* the word *doublethink* was invented by George Orwell, who described it as follows:

> . . . to hold simultaneously two opinions which cancelled out, knowing them to be contradictory and believing in both of them . . . to forget, whatever it was necessary to forget, then to draw it back into memory again at the moment when it was needed, and then promptly to forget it again, and above all, to apply the same process to the process itself.[22]

Jane Caputi gives a Radical Feminist analysis of the use of doublethink in the contemporary media in "Seeing Elephants," *Feminist Studies*, vol. 14 (1988).

drag queen, holy spirit as ⦿ **:** the third person of the all-male christian trinity, traditionally described as feminine (he is said to heal, bless, cleanse, spiritually nourish), who impregnates Mary, producing male offspring, in a dis-guised re-vision of Parthenogenesis

drag queen, pope John Paul Too as ○ **:** pop patriarch of the 1980s who uses the electronic media to proclaim his love for souls; granite-jawed, white-robed superstar who made his 1979 debut as visiting

Queen of Heaven, con-descending upon continent after continent in his special airplane; champion of imprisonment in the family, fetal rights, and discreet christian gynocide: Male Mother of the Decade

drag queens, obstetricians and gynecologists as : the holy ghosts of modern medicine who usurp female powers of birthing; trickers who represent an advanced stage of deception, not bothering with the guise of female attire, but manufacturing the illusion that it is *they* who have the capacity to bring Life into the world. *Catty Comment:*

> Who needs *them?* My mother (who, by the way, is a Beldam) did it perfectly well many times by herSelf. The Tabbies of our family consult only Gyn/Ecologists.
> —Ms. Wild Cat

drag queens, supreme court justices as : "justices," who, having blindfolded Justice, steal both her name and her skirts, pompously executing justice. *Example:* William Rehnquist

dryasdust *n* ["one that is uninteresting because of concentration on minutiae: PEDANT"—*Webster's*] : This definition has been awarded *Websters'* Intergalactic Seal of Approval. *Example:* John Dryden

dummy *n* ["an imitation, copy, or likeness of something intended for use as a substitute: EFFIGY"—*Webster's*] : a species of elementary: simulation of Elemental reality; any component of the plastic world. *See* **elementaries** (w-w 1)

dummydom *n* : any domain of dummies. *Examples:* wall street, the pentagon, harvard university

Dummy, the Great [*dummy adj* "having the appearance of acting independently or for oneself while really acting at the instruction of another"—*Webster's*] : Ronald Reagan ("the Great Communicator") in his role as presbot of the united states. *Cockaludicrous Comment:*

> They tell me I'm the most powerful man in the world. I don't believe that. Over there in the White House someplace, there's a fellow that puts a piece of paper on my desk everyday that tells me what I am going to be doing every 15 minutes. He's the most powerful man in the world.
> —Ronald Reagan[23]

elementary school ○ (Emily Culpepper[24]) **:** a school in which elementary subjects (e.g., ill-logic, woman-erasing history, manly grammar, psycho-ology, foolosophy, and the-ology) are taught

e-racer ○ *n* **1 :** a hacker who attempts to sever women from our Elemental roots, to arrest and destroy the Race of Women **2 :** any genocidal snool. *N.B.:* This word is derived from *e-raced,* which was Dis-covered by Anne Dellenbaugh in 1981.

eyeballer *n* **:** a deadeye dick; crude public peeper; pornography user/ woman-abuser

The inhabitants of the foreground, their activities and characteristics

"Faith of Our Fathers" : hideous hymn extolling a long dead faith of fatherland; perverted paean to dead faith, which is the patriarchal parody and reversal of Wholly Heathen Faith. *Compare* **Fey Faith** (w-w 1); **Ethnic Background** (w-w 2)

faker ○ *n* **:** a common variety of snool: one who is adept at the fakery which is prerequisite for success and status in fooldom: one who is likely to suckseed

family, patriarchal *n* [(derived fr. L *familia* servants of a household): "*archaic:* a group of persons in the service of an individual (he had a great family, that is to say . . . many slaves . . .)"—*Webster's*] **:** primary unit of the sadosociety, consisting of slaves organized in domestic and sexual service to a snool as their head. *Cockaludicrous Comments:*

> This order [of domestic society] includes both the primacy of the husband with regard to the wife and children, the ready subjection of the wife and her willing obedience.
>   —pope Pius XI[25]

> Wives are young men's mistresses, companions for middle age, and old men's nurses.
>   —Francis Bacon[26]

family, all-male᾿ : the "Family of Man"; the "human family"; the world of men, the society where women do not exist. *Cockaludicrous Comment:*

> [The catholic church will focus] on the world of men, the whole human family, so that this world might be fashioned anew according to God's design and reach its fulfillment.
>   —pope John Paul II[27]

See **full-fillment** (w-w 3)

fashion *n* [derived fr. L *factus* (past part. of *facere* to make)—*Web-ster's*] : a primary means by which phallocratic fixers fix, tame, and train women for their own designs; the bad magic by which fakers attempt to destroy female consciousness, embedding contagious anxieties and cravings, trying to trap women in houses of correction/houses of mirrors. *Cockaludicrous Comment:*

> My desire is to save them [women] from nature.
> —Christian Dior[28]

Canny Comment:

> Who's Max Factor
> Who's Max Factor
> He Fakes up
> our make-up
> Dirty old man
> with the Hollywood tan
> That's the man
> we must ban.
>
> What's the factor
> the factor in Max
> He's a bad actor
> Woman de-tractor
> Facts on Max
> Hex on Max.
> —Song to be sung to the tune of "Frère Jacques"[29]

fatherland [°] *n* : an amalgamation of all nations under god and the rule of his popocrats: SADOSOCIETY, FOOLDOM; territory forever foreign to Wild Women, animals, all of nature, and our Foresisters and Fore-Bears. *See* **foreground** (w-w 1)

fembot [°] *n* : female robot: the archetypical role model forced upon women throughout fatherland: the unstated goal/end of socialization into patriarchal womanhood: the totaled woman. *See* **totaled woman** (w-w 3)

feminitude[30] *n* : the state of idealized female servitude: FEMININITY

fetal identification syndrome [°] **1** : masculine identification with fetal tissue resulting from male apprehension that men "live" by con-

198

necting themselves to women and to "Mother Earth" as forever fetal inhabitors, possessors, and parasites. *Cockaludicrous Comment:*

> We as a society feel closer all the time to preterm children.
> —Henry M. Sondheimer, M.D.[31]

2 : fetal fixation/fetishization; fatherly obsession with fetuses and fetal rights; glorification of fetuses and the fetal state.[32] *See* **flying fetuses; hostage crisis** (w-w 3)

The inhabitants of the foreground, their activities and characteristics

fix ○ *v* ["to treat so as to make some condition permanent . . . to kill, harden and preserve . . . FASTEN, ATTACH, AFFIX . . . to hold fast: CAPTURE. . . . CASTRATE, SPAY . . . to remove a principal means of defense from (as a pet skunk) . . . get even with: PUNISH . . . to determine the outcome of (a contest) by bribery or other improper methods . . . to tamper with in advance (a horse fixed to lose a race)"—*Webster's*] : These definitions have been awarded *Websters'* Intergalactic Seal of Approval.

fixer ○ *n* : a snool whose occupation is to fix: FIX-MASTER

fix-master ○ *n* **1 :** one who continually aims to freeze life, to make Elemental be-ing stationary, nonvolatile, solid/stolid, killed, hardened, preserved, selectively bred, fastened, captured, castrated, made defenseless, bribed, tampered with **2 :** one who attempts to fix women in fixocracy, the State of Addiction. *See* **junkocracy** (w-w 3)

flapper *n* ["one that flaps. . . . a part that hangs or droops"—*Webster's*] **1 :** one obsessed with his flapper, i.e., his part that hangs or droops. *Example:* Freud **2 :** one who swings back and forth indecisively. *Example:* Hamlet

flasher ○ *n* : one who compulsively exposes his inadequacies

flatland ○ *n* : the zone of dullness, sameness, depression: PATRIARCHY, FOREGROUND; the place where Nothing grows

flopocracy *n* [*flop* *n* "a complete failure: DUD"; also *flop* *v* "to swing or bounce loosely"—*Webster's Collegiate*] : rule by flops; government by those who swing and bounce from one grotesque fiasco to another: FOOLOCRACY

flunky *n* : a successful snool: YES-MAN; a flop who has fully realized his potential. *Examples:* all of the twelve apostles. *See* **Yessir, Professor** (w-w 3)

flying fetuses ⁰ : astronauts in spaceships; technological offspring of male monogender mating; tube-fed orbiters who are mothered/monitored by ground controllers and their computers. *Cockaludicrous Comment:*

> SPACE FLIGHT ABORTED IN LAST SECONDS—headline,
> *New York Times*, June 27, 1984, p. 1

fool *n* [derived fr. L *follis* bellows, bag, akin to Gk *phallos* penis (found at *blow*)—*Webster's;* also derived from Indo-European root *bhel-* "to blow, swell; with derivatives referring to various round objects and to the notion of tumescent masculinity"—*American Heritage,* Appendix on Indo-European Roots] : archetypal player on the stage/foreground of phallocracy: bellowing fellow, windbag; cockaludicrous parader of "round objects"; exposer/exponent of tumescent masculinity

fooldom *n* **1** : the domain of wantwits and fools: PHALLOCRACY **2** : the common non-sense of the Numbed State; the accumulated "wisdom" (bull) of bullocracy

fool-fillment *n* : *See* **full-fillment** (w-w 3)

foolocracy *n* ["government by fools; a ruling class of fools"—*Webster's*] : This definition has been awarded *Websters'* Intergalactic Seal of Approval.

foolosophy *n* : fooldom parading as wisdom. *See* **academentia** (w-w 3)

foolproof *n* : demonstration performed according to the methods of foolosophical re-search, considered by fools to be cogent, incontestable, absolutely conclusive

fop *n* ["*obs* . . . a conceited pretender to wit or accomplishments . . . a man who is devoted to or vain of the exquisiteness or showiness of his dress: COXCOMB, DANDY, DUDE"—*Webster's*] : This definition has been awarded *Websters'* Intergalactic Seal of Approval. *Cockaludicrous Comment:*

> I'm a Yankee Doodle Dandy.
> —George M. Cohan

foreground feminism ○ : *See* **plastic feminism; pseudobonding** (w-w 3)

framer ○ *n* **1 :** a species of fixer: one who specializes in setting up Others. *Examples* **a:** the authors of Genesis **b:** the witch prickers **c:** attorneys who defend known rapists. *Canny Comment:*

> "Eve was framed."
> —popular feminist adage

2 : a professional objectifier; one who encloses and displays women for prurient purposes. *Examples* **a:** Bob Guccione (publisher of *Penthouse*) **b:** Norman Mailer (hack) **c:** Ingmar Bergman (phallosophical filmmaker)

Frankenstein phenomenon ◑ **:** phallotechnological fusion of male motherhood and necrophilia; scientific "progress" understood as leading to the destruction/elimination of women and all life. *N.B.:* Mary Wollstonecraft Shelley's novel *Frankenstein* is, in its entirety, an Uncanny Canny Comment on this phenomenon.

The inhabitants of the foreground, their activities and characteristics

fraternity of phallic fellers ○ **:** the ruling brother-hoods of phallocracy: fellowship of fools whose project is to fell the Tree of Life by forcing women to our knees and bringing down all of nature. *Canny Comment:*

> For the first time in human history the mother kneels before her son; she freely accepts her inferiority. This is the supreme masculine victory, consummated in the cult of the Virgin—it is the rehabilitation of woman through the accomplishment of her defeat.
> —Simone de Beauvoir, commenting on the christian cult of the Virgin Mary [33]

fraud ○ *n* **:** a prickish pretender, deceiver, tricker, reverser, cheat. *Example:* Sigmund Fraud, inventor of the vaginal orgasm, penis envy, and the colossal reversal that women "castrate" men

full-fillment ○ *n* **1 :** the saddest of the plastic passions: therapeutized perversion of the passion of joy **2 :** condition of women as vessels/vassals, as containers/carriers of plastic passions, ideas, self-images, and other waste products of junkocracy. *Canny Comment:*

> What we prayed for was emptiness, so we would be worthy to be filled: with grace, with love, with self-denial, semen and babies.
> Oh God, King of the universe, thank you for not creating me a man.

> Oh God, obliterate me. Make me fruitful. Mortify my flesh,
> that I may be multiplied. Let me be fulfilled.
> —Margaret Atwood, *The Handmaid's Tale* [34]

3 : the ultimate fulfillment of all necrophilic christian desire: the annihilation of all life. *Cockaludicrous Comment:*

> The extraordinary adventure of the World will have ended. . . .
> The dream of every mystic will have found its full and proper
> fulfillment.
> —Pierre Teilhard de Chardin, "The End of the World" [35]

full-osopher ° *n* [*philosopher* "one who seeks wisdom or enlightenment"—*Webster's*] **:** one who fails to seek wisdom, having deluded himself into believing that he possesses it: academented stuffed shirt. *Example:* Full Professor Yessir, Department of Ology, College of Knowledge. *See* **Yessir, Professor** (w-w 3)

full professor/fool professor **:** one who has found full-fillment in academentia

fundamentalist *n* [*fundament* "the part of the body on which one sits: BUTTOCKS . . . anus"—*Webster's*] **:** one who sermonizes from the fundament, spreading the "word": WINDBAG; a bibliolater, esp. one affected with logorrhea. *See* **logorrhea; sir-reverence** (w-w 3)

gaffer *n* [(prob. contraction of *godfather*) "old man, old fellow"; also fr. *gaff v* "DECEIVE, TRICK; also: FLEECE . . . FIX"—*Webster's*] **:** ghoulish godfather; deceptive old fellow who tricks, fleeces, and fixes women under the guise of godliness. *Examples:* fundamentalist smoothies.

gagger *n* **:** a species of dickspeaker: one who tries to stop the Musings of Muses, esp. by means of rules or ridicule; common preacher or dirty joker. *Examples* **a:** "saint Paul" (or one of his clones),[36] who droned:

> Let a woman learn in silence with all submissiveness. I permit
> no woman to teach or to have authority over men; she is to
> keep silent. For Adam was formed first, then Eve; and Adam
> was not deceived, but the woman was deceived and became
> a transgressor.
> —1 Tim. 2:11–14

b: Rudyard Kipling, who dribbled/scribbled:

And a woman is only a woman, but a
   good cigar is a smoke.[37]

goad-god ° *n* : the divine role model for the little goadfathers who goad, prick, spur, prod, and bore all natural creatures within their reach

godfather ° *n* **1** : worldly representative and role model for the heavenly god/rod; ventriloquist who manipulates and speaks through the dummy divinity of fatherland. *Examples* **a:** fathers Heinrich Kramer and James Sprenger, priestly inquisitors who piously proclaimed:

> And blessed be the Highest Who has so far preserved the
> male sex from so great a crime [witchcraft]: for since He
> was willing to be born and to suffer for us, therefore He has
> granted to men this privilege.[38]

b: godfather and presbot Harry S Truman, who intoned:

> We thank God it [the atomic bomb] has come to us instead of
> to our enemies; and we pray that He may guide us to use it
> in His ways and for His purposes.
>   —Radio address to the nation, Aug. 9, 1945 [39]

2 : fictional divine father of worldly godfathers; heavenly puppet of popocrats, which they have fashioned in their image and likeness and which functions as their figure/head

Godfather, Son & Company ● **1** : the christian trinity **2** : the church, the state, the family, and all other firms dedicated to the propagation of the male line

god/rod ° *n* **1** : projection by impotent prickers of an omnipotent, eternally erect divinity **2** : divine ruler of phallocrats possessed by penis envy, who obsessively compete, measuring/comparing their rods—e.g., guns, missiles, rockets. *Cockaludicrous Comment:*

> Why do men then now not reck his rod?
>   —Gerard Manley Hopkins, S.J.[40]

Canny Comment:

> Why do Crones then now not wreck his rod?
>   —Amazonian lullaby

grammar *n* : *See* **phallogrammar/fellowgrammar** (w-w 3)

The inhabitants of the foreground, their activities and characteristics

grave keepers of tradition ° : members of patriarchal professions: official guardians of the coffers/coffins in which dead bodies of knowledge are stored, re-stored, and re-covered

gross national product : any lethal or toxic commodity produced by a phallotechnological nation. *Examples:* pesticide-poisoned produce, pornography, nuclear weaponry

guising/dis-guising ° [*guise* "a superficial seeming: an artful or simulated appearance"—*Webster's*] : negative shape-shifting: endless conversion from one patriarchal position to another; shifty strategy of the State of Deception, whose players perpetually switch from one guise to another without ever effecting genuine change.

Gynocidal Society ° : patriarchy: the state of planned, systematic bodily and spiritual destruction of women. *See* **gynocide** (w-w 1)

gyrophobia *n* : fixers' fear of Spinning; the fright of framers/frauds/fakers at the sight of Spinning Spinsters

hack ° *n* : literary drudge who is over-rewarded for his prurient outpourings; pretentious pornographer who hacks at the integrity of women, inciting his followers/readers to complicity in the carnage. *Example:* Norman Mailer, who slobbered over his fellow hack Henry Miller:

> While nobody can be more poetic than Miller about fucking itself. . . . he still cannot write about fucking with love. . . . Miller nonetheless pounds away on the subject like a giant phallus trying to enter a child's vagina—in the pounding is one simple question: How do you get in?[41]

hackers ° *n* : manglers, dismemberers, mutilators; plug-uglies who attack/hack women, animals, and all of nature: hit-men for the higher powers of the sadostate. *Examples:* the hackers who murdered scientist Dian Fossey; the poachers and trophy hunters who hacked to death the gorillas with whom Fossey lived and worked for over twenty years.[42] *See* **plug-ugly** (w-w 3)

Happy Dead Ones ° : the inhabitants of patriarchal heaven, the final Stag-nation. *See* **Beatific Vision** (w-w 3)

haunted house-keepers ° : prepossessors of women who spook their victims into entrapment in the Domesticated State, haunting them with fears, anxieties, and a Self-defeating longing for belonging (to a man, to a family, to an "acceptable" social set). *See* **full-fillment; spooking** (w-w 3). *Compare* **Be-Longing** (w-w 1)

hero, cockocratic : an idolized and widely imitated snool, one who serves as a sacred role model in patriarchy, the State of Atrocity. *Examples* **a:** the Marquis de Sade, idolized by the pseudo-intellectual left[43] **b:** Daniel Boone—hunter, trapper and Indian killer **c:** Jack the Ripper, described by journalist Charles McCabe as

> that great hero of my youth, that skilled human butcher who did all his work on alcoholic whores.[44]

hetero-reality ○ *n* **:** "the world view that woman exists always in relation to man"—Janice G. Raymond.[45] *Cockaludicrous Comment:*

> Simone de Beauvoir without Sartre is difficult to imagine. . . . Whatever her skill as a writer or her own role as courageous supporter of many causes, she can only be assessed in relation to the Sartrian universe.
> —Douglas (Nobody) Johnson[46]

holeyness, his : title reserved by Crones for the popebot of Rome

home, patriarchal [akin to Gk *koiman* to put to sleep; etymologically connected with *cemetery—Webster's*] **:** the primary and paradigmatic unit of the Comatose State. *Cockaludicrous Comment:*

> Oh, woman, poets have sung of you, and men gone mad over thy beauty, but before you decide to divorce yourselves from the sphere over which you have held undisputed sway from time immemorial, let me remind you of the sweet words of John Howard Payne—"Home, Sweet Home, there is no place like home."
> —Abraham L. Kellog, antisuffragist, 1894[47]

homesick *adj* **1 :** sickened by the home **2 :** sick of the home; healthily motivated to escape the patriarchal home and family. *See* **family, patriarchal** (w-w 3)

hostage crisis ○ **:** repetitive scenario of snooldom's media (particularly in the 1980s) revealing the forever fetal identification of its fabricators, portraying captivity in the womb of the mythic Terrible Mother (The Enemy), followed by deliverance and return to the womb of the Good Mother (America). *Cockaludicrous Comment:*

The inhabitants of the foreground, their activities and characteristics

I want to say thank you to the world. Man, what a relief: it's
like you gave birth to 52.
   —Twin brother of one of the 52 American hostages held in
      Iran (1980–81), upon hearing of his brother's release[48]

See **fetal identification syndrome** (w-w 3)

housebroken *adj* [*housebreak v* "to teach acceptable social manners to:
accustom to indoor living: make tractable or polite . . . to break the
spirit of: TAME, SUBDUE"—*Webster's*] : condition of women taught/
trained to "live" in the Domesticated State: state of being tractable, polite, tamed, subdued, heart-broken/spirit-broken

huckster ○ *n* : adman/badman; mind molester who pimps images of
women's bodies, selling junk to junk junkies; tricker who trades in
overt and subliminal manipulation[49]

idiot-ology ◑ *n* : any dead body of knowledge that passes as professional expertise; professional "wisdom" forced upon women by the experts of fooldom, frequently taking the form of patronizing and even
lethal advice and prescriptions. *Example:* dr. S. Weir Mitchell's direc-
tives to Charlotte Perkins Gilman:

> Live as domestic a life as possible. Have your child with you
> all the time. . . . Lie down an hour after each meal. Have but
> two hours intellectual life a day. And never touch pen, brush
> or pencil as long as you live.[50]

ill logic ● (1985 ed.) *n* : the normal/normative, sick and sickening
"logic" of snooldom: invalid reasoning characterized by doublethink,
reversal, erasure, and other common forms of distortion and deception. *Example:* Comment of a spokesman for the all-male North
Korean delegation to the 1985 United Nations International Conference
on Women held in Nairobi:

> We do not discriminate between men and women, therefore
> there is no contradiction [in the makeup of the delegation].
> No more questions please.[51]

jabber ○ *n* : a disputatious snool: a finger-stabbing, poking, point-
making type who attempts to thrust his argument down any available
throat

jerk ○ *n* **1** : an ingrained reflex response: spasmodic conformity in-
culcated by patriarchy, e.g., military salutes, catholic genuflections,

snoolish jerking off to pornographic imagery **2 :** one who jerks; a common cock; jerk-off

jock ° *n* **:** an athletic supporter; a well-developed jerk

jockocracy ° *n* **:** patriarchy as the domain of jocks and their supporters/fans: the locker room society; back-slapping, butt-patting, ubiquitous boys' clubs. *Examples:* the military industrial complex, the Bosstown College football team, the Republican Party, the society of jesus

jockocratic ° *adj* **:** having the bearing and swagger of a jock, and being supported for this

junkocracy *n* **:** state of man-made addiction to toxic waste, e.g., junk food, junk mail, junk medicine, junk religion, junk politics, junk entertainment, chemical and nuclear junk

lackey *n* **:** a servile groveler: one characterized by the lack of everything—integrity, intelligence, passion, humor, courage, vitality, beauty, grace—in short, Potency. *Example:* Adam. *See* **Snot Boy** (w-w 3)

Laws of Lechery ° **:** old saws/laws of the Lecherous State, intended to oppress and harass Prudes, to thwart the practice of Pyromantic Virtues. *Examples:* anti-abortion laws; cardinal law

Lecherous Lackluster ° **:** a lascivious snool; one who lacks Ontological Lust and who lusts for Nothing; a leering dis-passionate deadhead

leech *n* ["*archaic:* PHYSICIAN, SURGEON. . . . a hanger-on who seeks advantage or gain: PARASITE"—*Webster's*] **:** These definitions have been awarded *Websters'* Intergalactic Seal of Approval. *Example:* J. Marion Sims, M.D., "father of gynecology," also known as "the architect of the vagina." Sims, a classic sadist, subjected many women to multiple experimental and excruciatingly painful procedures (without anaesthesia). For example, the Black slave Anarcha suffered thirty of his operations in his backyard stable. A decade later, between 1856 and 1859, an Irish indigent, Mary Smith, suffered the same number of his gruesome operations at The Woman's Hospital in New York.[52]

Legiti-Mates, The ° **:** the members of the all-male christian trinity, who function to legitimate all varieties of male monogender mating. *See* **luv story, archetypal** (w-w 3)

The inhabitants of the foreground, their activities and characteristics

lob *n* ["a dull, heavy person: LOUT. . . . *archaic:* a loosely hanging object"—*Webster's*] : a dull heavy deadfellow: one who gives too much weight to loosely hanging objects

logocide ° *n* : the systematic murder of logos (reason) in patriarchy, the State of Sleeping Death

logorrhea ° *n* : diarrhea of the mouth: communicable disease transmitted by paternal politicians and propagandists, exacerbated and spread by phallotechnic media

Looking Glass Society ● **1** : patriarchy: the house of mirrors, the world of reversals **2** : the society in which women serve as magnifying mirrors reflecting men at twice their natural size[53] **3** : society manufactured by phallocrats, who project their own deficiencies upon all Others, attempting to convert these into reflections of their own inadequate selves

Looking Glass War ● : basic preoccupation of the Looking Glass Society: compulsive and continual destruction of the world and its inhabitants; state of perpetual enmity engendered by patriarchal males' self-loathing and projection of their own hatefulness, soullessness, and sense of worthlessness upon all living be-ing

Lust-starvation ° *n* : the denial and blockage of Pure Lust, resulting in regression into and obsession with luv. *See* **luv** (w-w 3); **Pure Lust** (W-W I)

luv ● (1985 ed.) *n* **1** : the "love" for women and all other victimized persons which is ascribed to jesus/god by religious leaders and their full-filled followers. *Example:* the luv of jesus as depicted by Mother Teresa:

> She described how she told a dying cancer patient her pain meant she was so close to Jesus that he was kissing [sic] her: "She joined her hands together and said to me, 'Mother Teresa, please tell Jesus to stop kissing me!'" Laughter rippled across the stadium. "See how tender is God's love," Mother Teresa said.[54]

2 : the "love" for women professed by pimps, priests, popes, preachers, pornographers, and other protectors/possessors. *Example:* the "love" for women attributed to fashion photographer Helmut Newton. One of Newton's apologists, Edward Behr, meticulously "explains":

208

But above all, here is a man who loves women so passionately, so completely, that he has to carry this love to its ultimate conclusion. Look, he says, in a brace, a plaster cast, even in an artificial limb, she remains beautiful and desirable.[55]

3 : a plastic passion injected into women by the fixers and framers of phallocracy; a man-made addiction which progressively hooks women to woman-haters and destroys female Self-love: romantic love. *Canny Comment:*

> Romantic love, in pornography as in life, is the mythic cele-
> bration of female negation. For a woman, love is defined as
> her willingness to submit to her own annihilation. . . . For
> the female, the capacity to love is exactly synonymous with
> the capacity to sustain abuse and the appetite for it. . . .
> For the woman, love is always self-sacrifice, the sacrifice of
> identity, will, and bodily integrity, in order to fulfill and re-
> deem the masculinity of her lover.
> —Andrea Dworkin[56]

The inhabitants of the foreground, their activities and characteristics

luv story, archetypal : the dogma of the christian trinity: "the most sensational one-act play of the centuries, performed by the Supreme All-Male Cast; 'sublime' (and therefore disguised) erotic male homo-sexual mythos, the perfect all-male marriage, the ideal all-male family, the best boys' club, the model monastery, the supreme Men's Associa-tion, the mold for all varieties of male monogender mating"—*Gyn/Ecology,* p. 38.

M-A-Dness ⁹ : "Male Approval Desire"—Honor Moore

male-diction *n* **:** the droning of clones. *See* **dickspeak** (w-w 3)

maledom/staledom ° *n* **:** society crumbling in the patriarchal mold: Stag-nation

male-factor ⁹ *n* **1 :** male malefactor, evildoer **2 :** any of the ciphers which when multiplied together constitute the Absent State of patriarchy. *See* **cipherdom** (w-w 3)

male-function ⁹ *n* **1 :** characteristically unreliable performance of phallic equipment. *Example:* the explosion of the space shuttle *Chal-lenger* **2 :** archetypally endless ceremony or gathering of male-dom. *Examples:* diplomatic functions, church functions, White House functions

male-identification [9] *n* : malidentification of women with patriarchs as their misters/masters; depletion of the female Self prescribed by patriarchal laws and customs

male menstruation [9] : male attempts to mimic female creative powers and participation in Elemental rhythms. *Examples* **a:** christian priests' attempt to play at being female by "changing" wine into the "blood of Christ" in the sacrament of the eucharist **b:** subincision: a ritual mutilation performed as part of puberty rites among some native Australian and Fijian groups that involves slitting the underside of the penis with permanent opening of the urethra, the wound being called a vulva and its bleeding (caused by repeated reopening) being referred to by the people as "menses"[57]

male motherhood [9] **1** : fundamental reversal characteristic of patriarchal myth, e.g., god the father creating the world, Adam giving birth to Eve, Zeus bringing forth Athena **2** : male attempts to possess the creative powers of women, resulting in berserk and destructive simulations of motherhood—exemplified in the activities of obstetricians and gynecologists **3** : male endeavors to self-generate by means of necrological reproductive technologies which reduce females to the condition of incubators/vessels and which are inherently directed toward the annihilation of women[58]

male-ordered monotony [○] : wearisome sameness; the unrelenting tidy tedium that produces and reproduces Boredom; packaged uniformity that characterizes the male-ordered society

man-dated world [○] : *See* **clockocracy** (w-w 3)

man-infested [○] (Eleanor Mullaley[59]) *adj* : overrun by phallic presence of absence, both overt and subliminal. *See* **priest-ridden** (w-w 3); **presence of absence** (w-w 1)

masosadism [○] *n* : disorder injected into women in the sadostate, which begins with doubting the validity of one's own be-ing—a doubt experienced as Self-hatred—and which extends to doubting the validity of other women's be-ing, expressing itself finally in acts of horizontal violence

Master of Mister Cleans [○] : any male mythic model of tyrannical tidiness. *Example:* Apollo, who

. . . brought the Muses down from their home on Mount Helicon to Delphi, tamed their wild frenzy, and led them in formal and decorous dances.
    —Robert Graves[60]

Masters of Male Morality : apologists for every androcratic atrocity; species including ethicists, preachers, churchmen, and politicians who label natural acts "abominations" and evil behavior "good," "heroic," and "godly." *Example:* Pierre Teilhard de Chardin, s.j., who wrote:

> I shall not seek to discuss or defend the essential morality of this act of releasing atomic energy [explosion of the first atomic bomb]. . . . As though it were not every man's duty to pursue the creative forces of knowledge and action to their uttermost end![61]

The inhabitants of the foreground, their activities and characteristics

maze ◑ *n* : man-made set of tracks/traps leading nowhere which masks/hides the true Labyrinthine path leading into Wild Reality, the Background. *Compare* **Labyrinth** (w-w 2)

media potters/plotters ○ : propagandists who pot, can, stunt, and bury women's passions; popocrats who ritually plot and depict female failure, victimization, humiliation, and full-fillment as the inescapable script for women's lives. *See* **a-Musing** (w-w 3)

mindbindings ◑ *n* : layers of crippling patriarchal thought patterns comparable to the footbindings which mutilated millions of Chinese women for over one thousand years; master-minded myths and ideologies meant to mummify the spirit and maim the brain

mind-gynecologists ◑ *n* : psycho-logical professionals and semi-professionals who specialize in probing, humiliating, repressing and depressing women. *See* **Soap Opera Syndrome; the/rapist** (w-w 3)

mirrordom *n* : *See* **Looking Glass Society** (w-w 3)

Misbegotten State ○ [*misbegotten* "Illegally or abnormally begotten; especially, illegitimate"—*American Heritage*] **1** : state of illegitimacy and powerlessness inflicted upon women in fatherland **2** : condition of women who have been reborn/deformed according to male-made models and patterns; state of twice-born Athenas, the patriarchally begotten freaks of man: condition transcended by Metapatriarchal Journeyers. *Cockaludicrous Comment:*

As regards the individual nature, woman is defective and misbegotten, for the active force in the male seed tends to the
production of a perfect likeness in the masculine sex; while the
production of woman comes from defect in the active force or
from some material indisposition, or even from some external
influence; such as that of a south wind which is moist, as the
Philosopher [Aristotle] observes.
                                       —Thomas Aquinas[62]

WORD-WEB
THREE   **misterics** *n* : uncontrollable and mysterious fits (thought by some to
be caused by testicular disturbances): common psychoneurotic manifestation of mister-ectomy anxiety. *See* **mister-ectomy** (w-w 2)

museless/useless *adj* [*museless* "*archaic:* illiterate, uncultured"—*Webster's*] : inherently uninspired and meaningless: said of patriarchal
poets and patriarchal poetry. *Canny Comment:*

> Their origin and their history patriarchal poetry their ori-
> gin and their history patriarchal poetry their origin and their
> history. . . .
> Patriarchal Poetry is the same as Patriotic poetry is the same
> as patriarchal poetry is the same as Patriotic poetry is the
> same as patriarchal poetry is the same.
> Patriarchal poetry is the same.
> —Gertrude Stein[63]

mysteria *n* : unnatural frenzy/mania perpetually generated by phallocrats for the purpose of masking their true agendas, veiling male mysteries, and creating a State of Distraction. *Example:* the Witchcraze in
Western Europe. *See* **Mystery of Man, the** (w-w 1)

necro-apocalyptic *adj* : marked by a malignant intent to bring
about a holocaust that will purge the "unrighteous" and engulf the
Earth; characterized by expectations/hallucinations of the resurrection
of the "righteous" to a purified world of bliss, i.e., utter nonbe-ing.
Cockaludicrous Comment:

> Well, nuclear war and the Second Coming of Christ, Arma-
> geddon, and the coming war with Russia . . . none of this
> should bring fear to your hearts, because we are all going up
> in the Rapture before any of it occurs.[64]
> —Jerry Falwell

necrographer ○ (Emily Culpepper[65]) *n* : a "biographer" who ne-
gates the life of his "subject." *Example:* Quentin Bell[66]

212

necro-logical *adj* : marked by lethal ill logic. *See* **ill logic** (W-W 3). *Compare* **Bio-logical** (W-W 2)

¹**necrology** *n* : any patriarchal -ology: "science" which reduces living reality to objectified deadforms. *Example:* patriarchal medicine and "biology." *See* **-ologies** (W-W 3)

²**necrology** *n* ["The history of the dead"—*O.E.D.*] : patriarchal history. *See* **cock and bull story** (W-W 3)

necromantic *adj* : necrophilically romantic, said of luv that dooms its object to full-fillment/fool-fillment. *See* **luv** (W-W 3)

necropolis *n* [(derived fr. LL *necropolis* city of the dead): "CEMETERY; esp. a large elaborate cemetery. . . . a place . . . devoid of life and inhabited by or as if by only the dead"—*Webster's*] : These definitions have been awarded *Websters'* Intergalactic Seal of Approval. *Example par excellence:* Washington, D.C.

nocturnal emissions ● **1** : satellites and other christotechnological rubbish used to convert nearby outer space into a heavenly junkyard visibly polluting the beauty of the night sky   **2** : the nightly news

Nothing-lovers ◗ **1** : patriarchal narcissists who love Nothing, i.e., themselves   **2** : archetypical necrophiliacs whose fundamental desire is to reduce the entire cosmos to zero. *See* **necrophilia; pure lust** (W-W 1)

nothingness, his ●(1985 ed.)   **1** : title reserved by Crones for the papal bully, emphasizing his supreme absence of Presence   **2** : sum of the attributes and products of the patriarchal god/rod, e.g., his words, his plans, his mysteries, his luv, his presence, his presents. *See* **presence of absence** (W-W 1)

not-women ◗ *n* : cockocrats afflicted with cock-eyed womb envy; impotent prickers who crave/lust after Haggard Creative Powers. *See* **cock-eyed** (W-W 3)

Numbed State ○ : condition of those who have been psychically numbed/voided of E-motion: State of the Living Dead. *Canny Comment:*

> The question so often asked, "Would the survivors [of a nuclear war] envy the dead?" may turn out to have a simple

answer. No, they would be incapable of such feelings. They would not so much envy, as inwardly and outwardly, resemble the dead.

—Robert Jay Lifton[67]

numbot ○ *n* : species of fembot employed as a vessel/channel of psychic numbing,[68] esp. in televised performances. *Example:* Nancy Reagan as programmed in the role of First Lady

Numbot Chorus ○ : images of "happy" fembots filing through the foreground of fatherdom's dumb shows/fantasies, erasing Rage, setting the stage for numberless mummified/numb-ified copies. *Example:* the Miss America Pageant

olds, the : the same old stories: patriarchal "news" as reported/distorted by assorted officious olds agencies and disseminated in the daily oldspapers, the nightly olds, *Deadtime* and *Oldsweek* magazines, etc. etc.

-ologies ◑ *n* : static and stagnant bodies of knowledge; fetid pools of fraudulent "learning"; tidy fields/plots of academic cemeteries containing the consummate emptiness of patriarchal erudition. *Compare* **O-logy** (w-w I)

omniabsence ○ *n* : essential attribute of the wholly ghostly divine father, who is acclaimed by the-ological reversers as "omnipresent"; attribute of the dummy deity who is never there, not all there, and therefore does not and cannot care

Painted Bird ◑ **1** : symbol for the condition of women in the State of Possession who are full-filled with man-made-up self-images **2** : a tokenized/plasticized woman who is used to oppress her sisters, i.e., one who has been snatched from the Wild, domesticated, dolled up, and released only to function as "the ultimate weapon in the hands of the boys"[69]

paradise, patriarchal ◑ [derived fr. Gk *paradeisos* enclosed park . . . akin to Iranian *pairi* around + *daēza* wall—*Webster's*] : the perpetual after-life which is patriarchy, the State of Living Death; the enclosed a-Musement park whose inhabitants are perpetually parked, locked into the parking lots of the past; arena of games: playboys' playground: the foreground. *Canny Comment:*

Can you *imagine* being locked up in there with Adam forever?
I got out while the getting was good.
　　—Lilith, in her collection of Lusty memoirs, *Never a Rib*

Passive Voice ⁰ **1 :** a common structure of phallogrammar: means of disguising the agents of androcratic atrocities; verb form used to passify/passivize the victims of such atrocities.[70] *Example:*

In 1985 more women were raped.
　　—*Deadtime Magazine,* Feb. 30, 1986 a.d.

The inhabitants of the foreground, their activities and characteristics

2 : the call of the tame; the ubiquitous voice that subliminally spooks women, luring its victims into passivity, rendering them unable to recognize and Name the agents of their oppression. *See* **spooking** (w-w 3)

pedestal peddlar • (1968 ed.) : pseudo-glorifier of "Woman"; pusher/proponent of the archetypal "eternal feminine"; curator of "woman's mysteries." *Cockaludicrous Comment:*

I would not, and I say it deliberately, degrade woman by giving her the right of suffrage: I mean the word in its full signification, because I believe that woman as she is to-day, the queen of the home and of hearts, is above the political collisions of this world, and should always be kept above them. . . .
It is said that the suffrage is to be given to enlarge the sphere of woman's influence. Mr. President, it would destroy her influence. It would take her down from that pedestal where she is to-day, influencing as a mother the minds of her offspring, influencing by her gentle and kindly caress the action of her husband toward the good and pure.
　　—Senator G. [Windbag] Vest (Democrat, Missouri), 1887[71]

penis envy ⁰ **1 :** classic reversal and projection propagated by the fraud freud and co.; conceptual cover-up for the male's hidden shame and sense of inadequacy. *Canny Comment:*

I stared at Buddy while he unzipped his chino pants and took them off and laid them on a chair and then took off his underpants that were made of something like nylon fishnet. . . .
Then he just stood there in front of me and I kept staring at him. The only thing I could think of was turkey neck and turkey gizzards and I felt very depressed.
　　—Sylvia Plath[72]

2 : phallic feeling common among fellow members of the cockocratic Men's Association: elementary emotion of males obsessed with measurements of other members' members   **3 :** motivating emotion behind the missile build-up.[73] *See* **god/rod** (w-w 3)

phallic infinity : essential attribute of the Phallic State, the State in which Nothing happens: endlessness. *See* **endlessness** (w-w 1)

phallicism ○ *n* ["the worship of or reverence for the generative principle in nature as symbolized esp. by the phallus"—*Webster's*]   **1 :** the worship of or reverence for the degenerative principle in civilization, as symbolized esp. by the phallus; male self-worship; ideology and practice consequent upon and reinforcing the belief that "God" is male and the male is "God"   **2 :** phallic solipsism: the theory or view that the phallus is the only reality: the phallusy fallacy, the most pathetic fallacy

phallic morality ⦿ : morality completely unconcerned with right and wrong; system of ethics intended solely to uphold and legitimate the Phallic State; system of apology for every androcratic atrocity; the prevailing "ethical" climate in all patriarchal societies, north and south, east and west, right and left, rich and poor, "free" and "enslaved"

Phallic State ○   **1 :** state of intellectual, moral, physical, and metaphysical flaccidity   **2 :** condition of rigidity/frigidity: STATE OF RIGOR MORTIS

phallocentrism *n*   **1 :** a habitual disposition to fixate on the phallus and to indulge in worship of the phallus. *Cockaludicrous Comment:* ". . . the penis is the head of the body."—Norman O. Brown[74]   **2 :** a tendency to project/erect (erect) penises everywhere

phallocracy ○ *n* **:** rule by Godfather, Son, and Company. *See* **cockocracy; foolocracy** (w-w 3)

phallogeneric term : a pseudogeneric term which, while pretending to include women, in reality conveys the message that only men exist. *Example: man* (history of, evolution of, future of, philosophy of, et cetera, ad nauseam). *N.B.:* As Julia Penelope has pointed out, even seemingly innocuous terms function as pseudogenerics—a fact which can be ascertained from their context, e.g.: "People and their wives are invited to the faculty banquet."[75]

phalloglamour *n* **:** illusions systematically manufactured by snools in order to block the flow of Elemental communication and to maintain male mystery; the pseudoexcitement and attractiveness of the elementary world and its products. *Compare* **Glamour** (w-w 2)

phallogrammar/fellowgrammar *n* : fixed foreground ordering of speech that fixes Female minds into phallocentric molds. *Canny Comment:*

> The "I" [*Je*] who writes is alien to her own writing at every word because this "I" [*Je*] uses a language alien to her; this "I" [*Je*] experiences what is alien to her since this "I" [*Je*] cannot be "*un* écrivain." . . . *J/e* is the symbol of the lived, rending experience which is m/y writing, of this cutting in two which throughout literature is the exercise of a language which does not constitute m/e as subject. *J/e* poses the ideological and historic question of feminine subjects.
> —Monique Wittig[76]

The inhabitants of the foreground, their activities and characteristics

phallosophy *n* : inflated foolosophy: "wisdom" loaded with seminal ideas and disseminated by means of thrusting arguments. *Examples* **a:** "The bridge to the future is the phallus."[77]—D. H. Lawrence **b:** William Shockley's ludicrous legitimations of white supremacy

phallo-institutions ○ *n* : the building blocks of the Phallic State: sadosystems erected to block process, to confuse, ensnare, deceive, and defeat Journeyers; the major institutions of patriarchy, e.g., the all-male family, elementary schooling, necromantic luv, sado-religion, missile envy, apartheid

phallotechnology ◗ *n* : the technology of doomdom; technology which has rapism as its hidden agenda and destruction of life as its final goal; applied scientific fooldom. *See* **fooldom** (w-w 3)

plastic feminism ○ : elementary substitute/replacement for Original woman-identified bonding and movement; man-made pseudofeminism; rageless, humorless product of Boredom: fashionable, feminine "feminism"

plastic passion ○ : species of pseudopassion: mad-made feeling which lacks natural Wildness; blob in inner space which pre-occupies and paralyzes its victims—predominantly women—draining energies, preventing E-motion, distracting from the pursuit of Pure Lust; freefloating feeling characterized by lack of specific and nameable causes, which functions to mask the agents of repression/oppression. *Ex-*

amples: guilt, anxiety, depression, hostility, bitterness, resentment, frustration, boredom, resignation, full-fillment. *Canny Comment:*

> Wild Women don't get the blahs.
> —Diana Beguine[78]

See **potted passion** (w-w 3)

plastic virtue ○ : species of pseudovirtue: man-made counterfeit of genuine Virtue which functions to disguise and pervert the meaning of Virtue. *Examples:* the "prudence" of the presbot; the "justice" of the supreme court justices; the "courage" of the marines; the "temperance" of the puritans. *See* **potted virtue** (w-w 3)

plopocracy *n* : rule by the god-identified ploppers who flop/plop themselves everywhere: FLOPOCRACY. *Canny Comment:*

> Man corrupt everything, say Shug. He on your box of grits, in your head and all over the radio. He try to make you think he everywhere. Soon as you think he everywhere, you think he God. But he ain't. Whenever you trying to pray, and man plop himself on the other end of it, tell him to git lost, say Shug.
> —Alice Walker[79]

plug ○ *n* ["a male fitting used to make an electrical connection by insertion in a receptacle or body and having one or more contact-making parts or blades that serve to close a circuit"—*Webster's*] : a male who in his connections with women creates the illusion that he is always giving something while in fact he is draining energy, closing women's circuits, sapping the flow of Gynergetic currents so that these cannot circulate within/among women. *Examples* **a:** Gerald, a snoolish character in the novel *Women in Love* by D. H. Lawrence, described by the author as follows:

> Into her he poured all his pent-up darkness and corrosive death, and he was whole again. . . . And she, subject, received him as a vessel filled with his bitter potion of death.[80]

b: D. H. Lawrence

plug-ugly ○ *n* ["a member of a gang of disorderly ruffians often active in political pressure and intimidation"—*Webster's*] **1** : one of the grosser snoolish incarnations; henchman required for the smooth operation of fixocracy; a fixer who plugs himself into women and nature; everyday rapist, child-abuser, pimp, wife-beater, maimer, murderer, dismemberer **2 :** member of a group/blob of reputable ruffians, perpetually active in political pressure and intimidation. *Examples* **a:** CIA agent **b:** member of the "Moral Majority"

popebot *n* **:** the pope as he appears on television, the full-figured representative of holy mother church. *See* **presbot** (w-w 3)

popocracy *n* **:** rule by the papas of patriarchy; pop culture

Possessed State ○ **:** state of women separated from their Selves by the separaters/fracturers/batterers/flatterers who control their lives; state of women forcibly blocked from Be-Friending. *See* **separatism, phallic** (w-w 3); **Be-Friending** (w-w 1)

potted passion ○ *n* **:** species of pseudopassion: stunted, artificially contained, twisted, and warped version of a genuine passion; contorted/distorted passion, bent in unnatural directions, stopping at the wrong object. *Example:* the addictive "love" that is instilled into a prostitute by her pimp.[81] *See* **plastic passion** (w-w 3)

potted virtue ○ **:** species of pseudovirtue: stifled and stifling habit which stops at the wrong object; limited and distorted virtue which functions to inhibit Original movement and Realization of one's Final Cause. *Examples* **a:** the "prudence" of a woman who stops her Self from "going too far" **b:** the "courage" of Athena, who forgets and denies her Mother and Sisters, committing herself to fighting boys' battles, to serving the masters' purposes. *See* **plastic virtue** (w-w 3)

Predatory State ○ [*predatory* "Addicted to or characterized by a tendency to victimize or destroy others for one's own gain"—*American Heritage*] **:** state manufactured and ruled by snools addicted to predation. *Cockaludicrous Comment:*

> Man is the hunter; woman is his game.
> The sleek and shining creatures of the chase,
> We hunt them for the beauty of their skins;
> They love us for it and we ride them down.
>   —Alfred lord Tennyson, "The Princess," pt. V

pre-occupation ◑ *n* [derived fr. *praeoccupatio* act of seizing beforehand—*Webster's*] **:** method of reinforcing the State of Possession: patriarchal strategy of seizing women's Self-esteem, independence, vigor and vitality "beforehand," i.e., with the intent of permanently inhibiting Self-Realization; invasion and occupation of female bodies and

The inhabitants of the foreground, their activities and characteristics

minds through such means as incest, rape, enforced pregnancies, and the early implantation of such preoccupations as Self-doubt, anxiety, guilt, depression, and terror. *See* **passive voice** (w-w 3)

pre-possession ⁹ *n* : the final solution intended for women under fixocracy: the condensation and freezing of female be-ing; possession before a woman Realizes her Original Movement in be-ing

presbot ○ *n* : the president as he appears on television: the Talking Head of State; the president as robot: mechanical imitation of a political leader capable of experiencing emotion and thought processes. *Example par excellence:* Ronald Reagan

prestige ⁹ *n* ["*archaic:* a conjurer's trick: ILLUSION, DECEPTION"— *Webster's*] : prominence achieved through the use of trickery, illusion, deception, and sham; status and esteem accorded to the most pretentious, perverted, and "preferred" prigs and institutions of patriarchy

prick ○ *n* ["PENIS—usu. considered vulgar"—*Webster's*] : a self-important member of the thrusting throng; an especially contemptible and disagreeable dick. *See* **dick** (w-w 3)

pricker ○ *n* ["one who pricks suspected witches to determine their guilt or innocence"—*Webster's*] : professional torturer of women in the perpetual witchcraze which is patriarchy

prickery ○ *n* : the place where pricks and prickers preside, frequently as presidents and chairmen of the bored

priest ○ *n* [derived fr. Gk *presbyteros* priest, elder, older, compar. of *presbys* old man—*Webster's*] : a member of any of the hierarchies/liararchies of patriarchy, charged with Holy Orders to perform the necrophilic rites of the sadosociety. *Examples:* priests of religion; priests of science; priests of medicine; priests of war

priest-ridden *adj* ["controlled or oppressed by a priest"—*Webster's*] : controlled, oppressed, repressed, and depressed by priests. *Examples:* nuclear science and industry; the city of Boston; Italy

prig *n* [³*prig* "THIEF, PILFERER"; also ⁴*prig* "*archaic:* FOP, BUCK, DANDY"—*Webster's*] : a snool who steals women's words, ideas, and energy, foppishly displaying these as his own. *Example:* F. Scott Fitzgerald[82]

pseudobonding ⁹ *n* : negative mirror image of genuine feminist bonding, arising from weakness, fear, guilt, and male-identification

pseudofeminism ○ *n* : *See* **plastic feminism; pseudobonding** (w-w 3)

pseudopassion ○ *n* : feeling which is a product of patriarchy and which paralyzes its victim, containing and concealing Female Fire, true desire. *See* **plastic passion; potted passion** (w-w 3)

pseudovirtue ○ *n* : habit which is a product of patriarchy and which functions as a substitute/replacement for genuine Virtue. *See* **plastic virtue; potted virtue** (w-w 3)

The inhabitants of the foreground, their activities and characteristics

psycho-ology ○ *n* : disturbed and disturbing area of academentia: field favored by woman-haters. *Cockaludicrous Comment:*

> Who can look fairly at the bitterness, the hatefulness, the sadistic cruelty of Adolf Hitler without wondering what Hitler's mother did to him that he now repays to millions of other helpless ones? We must remind ourselves again and again that the men by whom women are frustrated are the grown-up sons of mothers who were chiefly responsible for the personality of those sons.
> —Karl Menninger[83]

Pure Act ○ : the perpetual performance of the eternally upright god/rod and his supporting cast. *See* **Mystery of Man, the** (w-w 1)

pure thrust ○ : the monodimensional track characteristic of all phallic arguments. *Example:* "The thrust of my argument is that we must destroy the earth in order to save it," from an interview with Professor Edward Feller of Lawrence Liverless Laboratories, *Technology Yesterday,* Dec. 31, 1999, a.d.

pyrophobia ○ *n* : craven snoolish fear of Elemental/Female Fire, manifested in such atrocities as witchburnings, widow burnings, electroshock "therapies," the dropping of napalm, and the strategic planning of nuclear holocaust

Queen of Heaven, pope as ○ : worldly, airborne representative of the patriarchal "Great Mother"; flamboyant Queen of Queens: the Flying Queen. *See* **drag queen, pope John Paul Too as** (w-w 3)

rake ○ *n* ["(abbrev. of RAKEHELL) a man of loose habits and immoral character; an idle dissipated man of fashion"—*O.E.D.*] **:** This definition has been awarded *Websters'* Intergalactic Seal of Approval. *Example:* Teddy Kennedy

re-acting ☽ **:** "fighting back" against the phallocrats on their own terms, in their own terms; becoming absorbed in boys' games—their rules and roles; moving in fixed circles, repeating and replicating male-ordered models endlessly

re-covering ☽ **:** a function of patriarchal re-search (including pseudo-feminist re-search): the systematic and repeated covering of phallocracy's global rapism and of the history of women's oppression, achievements, and unquenchable Genius. *See* ¹**re-search** (w-w 3); **erasure; rapism; reversal** (w-w 1)

re-form ☽ *n* **:** the deformation by fix-masters of women's bodies and minds, under the guises of improvement, health, beauty, sanity, and morality

re-hearsing ☽ **:** an elementary strategy of patriarchal conditioning: the endless reiteration by snoolmasters of refrains that restrain women's Selves; the enforced repeating of these refrains by women: a process that converts female bodies/minds into hearses/coffins—false selves which are containers of confined Selves. *Example:* the transmission of necromantic advice such as "Be a good listener," "Let him win," "It's *his* career that counts."

¹**re-search** ☽ *n* **:** a function of patriarchal scholarship (including pseudofeminist scholarship): circular academented game of hide-and-seek: pseudosearch for information which, in fact, has been systematically hidden by previous re-searchers, and which, when found, is then ritually re-covered by succeeding investigators, only to be re-discovered and re-covered endlessly: syndrome often described by Catty Crones as the "kitty litter box syndrome of patriarchal scholarship." *See* **re-covering** (w-w 3). *Compare* **Hag-ography; Searcher** (w-w 2)

²**re-search** *n* **:** "search" for the screamingly obvious which is then paraded as the latest scientific information. *Example:* the experiments of scientific re-searcher Harry Harlow, who induces mental disorders in infant monkeys by putting them into *complete* isolation for up to twelve months. Such experiments "prove" that touch and companionship are necessary for normal social development.[84]

re-sister [◑] *n* : the pseudosister, who stands against her Sister; reversed imitation, mirror image, "life-like" reproduction of a genuine Sister. *See* **plastic feminism** (W-W 3)

re-source [◑] *n* : derivative "source," regarded in academentia as authoritative and Original, recognized and used by Hag-ologists as containing fragments of and clues to our own stolen heritage. *Example: Webster's Third New International Dictionary of the English Language. See* **Hag-ology** (W-W 2)

restorationist syndrome [○] : basic syndrome of the sado-sublimated society, involving annihilation of Elemental reality, replacement of this reality with elementary imitations/substitutes, and the consequent obligatory gratitude of the victims of this syndrome to the sado-sublimators, coupled with their embrace of the re-formed "reality" inflicted upon them. *See* **Sadospiritual Syndrome: sado-sublimation** (W-W 1)

re-turning, phallocentric [◑] : "living" out, dying out the paradigmatic patriarchal myth of separation and return; processing in circles endlessly. *Cockaludicrous Comment:*

> A time for killing,
> A time for healing;
> A time for knocking down,
> A time for building. . . .
> A time for loving,
> A time for hating;
> A time for war,
> A time for peace.
> —Pete Seeger, re-turning to Eccles. 3:1–8[85]

re-verberator [○] *n* : species of dickspeaker: repeater of verbiage; clone-speaking inhabitant of babblespheres; little Sir Echo of "experts"; reflector of received opinions. *Example:* Hojatoleslam Akbar Hashemi Rafsanjani, speaker of the Iranian parliament, who in 1986 reiterated during prayers in Tehran that there is "no such thing as equality between men and women." Rafsanjani added that the measures being used to force all women into the Islamic veil are relatively mild and could be harsher.[86]

re-versing [◑] : the numbing/dumbing of potential Spell-Speakers through enforced rote memorizing and reciting of patriarchal reversals, as in sexist nursery rhymes, patriarchal poetry, "history" lessons, bible/babble lessons

ripper $^\circ$ *n* : hacker, snuffer, slasher. *Examples:* Jack the Ripper; Dr. Robert Battey, gynecologist who in 1873 invented "female castration" (removal of healthy ovaries as a cure for "insanity")

robotitude $^\bullet$ *n* : hollow/solid depthless state of servitude marked by the reduction of life to mechanical motion; state characterized by marking time hopelessly, by pure repetition of mechanical gestures. *Compare* **Roboticide** (w-w 2)

sado-euphemism *n* : a common feature of dickspeak: the use of deceptive terms and phrases to hide lethal intent. *Examples* **a:** *nuclear exchange* (for nuclear war) **b:** *termination with extreme prejudice* (for government-sponsored assassination)[87] **c:** *medical duties* (for the role assigned to animals who are tortured in laboratories)[88] **d:** *making love* (for rape)[89]

sadofeminism $^\circ$ *n* : a species of plastic feminism marked by malignant hatred of and/or indifference to women and characterized by scapegoating, sadomasochism (both physical and psychic) and attempts to destroy female creativity and bonding: the fathers' final solution to the problem of female bonding/be-ing. *See* **plastic feminism** (w-w 3)

sado-hagiography $^\circ$ *n* **1** : biographies of "saints": writings depicting scenes of masochistic wallowing in humiliation, torture, and martyrdom: "inspirational" writings designed to elicit the reader's approval, admiration, and emulation **2** : the common romance; the common soap opera. *Compare* **Hag-ography** (w-w 2)

sado-religion $^\circ$ *n* : worship of a sadist god; religion characterized by bondage and discipline, dominance and submission, and the forcing of women to their knees

sado-symbolism $^\circ$ *n* : the perversion/manipulation of Archaic symbols for the purposes of gynocidal/biocidal propaganda. *Example:* the necrophilic conversion/perversion of the Tree of Life into the torture cross—a dead body hanging on dead wood. *N.B.:* Clearly many other *sado-* words could be listed and defined. Any Crone is free to compose such words whenever she deems this necessary or appropriate.

sapper $^\circ$ *n* : *See* **fetal identification syndrome** (w-w 3)

schoolman *n* : common snoolmaster: re-searcher, re-coverer, reverberator; abominable arbiter of taste and merit. *Examples* **a:** the

224

nameless nobody who in his "review" of Aphra Behn's works when they were republished in the nineteenth century sneered:

> If Mrs. Behn is read at all, it can only be from a love of impurity for its own sake, for rank indecency . . . even in her own day, Mrs. Behn's works had a scandalous reputation . . . it is a pity her books did not rot with her bones. That they should now be disinterred from the obscurity into which they had fallen is surely inexcusable.[90]

b: Granville Hicks, who foolishly assessed Sarah Orne Jewett as "merely a New England Old Maid"[91]

See **usage, phallic** (w-w 3)

The inhabitants of the foreground, their activities and characteristics

separatism, phallic ○ **:** disorder at the core of patriarchal consciousness, engendered by phallocentric myths, ideologies, and institutions: state of disconnection from Biophilic purposefulness, exemplified in such atrocities as the worldwide rape of women, the rape of the Third World, and the soulless manipulation and torture of laboratory animals

sham ○ *n* **:** shameless imposter: TRICKER, FAKER, FRAUD. *See* **Uncle Sham** (w-w 3)

she-male (Janice G. Raymond[92]) *n* **:** male-to-constructed-female transsexual: an artifactual female produced by the he-mothers of "the transsexual empire"

sick transit [derived fr. *sic transit gloria mundi* (L): so passes away the glory of the world—*Webster's Collegiate*, Foreign Words and Phrases] **:** snoolish pseudojourneying: walking/talking in circles, flapping/flopping indecisively, going Nowhere. *Examples:* religious processions, academic processions, etc. *See* **deadly sins of the fathers: processions** (w-w 1)

sir *n* ["*Archaic.* A gentleman of rank"—*American Heritage*] **:** a rank gentleman

Sir Echoes, little : yabbering, yammering yes-men; servile, simpering sycophants. *Cockaludicrous Comment:*

> In language that is echoed again and again in the speeches of others, Cardinal Ratzinger describes the church as "a mystery."[93]

sirly *adj* [obsolete alter. of *surly* (at *surly*)—*Webster's*] : arrogant, domineering, ill-natured, churlish, esp. applied to snools of high status. *Example:* Alfred lord Tennyson, who scribbled:

> Woman is the lesser man, and all thy
>   passions, match'd with mine,
> Are as moonlight unto sunlight and as
>   water unto wine[94]

sir-reverence *n* ["*obs*—used as an expression of apology before a statement that might be taken as presumptuous or offensive. . . . *archaic* human excrement: FECES . . . a lump of human excrement"—*Webster's*] : used by Scolds as an expression of disdain before a statement that is meant to be taken as mocking or offensive

Sir Sirens of Siredom, little ᗬ : sweet-talking spookers who seduce women into the State of Sleeping Death. *Example:* Paul Anka, popular crooner of the pathetic pregnancy propaganda/anti-abortion song "Having My Baby" (circa 1975)

snarl ᗬ *n* **1** : a species of nonknot which is without harmony, order, sense, and which is characterized by inherent confusion **2** : sound made by a snool giving vent to anger or irritation in snide, sirly language

sneak ○ *n* : a mean-spirited, paltry, despicable, shifty, shabby, underhanded tricker

sniffler ○ *n* : *See* **snivelard** (w-w 3)

snitch ○ *n* : a sneak thief, especially one who steals women's money, jobs, and ideas: PRIG. *See* **prig** (w-w 3)

snivelard *n* ["*Obs. rare.* A sniveler"—*O.E.D.*] : a snool who snivels or whines. *Examples* **a:** Martin Luther, who whined: "God created Adam lord of all living creatures, but Eve spoiled it all."[95] **b:** "Tricky Dick" Nixon, who sniveled: "You won't have Dick Nixon to kick around anymore."

snivelization (Diana Beguine[96]) *n* : society and culture composed of and by snivelards: the white man's civilization: his "burden" inflicted upon the rest of the world. *Cockaludicrous Comment:*

> Take up the White Man's burden.
>   —Rudyard Kipling[97]

> If we have any true love for the stars, planets, the rest of
> Creation, we must do everything we can to keep white men
> away from them. They who have appointed themselves our
> representatives to the rest of the universe. They who have
> never met any new creature without exploiting, abusing, or
> destroying it. They who say we poor (white included) and
> colored and female and elderly blight neighborhoods, while
> they blight worlds.
>
> What they have done to the Old, they will do to the New.
>
> Under the white man every star would become a South
> Africa, every planet a Vietnam.
> —Alice Walker[98]

The inhabitants of the foreground, their activities and characteristics

> Civilization brought measles, whooping cough, chicken
> pox, diphtheria, small pox, tuberculosis, and syphilis.
> —Anne Cameron[99]

snooker ° *n* : a cock who snooks, especially one who pries about while sniffing and smelling: SNEAK. *Example:* any agent of elementary intelligence, e.g., FBI agent, KGB agent

snool ° *n* [*snool n* "*Scot* a cringing person"; also *snool v* "to reduce to submission: COW, BULLY . . . CRINGE, COWER"—*Webster's*; also *snool n* "a tame, abject, or mean-spirited person"—*O.E.D.*] : normal inhabitant of sadosociety, characterized by sadism and masochism combined; stereotypic hero and/or saint of the sadostate. *Examples:* Adam; saint Paul; the Marquis de Sade. *Canny Comment:*

> Remember all Men would be tyrants if they could.
> —Abigail Adams (1776)[100]

snool-daze *n* : common, everyday stupor characteristic of the sadosociety, the State of Stupefaction. *See* **Numbed State** (w-w 3)

snooldom ° *n* : the state in which snools rule, and snools are the rule: BOREDOM, FOOLDOM, DOOMDOM

snoolette (Nancy Kelly[101]) *n* : species of fembot: one who identifies with snools, foolishly embracing their roles and behaviors, endorsing and joining their games

snooltide (Linda Barufaldi) *n* : christmas season: snoolish replacement/displacement of Winter Solstice; tidy packaging of the great Heathen festivities surrounding Yuletide. *See* **christmas spirit** (w-w 3)

snot boy ° *n* : a common, typically inept, incomplete, insufficient, and inadequate companion. *Canny Comment:*

> Copper Woman was living with Snot Boy, the incomplete mannikin. . . . She taught the small strange creature as much as she could, but he never really seemed to learn properly. . . . When he built a fire it was either too hot or not hot enough, and often he would burn himself. When he was through using a thing, he would leave it, never remembering to put it away where he could find it again, and sometimes he would forget to come home when the meal was ready, then would complain bitterly if his food was overdone or cold. Copper Woman would tease him, make him forget his ill humor, laugh with him, and often she would sing for him. . . .
> —Anne Cameron [102]

N.B.: In this creation story related by native women of Vancouver Island, the incomplete mannikin, Snot Boy, was formed from the tears, mucus, and saliva of Copper Woman, who was alone on the island. This story is a Nag-noteworthy contrast to such creation myths as the biblical story of Eve's "birth" from Adam.

snudge ° *n* ["a miser, a mean, avaricious fellow"—*O.E.D.*] : species of lackey whose ontological impotence motivates acts of aggression, acquisition, and gross greed. *Examples:* archetypical american millionaires, vatican bankers and their bosses, the mafia

snuffer ° *n* **1** : a sex killer, esp. a producer of a "snuff film"—one in which an actress is actually tortured and murdered before the camera **2** : a professional hatchet-man, a physician, surgeon, politician, scientist, or military expert who kills in order to "cure." *Cockaludicrous Comment:*

> We had to destroy the village in order to save it.
> —U.S. military officer, Vietnam

Soap Opera Syndrome ⁹ : syndrome symptomatic of feminitude and its derivative, plastic feminism: therapeutic syndrome whose one basic Program can be entitled "How to Deal with Relationships"; complex of scripts which program women to be perpetual actresses, playing and identifying with clichéd roles in tidy timeworn scripts; syndrome reinforcing self-obsession, luv, and lack of motivation for Radical Feminist work

spiritbindings ⁹ *n* : products of sadospiritual fixers: sadoconditionings that tie up, tie back, and tie down the spirits of women and animals; fixes intended to maim and paralyze the psychic powers of Mediums. *Example:* taboos against Witchcraft. *See* **mindbindings** (w-w 3)

spooking ⁹ **:** the fabrication of confusion, disorientation, Self-alienation, and psychic numbing in women through the tactics of sadosublimination. *See* **Passive Voice** (w-w 3); **Sadospiritual Syndrome: sado-sublimination** (w-w 1)

Stag-nation ⁹ *n* **1 :** the eternally atrophied "Afterlife" of the Happy Dead Ones **2 :** nation governed by stag parties; the perpetually stagnant state

The inhabitants of the foreground, their activities and characteristics

Standstill Society ○ **:** *See* **Stag-nation** (w-w 3)

State of Animated Death ⁹ **:** the beautified, mummified state; the carefully arranged, made-up, wound-up world of numbots

State of Appeasement ○ **:** state in which women are bought off with things, praise, luv, "protection," assurances of "belonging"

State of Atrocity ⁹ **:** state in which atrocities are normalized, ritualized, repeated, legitimized, sacralized: PATRIARCHY. *See* **Sado-Ritual Syndrome** (w-w 1)

State of Degradation ○ **1 :** state in which women are the universal low caste within all castes, classes, and races: PATRIARCHY; state characterized by the all-pervasive, overt and subliminal negation of Self-esteem in women and all oppressed people **2 :** state marked by the continuous debasement of animals and all Elemental life

State of Emergency ○ **:** state in which some male-ordered activity is always made to appear prior in importance to the liberation and Self-Realization of women: State of Perpetual Distraction

State of Enmity ⁹ **1 :** the perpetually warring state of patriarchy **2 :** the man-made conditions that perpetuate horizontal violence among those oppressed by patriarchy

State of Estrangement ⁹ **:** the alienating state of patriarchy, from which Self-Realizing women choose to depart, Naming ourSelves Aliens, forming the Outsiders' Society—the Company of the Wild and the Strange

State of Fear ⁹ **:** state created, supported, and legitimated by ceaseless terrorism: phallocracy, snooldom. *Cockaludicrous Comment:*

For love befits the man; fear befits the woman. As for the slave, not only fear is befitting him, but also trembling.
    —saint Jerome [103]

Canny Comment:

> . . . one of the earliest forms of male bonding must have been the gang rape of one woman by a band of marauding men. This accomplished, rape became not only a male prerogative, but man's basic weapon of force against woman, the principal agent of his will and her fear. . . . It [rape] is nothing more or less than a conscious process of intimidation by which *all men* keep *all women* in a state of fear.
>   —Susan Brownmiller [104]

N.B.: In addition to those already defined, there are many other phallic States. These include:

State of:		
	Bondage	Rapism
	Depression	Restoration
	Feminitude	Reversal
	Fixation	Robotitude
	Fraternity	Schizophrenia
	Genocide	Separation
	Grateful Dead, the	Servitude
	Gynocide	Severance
	Holy Wedlock, Deadlock	Siege
	Lechery	Sleeping Death
	Living Dead, the	Stag-nation
	Martyrdom	Staledom
	Obsession	Sublimated Servitude
	Patriarchal Paralysis	Total Tokenism
	Possession	War, et cetera
	Racism	

sunday/sonday *n* : day devoted to Godfather, Son, & Company; day which induces and perpetuates the State of Depression: homeday, ho-humday

suckseed *v* : to conform to the role requirements for an up-and-coming young snool

the/rapist ⁰ *n* : a psycho-ologist who practices what he preaches/teaches. *See* **psycho-ology** (w-w 3)

the-ologian ○ *n* : species of schoolman: specialist in the most traditional field of academentia (formerly known as "sacred science"): one
versed in the-ology, the -ology of all -ologies

tidy bore ○ : time-keeper/space-keeper of bore-ocracy; waster of Life-
Time; a neat and necrophilic snool who attempts to break Elemental
rhythms, to contain the flow of Tidal Time

tidydom ○ *n* : the domain where individuality is cleaned up/erased:
CLONEDOM, CLOCKOCRACY. *N.B.:* For Canny commentary on tidydom, see the novel *The Stepford Wives* by Ira Levin (1972) as well as the
film based on the book.

tidy torture ○ : regime of endless tidiness imposed on women in the
State of Servitude: the Self-containment imposed by the inescapable
demands of the traditional feminine occupations and preoccupations,
e.g., housework, clerical labor, childcare, nursing (paid and unpaid),
personal maintenance, etc. *Canny Comment:*

> ———Achieve. Assist. Balance the budget. Balance the meals.
> Bandage cuts. Bawl in hiding. Blanche. Buy. Care for. Chill.
> Clear. Console. Cook. Cut out. Cut up. Darn. Do the dishes.
> Drive. Dry. Dry dishes. Economize. Educate. Empty the ash-
> trays. Empty the garbage cans. . . . Rinse. Roast. Rub. Serve.
> Set table. Sew. Shout. Shut (yourself) up. Stop (yourself)
> shouting. Sweep. Tidy. Use up leftovers. Wash. Wax. ETC.
>   —Louky Bersianik [105]

token eraser ○ : a woman who (often unwittingly) aids and abets the
erasers/obliterators of the experiences, perceptions, creative potential,
and actual achievements of her own kind. *Example:* a female academic
who uncritically teaches the grammar, history, literature, philosophy, et
cetera—of man

token torturer ❾ : a woman who (often unwittingly) pleases her masters by selling out her own kind, increasing the patriarchs' pleasure by
performing acts which are less than gentlemanly, thus obscuring the
identity of the primary torturers

tom, dick, and harry ○ ["persons taken at random: the common run
of humanity: EVERYBODY, EVERYONE"—*Webster's*] : the three persons
of a popocratic vulgar trinity; the common run of pops: NOBODY, NO
ONE. *See* **dick; tomfool** (W-W 3)

tomfool *n* ["one lacking in sense or good judgment: a great fool: BLOCKHEAD"—*Webster's*] : the first person of the vulgar trinity—tom, dick, and harry: Tom Fool

totaled woman ☽ : [*total woman* "(one who) caters to her man's special quirks, whether it be in salads, sex, or sports"—Marabel Morgan, *The Total Woman*] : one conditioned to cater compulsively to her master's "special" quirks, whether it be in salads, sex, or sports. *Sad Commentaries:*

WORD-WEB
THREE

> It is only when a woman surrenders her life to her husband, reveres and worships him, and is willing to serve him, that she becomes really beautiful to him.
> —Marabel Morgan [106]

> Try to spend a little time each day visualizing Jesus coming in the door from work. Then see yourself walking up to him, embracing him. Say to Jesus, "It's good to have you home, Nick."
> —Ruth Carter Stapleton [107]

tricker *n* [*trick* "*slang:* the customer of a prostitute"—*Webster's*] **1** : the consumer of a prostitute; one who practices the oldest profession: defrauding, tricking, using/abusing women, while creating the illusion that females are the manipulators/seducers/criminals as well as the beneficiaries of this cockocratic exchange/game **2** : common pricker, fraud, fake

Uncle Sham : the American Stag-nation personified

unctuous undertakers ○ : oily entrepreneurs of the necropolitan society. *Examples:* the mormon corporate elite; arab oil sheiks

usage, phallic : characteristic phallic practice of mistreating Others—women, words, and all of nature; unrelenting abuse intended to make women and animals "used to" such usage/abusage. *Cockaludicrous Comment:*

> We will fly women into space and use them the same way we use them on earth—for the same purpose.
> —Former U.S. astronaut James Lovell [108]

vampirism, veiled ☽ : essential component of the Mystery of Man: classic fetal-identified syndrome/scenario of snooldom: disguised necrophilic assimilation of Female/Elemental energy; the concealed sapping of Life Forces/Sources. *Examples* **a:** the draining of women's energy by husbands, fathers, and father figures, under the guise of love, as Named by Sylvia Plath in her poem "Daddy":

> If I've killed one man, I've killed two—
> The vampire who said he was you
> And drank my blood for a year,
> Seven years, if you want to know.
> Daddy, you can lie back now.

> There's a stake in your fat black heart . . .
> —Sylvia Plath [109]

b: the draining of the Earth's sources by technocrats, such as oil magnates, strip miners, animal "harvesters." *N.B.:* Veiled vampirism is legitimated by the "blood"-drinking syndrome of christian ritual, in which the Witch's Cauldron is ripped off, reduced, reversed into the chalice of the priest (Dracula), who pretends to change wine into blood and then drinks this and obliges others to do so.[110]

Vapor State ○ **:** ghostly state created by the process of sado-subliming; State consisting of the phantoms, delusions, specters which are the archetypes produced by patriarchs to legitimate the sadostate: State of Illusion/Confusion/Depression. *See* **Sadospiritual Syndrome: the sado-sublime** (W-W 1)

verbicide ○ *n* **:** form of biocide: the systematic murder of words: the reduction of living words to the condition of mere noises echoing each other through the hollow world of the hollow men. *See* **logocide** (W-W 3)

verbigeration ○ *n* ["continual repetition of stereotyped phrases"— *Webster's*] **:** a form of verbicide: the incessant, depressing, thought-stopping babble of babblespheres

Virulent State ○ **:** state characterized by viral/virile vice and viciousness: the Toxic State, the state in which poisons are everywhere. *Canny Comment:*

> A pretty girl in this society
> Is judged by looks alone.
> What you see on her face
> Is often the waste
> Of chemicals developed for the war.
> —Song to be sung to the tune of "A Pretty Girl Is Like a Melody"[111]

wangler *n* [*wangle* "to resort to trickery, makeshift, or devious methods. . . . to persuade or convince by cunning or devious methods"—*Webster's*] **:** species of fraud: a snool who works through deception, insinuation, and trickery to undermine a woman's reputation and position. *Cockaludicrous Comment:*

> "Well yes, she's published thirteen books, but we shouldn't promote her. She is emotionally unstable, unfriendly, doesn't smile enough, and never wears a skirt."
> —Professor Wadfellow Wangler to Professor Yessir, conversation overheard and reported by Ms. Wild Cat

wantwit *n* ["a person wanting wit: FOOL"—*Webster's*] **:** dangerous species of lackey: one who wants/lacks the most essential qualities of sense and intelligence: a necessary cog in the negatively spinning wheels of foolocracy. *Example:* Thomas K. Jones, deputy undersecretary of defense for strategic and nuclear forces, calming the populace's fears about the dangers of nuclear war (1982):

> Everybody's going to make it if there are enough shovels to go around. Dig a hole, cover it with a couple of doors, and then throw three feet of dirt on top. It's the dirt that does it.[112]

wasters *n* ["one that lays waste or ruins: DESOLATER, DESTROYER, DEVASTATOR"—*Webster's*] **:** the celebrated conquerors, missionaries, and heroes of civilization/snivelization. *Example:* Julius Caesar, who boasted:

> I came, I saw, I conquered.

Canny Comment:

> The male . . . has made of the world a shitpile.
> —Valerie Solanas[113]

Weirdless *adj* ["*Scottish:* Destined to ill fortune, ill-fated, unlucky"—*O.E.D.*] **:** marked by misfortune: said of those who fail to heed the wisdom of Witches and Weirds

white out *v* **:** to erase, obliterate, destroy. *See* **erasure** (w-w 1)

whiteout *n* **:** essential strategy of civilization/snivelization: attempted erasure, blotting out, negation by white men of all Otherness. *Example:* multiple massacres of the Aboriginal inhabitants of Australia by the white plug-uglies who brought snivelization to their continent, wrought havoc on the land, and continue to slaughter the animals, incarcerate Native people in reservations, and negate their heritage

windbag *n* : a fellow who bellows; one afflicted with chronic logorrhea: a blathering, blatant, flagrantly flatulent fool. *Example:* Martin Luther, who blathered in 1531:

> Men have broad shoulders and narrow hips, and accordingly they possess intelligence. Women have narrow shoulders and broad hips. Women ought to stay at home; the way they were created indicates this, for they have broad hips and a wide fundament to sit upon, keep house, and bear and raise children.[114]

The inhabitants of the foreground, their activities and characteristics

N.B.: It is Nag-noteworthy that Luther invented his doctrine of grace while seated in the privy.

Yahweh & Son ◉ : mythic paradigm for any corporation of cockocracy, for any all-male family business

Yessir, Professor ○ **1** : common academented snool **2** : common response of a common academented snool to a colleague of higher rank

THE THIRD PHASE | *Appendicular Webs*

WOVEN BY MARY DALY

APPENDICULAR WEB ONE

Exposing elementary terms and phrases: mummies, dummies, anti-biotics, and reversals

Websters are painfully aware that the foreground is filled with deadly distortions/simulations of Elemental reality. In the *Wickedary*, these foreground fabrications are Named *elementaries*. According to the sixteenth-century philosopher and alchemist Paracelsus, *elementaries* are artificial beings, created in the invisible worlds by man himself. They are of an evil, destructive nature, resulting from corruption of character or degeneration of faculties and powers.[1]

Springing off from this insight, the *Wickedary* defines the noun *elementaries* as "simulations of and planned replacements for the Elemental, the Wild; fabrications which distort experience of the Elements and which are largely invisible by reason of being all-pervasive . . ." (*Word-Web One*). Elementaries include the omnipresent solid products of phallotechnology (such as nuclear missiles), the poisonous fumes and radioactive emissions of such technology, as well as the transmissions of the popular media and other carriers of dis-eased traditional assumptions, such as the professions of popocracy/flopocracy. The adjective *elementary* is here defined as "characterized by artificiality, lack of depth, aura, and interconnectedness with living be-ing; marked by a derivative and parasitic relation to Elemental reality."

Both of these definitions apply to elementary terms* and phrases, which are similar to other elementary phenomena. They are simula-

---

*These are here Named *terms*, rather than *words*, because they are dead words that terminate thought.

239

tions of and substitutes for Elemental, Wild words. They mendaciously mediate our experience. Becoming more invisible as they become more pervasive, they are like poisonous fumes and radioactive emissions permeating the atmosphere. They function to terminate the life of the mind. Elementary terms are fabrications of phallocrats, characterized by lack of depth, radiance, resonance, harmonious interconnectedness with living be-ing. Their relationship to living words is parasitic.

It is important to understand that the process by which these terms and phrases are fabricated and perpetuated is starkly different from Crone-logical creativity. The latter is a process of Dis-covering, Re-membering. Wild words are New in a way that is not reducible to the inorganic "newness" of elementary terms, for Crone-identified creativity involves Acts of participation in Be-ing. This is what Websters mean when we say that we Muse words. That is, our inspirations to speak/write New Words are rooted in intuitions of Original integrity. We attain varying degrees of success, but the intent is to be true to such intuitions of Archaic wholeness.

The *Wickedary* is a book of Crone-created New Words. These are New because the Acts of Dis-covering which they reflect participate in the Tidal Time of woman-identified experience. Some of these words directly Name Elemental reality and experience. *Nag-Gnostic,* for example, is a combination of two ancient words reclaimed to describe the creative intellectual experience of women on the Boundary of patriarchy. Other New Words Name the pseudorealities of the foreground from the perspective of the Background, for example, *phallocracy.*

In contrast to New/Archaic Naming, the manufacture of elementary terms legitimates the pseudorealities of the foreground and is itself an obscene multiplication of foreground fabrications. The endless production/reproduction of foreground-legitimating labels results in the formation of films of deception by means of which the patriarchs cover Elemental reality. The proliferation of terms such as *plant,* used to describe a nuclear facility, and *bug,* used to label an electronic listening device, together with the man-made horrors which these represent, constitutes a deadland of dead ends, a state of terminal dis-ease.

the soullessness of the elementary world and the proliferation of elementary terms

The sadorulers are driven to destroy women, animals, trees, air, water—whatever they are able to touch. They are obsessed with substituting elementary artifacts for Natural be-ing. Clearly such an agenda must include the destruction and replacement of Elemental words, that is, words that Name Elemental reality. For the phallocrats fear all reminders of Elemental powers with which they fail to cooperate. Such reminders are ineffably odious to the doomers. As long as Elemental realities and the words that Name these are around, Deep Memories are accessible, at least to those whose senses have not been completely dulled.

The necrophilic dullers/doomers lust to destroy the Wild realities of the physical/spiritual Elemental world, including Wild words, because they are Alive, and Living/Ensouled be-ing perpetuates Living Memory. Only mass murder can reassure the necro-apocalyptic Nothing-lovers who dread confrontation with the knowledge of their own ineffable perversion and impotence.

Destruction of Elemental nature is inherently insufficient to reassure the doomers, however. They must also fill the void with replacements, immuring those who might still Re-member, walling us off from Elemental connections and Sources. This immurement of potential Re-memberers in prisons of man-made things—simulations/replacements of Wild reality—is also the manufacture of an infrastructure that can give apparent plausibility to the senescent symbol system of the sado-society. Moreover, this symbol system has as one of its chief means of propagation the continual fabrication of conglomerates of elementary terms.

The proliferation of elementary terms functions to destroy the ability of victims of phallotechnocracy/fellowtechnocracy to Name Wild reality, or what is left of that reality. At the same time, the incessant destruction and replacement of the Elemental world corrodes the ability of this society's inhabitants/captives to recognize and be in Touch with even the remnants of Deep Memory. The replacement and covering of wetlands with shopping malls, the conversion of wildlife refuges and sanctuaries into hunting grounds, the transformation of rivers and lakes into lethal soups of radioactive wastes and pesticides, the embedding of deadly subliminal messages into ads, news photographs, record albums, and television images—together with the social imperative to watch television—all of these phenomena exemplify the sadosociety's obscene determination to fabricate a soulless world.

Since this spread of soullessness is facilitated by and indeed requires the proliferation of elementary terms, which dull the capacity for hearing and speaking Wild words, it is essential that Websters consider such terms. Elementary terms basely fall into four classes. The task at hand is to expose each of these types in turn.

I. archetypal elementary terms: mummies

Archetypal elementary terms are the most ancient and the most widespread elementary terms. They are also the most respectable according to the norms of the Numbed State. Consequently their elementary character is almost invisible.

Archetypal elementary terms can be seen as precursors and role models for the more recently devolved classes. They are mummy terms, whose role is to mummify minds and memories, ensuring habituation/adaptation to mummification and manufacturing an atmosphere in which latter-day elementaries can thrive. They are man-made Great Mummies, bringing forth death of the mind.

APPENDICULAR WEB ONE Archetypal mummy terms, such as *civilization, mystery, custom, forefathers, history,** are hammered into the heads of pupils in elementary schools—the base schools of snooldom—and they are reiterated in the halls of academentia. They are the stock-in-trade of snoolmasters, who are the pillars of pedantocracy. They have a tendency to stick together, and therefore often appear in blobs, for example, in textbooks and in pseudosacred texts. They also commonly appear in blobular formations in the mass media.

Time, a popular mummy magazine, provides ample examples of this phenomenon. For instance, droning of the "inspirational document" entitled "Message to the People of God," which was issued at the close of the 1985 extraordinary synod of roman catholic bishops, *Time* points out that the document called the church "the *mystery* of the *love* of *God present* in the *history* of *men* [emphases mine]."[2]

Each of the italicized terms cited can be recognized by Eye-biting Spinsters as an archetypal mummy. *Mystery* has been exposed in *Preliminary Web One*. The elementary character of the term *love* (discussed in *Word-Web Three* under *luv*), particularly when it is combined with *God,* is self-evident. To Websters, *God* also is a self-exposing mummy. The term *present* in this context clearly has nothing to do with Real Presence. Moreover, *history*—as even Henry Ford recognized long ago—"is bunk." Finally, the term *men,* pretending in this context to refer to both sexes, is a pseudogeneric, falsely inclusive mummy term.

When Websters examine the conglomerate, i.e., the blob, formed by the combining of these terms in the churchly document cited above, we notice that such an amalgamation of mummies functions to scramble and ultimately to erase all genuine thought processes, replacing these with the verbigeration of babblespheres. When many such blobs/clumps

---

*Websters have assessed some of these archetypal elementary terms as unreclaimable, for example, *civilization, forefathers*. Others, such as *history* and *mystery,* require more complex consideration by Crones. When spoken within the parameters of the foreground, the elementary world, these are mere elementary terms. However, when Be-Spoken from the perspective of the Background, the Elemental world, they can be transmuted into real words. Thus *History* can be used by Crones in a Crone-logical context to refer to Crone-ology. *Mystery* can be converted into a Wicked word, as in the phrase *Mystery of Man* (see *Preliminary Web One* and *Word-Web One*).

of elementary terms occur together, as they do in this "inspirational document," the resultant formations are blobs of blobs, or megablobs. The ill-logical consequence is utter stupefaction/stupification of the reader/hearer.

Such elementary formations are the building blobs/blocks of the elementary world of "ideas," manifested not only in official/officious ecclesiastical and government documents, but in all the other dead bodies of knowledge that one finds perpetually lying around in the State of the Living Dead.

Exposing elementary terms and phrases

Archetypal elementary terms and phrases (mummies) are not usually difficult for Websters to detect. They are terms very commonly used in snooldom to describe or legitimate elementary phenomena from an elementary point of view. Both the context and the usage of the term point to its identity as mummy. When snoolmasters drone of *research,* for example, the context is the halls/walls of academented learning. The usual purpose of the term's usage is clear: to dignify and legitimate the senescent circles of re-covering and re-searching the same data endlessly, while giving the impression that something "new" is happening. A Crone listening with her Inner Ear can actually Hear *research* saying "search again . . . and again." (See **re-search,** *Word-Web Three.*) Searchers do not re-search, but really Search.

Another commonly used mummy is *revelation.* The unctuous and dogmatic contexts in which utterances about *revelation* usually appear are enough to make the term suspect. A common dictionary definition, "something that is revealed by God to man" (*Webster's*), adds to the miasma of mystification surrounding the term. Women familiar with the workings of patriarchal religion know well enough about the usage of this term by men who think that "God" has revealed something to them. The etymology also is clue-laden for Hearing Hags, for it is derived from the Latin *re-* plus *velare.* Since *velare* means "to veil" and since *re-* can mean "again," it is not hard to hear *revelation* as "re-veiling." Of course, we are told that revelation has to do with "tearing back" the veil that shrouds mystery, but a Webster whose Labyrinthine Sense is unblocked can detect levels of meaning unintended for her ears.

The term *civilization* also illustrates the nasty character of archetypal mummies. This term has accrued to itself such a history of arrogance, aggression, and hypocrisy that it is hardly accurate to put defensive quotation marks around it when speaking of the depravity perpetrated in its name. There is no pure meaning of *civilization* that can be salvaged. This point is demonstrated in one stark sentence in *Daughters of Copper Woman,* in which Anne Cameron recounts some of the myths and history of the native women of Vancouver Island:

> Civilization brought measles, whooping cough, chicken pox, diphtheria, small pox, tuberculosis, and syphilis.[3]

And as that entire work demonstrates, it also brought rape, degradation, woman-loathing, loss of Deep Memory, devastation of the Wild, poverty, psychic numbing, death.

Although archetypal elementary terms are old, they are not at all Archaic. There is no Deep Memory, no Originality in them. They stop short, having no Background. Pretending depth that they do not possess, appearing capable of taking us back to our roots or to first principles or sources, they in fact block access to Origins. These terms are the priests—the old men—of the world of elementary terms. They are the forefathers of phoney words, manufacturing and guarding mysteries. As priests they are male mother terms—mummies. Capable only of mystification and empty display, they commonly lend themselves to *mummery,* that is, "a ridiculous, hypocritical, or pretentious ceremony, observance, or performance" (*Webster's*). They are pseudoshapeshifters; that is, they are shifty.*

Archetypal elementary terms are self-erasing. They leave no profound impression, although they do function to prevent Original profound impressions. Writing or speaking that is filled with blobs of these terms is ineffably unmemorable; it erases itself. A sign of their presence, that is, their presence of absence, is the sense of boredom and frustration which they inevitably elicit in Soothsayers, whose Senses are Alive.

These boring old priestly terms are not only the building blobs of archetypal civilization; they are also the silly putty that holds it together, that is, apart. Be-Witching women, who See/Hear through these terms, recognize that they are also the weapons of the demon wardens who try to block our Passage on the Labyrinthine Journey of Exorcism and Ecstasy that leads into and through the Background.

Since the more recently fabricated elementary terms are chips off these old blockheads, we can now turn our attention to the newcomers/novices/upstarts, examining them in the light of our understanding of their archetypal mummies. First in line among these elementary upstarts are those terms that are most unnaturally close to their mummies, that is, the dummies.

II. dummies: the look-alike elementary terms and phrases

Dummy terms are the ill-logical offspring and pupils of the elementary society that is served and represented by such mummies as those dis-

---

* Other ideal candidates for the rank rank of mummy are the following: *androgyny, authority, brotherhood, charity, custom, democracy, divinity, equality, family, femininity, fulfillment, fundamental, humanity, resource, revolution.* The term *candidate* is also a fine candidate for mummy status.

gustedly discussed above. The role of dummy terms can be understood from the following definition of *dummy:* "an imitation, copy, or likeness of something intended for use as a substitute: EFFIGY" (*Webster's*). Within the world of elementary terms, dummies can be seen as those terms formed and groomed to become copies and substitutes for Elemental words. Just as the elementary things to which dummies refer are warped imitations and replacements for Elemental realities (as nuclear power plants are replacements for plants which are living organisms), dummy terms, such as *plant,* are formed to look and sound the same as the words which they mimic and which they are ultimately intended to replace. Within the elementary world, these terms are valued for copying well. Insofar as they succeed in making the Elemental world recede from consciousness they are serving their purpose. They are functioning to block Deep Memory of Elemental words and Other realities. The attainment of this end requires the construction and use of two general types of dummy terms. Hence these basely fall into two main groups.

Exposing elementary terms and phrases

In the first group are phallotechnological terms and brand names which are elementary spin-offs from these. The following passage from *Science Digest* is replete with phallotechnological dummies:

> A computer installed in a warhead converts a dumb warhead into a smart warhead. Smart warheads have radar eyes and electronic brains.[4]

Another example is the use of the term *daughter* to refer to a radioactive decay product.[5] Moreover, a *breeder* reactor is a nuclear reactor that produces more nuclear fuel than it consumes while generating power.[6] An *air-breathing missile* is a missile with an engine requiring the intake of air for combustion of its fuel, as in a ramjet or turbojet.[7] Experts speak of *third-generation* nuclear technology.[8]

Dummy terms and phrases have been fabricated to copy words that Name intelligence and memory. We constantly hear the phrase *artificial intelligence.* The dummy term *memory* has worked its way into dictionaries. Thus the *American Heritage Dictionary* gives the following as one definition of *memory:* "a unit of a computer that preserves data for retrieval." A *head* is "a device which reads, records, or erases information on a storage medium."[9]

There are dummy phrases copying the names of seasons (*nuclear winter*) and other Elemental phenomena (*mushroom cloud*). Commercial products have dummy labels copying words for emotions (*Joy*), oceanic phenomena (*Tide*), celestial phenomena (*Comet*), fruit (*Apple, Macintosh*), animals (*Jaguar, Mustang*). The dummy of dummies, deserving the dummy award for decadence in the nineteen-eighties, is *Star Wars.*

In the second group of dummies are terms intended to demean Elemental creatures, especially Wild women, animals, and Elemental Spirits by transmuting Elemental words into degraded and degrading labels and projecting these onto their victims. The dummy term *witch* is used to label a woman as despicable, ugly, and evil. *Chick, bitch, dog, pig* are intended to demean women and are also insulting to animals. *Angel* is shrunken and twisted to mean sweetheart-baby-honeypie. *Wild* is degraded into a label for a person or a behavior that in reality tamely conforms to patriarchal norms (*wild* girls at a *wild* party).

It is an observable phenomenon that the makers and users of dummy terms become dummy-like themselves. George Orwell was aware of this, when in *1984* he described a worker who held an important post in the Fiction Department of the Ministry of Truth. This person, seen through the eyes of Winston, was wearing spectacles which caught the light and presented two blank discs instead of eyes. Moreover:

> What was slightly horrible was that from the stream of sound that poured out of his mouth, it was almost impossible to distinguish a single word. . . . Whatever it was, you could be certain that every word of it was pure orthodoxy, pure Ingsoc. As he watched the eyeless face with the jaw moving rapidly up and down, Winston had a curious feeling that this was not a real human being but some kind of dummy. It was not the man's brain that was speaking; it was his larynx. The stuff that was coming out of him consisted of words, but it was not speech in the true sense.[10]

In the elementary world, then, the dummy-speaking inhabitants become dummies. It is not surprising that in such a world, which is defined/limited by elementary terms, Life is not valued and necrophilia prevails. This observation leads logically to an examination of the third class of such terms and phrases, that is, anti-biotics.[11]

III. anti-biotic terms and phrases

The word *antibiotic* means "tending to prevent, inhibit, or destroy life" (*Webster's*). Anti-biotic terms and phrases are anti-life. They are terms invented and promulgated by the phallotechnological establishment for the purpose of preventing, inhibiting, and destroying life. Of course, it can reasonably be argued that dummy terms and phrases, which are products of the same establishment, are all anti-biotic. While this is accurate, the word *anti-biotic* is reserved here to Name members of that class of phallotechnological terms that go even beyond dummies in

246

their degree of removal from words that Name Wild reality. As we have seen, dummy terms are designed to copy such words. This mechanism is readily detected in the cases of such dummies as *eye, brain, bug, plant*. By contrast, anti-biotic terms and phrases are so far removed from words that Name natural realities that they do not even have the deceptive resemblance to such words that characterizes dummies (except in the cases of a few acronyms).*

Among anti-biotic terms are many bizarre acronyms. SAINT, for example, means "Satellite Interceptor" (a U.S. anti-satellite program of the 1960s).[12] Other acronyms are MAD, meaning "Mutual Assured Destruction,"[13] and PENAIDS, meaning "Penetration Aids" (techniques and/or devices intended to increase the probability of a weapon's penetrating an opponent's defenses).[14]

Anti-biotic terms blatantly advertise the necrophilia and cynicism of their fabricators. Thus *bomblet* is a term meaning a "submunition" that searches out and attacks targets.[15] This term and its definition also illustrate the increasingly frequent phenomenon of one elementary term being defined by another.

The spread of anti-biotic terms is illustrated by the fact that such specimens as *fallout, nuke, meltdown, deployment,* and *plutonium* have penetrated the vocabularies of most English-speaking persons.† Another widespread anti-biotic is *deterrence,* defined as "the maintaining of vast military power and weaponry in order to discourage war" (*Webster's Collegiate*). Yet another well-known anti-biotic is *disinformation,* a CIA term for false information deliberately manufactured and spread by such agencies as the CIA, usually supported by forged documents. *Disinformation* often includes character assassination and divisive propaganda designed to create artificial conflicts within a society.[16] The CIA, a prolific producer of anti-biotics, also has gifted us with the term *neutralize,* meaning "to assassinate."[17]

An instructive and particularly horrifying example of an anti-biotic term is AIDS, the acronym for Acquired Immune Deficiency Syndrome. There is a cruel irony in the choice of this term to name an incurable disease which many suspect to have been "planted" deliberately in a tar-

---

*There are, of course, acronyms that look like words having something to do with Elemental reality, for example, GIRL, meaning "Generalized Information Retrieval Language." See *The Random House Dictionary of New Information Technology,* ed. by A. J. Meadows, M. Gordon, and A. Singleton (New York: Vintage Books, 1982). Another example is BAMBI, meaning "Ballistic Missile Booster Intercept" (a program of the 1960s). See Robert C. Aldridge, *The Counterforce Syndrome* (Washington, D.C.: Institute for Policy Studies, 1978), p. 79. However, these acronyms are not labels for elementary objects that (perversely) imitate natural realities—as radar "eyes" imitate real eyes. They are anti-biotic terms.

†Of course, the equivalents of these terms in other languages have multiplied and spread in a similar fashion.

get population of gay men. One might ask: Just what or whom is it that this disease "aids"? Pat Robertson and the rest of the army of right-wing heterosexist crusaders?

The man-akin character of anti-biotic terms is obvious.[18] In some cases it is blatant. We have already examined PENAIDS. Another example is *Quick Thrust*. This was a code term for an exercise intended to train troops in what is known as "Airland Battle," which calls for fast-moving, well-dispersed tactics.[19] Anti-biotic language is well suited to express the seminal ideas of necrophilic Stag-nation.

The multiplication and metastasis of anti-biotic language keeps pace with the growth of the anti-biotic society. The term *terraforming* gives a chilling clue concerning the intended extent of such gruesome growth. This term is said to mean "the artificial alteration of the physical and biological conditions of a planet or moon with the ultimate goal of making it habitable for earth life forms."[20]

The horror of the anti-biotic intent is self-evident. This intent is masked by the most complex and deadly form of elementary usage of terms and phrases, that is, reversal. Reversal is a mechanism that functions to hide the State of Atrocity utterly, to cover the eyes and close the lips of its inhabitants in the face of its necro-apocalyptic intent. Terms and phrases thus used/abused by the reversers who rule the State of Reversal—phallocracy—are converted into mind-twisters/tongue-twisters that thwart thought and communication. It is therefore imperative that we proceed to an analysis of this elementary phenomenon.

IV. *reversals*

Reversal is the fundamental mechanism in the process of the patriarchs' construction and maintenance of their world, which is mirrordom. Reversal is omnipresent within patriarchy. It is inherent in all patriarchal language, myths, ideologies, institutions, strategies, and behaviors. Reversal is closely associated with *doublethink,* which can be defined as "the keeping of two contradictory ideas or opinions in one's mind at the same time and the conscious belief in both of them" (*Webster's*).[21] Doublethink is the internal/infernal nonthought process which continually generates reversals and which is itself sustained by the reversals that are embedded into all of the structures of the patriarchal world and into the psyches of all of its prisoners. This endless re-cycling of doublethink and reversal is essential to maintain the plausibility and indeed the very existence of patriarchy.

Astute feminists have always recognized the mechanism of reversal. In 1898 Mme. Celine Renooz published a book, now extinct, in which she discussed one form of this:

Modesty is *masculine shame attributed to women* for two reasons: first, because man believes that woman is subject to the same laws as himself; second, because the course of human evolution has reversed the psychology of the sexes, attributing to women the psychological results of masculine sexuality. . . . This reversal of psychological laws has, however, been accepted by women with a struggle.[22]

In 1967 Valerie Solanas carried on in this tradition of reversal-detecting in her inimitable and forthright manner. She wrote:

Exposing elementary terms and phrases

Being an incomplete female, the male spends his life attempting to complete himself, to become female. He attempts to do this by constantly seeking out, fraternizing with and trying to live through and fuse with the female, and by claiming as his own all female characteristics—emotional strength and independence, forcefulness, dynamism, decisiveness, coolness, objectivity, assertiveness, courage, integrity, vitality, intensity, depth of character, grooviness, etc.—and projecting onto women all male traits—vanity, frivolity, triviality, weakness, etc. It should be said, though, that the male has one glaring area of superiority over the female—public relations. (He has done a brilliant job of convincing millions of women that men are women and women are men.)[23]

Once the reversal mechanism is understood, it can easily be detected in phallocracy's myths (Adam giving birth to Eve), ideologies (women labeled "the weaker sex"), institutions (the United States government's "Department of Defense"), strategies (blaming the victim; universal scapegoating of mothers), activities (the "revolutionary" activities by the "contras" in Nicaragua). Clearly, there are multiple levels of reversals.

A glance through any newspaper (oldspaper) substantiates this assessment of the omnipresence of reversals. The *Boston Globe* lies/lies on the table. It carries the following headline: "Do Mice Hold Too Much Power Over Us?"[24] The article under this "clever" headline seriously complains that laboratory experiments involving the injection of carcinogens into mice are "depriving" people of substances that cause cancers in mice but only *might* cause disease in humans.

Lying/lying on the same table is a copy of the *New York Times* which contains a story entitled "For Thriving Furriers, Protesters Pose Threat." The story contains the following statement by Fred Schwartz, a furrier:

"We want people to understand that we're an industry in harmony with nature."

This thought is completed by Henry Foner, who is identified as "president of the Fur, Leather and Machine Workers Union and chairman of the committee on wildlife conservation and legislation for the American Fur Industry, the New York-based trade group." Foner is quoted as saying:

> "We want to get past the emotional issue, the Bambi syndrome where people think animals talk to you, and get to the actual issue of what constitutes effective management of the species. . . . Since these animals must be harvested, the industry is playing a constructive role. . . . The fact that there is an economic incentive just makes it easier for that balance to be achieved."[25]

As such reversals of patriarchy multiply and spread, they become less and less visible to the victims of these mindbinding devices. It is essential, therefore, that they be exposed, studied, and categorized. The following analysis uncovers five types of reversal.

1. simple inversion

Many of patriarchy's reversals are the products of direct inversion. According to *Webster's, inversion* means "an act or result of turning inside out or upside down." *Simple inversion* is taken here to mean the usage of terms and phrases to label persons, things, groups, qualities, activities as the opposite of what they really are. In simple inversion, the terms and phrases are not inherently self-contradictory. Rather, the contradiction, or lie, consists in their misapplication. Thus Ronald Reagan is called "The Great Communicator." The MX missile has been called "Peacekeeper." Animal rights activists who oppose violence against any creature are labeled "terrorists."

The same mechanism is observable when groups opposing women's right to choose abortion—groups manifesting callous indifference to women's lives and to the lives of unwanted children—label themselves "pro-life" and "right-to-lifers." In a society that accepts such inversion, Coca-Cola can pass as "The Real Thing" and makeup can be labeled "The Natural Look," while women who refuse to wear makeup are called "unnatural."

This elementary world of inversions is legitimated and propagated by "the news," which is in reality the olds, the same old stuff, having the deceptive appearance of newness. Thus, on "the news" one hears of the "Strategic Defense Initiative" (or "Star Wars") which is a program for the aggressive/*offensive* militarization of space, involving the most extensive weapons research since World War II and manically accelerating the arms race.

Women's minds are battered by the incessant barrage of reversals, including pseudofeminist reversals. A small group that was organized in the mid-eighties solely to obstruct the attempts of feminists to enact anti-pornography legislation labeled itself FACT ("Feminist Anti-Censorship Task Force"), thereby reversing the meaning of the word *feminist* into a mere elementary term, manufacturing the illusion of a "split" in the "feminist movement" and reversing the meaning of anti-censorship by labeling a woman-silencing organization (themselves) as "anti-censorship."[26] During the same period a group called "Feminists for Life" proclaimed that a woman cannot be a feminist and be for abortion, claiming that abortion is "a perversion of feminism, fostering sexist attitudes, since by rejecting pregnancy, a woman is rejecting a fundamental aspect of her sexuality."[27] That same year Dr. Bernard Nathanson, producer of the anti-abortion propaganda film entitled "The Silent Scream," which pretends to depict abortion from an intra-uterine perspective, referred to his production as a "snuff film," thereby equating all women who have abortions with the sex killers who produce "snuff films" in which actresses are literally tortured and murdered before the camera.[28]

Exposing elementary terms and phrases

Particularly insidious is the pseudofeminist usage of the term *essentialist* to label and discredit all feminist writing that dares to Name and celebrate the Wild and Elemental reality of women who choose to think and to be beyond the prescribed parameters of patriarchal mandates. Using this label, self-appointed thought police have campaigned to exclude Radical Feminists from possibilities of teaching and publishing and, indeed, surviving. The fallacy involved in abusive political usage of the term *essentialist* is simple inversion. For patriarchal ideology is utterly essentialist, having as its hidden basic assumption the idea that there is a "human essence" possessed by males alone, relegating women to the category of a subspecies that can conveniently be contained within or excluded from this pseudo-universal "human" essence, according to the shifty whims of the masculinist strategists of patriarchy. The projection of the label "essentialist" onto women (Radical Feminists) who strive for Self-definition beyond the amorphous blob-concept of "human essence"/"human nature" is typical patriarchal usage of reversal.* The projection of the accusatory label "essentialist" onto Radical Feminist thought and be-ing is not merely deceptive; it is

*The reversal involved in accusing Radical Feminists of "biological determinism" involves false reasoning similar to the fallacy analyzed here in connection with accusations of essentialism.

251

evil. It elicits the patriarchally embedded Self-censor in women attempting to create in woman-identified ways. This reversal/projection can function tragically and malignantly to inhibit and even cripple Female Spinning Creativity by allowing legitimacy only to that aspect of feminism which is in perpetual struggle against oppression—a struggle which itself cannot be maintained without the Force and Focus that arises from Spinning. In other words, the expression of Original Powers and of the Ecstatic existential experience of women breaking free from patriarchal mindbindings is stigmatized by the label "essentialist," leaving only the grimness of oppression as that which women have in common. Ultimately this reversal/usage functions to negate Hope for Life that transcends the illusion of inclusion in forever male-identified "humankind."*

APPENDICULAR WEB ONE

The enormity of the lies that are made to appear plausible by labeling things as the opposites of what they are is illustrated in the stupendously stupefying statements of the renowned jesuit philosopher-anthropologist and screamer Pierre Teilhard de Chardin. In an essay entitled "The Spiritual Repercussions of the Atom Bomb" (in *The Future of Man*) Teilhard screeched misterically:

> Whatever may be the future economic repercussions of the atom bomb, whether over- or under-estimated, the fact remains that in laying hands on the very core of matter we have disclosed to human existence a supreme purpose: the purpose of pursuing ever further, to the very end, the forces of Life. In exploding the atom we took our first bite at the fruit of the great discovery, and this was enough for a taste to enter our mouths that can never be washed away: the taste for *super-creativeness* [emphasis mine].[29]

Thus we come full circle in reversal land: total destructiveness is labeled "super-creativeness." With this grand culmination in mind, we are pre-

---

*The susceptibility of women who are feminists to intimidation by the inverted label *essentialist* is explained in part by their recognition of the fact that the "eternal feminine" is a hideously restrictive archetype. It is important to remember that this is a man-made projection of a special "essence" onto "woman" and has nothing whatever to do with Radical Feminism and the Spinning Creativity which this inspires and celebrates. It is also crucial to understand that the *core* of patriarchal essentialism is not simply this all-too-obvious "eternal feminine" category, but the "eternal masculine" that is hidden in and merges with "humankind" and forever functions to exclude women from the "human species" which *is* the male species. Radical Feminists do not tend to waste time grieving over this exclusion or trying to remedy it, since we are happily engaged in Dis-covering our own potentialities and conveying this possibility to other women. Moreover, the inclusion of Self-identified women in the man-made "humankind," which is *man*kind, is not merely undesirable but inherently contradictory.

pared to proceed further in our analysis of the reversal mechanism's operations.

2. reversals that posit the elementary world as the model for natural phenomena

Another shape taken by the reversal mechanism is the positing of the elementary world and its fixtures as the model for labeling Elemental realities. This abusive usage marked the early modern period, setting a precedent for contemporary reversal-speak. Thus in 1605 Johannes Kepler wrote:

Exposing elementary terms and phrases

> My aim is to show that the celestial machine is to be likened
> not to a divine organism but to a clockwork.[30]

Descartes likened animals to mere machines.[31] The idea that machines are the models of nature was thus legitimated and propagated.

This kind of reversal has become so all-pervasive that it usually escapes unnoticed. The heart is commonly referred to as a "pump" and also as a "ticker"—usages accepted and legitimated in *Webster's* and in other dictionaries. The excretory system is called "plumbing." The sense of natural, Tidal Timing in animals is tediously labeled "animal clocks." The more widely used expression, which is snoolishly applied also to the Bio-logical rhythms of women, is "biological clocks."

The body is commonly likened to a "machine" and the brain to a "computer." Consistent with this view are expressions such as "turn on," "tune in," "nervous breakdown." Often speakers unwittingly refer to themselves as computers, when making such statements as "I want to *process* that information" or "We should *interface* with women of various religions." Clearly also the automobile is a model for natural processes. One often hears expressions such as "You'd better put your brakes on."

3. reversals that project patriarchal male qualities onto women and nature

Almost ubiquitous in patriarchal speech is the hidden assumption that women are possessed by the grotesque motivations and compulsions that in fact characterize the patriarchal male's behavior toward women and all of nature. Thus Self-affirming women are said to have "penis envy." In reversing such a reversal it is essential that Websters refuse to stop short in our analysis. It is not sufficient to see, for example, that the attribution of "penis envy" to women is an inversion of "male womb envy." The fact that patriarchal scholars such as Philip Slater have been all too willing to acknowledge this level of reversal is a clue that there is more to be uncovered.[32] Lifting the male veils, Websters note the hidden phenomenon of *male* penis envy, which often takes the form of "missile envy" and which is sufficiently malignant to give rise to a military system intent upon the destruction of all life.[33]

This form of reversal is involved in the labeling of all strong women as "man haters" in a society founded upon and sustained by the collective victimization of women, that is, woman hating. Again, patriarchs label Strong, Proud, Bitchy women as "castrating," when in fact it is under male orders that women—and some men—are routinely castrated.[34] The list of such reversals can go on indefinitely. Women are labeled "masochistic," "passive," "narcissistic," "humorless," "irrational," "vain," "slaves to their biology," et cetera, ad nauseam. Such instances of reversal become screamingly obvious to any Hag who has once grasped the *mechanism* of reversal and thus cracked the mirrors of mirrordom.

APPENDICULAR WEB ONE

There are also countless instances of the projection of patriarchal male characteristics onto animals and all of nature. Thus many animals are labeled "cruel" and "predatory." In some cases the reversal doubles back on itself and the speaker projects the projection onto a member of his own kind, by means of such labels as "mere animal," "vegetable," "bird brain," "stupid ape," "dirty rat," "brute," and so forth. Clearly, the problem is with the reversal-speaker and has nothing to do with animals and other natural realities in themSelves.

4. *reversals by means of which patriarchal males appropriate capacities and qualities of women*

Another type of reversal is specifically designed as an aid in the usurping, arrogating, confiscating of women's creative powers. Many of these reversals are so old and so deeply embedded in the English language that they can easily pass unnoticed.

The word *obstetrician* is derived from the Latin *obstetrix,* meaning "midwife, literally an assistant, stander near" (*Skeat's*). The implication in this etymology is that the obstetrician is a woman who *assists* women in the process of giving birth. Beginning in the late sixteenth century, however, obstetrics was gradually transformed into a male province. Today, of course, the vast majority of "obstetricians" are males. These are "man-midwives," and the history of their profession indicates that it has in large measure functioned as an obstacle* to the bringing forth

---

*Crones might note with interest that the word *obstetrician* is somewhat ambivalent in its etymological associations. On the one hand, as we have seen, it is derived from the Latin word for midwife, one who assists. Yet it is also etymologically re-of life.[35] The picture becomes grimmer all the time. As Gena Corea has pointed out, there is little concern for women in the politics of this profession:

> Increasingly, obstetricians are viewing themselves as "physicians to the fetus." They are establishing high-risk obstetrical clinics and intensive care delivery rooms to better salvage endangered fetuses.[36]

In other words, the fetus is the only patient.

A similar reversal is implied in the term *gynecologist*. Derived from the Greek *gyne*, meaning "woman," plus *-ology*, meaning "a branch of knowledge: SCIENCE," this word, as applied to a patriarchal male, is, to say the least, problematic. The term *gynecology*, applied to a branch of patriarchal medicine invented in the nineteenth century as an oppressive/repressive response and antidote to the first wave of feminism in the United States and Europe, is firmly ensconced in the reversal world.[37]

The reversals discussed above are related to the elementary phenomenon of male motherhood.[38] Not surprisingly, *mother* (in various forms) is often used as an elementary term to label patriarchal institutions, as in the expressions "Holy Mother Church," "alma mater," and "Ma Bell." The entities thus described, unlike real mothers, are not sources of life and nurturance, but rather are elementary imitations and replacements of spiritual/intellectual/life-communicating sources.

The male motherhood syndrome is writ large in the usage of the archetypal elementary term *God,* the great mummy, the he-goddess displaying the hubris of the he-men's religious fantasy. This syndrome also is reflected in the usage of the label *priest* (derived from the Greek *presbys,* meaning "old man") by the old men who control patriarchal religion and who attempt to imitate and become replacements for the Crones/Witches/Soothsayers of Pagan Times.

A society controlled and legitimated by patriarchal priests inevitably spawns more and more reversals. Not surprisingly, then, yet another category of reversals "merits" attention here.

---

lated to the word *obstacle,* since, as *Webster's* points out, both words are ultimately derived from the Latin *ob-*, which can mean "to, before, near, or against," plus *stare,* meaning "to stand." Historically there has been a woman-negating transition from the flourishing of midwifery, which involved women standing near and assisting a woman in childbirth, to the rise of a male-controlled "branch" of medical science which in many ways stands against women. It is useful to recall that *midwife* is from the Anglo-Saxon *mid,* meaning "together, with," plus *wif,* meaning "a woman." "Thus the literal sense is 'a woman who is with another,' a helper" (*Skeat's*).

255

5. reversals by redundancy and contradiction

On January 31, 1984, the *New York Times* cited a young physicist from the Lawrence Livermore Laboratory who was questioned about the morality of working on "weapons of death." The scientist, Lawrence C. West, replied:

> I don't think I fall into that category, of working on weapons of death. . . . We're working on weapons of life, ones that will save people from weapons of death.[39]

Any Shrewd Prude can see that there is something wrong with such an expression as *weapons of life*. The following analysis exposes the illlogic involved: The genus *weapons* has been fallaciously expanded to include two opposing subcategories, one of which (*weapons of death*) is included in the very definition of the genus and the other of which (*weapons of life*) contradicts the definition of the genus—that is, it is falsely included. Thus the first subdivision is redundant. (All weapons, especially nuclear weapons, are weapons of death.) The second subdivision is an absurd contradiction. The possibility of the speaker's getting away with this absurdity is facilitated by the redundancy of *weapons of death,* which sets up the reader to imagine that there might be an opposite kind of weapon.

The phrase *just war,* which has been obsessively used by moralists, especially roman catholic moralists, works in a similar way. The hidden assumption, of course, is that the genus *war* contains two subcategories: *just war* and *unjust war*. Given this assumption it is always possible to claim that the war in which one is engaged (that is, the side on which one is fighting) is "just."* By implication, the enemy is fighting an *unjust war*. To Websters, it is obvious that the subcategory *unjust war* is redundant, since injustice is implied in the very definition of *war*. The subcategory *just war,* then, is inherently self-contradictory.

An interesting variation of this strategy of reversal by redundancy and contradiction has been its usage by proponents of "transsexual operations." These operators have coined the elementary phrase *native women* to refer to women who were (naturally!) born female, thus legitimating their assumption that there exist *non-native women,* that is, "women" who have been "trapped inside male bodies" and therefore require extensive/expensive surgery to be "transsexed." Searchers will find that in this instance it is the redundant subcategory, *native women*—as if all

---

*This, of course, is precisely what some members of the roman catholic hierarchy in nazi germany did claim, while their counterparts among the "allied nations" made the same claim. The righteousness of the latter extended to approval of the dropping of atomic bombs on Hiroshima and Nagasaki.

women were not "native"—that has been made explicit in order to make room for the self-contradictory subcategory *non-native women*. This pseudodistinction reduces the word *woman* to an elementary term, making it possible/plausible for a male who has undergone such an operation, or who even has considered himself a candidate for such surgery, to call himself a "woman," thereby reversing the Original meaning of the word *woman*. This contradiction/reversal has been necessary for the operation of "the transsexual empire."[40]

An especially important example of reversal by redundancy and contradiction is the elementary phrase *forcible rape*. All rapes are by definition forcible. This fallacious extension of the genus *rape* to include the redundant subcategory *forcible rape* opens the way for the absurdly contradictory subcategory *benign rape*. Indeed, re-searchers have actually referred to a pornographic depiction of rape that results in orgasm for the woman as a "benign rape."[41] This phrase, of course, is a woman-battering device which invites and legitimates exploitation of women who cannot prove that their rapes were "forcible." The usage of this particular reversal paves the way for the legitimation of all sorts of woman-victimizing behaviors.

Exposing elementary terms and phrases

A particularly baffling example of this type of reversal is the phrase *reverse discrimination*. Shrewd Shrews will notice that this requires a good deal of unreversing/unraveling. The expression is particularly difficult to unravel because *discrimination* is a weak elementary term, a euphemism used to disguise the horrors of oppression. However, if we replace *discrimination* with the word *oppression*, which Names what is actually going on, then we have something reality-based to work with. The ludicrousness of *reverse oppression* is more obvious, since *oppression* is an explicit word, meaning "unjust or cruel exercise of authority or power especially by the imposition of burdens" (*Webster's*). We can see that oppression is something done *by the institutionally powerful* to the powerless. That is, the agent is exposed. As Virginia Woolf would say: "The cat is out of the bag; and it is a Tom."[42] We can then see that "reverse oppression" would imply oppression *of the institutionally powerful,* an obvious and absurd self-contradiction, implying that the oppressors are the institutionally powerless. Applying the paradigm of reversal by redundancy and contradiction, we can see that the genus operative here is *oppression* and that the redundant subcategory is *oppression by the institutionally powerful,*which makes way for its self-contradictory opposite: *oppression by the institutionally powerless*. The latter is, in fact, what is meant by the slippery phrase "reverse discrimination"—a victim-blaming device used most frequently by white patriarchs against women and people of color—all in the names of "fairness," "justice," and "equal rights" and intended to keep the oppressed in their rightful place, which is, as always, on the bottom.

Shrewd Prudes can recognize the strategy of reversal by redundancy and contradiction as it operates in countless instances. Thus the elementary phrase *intelligent life* implies by its redundancy that there is such a thing as *nonintelligent life*—an assumption that legitimates animal experimentation and all kinds of exploitation of the Wild—of animals, trees, mountains, rivers, oceans, the air. Such reversals multiply endlessly, forming dead and deadly blobs of elementary terms and phrases that "hang around" together, comprising the logorrhea of babblespheres. These blobs are the glue that holds together the misbegotten illusions that keep the elementary world "alive."

Crackpot Crones enjoy exposing these blobs and making them march in processions. This is appropriate, since they are in large measure "the sons of educated men," and, as Virginia Woolf explained, these never tire of marching round and round in processions.[43] The following True Story is but one example of such a Furious Flight of Fancy/Fantasy.

an account of the processions of mummies, dummies, anti-biotics, reversals, and other sons of educated men

At a conventional convention of the Academented Fellows of America, held at the Death Valley Sado-Sheraton on Memorial Day, 1991 a.d. (archetypal deadtime), many snools are gathered from academentia all over the globe. The keynote spooker, introduced by professor Yessir from the College of Knowledge, is the reverend C. Roach, whose announced subject is "The Fetal Majority: An Historic Force in the March of Civilization?" So highly regarded is this spooker that he is commonly called "Sir-Reverence" by the younger fellows.*

As reverend Roach begins to speak/spook, processions of elementary terms and phrases emerge from his lips, filling the air with the odor of Stag-nation. These gradually form a circle, marching clockwise above the heads of the half-listening academented fellows who are seated in the balls-room where the lecture is being delivered. Most of the stupified members of the audience fail to notice the procession.

The terms process in lockstep, in strictly regimented order. The archetypal mummies take the lead. These are followed by the dummies, who are determined to suckseed. Next follow the anti-biotic terms, while the reversals take up the rear. Each group is appropriately appareled. The mummies wear priestly robes over their mummy-bindings, befitting their hierarchically rank ranks. The dummies wear academic

---

* See **sir-reverence** (*Word-Web Three*).

costumes, with mortarboards set squarely on their heads. Some of the anti-biotic terms wear lab coats, while some wear military uniforms, indicating their respective lines of work. The reversals wear police officers' uniforms. Serving as rear guard, they cooperate with the mummies in seeing to it that all of the terms march clockwise.

One segment of the "listeners"—a group that has carefully infiltrated the fellowship and whose members have seated themselves strategically around the balls-room—is intensely aware of all that is happening. These Infiltrators are all females, posing as tokens. They are treated with masked contempt by the hypocritical fellows, who label them with ugly names behind their backs. Thus some are called "hags." Others are called "crones," "nags," "prudes," and "spinsters." Still Others are mocked as "trivial." The more daring are labeled "dykes," "viragos," "witches," "bitches"—sometimes with the addition of insulting adjectives, such as "wicked" and "weird." The younger members of the group are referred to as "chicks," while the older ones are sneeringly labeled "dogs" and "pigs."

Exposing elementary terms and phrases

The Infiltrators, of course, are aware of this labeling. However, they also know the true Background of these labels (having studied *Word-Web Two* of the *Wickedary*). They therefore proudly Be-Spell the Elemental Names which these elementary labels are intended to mimic and replace. Their Be-Spelling/Be-Speaking sends forth Biophilic vibrations, which Naturally Spin Counterclockwise. These vibrations have a disturbing effect upon reverend Roach, who soon begins to show signs of a breakdown. His spooking patterns become more disorganized.

The elementary terms and phrases dribble confusedly from the keynote spooker's mouth. Gradually his address begins to resemble the Sado-Sheraton's luncheon menu. When he tries to say "bomblet" he can only say "omelet." He describes a "meltdown" as grilled cheese. Referring to "Apple" he describes at length a piece of pie. He castigates "dinners" instead of "sinners." Switching to military subjects, such as "PENAIDS," Operation "Quick Thrust," and "proliferation," he displays inappropriate agitation. The fellows, many of whom are dozing, fail to notice the change.

As the spooker becomes more excited, the processing terms become more disorganized. They begin to lurch into each other. The mummies' bindings come unwound and begin to hang out from under their priestly robes. The dummies swing their plastic arms and legs in all directions, swatting and kicking each other as their heads swivel bizarrely. The anti-biotics begin proliferating, filling the airwaves. The reversals "spin" senselessly like mechanical tops that have gone berserk.

Observing this general breakdown, the Infiltrators Conjure their own Names with intensified intention. Finally one Hag, unable to contain her cackles, Laughs Out Loud. So contagious is her Laughing that her Sister Conspirators join in a chorus of Cackling/Crackling. The Prudes, Crones, Nags, Spinsters, Witches, Bitches, Chicks, and Pigs all Laugh in their own styles and rhythms.

The reverend C. Roach finally collapses, followed by professor Yessir. None of the fellows notices. While the snools remain seated in comatose postures, the Weird Infiltrators begin to dance. They are led by the Nags, who urge them to Prance. Prancing Counterclockwise, they howl their Counterclock Whys.

These Re-Sounding vibrations set the balls-room on fire, causing the mummies, dummies, anti-biotics, and reversals to explode in gusts of hot air. While the fellows doze on, the Infiltrators quickly fly away. And that is the story of the Happy Ending of elementary terms and phrases and their users. The Question this raises is: What is the nature of Be-Laughing? This will be Spun about, made Fun about, in the next Appendicular Web.

APPENDICULAR WEB TWO

Be-Laughing:
Nixing, Hexing, and X-ing

Be-Laughing women see snools as fools and Denounce them as such. Such Denouncing is not mere "fooling around." It is Pronouncing snoolish stupidity to be blameworthy and evil. It punctures the pomposity of wantwits and windbags whose malignant mindlessness would destroy the world. Moreover, Be-Laughing is an expression of Elemental humor, carrying Lusty Leapers/Laughers into the Background. It is ontological laughing.

Be-Laughing Searchers are intrigued with the etymology of the word *fool*. It is derived from the Middle English *fol*, from the Old French *fol*, from the Latin *follis*, meaning "bellows, windbag" (*American Heritage*). *Follis* is akin to the Greek *phallos*, meaning "penis," and the Sanskrit bhānda, meaning "pot." The basic sense is "to swell" (*Webster's*).[1]

The etymological Search for the roots of *fool* becomes even more intriguing when Searchers find that the origins of this word can be traced to the Indo-European root *bhel-*, which is defined as follows: "To blow, swell: with derivatives referring to various round objects and to the notion of tumescent masculinity." *Bhel-*, of course, is also the root of *phallos*. (See *bhel-*[2] in the Appendix on Indo-European Roots, *American Heritage*.) The ultimate convergence of fooldom and phallocracy has been foretold in this etymological history.

The identity of snoolishness with foolishness is writ large in the politics, postures, pornography, and piety of popocrats/flopocrats, the deadly serious sages and saviors of the sadostate. Of course, the sadorulers have always striven to fabricate illusions of extreme opposition to foolishness. Therefore, institutionally powerful and officious snools have required the existence of those who are popularly acclaimed *as fools* (or phallocratically identified foolettes).[2] In fact, the jesters/clowns who are acknowledged and rewarded as fools in phallocracy/foolocracy function to sustain the credibility of those invested with authority by serving as seeming mirror opposites of these fatherly figureheads, whose apparent rationality is highlighted by this illusion of contrast.[3]

One sociologist describes the legitimating function of traditional fools and folly as follows:

> Reality needs the looking-glass function of folly and this fact has been neglected by Rational Man to his own detriment. But the reverse is also true: folly needs reality, an existing institutional order which it can reflect contrariwise.[4]

Reading this passage, Contrary-Wise Crones will note that the "reality" under discussion is man-made. It is the socially constructed/constricted world. The maintenance of such a world indeed requires fools and folly.

The role of the traditional fool in patriarchy is in fact conservative. The same author states:

> If folly would venture to emancipate itself from an existing status quo, erecting as it were its very own autonomous reality, it would have to break the looking-glass which is itself. This would no longer be folly but lunacy, schizophrenia.[5]

This text unintentionally describes the Real Acts of Be-Laughing women. For it is by Laughing Out Loud at the false opposition within the Looking Glass Society between the somber fools in positions of authority and the "funny" fools who reflect these serious men that we break the snool-legitimating looking glass. And indeed this will be labeled "schizophrenia" by the doublethinkers of daddydom, for Be-Laughers split apart the set-up of mutually reinforcing mirrors, causing Dreadful Disorder.

Such mirror-cracking, moreover, is a manifestation of Lusty Lunacy. The word *lunatic,* derived from the Latin *luna,* meaning "moon," is defined as "one who is wildly eccentric: one capable of crazy actions or extravagances: CRACKPOT" (*Webster's*). Crackpot Crones choose to be Wildly Eccentric, moving Out from the centers of sadoseriousness and snoolish folly and forming the Lunatic Fringe on the Boundary of bore-ocracy/buffoonery.*

---

*The application of the word *buffoonery* here to the activities of phallocratic fools requires clarification. If *Webster's* is right, *buffoon* is derived from the Latin *bufo,* meaning "toad." All Websters recognize that any resemblance of bore-ocracy's buffoons to Elemental Toads is purely elementary.

Be-Laughing, then, is a Primal Act of Power. It is breaking the Taboo against Elemental humor, which splits/cracks man-made "reality," unveiling man's mysteries. Lusty Lunatics Laughing Out Loud together break the Terrible Taboo against women Intimately/Ultimately Touching each Other, for Be-Laughing Touches the spirits of women, enlivening auras, awakening hope.[6]

Be-Laughing is not mere reacting to patriarchy's horrors. It is an activity that carries Laughers into the Background. It is be-ing Silly together. The word *silly* is derived from the Middle English *sely, silly,* meaning "happy, blessed." Silly Soothsayers actually do the thing which mysterious men most dread. By Laughing Out Loud we not only cause the shrinkage of masculine tumescence but expand our auras and those of Others, including, of course, Lusty animals.

The laughter of Silly women and animals explodes in Gales. The etymology of the word *gale* helps to describe such explosions. It is believed to be derived from the Norwegian *galen,* meaning "bad," and probably from the Old Norse *galinn,* meaning "bewitched, enchanted," from *gala,* meaning "to sing, enchant, bewitch" (*American Heritage*). A Silly Gale is a Be-Witching, Enchanting force released by the Laughing Out Loud of Lusty crowds of women and animals, including laughing frogs, laughing geese, laughing gulls, laughing hyenas, laughing jackasses, and laughing owls. Such Gales of laughter clear the air, lighting up Wild Eyes, Eye-Biting Eyes, encouraging Contrary Whys.

Silly women, glad to identify with Silly geese, create spaces/times in which women can overcome the man-made impediments to Be-Laughing. Shameless Hussies encourage Others to shed the plastic and potted passions that have been embedded in our psyches to inhibit our Laughing Out Loud. Cackling Crones and Gorgons Stare back at the staring studs/duds with Active Eyes and turn to each Other with Real Eyes.

As Self-conscious Seers, Be-Laughing women are engaged in the Metamysterious work of Metafooling. Disdaining the fooling of snools, we learn to See and Act in ways that transcend the rules of fools. Refusing Fool-fillment, we escape the state of totaled women. Refuting the foolproofs of foolosophical re-search, we avoid absorption by academentia. In short, Metafooling is Outrageous Contagious Departure from phallic fixations. It consists of riotous transformations.

The Metafooling herein described is threefold: First there is Nixing. Next there is Hexing. Third, there is X-ing. These are interwined, interwoven wondrous workings/wordings that are Dis-covered and passed on among Silly Shrews and Gossips and Other Weirdward Intergalactic Galloping Nag-Gnostic Voyagers.

Nixing

According to *Webster's*, the verb *nix* means "VETO, FORBID, PROHIBIT, BAN, REJECT, CANCEL." Nixes veto, forbid, and ban the boring behavior of snools, portending the end of snooldom. Thus *Nixing* means Denouncing the drooling of fools, the droning of clones, the mindless devastations wrought by Stag-nations.

APPENDICULAR
WEB TWO
As usual, Websters can find etymological information inspiring. Consulting *Webster's*, we find that the verb *nix* is derived from the German *nichts*, meaning "nothing." Nixes ban by our very be-ing the nonbe-ing of Nothing-lovers. We employ the title "his nothingness" to designate a supreme bully of nothingdom, for example, the papal bully. Moreover, we use this expression to Name the sum of the attributes and products of the patriarchal god/rod, e.g., his "word," his plan, his mystery, his luv, his presence, his presents.

Lifting the male veils, Nixes See the quintessential Nothing which is the priceless secret of the fellowship of fools. We See the naught, the zero, the nil which is the sum total of the treasures of cipherdom. *Cipherdom*, as defined in the *Wickedary*, means "STATE OF THE GRATEFUL DEAD. . . . normal condition of any clone, drone, or bore" (*Word-Web Three*).

Nixes say "Nix!" to this nothingness, bidding farewell to the Numbed State. Some Nixes recall an old folk joke, attributed to Gloria Steinem: "When Nixon is alone in a room, is anyone there?" Others speculate about the real absence of The President (presbot) and of the popebot on television and in the flesh.* Some comment on the techniques of cipherdom's advertisers, who attribute power, brains, beauty, charm, and other talents to such gross national products as automobiles and electric razors.

Nixing Nixes Nixname the Nothing-lovers, ripping to shreds their veils, reducing the masters of mystery to mysterics. We Nix them as blobbers, as robbers, as rippers and jerks. We Denounce them as dry-asdust pedants and chauvinist bores, as flappers and jabbers and jerk-alike jocks, as lickspittles, louts, cockaludicrous cocks. Nixes Nixname the sirly snivelards and snot boys whose snivelization is epitomized in the fakery of Uncle Sham.

---

*On December 18, 1985 the Vatican announced that catholics who would follow the pope's annual christmas benediction on television or radio could partake for the first time in the plenary indulgence reserved until now for those who were physically present at the service. According to an article in the *New York Times* (December 19, 1985, p. A8): "in a single-page decree in Latin signed by Luigi Cardinal Dadaglio . . . the Vatican said improvements in electronic technology made the change possible."

Nixes Nill the nothing, the nil. According to *Webster's*, the verb *nill* (derived from the Old English *ne,* meaning "not," plus *wyllan,* meaning "to wish"), has "archaic" definitions, i.e., "to be unwilling" and "not to will: REFUSE, REJECT, PREVENT." Nixes Be-speak this word's Archimagical Archaic meanings, declaring our Selves Unwilling to permit the atrocities of fooldom. We Refuse, Reject, and Will to Prevent the swelling and proliferation of tumescent phallocracy.

Nixes know that such Refusing of "unreal loyalities"[7] is essential for Re-fusing, that is, the Self-Realizing by means of which Hags reunite/re-fuse powers within ourSelves—such as thinking, feeling, sensing—that have been artificially split/splintered in the State of Severance. Thus the Nilling of Nixes leads us to the Positively Revolting subject of Hexing.

Hexing

The verb *hex* is said to mean "to practice witchcraft upon: put a hex on" (*Webster's*). Be-Witching women practice Hexing, casting Spells. The Hexing of Be-Laughing Witches does not deceive/delude. Rather, it unmasks the mysterious masters, undoes the dupers, the deadly dudes, Pronouncing the Doom of doomdom.

The noun *hex,* meaning "a person who practices witchcraft: WITCH" (*Webster's*), has an astonishing etymological history. According to that dictionary it is derived from the Pennsylvania German *hex* plus the German *hexe,* from the Middle High German *hecse, häxe.* It is akin to the Old High German *hagzissa, hagazussa,* meaning "harpy, witch." Having divulged this much information, *Webster's* invites the Searcher to "see more" at *hag.* Looking under *hag,* we find that this word also is akin to *hagzissa, hagazussa,* whose roots are akin to the Old English word *haga,* meaning "hedge," and to the German dialect word *dūs,* meaning "devil." A hedge, of course, is a boundary. Thus Hexing Hags can Dis-cover our Boundary-based, Daredevil situation depicted in the very etymologies of *Hex* and *Hag.*

The Boundary Living of Witches/Hexes/Hags was acknowledged many centuries ago. One scholar writes:

> As late as the Middle Ages, the witch was still the *hagazussa,* a being that sat on the *Hag,* the fence, which passed behind the gardens and separated the village from the wilderness. She was a being who participated in both worlds. As we might say today, she was semi-demonic.[8]

HEXING: *Positively Revolting Willing the Way Out of fooldom: Be-Wishing*

A Witch, since she is in Touch with her Demon/Genius/Muse, is engaged not only in Boundary Living but also in Boundary Breaking. She Presentiates the Background in the midst of foreground conditions by communicating contagious Courage, Pride, Rage, and Other Haggard Virtues, including the Virtue of Laughing Out Loud. Sitting on the Fence between the worlds, she summons/beckons Other women into the Wilderness, the Wild.

Clearly, then, the Boundary Living/Boundary Breaking of Hexes/Hags is utterly Other than the pseudoboundary buffoonery of phallocracy's traditionally approved fools. Whereas the latter perform on illusory boundaries, safely within the sadosanctuaries provided for them, Hags are Dreadless Daredevils who Dis-close ways out of the hedged-in gardens of fooldom/ghouldom, opening hidden gateways to the Wild. Such Dis-closing is essential to Hexing.

Hence, whereas the Nixing of Be-Laughing women is Nilling, Hexing implies Positively Revolting Willing. Hexing Hags Will the Way Out of fooldom. In Other words, Hexing is Be-Wishing. One dialectal definition of the Verb *wish* is "To influence in a magical or occult way by wishing; to bewitch by a desire or imprecation" (*O.E.D.*). *Be-Wishing*, according to the *Wickedary*, means "to influence in a Magical way by ontological Wishing; to Be-Witch by a desire or inspiration" (*Word-Web One*). *Be-Wishing*, then, is a form of *Be-Witching*.

The intensity of Haggard Willing/Be-Wishing/Be-Witching carries Hags through, under, and over the fathers' fences. Our laughter blasts holes in the barriers built by bores. Hexing Hags/Hexes hop and fly by means of Willpower, Howling all the way.

The Be-Wishing/Hexing that carries Willful Witches through and over the fences of fatherland is Canny. An "obsolete" Scottish definition of *canny* is "supernaturally wise, endowed with occult or magical power" (*O.E.D.*). Be-Wishing is Super Naturally Wise activity and therefore it is endowed with Magical Power. It is Willing that is Wise in a practical, realistic way, taking into account foreground foolishness as well as Background reality. Therefore, Be-Wishing is also Uncanny. *Uncanny* is said to mean "arousing feelings of dread or of inexplicable strangeness . . . EERIE, MYSTERIOUS, WEIRD" (*Webster's*). Be-Wishing/Hexing arouses feelings of dread in fooldom, for it is inexplicable within foolish categories. It is Strange, Metamysterious, and Weird.

The Canny/Uncanny Be-Laughing of Hexing Hags is the laughter of Seers who See the Other side of the hedge and thus have Pixilated Peripheral Vision. It exposes the dreariness of cockocracy's tragicomedies and canned laughter. It explodes the cans/containers intended to confine Female Fury and Hilarity, hurling us further on expeditions into the Wilderness.

Clearly such Boundary Breaking/Hexing is Contrary-Wise. This brings us to the fascinating subject of X-ing.

X-ing

X is the symbol for the Unknown and Variable Qualities of Questing women. *X-ing* is a metaphoric way of Naming the Contrariwise Qualitative Leaps of such women and of foretelling the emergence of the X-factor among Weirdward Journeyers. It is also a way of Announcing the convergence of conditions for cosmic encounters and for receiving Be-Tidings. The X-ing of Metafooling Muses can be considered under several aspects.

First, X-ing implies the Contrary-Wise activities of Be-Wildering Witches. It has long been known that Witches are Contrary. Knowledge of this fact persisted into christian times:

> Even in Christian times, witches often had their plaits arranged on their heads anti-clockwise. Looking into their eyes, a person saw his image in their pupils upside-down. At the sabbat, they also danced in a reversed manner.[9]

X-ing women are, of course, Anticlock-Wise. Moreover, it is not surprising that a "person" looking into Eyebiting Eyes would see in their pupils *his* image upside down, that is, as the opposite of his own image of himself. As for dancing "in a reversed manner"—this can be a ritual conjuring of powers to reverse the reversals of fooldom. X-ing Witches dance, look, speak, act the Wrong Way, that is, contrary to customary procedures.

In the Middle Ages, Witches' dances were performed in a circle. The dancers moved Widdershins—Counterclockwise—which is the direction of the moon, or the "left-hand path."[10] Moreover, they practiced back-to-back dancing. According to a seventeenth-century text on this subject:

> At theyr meetings, [they] do all thinges contrary to the custome of Men, dauncing, back to back, hip to hip, theyr handes ioyn'd, and making theyr circles backward, to the left hand, with strange phantastique motions of theyr heads, and bodyes.[11]

X-ing women indeed do all things "contrary to the custome of Men," that is, Naturally, Elementally, upending/ending the reversals of cockocracy/clockocracy. Such Wickedness requires Moving Widdershins.

X-ING: *Contrariwise Qualitative Leaping of Questing Women*

An "obsolete" definition of the adverb *withershins, widdershins* is "in a direction opposite to the usual; the wrong way; *to stand* or *start withershins,* (of the hair) to 'stand on end'" (*O.E.D.*). By be-ing her Self, an X-ing woman does make her own hair stand on end. She also Inspires Other Hair-Raising Hags to become Gorgon-identified, Gorgon-headed.*

Second, X-ing involves acts of conjuring Real Presence. We have seen that the Nothing-lovers continually attempt to negate Real Presence, replacing this with robotized presences of absence whose nothingness is veiled by man's mysteries. As Nixes, Be-Laughing women Nill the nil-fellows, and as Hexes we Be-Wish/Will ourSelves outside the boundaries of all their zeros, which are the institutions and other products of the Phallic/Foolish State. As XXes, Metafooling women conjure Presence, presentiating ourSelves and Others.

Clearly, phallotechnology, especially as it works through the master-minded media—functions to block and distract women from our Presentiating process. The diversionary strategy consists in large measure in substituting pseudopresence for Real Presence, tricking the victims of this ruse into believing that the substitute is "real."[†]

* The most terrible of Gorgon figures is Medusa, whose Furious Look turned men to stone and from whose head swirled hundreds of snakes. Stories of Medusa and other Gorgons go back to Africa. See Helen Diner, *Mothers and Amazons,* ed. and trans. by John Philip Lundin (New York: The Julian Press, Inc., 1965), pp. 120–40. Emily Culpepper has written that the Amazon Gorgon face is Female Fury personified. She depicts her personal experience of being attacked by a man who pushed his way into her home and of the "emergence of my will to fight, my Gorgon spirit." She describes the moment of conflict, as recorded in her journal: "NOW! PUSH his body BACK! KNOCK his hand AWAY! Shove and—loud—yell, 'GET OUT! GET OUT! GET OUT!' I am staring him out, pushing with my eyes too. My face is bursting, contorting with terrible teeth, flaming breath, erupting into ridges and contours of rage, hair hissing. It is over in a flash. I *still* see his eyes, stunned, wide and staring, almost quizzically, at me, as if *I* am acting strange, as if *I* were acting wrong! As soon as I realize I've succeeded in shoving him outside onto the porch, I slam the door." See Emily Erwin Culpepper, "Ancient Gorgons: A Face for Contemporary Women's Rage," *Woman of Power,* Issue Three (Winter/Spring 1986), pp. 22–24, 40. This article is an excerpt from Culpepper's forthcoming book, *Revolt of the Symbols.*

† American media coverage of the explosion of the space shuttle *Challenger* on January 28, 1986 (together with the lengthy and elaborate pre-launch publicity), was a stunning example of the manufacture and manipulation of pseudopresence, laying the groundwork for the fabrication of pseudomemory (elementary memory) and pseudopassions. A front-page article in the *New York Times* stated: "It seemed to be one of these scenes, enlarged and frozen, that people would remember and recount for the rest of their lives—what they were doing and where they were when they heard that the space shuttle Challenger had exploded. The need to reach out, to speak of disbelief and pain, was everywhere." (Sara Rimer, "Afterward, a Need to

Overcoming the man-made pseudopresences requires continuing Leaping through Realms of Reality beyond the banal boundaries set by foolish deadfellows. This implies nothing less than Dis-covering and Re-Weaving strands of the X-factor, that ever evolving convergence of Strange, Variable, and Diverse Qualities that characterize Questing women.[12] Such converging of Questing Qualities is the Weaving of living tapestries—of Original Selves. Paradoxically, it implies divergence, that is, expansion/expression of the Radiant Diversity that is possible only for unique Selves.[13] Converging implies diverging also in the sense that only Original Selves are capable of real choices—of moving decisively at crossroads and continuing on to Other crossroads.[14]

Be-Laughing: Nixing, Hexing, and X-ing

This convergence/divergence is unknown within the confines of fooldom, and it is partially Unknown even to Questers who have broken through hedges/boundaries to range/roam through uncharted Realms of the Wild. For the X-factor is always surprising. It is Changing/Shifting/Spiraling. It is not stasis. Rather, it is continual helical movement of the verb/verbs within X-ing women that constitute who we Are, who each one Is, when moving in Metamorphic resonance with our Selves.

Conjuring Real Presence, then, is Realizing Primal Potential, Seeing this with Real Eyes. This Activizes Archaic Ties—those bonds of the Original Self with those of her own kind, whom she knows and Re-calls in her experience of Tidal Time.

Hence the third aspect of X-ing is Be-Tiding, that is, moving in the flow of Tidal Time, in harmony with the Fates, Realizing Elemental Encounters. X-ing women experience coincidences, synchronicities. Forgetting the rules of fooldom and Unforgetting our Selves, Meta-fooling Furies find our friends and meet the Fates, the Norns—those Weird Sisters who guide Journeyers Weirdward through Spiraling Galaxies of Present, Past, and Future.

Reach Out and Share Grief," *New York Times,* January 29, 1986, p. 1.) There was no acknowledgment in the media (of course) of the implausibility of the "grief" and "pain" attributed by the media to millions around the globe over the deaths of seven americans in a space shuttle.

The displacement of attention and emotion away from massive tragedies—world famine, oil spills, pesticide contamination, the cancer plague—is made possible by planned substitution of pseudopresence for Real Presence. Viewers were conditioned by television—the extension of "vision"—to feel that Christa McAuliffe and the astronauts were "real" and really present to them in ways that the nameless millions dying of starvation in Africa and throughout the world could never be. The manufactured "presence," which made possible controlled and misdirected release of emotion and subsequent re-turn to the normal nuclear state of psychic numbing, was a manipulation of the masses comparable to the "Two Minutes Hate" required of the citizens of Ingsoc in George Orwell's *1984.*

As these encounters occur more frequently/Irregularly, X-ing Voyagers Dis-cover Happiness. One Real response to this Dis-covering is Laughing Out Loud. And that is how it happens that Be-Laughing women keep a Silly Sense of Humor and regain a Sinful Sense of Direction. This brings us to the subject of the following Appendicular Web.

APPENDICULAR WEB THREE

Spinning Beyond the Compass:
Regaining the Sense of Direction

S ibyls who are Re-membering our Sinful Sense of Direction practice Space-Craft. This is the art of Spinning beyond the compass. It is also skill in walking/talking the Wrong Way, moving in
Wicked directions, opening doors to Other dimensions, Other Spatial
perceptions. By reversing the reversals of the snoolish space controllers,
we enter a different context. This is Metapatriarchal Space/Time, beyond the measurements of compasses and maps.

Women who roam into these Wild Realms require Other navigational devices. Since we are traveling Widdershins, it is helpful to begin
by noting that the word *widdershins,* or *withershins,* is derived from the
Middle High German *widersinnes,* meaning "counter-course," which is
made up of *wider,* meaning "against," plus *sinnes,* the genitive of *sin,*
meaning "journey" (*American Heritage*). Following the etymological
trail further, we find that *sin* is traceable to the Indo-European root
sent-, meaning "to head for, go" (*American Heritage,* Appendix on
Indo-European Roots). According to the same Appendix, *sent-* is also
the root of the Old English *sand,* meaning "message, messenger," and
it may be the root of the Latin *sentire,* meaning "to feel" (i.e., "to go
mentally"). If this is the case, the same root is the source of the English
words *scent, sense, sentence, sentient, sentiment, consent, presentiment.*
This etymological information provides Sensible Websters/Journeyers
with significant clues concerning our New/Archaic Navigational Aids.

Journeyers traveling Widdershins are not too surprised when we
Sense Metapatriarchal messages. These, of course, imply the existence
of Senders, or Messengers. Seers recognize these Messengers as our

SPINNING BEYOND THE COMPASS—WIDDERSHINS

friends, the Angels. The word *Angel,* derived from the Greek *angelos,* meaning "messenger," is defined in the *Wickedary* as "an Elemental Spirit of the universe whose duration and movement are outside the limitations of tidy time and whose principal activities are knowing and willing; bearer of Archaic knowledge and wisdom" (*Word-Web One*).

The messages sent by these Elemental Messengers are conveyed through our Senses, all of which are enlivened and strengthened by the fact that we are traveling Widdershins. Thus the sense of smell becomes the Searcher's Sense of Scent, which brings us Dangerously near to hidden truths, leading us on the trails of Memory. This process is suggested by Virginia Woolf's Shrewd sentence: "The pen gets on the scent." [1]

Spinning Beyond the Compass: Regaining the Sense of Direction

Fore-Crone Woolf knew that Memories come in ribbons [2] and that in the process of writing (or speaking)—of Spinning out sentences—they are pulled to the surface. Thus Searchers who chase the Race of Wild Words catch the threads of Elemental Memory, that is, Deep Memory, grounded in primal experience of the Elements, beyond the fabricated elementary "recollections" of the foreground.

Catching these threads, we enter Realms of Metamemory—Deep, Ecstatic Memory of participation of Be-ing that eludes the categories and grids of patriarchal consciousness, reaching into the Past, carrying Vision forward. Here we Re-call Archaic Time, Touching Memory beyond civilization. Here also we glimpse and create Memories of the Future. Participating consciously in Tidal Time, we transcend the categories of tidy time, connecting with Sources of instinctive, ecstatic knowledge.

Space-Crafty Travelers entering these Realms become more Sentient in Other ways. The Scent of such Memory/Memories makes possible Prudish Presentiments, so that we have practical knowledge concerning which ways to turn in hitherto uncharted territories. Moreover, since there is a network of Re-memberers, we con-sense and consent to the Direction of the Metapatriarchal Journey. Of course, this con-sensing/consenting concerns the general Direction of the Journey in the widest/Wildest Sense of the word *Direction.* Prudes know that there are countless pathways and modes of traveling. Our choices are in large measure a matter of sentiment as well as presentiment. That is, since Elemental Memory is E-motional, stirring Deep Passion, it generates various forms of Movement out of the Fixed State. In Diverse ways, Elemental Passion moves Wild women out/away from the framed State of Stagnation, propelling us onward, urging us to overcome the psychic numbing of the necrophilic psycho-society.

Since Journeyers are Nags, our choices are also a matter of individual Horse Sense. This is a subject deserving special attention.

Horse Sense

The ability to get in Touch with our Elemental Sense of Direction can be called Plain Horse Sense. According to *Webster's, horse sense* means "plain shrewd unsophisticated common sense." Naturally, the Common Sense of Weirdward Intergalactically Galloping Nags is quite unlike the "common sense" that is praised by the pseudosages of snooldom. The High-Spirited Horse Sense of Nags is unadulterated by the unsophistication as well as the sophistication of the sadosociety. It is Shrewd.

Indeed, the Horse Sense of Nags/Hags is nothing less than a Canny capacity to See, Hear, Touch, Taste, and Sniff out the Angelic/Elemental messages that come to us from all directions. In this sense, Horse Sense is a Primal Navigational Aid. Moreover, it heightens and brings into focus the ordinary senses of those who are escaping from dummydom. Hence it helps us to detect and refuse the poisoned apples and other elementary "wonders" dispensed by wasters disguised as wizards—the bad alchemists of snooldom.

With the aid of Horse Sense, Nags are also freed to reclaim the ability/agility required to Sense the Senses of words that are our Guides. Galloping beyond the inane verbiage of babblespheres, we Re-call the Labrys-like character of Wild words. We note that the word *Be-Longing,* for example, Magnetizes Musing women, reminding us of our true course/cause, and that at the same Time it aids us in warding off the prevailing banality of the State of Depression/Repression/Oppression, which is marked by the embedding of false needs to "belong." Such words help Hags to fend off the paralyzing plastic and potted passions, together with the elementary terms—such as the pseudowords of psychobabble—which sustain these false emotions.

The expression *Horse Sense* is itself a strong reminder that we must Re-member Senses that we have in common with Animals. As the *Wickedary* explains, Animals are "elementally ensouled beings characterized by rich Diversity; instructors in the arts of Spinning, healing, communication, navigation; Helpers/Guides on the Journey beyond the State of Extinction into the Realms of Elemental Reality" (*Word-Web One*). The Senses that we have in common with these Wise beings (in varying modes and degrees) include not only the conventionally acknowledged "five senses" but also Others. Among these we Dis-cover a Sense known to medieval philosophers as the "estimative power," which enables an Animal to judge or estimate what is good or harmful, useful or useless for her life.[3] Clearly, this Sense is indispensable for Journeyers/Searchers.

Shrews/Spinsters/Nags Spinning beyond the compass are reclaiming our Elemental Estimative Sense, our Archaic instinctive ability to judge what is Good and useful from what is harmful or useless for Life.

276

In the process of reclaiming this Radical Sense, we Dis-cover Other Lost Senses, which have faded from consciousness in the miasma of patriarchy.

Horse Sense aids Nags/Hags in the hunt for these Lost Senses, which are necessary aids on the Metapatriarchal Voyage. Among these are such Normal Senses as telepathy and clairvoyance (labeled in snooldom as "paranormal" and frequently as delusionary). Pivotal among the Lost Senses are the Haggard Sense of Humor and the Sense of Wonder. It is Horse Sensible to consider each of these in turn.

The Haggard Sense of Humor

Women gifted with Horse Sense are often accused of "lacking a sense of humor." This accusation is predictable in the State of Reversal. Naturally, Hags possess a Haggard Sense of Humor. The word *haggard*, according to *Webster's*, means "intractable, willful, wanton." Intractable, Willful, Wanton women See, Hear, Taste, Touch, Smell through the deceptions of phallocracy. A Natural expression of such perceptions is Horselaughing. Indeed, Horsey women/Nags frequently indulge in Horselaughing.

The expression of our Haggard Sense of Humor is often condemned by means of such epithets as "tasteless, inappropriate, weird." Tasteless Hags gladly take on these words as Names. Some proclaim ourSelves as Weird as Gooneys. We invite the labelers to consult the *Wickedary* for a definition of the word *Gooney,* which is "an albatross: much maligned Weird bird who possesses an impeccable sense of humor and direction and who habitually wanders on long, tireless flights . . . a woman who participates in the qualities of a Gooney" (*Word-Web Two*).

Gooney Gossips proclaim that our impeccable Sense of Direction implies a delicate balance between the Sense of Levity and the Sense of Gravity. This balance makes possible our long, tireless flights beyond the range of maps and compasses.

The Sense of Wonder

The purposefulness of such flights is rooted in the Sense of Wonder,* which is inherently infinite. Because the Final Cause is always/all ways

---

* Websters who have wondered about the word *wonder* will be interested in the fact that one of its synonyms is *marvel,* which is derived from the Indo-European root *smei-,* meaning "to laugh, smile" (*American Heritage,* Appendix on Indo-European Roots). Clearly, there is a connection between humor and wonder.

277

beckoning, Spinning beyond the compass is never ended. Unlike the phallic finishers/fixers, whose goal is to finish/obliterate life, Searching women generate/regenerate Life with Leaps of Imagination and Daring. Such boundless bounding, because it is Super Natural, is Hopping/Hoping in harmony with Other worlds. Such Springing breaks the dead beat of doomdom's funereal processions. That is, it is Bio-rhythmic.

Bio-rhythmic Movement Magnetizes others into its whirling vortices. Whirling dervishes vault over the sound barriers of snooldom, generating sequences of Gynergetic vibrations among our Selves, inspiring/inviting concomitant Qualitative Leaping by more and more Others. The resonance of these vibrations has an inherent tendency to expand and attract,[4] moving beyond Stag-nation, reaching for the stars.

Guided by Angelic Forces, Travelers glimpse near and farther galaxies. Breaking out from man-made mazes, Sibyls Sense Diverse Directions and become Intergalactic Travel Agents. Pixie-led Prudes book passage for Outer/Inner Space Voyages.

Horselaughing Nags whinny at the foolish "space programs" of the phallotechnic fellows. Hags howl at the flops/plops of fundamentalist phallocrats as they lurch toward "heaven." Gooneys giggle at the "space races" of flopocracy's flying fetuses, whose pinoramic bore's-eye-view of "space voyaging" brings tears of laughter to Eyebiting Eyes.

The whinnying, howling, and giggling of Spinning Space Voyagers raises Terrible Tempests, providing Elemental Energy for the trip. These Wicked blasts of Weird wind arrive in the nick of Crone-Time, just as the cosmic Crone-Powered clock strikes Thirteen. This brings us to the subject of jumping off the doomsday clock, which will be discussed in the following, and final, Appendicular Web.

APPENDICULAR WEB FOUR

Jumping Off the doomsday clock: Eleven, Twelve . . . Thirteen

Spinsters Spinning Widdershins—turning about-face—feel/find an Other Sense of Time. We begin by asking clock-whys and then move on to counter these clock-whys with Counterclock Whys—Questions that whirl the Questioners beyond the boundaries of Boredom, into the flow of Tidal Time/Elemental Time. This is Wild Time, beyond the clocking/clacking of clonedom. It is the Time of Wicked Inspiration/Genius, which cannot be grasped by the tidily man-dated world.

The man-dated world is clockocracy—the society that is dead set by the clocks and calendars of fathered time. It is marked by measurements that tick off women's Lifetimes/Lifelines in tidy tidbits. It is the world of dismembered time, surgically sewn together to mimic and replace Tidal Time. It is the society of tedious time spent under the tyranny of tidy demons—those projections/emanations of the tyrants who seek to impose tidy order, to tie women down, to stop the flow of each woman's creativity, cutting her off from her Genius/Demon/Muse.

Clockocracy is marked by male-ordered monotony that breaks Biorhythms, preparing the way for the fullness of fathered time, that is, doomsday. The fathers' clocks are all doomsday clocks, meting out archetypal deadtime, marking the beat of the patriarchal death march. They are measures of the untime of the State of Possession—tidy time, nuclear time, doomed time.

Since 1947 a.d. (archetypal deadtime), the *Bulletin of the Atomic Scientists* (a prestigious american journal)* has displayed a picture of a

---

* See **prestige** (*Word-Web Three*).

Norn releasing the Doomsday Wolf . . . *Dooming the doomers*

"doomsday clock" which represents the degree of nuclear peril as perceived by the editors. In this symbol, "midnight" represents the hour of nuclear holocaust. Only twice have the clock's hands been set as close as three minutes to midnight—first, in 1953 (in response to the advent of the hydrogen bomb), and second, in 1984 (in response to the nuclear arms race and the almost complete breakdown of communication between the superpowers). As the *Wickedary* goes to press, the "doomsday clock" remains set at this same moment of atomic/archetypal deadtime.[1] The terrible extent of the effects of the meltdown at Chernobyl as well as other nuclear "accidents" continues to be erased by the erasers/e-racers.[2]

Jumping Off the doomsday clock: Eleven, Twelve . . . Thirteen

This nonacknowledgment is one enormous manifestation of clockocratic doublethink—that nonthought process by which patriarchal reversals are generated and which makes belief in these absurdities possible. Doublethink and reversal characterize the madtime/badtime of the clockocrats—those doomsday men who generate and perpetuate the psychic numbing which, as Robert Jay Lifton states, is associated with "a lifelong psychological immersion in death: permanent fear of invisible contamination." As Lifton describes the situation:

> While one can speak of invisible contamination in connection with exposure of toxic chemicals, radiation disasters have an added aura of dread associated with limitless danger, fearful mystery, and images of Hiroshima and Nagasaki.[3]

Indeed, radiation disasters such as Chernobyl do spread a miasma of mystery, that is, the Mystery of Man. This is the mystery of the flopocratic pops of patriarchy who swing and bounce from one grotesque fiasco to another—the mysterical men whose fundamental dispassionate lust is for the destruction of all life. The invisible tentacles of these male-factors maintain the inhabitants of clockocracy in a psychically numbed state, wrapped and strangled in mindbindings/spiritbindings that stop Movement.

Raging/Be-Laughing Websters unwind these bindings that would numb us, dumb us. With Eyebiting Eyes/I's we See through and Name man's interconnected atrocities—his rapism, his witchcrazes, his vile medical experimentation, his intended annihilation of the animals, the trees, the rivers, and seas. We Proclaim that the primary product of man's civilization/snivelization is toxic waste and that patriarchy/phallocracy/fatherland is the world of wasters: It is Wasteland.

Spinsters Spinning about-face face the fact that clockocracy's clocks are elementary moons. Whirling Witches Announce that the subject of clocks and calendars is about Face. Will we Face down the faceless "face-saving" fools who are the fathers of phallocracy/foolocracy? Lusty women, in tune with the Moon, pose the poignant Question: Is the Moon's Face the Face that can stop the doomsday clock?

The Moon in her various aspects awakens our knowledge of Gorgons, of Weirds, of Fates, of Norns. In the face of impending disaster, these Sidereal Sisters draw us onward, sharing their Powers.

Empowered by this Company, women as Gorgons look toward the madmen and turn them to stone—the doomsday men with their doomsday clocks whose tick-tocks mimic the rhythms of Lunar Time. Gorgons glare outward, refusing to serve the masters' commands to peer into mirrors. We tear off the blindfold from captive Justice, crying that the Time has come to Activize, to See with Active Eyes. We actualize Archimagical Powers, Beaming through the archetypal images that block Vision. We say that Eye-Beams/I-Beams can stop the doomsday clock—that Moonward-turning Eyes can break the spells of twelves, Spelling *Thirteen*.

Twelve is the measure of the master-minded monotony of the foreground. Nags need only think of the twelve apostles, the twelve days of christmas, twelve men on a jury, twelve hours on clock, twelve months on a cockocratic calendar. In general, Websters prefer a baxter's dozen[4]—a coded reminder of the Elemental number *Thirteen*. Lusty women Sense the primal potency of the Elemental, Thirteen-month Lunar year.

Thirteen represents the Other Hour, beyond the direction of disaster. It signals the Presence of the Otherworld—Metamorphospheres—true Homeland of all Hags, Crones, Furies, Furries, and Other Friends. It represents the Realm of Wild Reality, the Background, the Time/Space when/where auras of plants, planets, stars, animals, and all truly animate be-ing connect. It points to Living Worlds utterly foreign to foolocracy—Worlds that are Eccentric, Erratic, Odd, Queer, Quaint, Outlandish, Weird.

Thirteen signals Spheres of Macromutational events, where Prudes explore the States of Grace, where Websters see Stamina as its own reward, where Dragons are in our Elements, and where Muses Muse, Compose, Create.

Thirteen Spells Doom to the would-be doomers. It signals the release of the Doomsday Wolf that Fates/Norns had hitherto restrained.[5] It Spells awakening of Memory, of Metamemory, the Self-unveiling of Metamysterious Crones, whose Eye-Bites snap the chains of fettered Time.

The awakening of Metamemory is crucial to the Eyebiting Power of the Crone. Since Metamemory is Deep Ecstatic Memory of participation in Be-ing, it is also the Broom of the Crone, enabling her to jump off the doomsday clock of doomdom, to hop into the Hour of Hope, the Be-Witching Hour of *Thirteen*.

Lusty, Wicked women are increasingly aware that the Thirteenth Hour is the Hour of the Crone, who Alone can clearly See that the sadosociety is ruled by weak, doddering old fools whose overt and subliminal Lies permeate the man-made atmosphere as insidiously as their radioactive and chemical poisons. These old fools/snools are the priests of patriarchal religion, government, nuclear science and industry, and all the academented fields of fatherland. Crones (of all Ages) can say No to these men. Barbara Walker has written:

Jumping Off the doomsday clock: Eleven, Twelve . . . Thirteen

> Most of all, the Crone can represent precisely the kind of power women so desperately need today, and do not have: the power to force men to do what is right, for the benefit of future generations and of the earth itself. Forcing seems to be necessary. Men do not voluntarily relinquish their ego trips, war toys, and money games. . . . Men feared the judgmental eye of the wisewoman even when she was socially powerless. This, then, is the chink in the armor of patriarchal establishments. When many women together say no and mean it, the whole structure can collapse.[6]

Walker brings her argument to a stunning conclusion:

> Women, who have suffered so much at the hands of patriarchal mythmakers, need no longer pretend not to understand their motives. God can't, but woman can call man to account for his gynocidal, genocidal behavior.
>
> She had better do it soon, for he is already counting down to doomsday.[7]

It is not only her clear Knowledge and Memory of patriarchal evil that is the key to the Crone's Eyebiting Powers, however. It is her Ecstatic, Metamysterious Vision that makes *Thirteen* the Possible Dream. Such Vision is grounded not only in suffering but especially in the experience of Happiness, of Living in harmony with Wonderlusting energies that beckon us further and further from the confines of the fathers' foreground.

To Crone-logically Leaping Intelligence, *Thirteen* Spells the hitherto/as yet Unknown, the Elemental Forces/Sources that can save even planets doomed to destruction. It signals events that are not measurable, controllable, predictable—the Call of the Wild, the ever recurring Spring of New Creation. It Spells the Dawn of the Dream, the Sunrise and Moonrise, and further still, the Spinning of Spiral Galaxies whose majestic arms ponderously rotate in magnificent celestial ballets.

This context Spells Hope—the Hope of jumping off the parameters of the predators' predictability. The context that is suggested by Meta-phoric/Metamorphic *Thirteen* is the context of Leaping, of carrying Threads of Life through galaxies of Gynergetic/Gynergenetic Creation. The Tapestries thus woven are records of Re-membering and Foretelling Future Memories. They are recordings of celestial sound waves and light waves, chorusing morphogenetic resonances with stars.

Thirteen Re-calls possibilities of Metamorphosis, inspiring those who will to shift the shapes of words, of worlds. It points to Spaces/Times of New beginnings, of whirring whirls. It conjures whirlpools, whirlwinds, whose force unwinds the doomers' clocks, unlocks pent-up Elemental flocks of Weaving Spirits.

In this Be-Witching Hour, then, Crones are joined by Other participants in Elemental Be-ing. Moreover, as we have seen, Journeyers are Guided by many Mediums, who act as channels into the Background.* These include the stars, sun, and moon, as well as Other planets. Present, too, are the earth, air, fire, and water. Rivers, trees, mountains, seas also Act as Guides. Angels Presentiate their Selves on the Journey, bringing messages and protection. Foresisters are Here/There, accompanied by their/our Familiars—the hopping, leaping, prancing, soaring, splashing, diving, roving, lumbering crowd of hairy, feathery, finny, furry Friends who are at Home in the Thirteenth Hour. As the Toads say: "This is Toadal Time." As the Gorgons cry: "It's Time to get Gorgonized!"

Thirteen, then, is the time of Metamysterious Meetings, of synchronicities—"coincidences" experienced by Crones as Strangely significant. It is the Time of Realizing Star-Lust—the longing for knowledge of Astral connections, for scintillating cosmic conversations. Hence it is the Crone-logical Time for Weaving and Spinning Crone-ography and Crone-ology. It is the Time when Sibyls and Muses soar with the Race of Radiant Words. And of course it is the Hour when/where *Wickedaries* appear and Wicked women Announce our Departure from the State of Patriarchal Paralysis and our Arrival in Metamorphospheres.

Thirteen is when/where a Positively Revolting Hag Hears her own Name and finds the Courage to Be, to See, to Live, to Grieve, to Rage, and to Laugh Out Loud. And that is the End and the Beginning of *Websters' First New Intergalactic Wickedary of the English Language* and Other Archaic adventures/ventures of Weird women who cast our lot with the Fates, the Spinners of Stamina, the Forces who can save the world.

* See *Preliminary Web Five.*

NOTES

Preface

1. Judy Grahn, in *The Queen of Wands* (Trumansburg, N.Y.: The Crossing Press, 1982), p. xiii, has introduced the Name *Webster*. She writes: "This spirit is a weaving spider, a fate spinner from whose very body comes the cloth of life and time and understanding. I named this spirit *webster*, or Spider Webster. Webster is a word that formerly meant 'female weaver,' the 'ster' ending indicating a female ancestor, or female possession of the word."

2. These Word-Works by Mary Daly are:

> *The Church and the Second Sex* (Boston: Beacon Press, 1985). This recent edition contains the text of the original edition (New York: Harper and Row, 1968) and the "Autobiographical Preface" and "Feminist Postchristian Introduction by the Author" from the Harper Colophon edition (1975), as well as the 1985 "New Archaic Afterwords."

> *Beyond God the Father: Toward a Philosophy of Women's Liberation* (Boston: Beacon Press, 1973, 1985). The 1985 edition contains the "Original Reintroduction by the Author."

> *Gyn/Ecology: The Metaethics of Radical Feminism* (Boston: Beacon Press, 1978).

> *Pure Lust: Elemental Feminist Philosophy* (Boston: Beacon Press, 1984).

3. Some of these conversations with Cronies are recorded in the books cited in note 2 as well as in the notes to the various Webs of the *Wickedary*.

4. I have explained and elaborated upon the theme of this Journey in *Gyn/Ecology: The Metaethics of Radical Feminism*, pp. 1–34.

5. The concepts *Background* and *foreground* were first Named by Denise D. Connors during a conversation in Boston, October 1976. See Daly, *Gyn/Ecology: The Metaethics of Radical Feminism*, pp. 2–3.

The Wickedary: Its History/Metamystery

1. Tidal Time, which is Archaic Time, is Original Creative Time, Measurable only by Qualitative Leaps of Wicked Inspiration and Courage. It cannot be measured by the clocks of father time.

2. This expression was first Realized by Denise D. Connors (Conversation, Leverett, Mass., January 1983).

3. Not only dictionaries but all sorts of masculine inventions and "masterpieces" are in reality the products of plunderers/exploiters. Victims of such exploitation include Rosalind Franklin, Zelda Fitzgerald, Mary Leakey, Fanny Mendelsohn, Dorothy Wordsworth, and countless other wives, sisters, daughters, helpers, researchers, editors, etc., who have actually supplied many or most of the creative ideas and done much of the hard work. See Anne Sayre, *Rosalind Franklin and DNA* (New York: W. W. Norton, 1975); Nancy Milford, *Zelda* (New York: Avon, 1970); and Tillie Olsen, *Silences* (New York: Delacorte Press/Seymour Lawrence, 1965, 1972, 1978), esp. pp. 177–258.

4. It can be argued that the Eleusinian mysteries of ancient Greece were woman-centered. However, we hear of these as existing within the context of a patriarchal culture. It seems highly unlikely that such "mysteries" would be necessary in a truly Gynocentric/Gynocratic society.

5. One sterling, strident, and stunning example of such a Notice and Announcement is the historically momentous *SCUM Manifesto* by Valerie Solanas, first published in New York (Olympia Press, 1967, 1968, 1970). See Valerie Solanas, *Scum Manifesto* (London: The Matriarchy Study Group, 1983). This edition can be obtained by writing to The Matriarchy Study Group, c/o 190 Upper St., London, N.1.

6. For example, the mysterious men of the Vatican continually re-veil their inherent evil, hypocrisy, and cynical exploitativeness. A number of exposés of Vatican intrigue have appeared in the 1980s, for example, Richard Hammer, *The Vatican Connection* (New York: Holt, Rinehart and Winston, 1982); Paul I. Murphy with R. René Arlington, *La Popessa* (New York: Warner Books, 1983). An interesting point revealed in *La Popessa* concerns the Vatican's economic interest in birth control products, beginning in the 1930s, "specifically, the Vatican's purchase of controlling stock in a drug company, Instituto Farmacologico Serono di Roma, Italy's largest manufacturer of birth control products" (p. 99). Decades later, pope Pius XII "appointed his nephew, Giulio Pacelli, chairman of the board of the drug company making birth-control pills" (p. 109).

7. For a wonderfully Be-Laughing exposé of ridiculous ritualism, see Virginia Woolf, *Three Guineas* (New York: Harcourt, Brace & World, 1938; Harbinger Books, 1966), especially pp. 19–21.

8. For an excellent feminist analysis of the patriarchal degradation of nature, see Andrée Collard, "Rape of the Wild," *Trivia: A Journal of Ideas*, no. 2 (Spring 1983), pp. 64–86. These ideas are further expanded in Collard's forthcoming book, *Rape of the Wild* (London: The Women's Press, 1988).

9. Of course, not all nurses participate in the mysteries of patriarchal medicine. Rather than protecting doctors' silences, some nurses Name their games. For example, see Denise Donnell Connors, "Sickness unto Death: Medicine as Mythic, Necrophilic, and Iatrogenic," *Advances in Nursing Science*, vol. 2, no. 3 (April 1980), pp. 39–51, for an explanation and discussion of doctor-caused disease. Connors further develops this analysis in "Women's Sickness: A Case of Secondary Gains or Primary Losses," *Advances in Nursing Science*, vol. 7, no. 3 (April 1985), pp. 1–17. An

organization of radical nurses who work to unveil male medical mystery and move on to Re-member their own healing power is Cassandra: Radical Feminist Nurses Network. To receive their newsjournal, which provides informative articles, important announcements, and lists of contact women, write to *Cassandra*, P.O. Box 341, Williamsville, N.Y. 14221.

10. Lewis Spence, *The Magic Arts in Celtic Britain* (New York: Rider and Co., n.d.), p. 102.

11. This expression was invented by Virginia Woolf. See *Three Guineas*, pp. 93–97.

PRELIMINARY WEB TWO

Spelling: The Casting of Spells

1. Morris Bishop, "Good Usage, Bad Usage, and Usage," in *The American Heritage Dictionary of the English Language* (Boston: Houghton Mifflin Company, 1976), p. xxi.

2. This section can be seen as a discussion of Metamorphic Morphology. According to *Webster's*, one definition of *morphology* is "a study and description of word-formation in a language including inflection, derivation, and compounding—distinguished from *syntax*."

3. Heinrich Kramer and James Sprenger, *The Malleus Maleficarum*, trans. with introductions, bibliography, and notes by the Rev. Montague Summers (London, 1928; New York: Dover Publications, Inc., 1971), The Second Part, Question I, Chapter XV, pp. 147–49.

4. Julian Jaynes, *The Origin of Consciousness in the Breakdown of the Bicameral Mind* (Boston: Houghton Mifflin Company, 1976), p. 73.

5. Be-Spelling women can learn a great deal about dealing with drones from our sisters, the Worker Bees. The drone—whose brain is smaller than that of both worker and queen—has as the sole justification of his existence the necessity of fertilizing the queen. Once the young queens have ceased to fly, the hundreds of excess drones in a colony are treated as eminently disposable. Karl von Frisch, a specialist, discussing the fate of drones, writes: "The workers start plucking and biting those very drones whom up to now they have nursed and fed, pinching them with their firm jaws wherever they can get hold of them. Grasping their feelers or their legs, they try to pull them away from the combs, and to drag them toward the door of the hive. . . . Once they are turned out of the hive, the drones, unable to fend for themselves, are doomed to die of starvation. With great obstinacy they try to force their way back, only to be received again by the workers' biting jaws, and even by their poisonous sting, to which they yield without offering any resistance. For drones do not possess a poisonous sting, nor for that matter the least fighting spirit. Thus they find their inglorious end at the portals of the bee dwelling. . . . From that time onwards until the following spring, the females of the colony, left to themselves, keep an undisturbed peace." See *The Dancing Bees: An Account of the Life and Senses of the Honey Bee*, trans. by Dora Ilse (New York: Harcourt, Brace and Company, 1955), pp. 31–32.

6. Suzette Haden Elgin, in her remarkable novel *Native Tongue* (New York: Daw Books, Inc., 1984), describes the liberation of women through the invention of "Láadan"—a language developed and known by females only. The invention of this language is a catalyst for leaps of Metamorphosis in women's lives.

7. In *Native Tongue*, Elgin imaginatively illustrates how the creation of a woman-

identified language could change reality in completely unpredictable ways. See especially the last chapter (pp. 284–97).

8. This ancient traditional meaning of *element* is spelled out in Raymond T. Stamm, Exegesis of the Epistle to the Galatians, 4:3, in *The Interpreter's Bible*, 12 vols. (New York: Abingdon-Cokesbury Press, 1952–57), X, 521.

9. The idea of the *Wickedary* as an Abecedarium and of Websters as Abecedarians was suggested by Emily Culpepper (Conversation, Boston, February 1986).

10. Robert Graves, *The Greek Myths*, 2 vols. (Baltimore: Penguin Books, 1955, 1960), I, 52.2.

PRELIMINARY WEB THREE

Grammar: Our Wicked Witches' Hammer

1. W. Nelson Francis, "The English Language and Its History," *Webster's New Collegiate Dictionary*, 1975, p. 22a.

2. Julia Penelope (Stanley) has most clearly identified "syntactic exploitation" of women by patriarchal authors. This is deceptive manipulation of grammatical constructs and sentence structure. A common form of syntactic exploitation is "agent deletion," which involves suppressing information about the identity of the agent of an action—information that is required by the reader or hearer for understanding the message or meaning of a sentence. Agent deletion is often accomplished through the use of the passive voice, as in the sentence "Many women are battered." Agent (and victim) deletion often involves the use of pseudogenerics. This is exemplified in sentences such as "Many children are victims of incestuous abuse by their parents." See Julia P. Stanley, "Passive Motivation," *Foundations of Language*, vol. 13, pp. 25–39. See also Julia P. Stanley and Susan W. Robbins, "Truncated Passives: Some of Our Agents Are Missing," *Linguistic Theory and the Real World*, vol. 1, no. 2 (September 1976), pp. 33–37. Julia Penelope has developed her ideas in numerous papers and articles.

3. Many pedants idealized Latin, since it was a dead language, and saw this idealized corpse as a model for fixed English. The forgotten "poet" Waller bemoaned living language in the following words:

> But who can hope his lines should long
> Last, in a daily changing tongue?
> While they are new, Envy prevails;
> And as that dies, our language fails. . . .
>
> Poets that Lasting Marble seek,
> Must carve in Latin or in Greek;
> We write in Sand. . . .

Cited in Albert C. Baugh, *A History of the English Language* (New York: D. Appleton-Century Company, Inc., 1935), p. 322.

4. Jonathan Swift, *A Proposal for Correcting, Improving and Ascertaining the English Tongue, 1712* (Menston, England: The Scolar Press, 1969), p. 31.

5. Samuel Johnson, Preface, 1755, in *Johnson's Dictionary: A Modern Selection*, ed. by E. L. McAdam, Jr., and George Milne (New York: Pantheon, 1963), p. 26.

6. Samuel Johnson, *The Plan of a Dictionary, 1747* (Menston, England: The Scolar Press, 1970), p. 11.

288

7. Johnson, Preface, 1755, p. 27.

8. Ibid., p. 26.

9. Virginia Woolf, BBC radio broadcast, late 1930s.

10. Otis Tufton Mason, *Woman's Share in Primitive Culture* (New York: Macmillan, 1895), p. 190.

11. Virginia Woolf, BBC radio broadcast, late 1930s.

12. Monique Wittig describes tamed women as "prisoners of the mirror." See her book *Les Guérillères,* trans. by David Le Vay (New York: The Viking Press, 1969, 1971), p. 31.

13. According to popular belief, breaking a mirror is bad luck (and so also are encounters with black cats and the number thirteen). Wicked women, smashing mirrors, crossing paths with cats, and adopting Thirteen as our lucky number, declare these events auspicious/fortunate.

14. Lewis Spence, *Encyclopedia of Occultism* (New Hyde Park, N.Y.: University Books, 1960), p. 184.

15. Gertrude Stein, "Poetry and Grammar," in *Gertrude Stein: Writings and Lectures, 1909–1945,* ed. by Patricia Meyerowitz (Baltimore: Penguin Books, Inc., 1967), p. 126.

16. It is interesting to note that the Middle English word *gramary* (also, more archaically, *gramarye*) meant "1) Grammar; hence, learning in general; erudition, and 2) Magic; enchantment." In both of these senses the *Wickedary* is a book of gramary. See Sherman Kuhn and John Reidy, eds., *Middle English Dictionary* (Ann Arbor: University of Michigan Press, 1963), p. 2594. It is also fascinating to find that *gramarye* (or *gramary*) is derived from Middle French *gramaire,* meaning "grammar, grammar book, book of sorcery" (*Webster's*). An alternative form of *gramaire* is *grimoire,* meaning "a book of conjuring or magic" (*Middle English Dictionary*).

17. For a historical and philosophical analysis of this concept, see Daly, *Beyond God the Father: Toward a Philosophy of Women's Liberation,* pp. 179–98.

18. This expression is used by Nelle Morton to describe the prevailing "reasoning" of patriarchy, characterized by the assumption that words (male words) precede and authenticate all female experience. See Nelle Morton, "Beloved Image," *The Journey Is Home* (Boston: Beacon Press, 1985), p. 127.

19. Women tricked by these tricksters are sometimes mesmerized into believing that pornography is "exciting" and even "liberating." Some have been fooled into believing that such an attitude is "feminist." Be-Speaking Grammarians point out that such obsessions are not at all Wicked, but woman-hating, Self-hating. The same Prudish reasoning applies to all manifestations of sadomasochism. Since a truly Feminist stance on these phallic phenomena—i.e., that they are utterly opposed to the Good for women—is nonnegotiable, any talk of a "split among feminists" on these "issues" is pure phalloglamour.

PRELIMINARY WEB FOUR

Pronunciation: Denouncing, Pronouncing, Announcing

1. Wayne O'Neil, "The Spelling and Pronunciation of English," in *The American Heritage Dictionary of the English Language* (Boston: Houghton Mifflin Company, 1976), p. xxxv.

2. In the 1970s many women took on the epithet "Bitch" as a defiant affirmation

of strength. See Joreen, "The Bitch Manifesto," in *Radical Feminism,* ed. by Anne Koedt, Ellen Levine, and Anita Rapone (New York: Quadrangle Books, 1973), pp. 50–59.

3. Animals have been major targets of patriarchal users. An example of such an experimenter is Professor Harry Harlow, who, together with his wife, M. K. Harlow, proclaimed: "Another excellent reason for using other species is that we can subject them to conditions that cannot be imposed upon human beings. We can expose them to long periods of social or sensory deprivation. . . . We can also damage the brains of laboratory animals." Cited in Richard Ryder, "Experiments on Animals," in *Animals, Men and Morals: An Enquiry into the Maltreatment of Non-Humans,* ed. by Stanley and Roslind Godlovitch and John Harris (New York: Taplinger, 1972), p. 75. Harlow's experiments included trying to induce mental disorders in infant monkeys by putting them into complete isolation for up to twelve months. Working with his colleague Stephen Suomi, Harlow strove to induce depression in infant monkeys by attaching them to artificial surrogate mothers. These cloth and wire contraptions were both "mothers" and torture devices which could eject high-pressure compressed air, rock so violently that the babies' teeth would rattle, or (on the scientists' command) eject brass spikes into the babies' skin. Not content with the artificial "monster" mothers, Harlow and Suomi produced living ones by taking female monkeys who had been raised in isolation and therefore would not accept sexual relations with males and placing these on what they termed a "rape rack," so that they were forced to conceive. After the babies were born, the mothers were often lethally abusive to them. See also Harry F. Harlow, *Learning to Love* (San Francisco: Albion, 1971). See Peter Singer, *Animal Liberation: A New Ethics for Our Treatment of Animals* (New York: Avon Books, 1975), pp. 41–44. Andrée Collard, in her forthcoming book *Rape of the Wild* (London: The Women's Press, 1988), analyzes these and other atrocities against animals from the perspective of Radical Feminism. See especially Chapter Three, "Animal Experimentation," and Chapter Four, "Life with Father."

4. Nelle Morton, "Beloved Image," in *The Journey Is Home* (Boston: Beacon Press, 1985), pp. 128–29.

5. See J. C. Cooper, *An Illustrated Encyclopedia of Traditional Symbols* (London: Thames and Hudson, 1978), p. 24. In his entry under "Book," Cooper states: "The book is connected with tree symbolism and the Tree and Book can represent the whole cosmos. In Grail symbolism the book can also typify the Quest, in this case for the lost Word."

6. The basic reason for the tedium of such terms as *chronology* and *chronological* is that the chroniclers erase all woman-identified and Elemental events. An example of Crone-ology can be found in Susan Griffin, *Woman and Nature: The Roaring Inside Her* (New York: Harper and Row, 1978), pp. 15–17. An example of Crone-logical writing is this Web/essay.

7. Woolf first wrote of the "processions of the sons of educated men" in *Three Guineas* (New York: Harcourt, Brace & World, 1938; Harbinger Books, 1966), pp. 60–84. This idea is further developed in Daly, *Gyn/Ecology: The Metaethics of Radical Feminism,* pp. 30–105.

8. The concept of the Boundary is discussed in Daly, *Beyond God the Father: Toward a Philosophy of Women's Liberation,* pp. 40–43.

9. Patriarchal myth reflects the dearth of prophetic powers in males and their subsequent attempts to associate themselves with oracular sites and powers. Robert Briffault reports that the Norse god Wotan, or Odin, "was, in spite of the exalted position he occupied, deficient in prophetic powers. When he wanted to know the

future he was compelled to have recourse to goddesses, in the same manner as his earthly counterparts had to resort to prophetic women." See Robert Briffault, *The Mothers: A Study of the Origins of Sentiments and Institutions,* 3 vols. (New York: Macmillan, 1927), III, 67–68. It is significant that in Greek myth the god Apollo took over the Oracle of Gaea at Delphi but retained the priestesses. It is also noteworthy that when women visit ancient holy sites such as the cathedrals built to Mary in Europe, they often experience a Divining Presence. This can be attributed to the fact that such edifices were built over ancient "pagan," woman-centered, sacred places. Similarly, the Kaaba, shrine of the sacred stone in Mecca and now regarded as the holy center of patriarchal Islam, was formerly dedicated to the pre-Islamic Triple Goddess Manat, Al-Lat, and Al-Uzza, the "Old Woman." See Barbara G. Walker, *The Woman's Encyclopedia of Myths and Secrets* (San Francisco: Harper and Row, 1983), p. 487.

10. This idea was developed at length by Joyce Contrucci in a lecture entitled "Women, Common Sense, and Psychology," in which she analyzed the reductionistic and materialistic world view at the core of the discipline of experimental psychology. Contrucci's talk, given on October 17, 1985, in Cambridge, Mass., was one of a series of lectures sponsored by W.I.T.C.H. (Wild Independent Thinking Crones and Hags).

11. Virginia Woolf, *A Room of One's Own* (New York: Harcourt, Brace & World, 1929; Harbinger Books, 1957), pp. 35–36.

12. Ibid., p. 36.

13. As Ernest Schachtel points out: ". . . the memories of the majority of people come to resemble increasingly the stereotyped answers to a questionnaire, in which life consists of time and place of birth, religious denomination, residence, educational degrees, job, marriage, number and birthdates of children, income, sickness, and death." See Ernest G. Schachtel, *Metamorphosis: On the Development of Affect, Perception, Attention, and Memory* (New York: Basic Books, Inc., 1959), p. 287.

14. "One of the medieval names for the owl was 'night hag'; it was said to be a witch in bird form." See Walker, *Woman's Encyclopedia of Myths and Secrets,* p. 754.

15. *Magpiety* is defined in the *Oxford English Dictionary* as a jocular word. The following example is given from 1845: "Not pious in its proper sense, But chattring like a bird, Of sin and grace—in such a case Mag-piety's the word."

PRELIMINARY WEB FIVE

Guides to the Wickedary

1. For a philosophical discussion of Final Causality, see Daly, *Beyond God the Father: Toward a Philosophy of Women's Liberation,* pp. 179–98. The idea of a woman "leading her own life" is horrifying to snools. A classic expression of this horror is the droning of pope Pius XII in his "Address to Women of Catholic Action," Oct. 21, 1945, in which he bemoans the fact that the daughter of a working mother "will want to emancipate herself as early as possible and, according to a truly sad expression, 'live her own life.'" Cited in Daly, *The Church and the Second Sex: With the Feminist Postchristian Introduction* and *New Archaic Afterwords* by the Author, p. 116.

2. See **Passive Voice**, *Word-Web Three.* For more on this concept, see Daly, *Gyn/Ecology: The Metaethics of Radical Feminism,* pp. 324–29.

3. Janice G. Raymond discusses the value of discernment in relation to female

friendship in her book *A Passion for Friends: Toward a Philosophy of Female Affection* (Boston: Beacon Press, 1986), pp. 171–73.

4. For additional material about sources already cited on torture and exploitation of animals in the name of science, see Hans Ruesch, *Slaughter of the Innocent* (New York: Bantam Books, Inc., 1978).

5. Dunsany, Edward (Lord), *The Curse of the Wise Woman* (New York: Longmans, Green and Co., 1933), p. 242.

6. Ibid.

7. See Daly, *Pure Lust: Elemental Feminist Philosophy,* pp. 260–88.

8. Ibid., pp. 200–207.

9. See Margaret A. Murray, *The Witch-Cult in Western Europe* (Oxford: Oxford University Press, 1921), p. 222.

10. Ibid., p. 206.

11. Oshun is Goddess of love and beauty in West Africa and in the African-Brazilian Macumba religion. Her earthly domains are inland waters, rivers, and streams. See Judy Grahn, *The Queen of Wands* (Trumansburg, N.Y.: The Crossing Press, 1982), p. 95.

12. Chih Nu is one of the most beloved Goddesses of China. See Patricia Monaghan, *The Book of Goddesses and Heroines* (New York: E. P. Dutton, 1981), p. 64.

13. Judy Grahn writes of the beliefs of Pueblo Indians concerning Spider Grand-mother/Thought Woman: "Because She thinks, we are. Her thoughts are like a psychic net dropped over the universe, as if a golden apple were spun into the tiniest possible molecules of light, electrons of inspiration, and dropped over us as a universal mind, one we enter in psychic and dream states, and through which knowledge passes to us." See Grahn, *The Queen of Wands,* pp. 98–99. See also Merlin Stone, *Ancient Mirrors of Womanhood* (1979; Boston: Beacon Press, 1984), pp. 284–312.

14. See Monaghan, *The Book of Goddesses and Heroines,* p. 110.

15. See Barbara G. Walker, *The Woman's Encyclopedia of Myths and Secrets* (San Francisco: Harper and Row, 1983), pp. 325–26.

16. See Walker, *The Woman's Encyclopedia,* pp. 628–29.

WORD-WEB ONE

Elemental Philosophical Words and Phrases and Other Key Words

1. This definition takes off from a discussion of allocentric perception by Ernest G. Schachtel in his book *Metamorphosis* (New York: Basic Books, 1959), pp. 176–85.

2. This word was invented by Louky Bersianik in *Les agénésies du vieux monde* (Outremont, Quebec: L'Intégrale, éditrice, 1982).

3. This word was first Dis-covered by Denise D. Connors (Conversation, Boston, Mass., October 1976).

4. Robin Morgan, "Monster," in *Monster* (New York: Random House, Vintage Books, 1972), pp. 81–86.

5. The image of a Lesbian nation was first conjured by Jill Johnston, *The Lesbian Nation: The Feminist Solution* (New York: Simon and Schuster, Touchstone Books, 1974).

6. Willie Tyson, "The Witching Hour," *Debutante,* Urana Records, STWWE-82.

7. This word was Newly Dis-covered by Anne Dellenbaugh (Conversation, Leverett, Mass., 1981). *Biocide* was previously Dis-covered by Rachel Carson in 1962.

8. Rachel Carson, *Silent Spring* (1962; New York: Ballantine Books, 1982), p. 18.

9. For a feminist discussion of Chinese marriage resisters see Janice G. Raymond, *A Passion for Friends: Toward a Philosophy of Female Affection* (Boston: Beacon Press, 1986), pp. 115–47.

10. A feminist analysis of the Beguines can be found in Raymond, *A Passion for Friends,* pp. 75–77, 81.

11. This definition takes off from ideas expressed by Paul Tillich in his book *The Courage to Be* (New Haven: Yale University Press, 1952).

12. For information on Mitchell's "rest cure," see G. J. Barker-Benfield, *The Horrors of the Half-Known Life: Male Attitudes Toward Women and Sexuality in Nineteenth-Century America* (New York: Harper and Row, 1976), p. 130. Significantly, Mitchell prescribed this "cure" for Charlotte Perkins Gilman, the great feminist activist, lecturer, and author, directing that she devote herself to domestic work and to her child, confine herself to, at most, two hours of intellectual work a day. See *The Living of Charlotte Perkins Gilman: An Autobiography* (New York: Appleton-Century, 1935), p. 96.

13. The vicious fragmentation of animals by agribusiness is discussed by Jim Mason and Peter Singer in *Animal Factories* (New York: Crown Publishers, 1980). These authors describe the effects of abuse, confinement, and stress on animals' psyches: "Some animals may become so fearful that they dare not move, even to eat or drink. They become runts and die. Others remain in constant, panicked motion, a neurotic perversion of their instinct to escape" (pp. 23–24).

14. Nelle Morton, "Beloved Image," *The Journey Is Home* (Boston: Beacon Press, 1985), pp. 127–28.

15. Muriel Rukeyser, "Käthe Kollwitz," *Collected Poems of Muriel Rukeyser* (New York: McGraw-Hill, 1982), p. 479.

16. The Elementals are discussed by Paracelsus in "Book of Nymphs, Sylphs, Pygmies, and Salamanders, and Kindred Beings," in *The Mystical and Medical Philosophy of Paracelsus* by Manly P. Hall (Los Angeles: The Philosophical Research Society, Inc., 1964), pp. 67–78.

17. Rachel Carson, *The Edge of the Sea* (Boston: Houghton Mifflin Company, 1955), p. 27.

18. The traditional biblical understanding of Elemental Spirits is, according to Raymond T. Stamm: "the spirits, angels, and demons which were believed to ensoul the heavenly bodies, traverse all space, and inhabit every nook and cranny of earth, particularly tombs, desert places, and demented persons." Raymond T. Stamm, Exegesis of the Epistle to the Galatians, 4:3, in *The Interpreter's Bible,* 12 vols. (New York: Abingdon-Cokesbury Press, 1952–57), X, 521.

19. The term *elementary* is borrowed from the philosopher and alchemist Paracelsus. As Manly P. Hall summarizes his views: "Most elementaries seem to be of an evil or destructive nature. They are generated from the excesses of human thought and emotion, the corruption of character, or the degeneration of faculties and powers which should be used in other, more constructive, ways." See Hall, *The Mystical and Medical Philosophy of Paracelsus,* p. 54.

20. This information was Gossiped Out by Diana Beguine. For further discussion see *Sappho: A New Translation,* ed. and trans. by M. Barnard (Berkeley: University of California Press, 1958); Arthur Weigall, *Sappho of Lesbos: Her Life and Times* (New York: Fred A. Stokes, 1932), pp. 318–21; Sappho, *Lyrics in the Original Greek,* with translations by Willis Barnstone (Garden City, N.Y.: Doubleday, Anchor Books, 1965), pp. xx–xxiii.

21. Sappho, Fragment No. 60 in *Sappho: A New Translation,* ed. and trans. by M. Barnard.

22. Elizabeth Oakes Smith, speech delivered at the National Woman's Rights Convention, 1852, in *History of Woman Suffrage,* ed. by Elizabeth Cady Stanton, Susan B. Anthony, and Matilda Joslyn Gage (New York: Fowler and Wells, 1881), I, 522–23.

23. This word was first Dis-covered by Denise D. Connors (Conversation, Boston, Mass., October 1976).

24. Raymond, *A Passion for Friends,* pp. 7–9.

25. The *Oxford English Dictionary* defines *gynecology* as "that department of medical science which treats of the functions and diseases peculiar to women; also *loosely,* the science of womankind."

26. This word was invented by Emily Culpepper. See Emily Culpepper, "Female History/Myth Making," *The Second Wave,* vol. 4, no. 1 (Spring 1975), pp. 14–17.

27. Raymond, *A Passion for Friends,* p. 7.

28. Zora Neale Hurston, *Dust Tracks on a Road,* 2nd ed., ed. and with an introduction by Robert E. Hemenway (Urbana, Ill.: University of Illinois Press, 1942, 1970, 1984), pp. 20–21.

29. Barbara Starrett, "I Dream in Female: The Metaphors of Evolution," *Amazon Quarterly,* vol. 3, no. 1 (November 1974), p. 13.

30. George Orwell, *1984* (1949; New York: New American Library, 1961), p. 32.

31. *The Trip to Bountiful,* dir. Peter Masterson, Bountiful Film Partners © 1985.

32. Virginia Woolf, *Moments of Being: Unpublished Autobiographical Writings,* ed. and with an introduction by Jeanne Schulkind (New York: Harcourt Brace Jovanovich, 1976), pp. 64–65.

33. Ibid., p. 67.

34. Robin Morgan, "The Network of the Imaginary Mother," in *Lady of the Beasts* (New York: Random House, 1976), pp. 85–86.

35. This word was invented by Denise D. Connors (Conversation, Maine, 1982).

36. For an enlivening discussion of Metaphor see Morton, *The Journey Is Home,* especially pp. 152–75, 212–23.

37. Cited in Donald Spoto, *The Dark Side of Genius: The Life of Alfred Hitchcock* (New York: Ballantine Books, 1983), p. 431.

38. Kenneth A. Briggs, "Synod Bishops Get Pope's Approval to Issue Report," *New York Times,* Dec. 8, 1985, Sec. 1, pp. 1, 19.

39. Arthur C. Clarke interviewed in Gene Youngblood, *Expanded Cinema* (New York: E. P. Dutton, 1970), p. 149.

40. Valerie Solanas, *SCUM Manifesto* (1967, 1968; London: The Matriarchy Study Group, 1983), p. 31.

41. Gage's unequivocal Naming of the primal creative powers of women is elaborated in an address written in 1884 and later published in *History of Woman Suffrage* (1883–1900), ed. by Susan B. Anthony and Ida Husted Harper (1902; Salem, N.H.: Ayer Company Publishers, Inc., 1985), IV, 28–30. See also Elizabeth Gould Davis, *The First Sex* (New York: G. P. Putnam's Sons, 1971).

42. For more information on Rosa Parks and the Montgomery bus boycott see Paula Giddings, *When and Where I Enter: The Impact of Black Women on Race and Sex in America* (New York: William Morrow and Co., Inc., 1984), pp. 261–67.

43. Cited in Wendy Martin, ed., *The American Sisterhood: Writings of the Feminist Movement from Colonial Times to the Present* (New York: Harper and Row, 1972), p. 102.

44. *Wildrose,* dir. John Hanson, New Front Films; Red Ghosts Films, Ltd. © 1983.

45. Pierre Teilhard de Chardin, S.J., "Some Reflections on the Spiritual Repercussions of the Atom Bomb" (1946), *The Future of Man,* trans. by Norman Denny (New York: Harper and Row, 1964), p. 146.

46. Olive Schreiner, cited in "Rebel Thoughts," *The Woman Rebel,* vol. 1, no. 3 (May 1914), p. 19.

47. Alice Walker, *The Color Purple* (New York: Harcourt Brace Jovanovich, 1982), pp. 175–76.

48. Reported by Reuters News Service, March 8, 1980, from Iki Island, Japan.

49. This word was invented by Denise D. Connors (Conversation, Leverett, Mass., January 1983).

50. Recounted by Ann Petry, *Harriet Tubman: Conductor of the Underground Railroad* (New York: Crowell, 1955), p. 101.

51. Wicked Witticism attributed to Gloria Steinem.

52. "Unreal loyalties" are discussed by Virginia Woolf in *Three Guineas* (New York: Harcourt, Brace & World, 1938; Harbinger Books, 1966), p. 78.

53. Cited in Herbert B. Workman, *The Evolution of the Monastic Ideal* (Boston: Beacon Press, 1962), p. 321.

54. Robert Oppenheimer: *Letters and Recollections,* ed. by Alice Kimball Smith and Charles Wiener (Cambridge, Mass.: Harvard University Press, 1980), p. 156.

55. Jane Caputi has written a comprehensive feminist analysis of the phenomenon of contemporary sexual murder in *The Age of Sex Crime* (Bowling Green, Ohio: Bowling Green University Popular Press, 1987).

56. See Daly, *Gyn/Ecology: The Metaethics of Radical Feminism,* pp. 130–33.

57. Pauli Murray to Rep. Edith Green's Special Subcommittee on Education, 1970, *Discrimination Against Women* (Washington, D.C.: Government Printing Office, 1971).

58. James Vogh, *Arachne Rising: The Thirteenth Sign of the Zodiac* (London: Hart-Davis, MacGibbon, 1977), p. 85.

59. Helen Diner, *Mothers and Amazons: The First Feminine History of Culture,* ed. and trans. by John Philip Lundin (New York: The Julian Press, Inc., 1965), p. 22.

60. Ida Cox, "Wild Women Don't Get the Blues," *Paramount* PM 12228. Ida Cox (1889–1968) was a Blues musician from Tennessee who made records from the 1920s through the early 1960s. "Wild Women Don't Get the Blues" was recorded on 78 rpm records between June 1923 and October 1929.

61. These lines are excerpted from "La Loba," a poem by Alfonsina Storni (Argentina, 1892–1938). These words were translated from the Spanish and set to music (with additional lyrics) by Teddy Holtz, 1976.

62. Rachel L. Carson, *The Sense of Wonder* (New York: Harper and Row, 1956), pp. 42–43.

WORD-WEB TWO

The Inhabitants of the Background, Their Activities and Characteristics

1. Alix Dobkin, "Amazon ABC," *Living with Lesbians,* Women's Wax Works, A001, 1976.

2. Robin Morgan, "A Country Weekend" (June 1970), in *Going Too Far: The Personal Chronicle of a Feminist* (1977; New York: Random House, Vintage Books, 1978), p. 142.

3. Brenda Walcott, "Amazons of Dahomey," *Slave of a Slave* (Cambridge, Mass., privately published by the author, 1974), n.p.

4. Monique Wittig and Sande Zeig, *Lesbian Peoples: Material for a Dictionary* (1976; New York: Avon Books, 1979), p. 5.

5. Sonia Johnson, *From Housewife to Heretic* (Garden City, N.Y.: Doubleday, 1981), p. 119.

6. Elmer G. Suhr, *The Spinning Aphrodite* (New York: Helios Books, 1969), p. 48.

7. Martha Jane Cannary Hickok, *Calamity Jane's Letters to Her Daughter* (San Lorenzo, Calif.: Shameless Hussy Press, 1976), letter of Sept. 1880.

8. Jane Ellen Harrison, letter (n.d.) quoted in *Jane Ellen Harrison: A Portrait from Letters,* ed. by Jessie G. Stewart (London: The Merlin Press, 1959), p. 5.

9. Vita Sackville-West, "The Bees Under My Bonnet," in *Time and Tide Anthology,* ed. by Anthony Lejeune (London: André Deutsch, 1956), p. 182.

10. Taped interview with Ms. Wild Cat, cited in *Pure Lust,* p. 414.

11. Joreen, "The Bitch Manifesto," in *Radical Feminism,* ed. by Anne Koedt, Ellen Levine, Anita Rapone (New York: Quadrangle Books, 1973), p. 5. This article first appeared in *Notes from the Second Year,* c. 1970 by Joreen. Many of the characteristics in the *Wickedary* definition of *Bitch* were drawn from this article.

12. Jean McMahon Humez, ed., *Gifts of Power: The Writings of Rebecca Jackson, Black Visionary, Shaker Eldress* (Amherst: The University of Massachusetts Press, 1981), p. 9.

13. Cited in Louise Bernikow, *Among Women* (New York: Harmony Books, 1980), p. 150.

14. Sylvia Beach, *Shakespeare and Company* (1956; New York: Harcourt Brace, 1959), p. 101.

15. Sojourner Truth, "Speech to the Convention of the American Equal Rights Association, New York City, 1867," in *Black Women in White America: A Documentary History,* ed. by Gerda Lerner (1972; New York: Vintage Books, 1973), p. 570.

16. Quoted in Karen Petersen and J. J. Wilson, *Women Artists: Recognition and Reappraisal from the Early Middle Ages to the Twentieth Century* (New York: Harper Colophon, 1976), p. 41. See especially Fini's painting "The Ideal Life" (1950).

17. Jane Frances (Lady) Wilde, *Ancient Legends/Mystic Charms and Superstitions of Ireland, with Sketches of the Irish Past* (London: Chatto and Windus, 1902), p. 14.

18. Conversation, Newton, Mass., January 1986.

19. Hsieh Ping-Ying, *Autobiography of a Chinese Girl* (London: Geo. Allen and Unwin, 1943), p. 207.

20. Virginia Woolf, *Three Guineas* (New York: Harcourt, Brace & World, 1938; Harbinger Books, 1966), p. 63.

21. Jane Anger, *Protection for Women,* excerpted in *by a Woman writt,* ed. by Joan Goulianos (1973; Baltimore: Penguin Books, 1974), p. 27.

22. The idea of "cosmosis" was invented and developed by Linda Barufaldi and Emily Culpepper in "Pandora's Box," *Proceedings of the Working Group on Women and Religion,* 1972, ed. by Judith Plaskow Goldenberg (Published by American Academy of Religion), p. 51.

23. Matilda Joslyn Gage, *Woman, Church and State* (1893; reprint ed. Watertown, Mass.: Persephone Press, 1980).

24. Susan Griffin, *Woman and Nature: The Roaring Inside Her* (New York: Harper and Row, 1978).

25. These lines are from the song "Buried Alive," words and music by Teddy Holtz, 1976.

26. WITCH Documents, 1969, in *Sisterhood Is Powerful: An Anthology of Writings from the Women's Liberation Movement,* ed. by Robin Morgan (New York: Random House, 1970), p. 553.

27. Gertrude Pridgett ("Ma" Rainey), "Prove It On Me Blues," Paramount 20665-2, 1928. This record has been reissued several times, including on the album *Ma Rainey* (Classic Jazz Series), Milestone Records M-47021, 1974.

28. Robert Southey, Letter of March 1837 to Charlotte Brontë, in *The Brontës: Their Lives, Friendships and Correspondence*, ed. by Thomas J. Wise and John A. Symington, 2 vols. (Philadelphia: Porcupine Press, Inc., 1980), I, 155.

29. Margaret Fuller, *Woman in the Nineteenth Century* (1855; New York: W. W. Norton, 1971), p. 56.

30. William Drake Westervelt, *Legends of Gods and Ghosts (Hawaiian Mythology)* (Boston: Press of Geo. H. Ellis, 1915), p. 130.

31. For more information on Jiu Jin see *Sisterhood Is Global: The International Women's Movement Anthology*, ed by Robin Morgan (Garden City, N.Y.: Anchor Press/Doubleday, 1984), p. 148.

32. Chris Albertson, *Bessie* (New York: Stein and Day, 1972), pp. 132–33.

33. Alice Walker, *The Color Purple* (New York: Harcourt Brace Jovanovich, 1982), p. 167.

34. Sylvia Townsend Warner, Letter to Bea Howe, Aug. 29, 1921, in Sylvia Townsend Warner, *Letters*, ed. by William Maxwell (New York: The Viking Press, 1982), p. 1.

35. Woolf, *Three Guineas*, p. 109.

36. Heinrich Kramer and James Sprenger, *The Malleus Maleficarum*, trans. with introductions and notes by the Rev. Montague Summers (London, 1928; New York: Dover Publications, Inc., 1971), p. 17n.

37. For historical information concerning Fairies, see Barbara G. Walker, *The Woman's Encyclopedia of Myths and Secrets* (San Francisco: Harper and Row, 1983), pp. 298–301.

38. *Greek Folk Songs*, ed. and trans. by Lucy M. J. Garnett (London: Eliot Stock, 1885), p. 111.

39. Woolf, *Three Guineas*, p. 36.

40. Jane Ellen Harrison, *Reminiscences of a Student's Life* (London: Hogarth Press, 1925), p. 70.

41. Matilda Joslyn Gage, in *National Citizen and Ballot Box*, May 1880. (This was a newspaper that Gage founded and edited.)

42. See Robert Briffault, *The Mothers: A Study of the Origins of Sentiments and Institutions*, 3 vols. (New York: Macmillan, 1927), I, 466. Briffault writes: "The art of pottery is a feminine invention; the original potter was a woman."

43. See Lucy R. Lippard, *Overlay: Contemporary Art and the Art of Prehistory* (New York: Random House, Pantheon Books, 1983), p. 57. Lippard writes: "A thousand years ago, the great Anasazi 'apartment buildings' of the Southwest, like Pueblo Bonito in Chaco Canyon, were built of stone and adobe by women."

44. Matilda Joslyn Gage, speech delivered at the National Woman's Rights Convention, Syracuse, N.Y., September 1852. Cited in *History of Woman Suffrage*, ed. by Elizabeth Cady Stanton, Susan B. Anthony, and Matilda Joslyn Gage (New York: Fowler and Wells, 1881), I, 529.

45. Kate Clinton, "Making Light: Notes on Feminist Humor," *Trivia: A Journal of Ideas*, 1 (Fall 1982), pp. 38–39.

46. Anger, *Protection for Women*, in *by a Woman writt*, pp. 27–28.

47. Walker, "In Search of Our Mothers' Gardens," in *In Search of Our Mothers' Gardens* (New York: Harcourt Brace Jovanovich, Harvest Books, 1983), p. 233.

48. Kramer and Sprenger, *Malleus Maleficarum*, Part II, Q. I, Ch. VII.

49. Ibid., Part I, Q. IX.

50. Lippard, *Overlay*, p. 57.

51. Daly, *Pure Lust: Elemental Feminist Philosophy*, p. 362.

52. Monique Wittig, *Les Guérillères*, trans. by David Le Vay (New York: The Viking Press, 1971), p. 90.

53. See John M. Leighty, "It's Gooney Time at Midway," *Boston Globe*,

Dec. 7, 1985, p. 2. Leighty reports that six gooneys were taken from their home on Midway Island and flown to Los Angeles, driven to Seattle and released. "Within 48 hours . . . all six had found their way back to Midway, a tiny dot on the map some 1,380 miles west of the Hawaiian Islands."

54. Dale Spender, *Man Made Language* (Boston: Routledge & Kegan Paul, 1980), p. 92.

55. The Girlillas have independently produced a tape of their songs entitled "Urban Scrawl, Suburban Crawl," August 1984.

56. Diana Beguine, personal communication, Feb. 25, 1986.

57. Aeschylus, *Prometheus Bound,* in *An Anthology of Greek Tragedy,* ed. by Albert Cook and Edwin Dolin (Indianapolis: Bobbs-Merrill, 1972), p. 89.

58. Walker, "In Search of Our Mothers' Gardens," in *In Search of Our Mothers' Gardens,* p. 241.

59. Walker, *The Color Purple,* p. 167.

60. Elizabeth Gould Davis, *The First Sex* (New York: G. P. Putnam's Sons, 1971), p. 15.

61. Cited by Laurie Lisle, *Portrait of an Artist: A Biography of Georgia O'Keeffe* (New York: Seaview Books, 1980), p. 190.

62. *Gaelic Proverbs,* ed. by Alexander Nicholson (Edinburgh: MacLachlan and Stewart, 1882), p. 179.

63. See Anne Cameron, *Daughters of Copper Woman* (Vancouver, British Columbia: Press Gang Publishers, 1981).

64. Sojourner Truth used the title *Book of Life* to Name her personal archives. This collection includes correspondence, newspaper interviews and accounts of her speeches, autographs of famous people she met, notices of her speeches, and other memorabilia. See *Narrative of Sojourner Truth* (Chicago: Johnson Publishing Company, Inc., Ebony Classics, 1970). The work contains a "History of Her Labors and Correspondence Drawn from Her *Book of Life.*"

65. See Lynn V. Andrews, *Flight of the Seventh Moon: The Teaching of the Shields* (New York: Harper and Row, 1984), p. 50.

66. Susan B. Anthony, personal correspondence, cited in Ida Husted Harper, *The Life and Work of Susan B. Anthony* (Indianapolis: The Hollenbeck Press, 1898), p. 366.

67. "Nonchapter Thirteen: Cat/egorical Appendix," in Daly, *Pure Lust: Elemental Feminist Philosophy,* p. 414.

68. Andrea Dworkin, *Right-wing Women* (New York: G. P. Putnam's Sons, Perigee Books, 1983), p. 237.

69. This word was invented by Jan Raymond (Conversation, November 1972).

70. J. E. Cirlot, *A Dictionary of Symbols,* trans. by Jack Sage (New York: Philosophical Library, 1962), p. 165.

71. Helen Diner, *Mothers and Amazons: The First Feminine History of Culture,* ed. and trans. by John Philip Lundin (New York: The Julian Press, Inc., 1965), p. 24.

72. Davis, *The First Sex,* p. 80.

73. From "The March of the Women," words by Cicely Hamilton, music by Ethel Smyth; copyright 1911 by Ethel Smyth (London: J. Curwen and Sons, Ltd., 1911). This song was sung by British suffragists in marches and in various prisons when captured.

74. Edith Sitwell, "Three Poor Witches," in *The Collected Poems of Edith Sitwell* (New York: Vanguard Press, 1968), pp. 13–14.

75. John Packs, *A Glossary of Arms Control Terms* (Washington, D.C.: Arms Control Association, 1979).

76. Sylvia Beach, *Shakespeare and Company,* p. 99.

77. Rachel L. Carson, *The Sea Around Us,* rev. ed. (New York: New American Library, Mentor Books, 1961), p. 142.

78. Rachel L. Carson, *The Edge of the Sea* (Boston: Houghton Mifflin Company, 1955), p. 14.

79. Emily Erwin Culpepper, "Mermaids: A Symbol for Female-Identified Psychic Self-Reflection," *Woman of Power* (Spring 1984), pp. 42–45. See also Emily Erwin Culpepper, "Philosophia in a Feminist Key: Revolt of the Symbols" (unpublished Th.D. dissertation, Harvard University, 1983), pp. 381–408.

80. T. S. Eliot, "The Love Song of J. Alfred Prufrock," cited in *Bartlett's Familiar Quotations,* p. 1001a.

81. Diana Beguine, personal communication, Winter Solstice, 1985.

82. Eudora Welty, *One Writer's Beginnings* (Cambridge, Mass.: Harvard University Press, 1984), p. 10.

83. For more on "loose women" see Janice G. Raymond, *A Passion for Friends: Toward a Philosophy of Female Affection* (Boston: Beacon Press, 1986), pp. 62, 64–70, 73–79, 98–108.

84. Virginia Woolf, *A Room of One's Own* (New York: Harcourt, Brace & World, 1929; Harbinger Books, 1957), p. 86. Woolf is referring to a passage from Mary Carmichael's first novel, *Life's Adventure,* published in October 1928.

85. This song was collected and sung by Bessie Jones, folklorist and musician from the Georgia Sea Islands, Georgia, U.S.A. See Bessie Jones and Bess Lomax Hawes, *Step It Down* (New York: Harper and Row, 1972), p. 204.

86. Walker, *The Woman's Encyclopedia,* p. 243.

87. Ibid., p. 730.

88. Carolina Maria de Jesus, *Child of the Dark,* trans. by David St. Clair (New York: New American Library, Signet Books, 1962), p. 21.

89. Emily Brontë, *Wuthering Heights* (New York: Random House, The Modern Library, 1950), p. 93.

90. Holly Near, "Mountain Song," sung by Meg Christian on *Face the Music,* Olivia Records, LF-913-B-RE-1, 1977.

91. Raymond, *A Passion for Friends,* pp. 41–42.

92. Meg Christian, "Song to My Mama," *I Know You Know,* Thumbelina Music, Olivia Records, LF 902, 1974.

93. See Woolf, *Three Guineas,* pp. 106–20.

94. This word was invented by Denise D. Connors (Conversation, Boston, Mass., December 1975).

95. For a further discussion of Parthenogenesis, see Anne Dellenbaugh, "She Who Is and Is Not Yet: An Essay on Parthenogenesis," *Trivia: A Journal of Ideas,* 1 (Fall 1982), pp. 43–63.

96. This definition is developed and expanded in Emily Erwin Culpepper, "Philosophia: Feminist Methodology: Constructing a Female Train of Thought," *Journal of Feminist Studies in Religion,* vol. 3, no. 2 (Fall, 1987).

97. This definition is developed by Emily Erwin Culpepper in "Philosophia in a Feminist Key: Revolt of the Symbols," esp. pp. 1–53.

98. Sylvia Plath, "Lady Lazarus," *Ariel* (New York: Harper and Row, 1961), p. 9.

99. See Katharine Briggs, *An Encyclopedia of Fairies* (New York: Pantheon Books, 1976), p. 230.

100. Cited in Morgan, *Sisterhood Is Global,* p. 28.

101. Cited in Nicholson, *Gaelic Proverbs,* p. 129.

102. Toni Morrison, *Sula* (New York: Alfred A. Knopf, 1973).

103. Diana Beguine, "War Stories," unpublished manuscript, 1984.

104. Zora Neale Hurston, *Dust Tracks on a Road,* 2nd ed., ed. and with an intro-

duction by Robert E. Hemenway (Urbana, Ill.: University of Illinois Press, 1942, 1970, 1984), p. 40.

105. Aphra Behn, Epilogue from *Sir Patient Fancy,* reprinted in Angeline Goreau, *Reconstructing Aphra: A Social Biography of Aphra Behn* (New York: The Dial Press, 1980), p. 234.

106. See Hurston, *Dust Tracks on a Road,* esp. pp. 57–60.

107. Mina Loy, "Feminist Manifesto" (1914) in *The Last Lunar Baedeker* (Highlands, N.C.: The Jargon Society, 1982), p. 269.

108. See Thomas Aquinas, *Summa theologiae* I, Q. 81.

109. Christine de Pizan, *The Book of the City of Ladies* (1405), trans. by Earl Jeffrey Richards (New York: Persea Books, 1982), pp. 99–100.

110. Andrea Dworkin, *Pornography: Men Possessing Women* (New York: G. P. Putnam's Sons, Perigee Books, 1979, 1980, 1981), p. 53.

111. Paracelsus, "Book of Nymphs, Sylphs, Pygmies, and Salamanders, and Kindred Beings" (1616), in *The Mystical and Medical Philosophy of Paracelsus,* by Manly P. Hall (Los Angeles, Calif.: The Philosophical Research Society, 1964), p. 78.

112. Florynce R. Kennedy, quoted in Gloria Steinem, "The Verbal Karate of Florynce R. Kennedy, Esq.," *Ms.,* March 1973.

113. See Diane Wolkstein and Samuel Noah Kramer, *Inanna, Queen of Heaven and Earth: Her Stories and Hymns from Sumer* (New York: Harper and Row, 1983), p. 36.

114. Monica Sjöö and Barbara Mor, *The Great Cosmic Mother: Rediscovering the Religion of the Earth* (San Francisco: Harper and Row, 1987), p. 97.

115. Alfonsina Storni, "It May Be" (trans. from the Spanish) in *The Other Voice: Twentieth Century Women's Poetry in Translation,* ed. by Joanna Bankier et al. (New York: W. W. Norton, 1976), p. 20. Storni (1892–1938) lived and worked in Argentina.

116. Ms. Wild Cat, *Prolegomenon to the Musings of Ms. Wild Cat* (Catatonia, N.H.: Feline Press, 1990 A.F.), p. 13.

117. Readers are requested to send personal narratives of Syn-Crone-icities to Ms. Wild Cat, who is currently engaged in compiling a collection of "coincidences" for her forthcoming work, *Meetings at Crossroads of Species.* Please send material to Ms. Wild Cat, c/o Beacon Press, 25 Beacon St., Boston, MA 02108.

118. Elizabeth Cady Stanton, Letter to Woman's Suffrage Convention, 1851, in *History of Woman Suffrage,* ed. by Elizabeth Cady Stanton, Susan B. Anthony, and Matilda Joslyn Gage (New York: Fowler and Wells, 1881), I, 816.

119. Humez, *Gifts of Power,* p. 42.

120. Cited in Humez, *Gifts of Power,* p. 44.

121. William Blake, "The Tyger," in *The Complete Poetry and Prose of William Blake,* newly revised edition, ed. by David Erdman (Garden City, N.Y.: Anchor Press/Doubleday, 1982), p. 24.

122. Warner, Letter to Martha Bacon Ballinger, Nov. 11, 1961, in *Letters,* p. 195.

123. For further information see C. Kerényi, "Kore," in C. G. Jung and C. Kerényi, *Essays on a Science of Mythology: The Myth of the Divine Child and the Mysteries of Eleusis* (Princeton, N.J.: Princeton University Press, 1969).

124. This journal can be obtained by writing to *Trivia,* P.O. Box 606, N. Amherst, Mass. 01059.

125. Cirlot, *A Dictionary of Symbols,* p. 165.

126. *You Have Struck a Rock: Women and Political Repression in South Africa* (London: International Defense Aid Fund for Southern Africa, 1980), p. 17.

127. Johnson, *From Housewife to Heretic,* pp. 106–107.

128. Judy Grahn, *The Queen of Wands* (Trumansburg, N.Y.: The Crossing Press, 1982), p. xiii.

129. Gage, *Woman, Church and State,* p. 105.

130. Kramer and Sprenger, *Malleus Maleficarum,* Part II, Q. I, Ch. VII.

131. Barbara G. Walker, *The Crone: Woman of Age, Wisdom, and Power* (San Francisco: Harper and Row, 1985), p. 13.

WORD-WEB THREE

The inhabitants of the foreground, their activities and characteristics

1. This word was invented by Diana Beguine, personal communication, June 1984.

2. Virginia Woolf, *Three Guineas* (New York: Harcourt, Brace & World, 1938; Harbinger Books, 1966), p. 94.

3. For a poetic commentary on the a-Musing of Sylvia Plath, see Robin Morgan, "Arraignment," in *Monster* (New York: Random House, Vintage Books, 1972), pp. 76–78.

4. Cited in Arlene Eisen, *Women and Revolution in Viet Nam* (London: Zed Books Ltd., 1984), p. 12.

5. Valerie Solanas, *Scum Manifesto* (1967, 1968; London: The Matriarchy Study Group, 1983), p. 28.

6. For an enlightening discussion of male comradeship, see J. Glenn Gray, *The Warriors: Reflections on Men in Battle* (New York: Harper Torchbooks, 1967), p. 102.

7. D. H. Lawrence, *Studies in Classic American Literature* (New York: Viking Press, 1964), p. 169.

8. Andrea Dworkin, "The Root Cause," in *Our Blood: Prophecies and Discourses on Sexual Politics* (New York: G. P. Putnam's Sons, Perigee Books, 1976), p. 103.

9. *Boston Globe,* April 23, 1982.

10. See Barbara Roberts, M.D., "Psychosurgery: The 'Final Solution' to the 'Woman Problem'?" *The Second Wave* II, no. 1 (1972), p. 13. See Walter Freeman and James W. Watts, *Psychosurgery in the Treatment of Mental Disorders and Intractable Pain* (Springfield, Ill.: Charles C. Thomas, Publisher, 1942, 1950), pp. 215–18.

11. Cited in Marc Ian Barasch, *The Little Black Book of Atomic War* (New York: Dell Publishing Co., Inc., 1983), p. 20.

12. Ibid., p. 20.

13. Hannah Tillich, *From Time to Time* (New York: Stein and Day, 1973), p. 14.

14. See Sandra M. Gilbert and Susan Gubar, *The Madwoman in the Attic* (New Haven: Yale University Press, 1979), p. 6.

15. William Broyles Jr., "Why Men Love War," *Esquire,* November 1984, p. 56.

16. Pandita Ramabai Sarasvati, *The High-Caste Hindu Woman* (New York: Fleming H. Revell, 1901), p. 52.

17. John Donne, Elegie XIX, "Going to Bed," in *Poems of John Donne,* ed. by Herbert Grierson (London: Oxford University Press, 1957), p. 107.

18. Cited in E. J. Dionne, Jr., "Pope Tells Synod View on Vatican II," *New York Times,* Dec. 8, 1985, p. 17.

19. Robert Southey, Letter of March 1837 to Charlotte Brontë, in *The Brontës: Their Lives, Friendships and Correspondence,* ed. by Thomas J. Wise and John A. Symington, 2 vols. (Philadelphia: Porcupine Press, Inc., 1980), I, 155.

20. John Greenway, "What Really Went on in Eden" ("review" of *The First Sex* by Elizabeth Gould Davis), in *National Review,* Oct. 22, 1971, p. 1183.

21. For a brief history of the "doomsday clock," see "Three Minutes to Midnight," *Bulletin of the Atomic Scientists,* January 1984, p. 2.

22. George Orwell, *1984* (1949; New York: New American Library, Signet Classics, 1961), pp. 32–33.

23. Cited by Lou Cannon in "The Year's Reaganisms," *Boston Globe,* Dec. 31, 1984, p. 11.

24. This expression was Dis-covered by Emily Culpepper, during a conversation in Leverett, Mass., in April 1983.

25. pope Pius XI, Encyclical Letter, *Casti Connubii,* Dec. 31, 1930.

26. Francis Bacon, "Of Marriage and Single Life," in *Essays,* cited in *Bartlett's Familiar Quotations,* p. 208a.

27. pope John Paul II, in his concluding address to the "extraordinary Synod of Roman Catholic Bishops," cited in James L. Franklin, "Synod Seen Proving Unity of Church," *Boston Globe,* Dec. 9, 1985, p. 1.

28. Cited in R. Donovan, "That Friend of Your Wife's Named Dior," *Colliers,* June 10, 1955, pp. 34–39.

29. Song cited in *Sisterhood Is Powerful,* ed. by Robin Morgan (New York: Random House, 1970), p. 555.

30. This word was invented and explained by Françoise d' Eaubonne, in *Le Féminisme ou la mort* (Paris: Pierre Horay, 1974), pp. 15–83.

31. Henry M. Sondheimer, M.D., Letter, *The Hastings Center Report,* August 1983, p. 50.

32. For an analysis of fetal identification as it operates in the 1975 film *Jaws,* see Jane E. Caputi, "'Jaws' as Patriarchal Myth," *The Journal of Popular Film,* vol. 6, no. 4 (1978), pp. 305–25.

33. Simone de Beauvoir, *The Second Sex,* trans. and ed. by H. M. Parshley (1952; New York: Random House, Vintage Books, 1974), p. 193.

34. Margaret Atwood, *The Handmaid's Tale* (Boston: Houghton Mifflin Company, 1986), p. 194.

35. Pierre Teilhard de Chardin, S.J., "The End of the World" (1924), *The Future of Man,* trans. by Norman Denny (New York: Harper and Row, 1964), p. 308.

36. This text is no longer generally believed to have been written by paul; however, it surely was written under the influence of the pauline tradition.

37. Rudyard Kipling, "The Betrothed," stanza 25, cited in *Bartlett's* [all too familiar] *Quotations,* p. 871b.

38. Heinrich Kramer and James Sprenger, *The Malleus Maleficarum,* trans. with introduction, bibliography, and notes by the Rev. Montague Summers (1928; New York: Dover Publications, Inc., 1971), Part I, Question VI, p. 47.

39. Cited in Paul Boyer, *By the Bomb's Early Light: American Thought and Culture at the Dawn of the Atomic Age* (New York: Pantheon Books, 1985), p. 6.

40. Gerard Manley Hopkins, "God's Grandeur," in *The Norton Anthology of Modern Poetry,* ed. by Richard Ellman and Robert O'Clair (New York: W. W. Norton, 1973), p. 80.

41. Norman Mailer, *Genius and Lust: A Journey Through the Major Writings of Henry Miller* (New York: Grove Press, Inc., 1976), p. xiii.

42. For more on Dian Fossey, see Sheila Rule, "Slain Naturalist's Life: Clues to the Mystery?" *New York Times,* Jan. 24, 1986, p. 1.

43. See Andrea Dworkin, *Pornography: Men Possessing Women* (New York: G. P. Putnam's Sons, Perigee Books, 1979, 1980, 1981), pp. 70–100.

44. Charles McCabe, in *San Francisco Chronicle,* Oct. 7, 1971, p. 43. Cited in Susan

Brownmiller, *Against Our Will: Men, Women and Rape* (New York: Simon and Schuster, 1975), p. 294.

45. Janice G. Raymond, *A Passion for Friends: Toward a Philosophy of Female Affection* (Boston: Beacon Press, 1986), p. 3.

46. Cited in Raymond, *A Passion for Friends*, p. 4. Johnson's comments first appeared in his "Managing the Great Man's Memory," review of *Adieux: A Farewell to Sartre*, by Simone de Beauvoir, in *New York Times Book Review*, May 6, 1984, p. 11.

47. Cited in *Up from the Pedestal: Selected Writings in the History of American Feminism*, ed. by Aileen S. Kraditor (Chicago: Quadrangle Books, 1968), p. 197.

48. *Boston Globe*, Jan. 21, 1981, p. 14.

49. For information concerning the techniques of subliminal manipulation see Wilson Bryan Key, *Subliminal Seduction* (New York: New American Library, Signet Books, 1973). See also Key's book *Media Sexploitation* (Englewood Cliffs, N.J.: Prentice-Hall, Inc., 1976).

50. See Charlotte Perkins Gilman, *The Living of Charlotte Perkins Gilman: An Autobiography* (New York: Appleton-Century, 1935), p. 96.

51. Cited in Colin Nickerson, "Third World Delegates Protest Speech by Israeli Women," *Boston Globe*, July 23, 1985, p. 8.

52. For more information on Sims, see G. J. Barker-Benfield, *The Horrors of the Half-Known Life: Male Attitudes Toward Women and Sexuality in Nineteenth-Century America* (New York: Harper and Row, 1976), pp. 91–119.

53. See Virginia Woolf, *A Room of One's Own* (New York: Harcourt, Brace & World, 1929; Harbinger Books, 1957), p. 35.

54. Jean Caldwell, "6,000 Hear Mother Teresa at UMass," *Boston Globe*, June 23, 1985, p. 25.

55. Edward Behr, Introduction to Helmut Newton, *Sleepless Nights* (New York: Congreve, 1978), unpaged.

56. Dworkin, "The Root Cause," in *Our Blood*, p. 105.

57. For more information, see Gena Corea, *The Mother Machine: Reproductive Technologies from Artificial Insemination to Artificial Wombs* (New York: Harper and Row, 1985), p. 284.

58. For detailed information on reproductive technologies, see Corea, *The Mother Machine*.

59. This word was Dis-covered by Eleanor Mullaley (Conversation, Boston, 1980).

60. Robert Graves, *The Greek Myths*, 2 vols. (Baltimore: Penguin Books, 1955, 1960), I, 21. 0.

61. Pierre Teilhard de Chardin, S.J., "Some Reflections on the Spiritual Repercussions of the Atom Bomb" (1946), in *The Future of Man*, p. 140.

62. Thomas Aquinas, *Summa theologiae* I, q. 92, a. 1, ad 1.

63. Gertrude Stein, "Patriarchal Poetry," in *Bee Time Vine and Other Pieces (1913–1927)* (New Haven: Yale University Press, 1953), pp. 263–64.

64. Cited in F. H. Knelman, *Reagan, God, and the Bomb: From Myth to Policy in the Nuclear Arms Race* (Buffalo, N.Y.: Prometheus Books, 1985), pp. 182–83.

65. This word was invented by Emily Culpepper (Conversation, Leverett, Mass., May 1983).

66. Quentin Bell, *Virginia Woolf: A Biography* (New York: Harcourt Brace Jovanovich, Harvest Books, 1972).

67. Robert Jay Lifton and Kai Erickson, "Nuclear War's Effect on the Mind," in Robert Jay Lifton and Richard Falk, *Indefensible Weapons: The Political and Psychological Case Against Nuclearism* (New York: Basic Books, Inc., 1982), p. 278.

68. The concept of "psychic numbing" has been developed at length by Robert

Jay Lifton. See Robert Jay Lifton, *Death in Life: Survivors of Hiroshima* (New York: Simon and Schuster, Touchstone Books, 1967). See also Lifton and Falk, *Indefensible Weapons.*

69. From Morgan, "The One That Got Away or The Woman Who Made It," in *Monster,* p. 70.

70. An analysis of the passive voice was first developed by the linguist Julia Penelope (Stanley). See her article "Prescribed Passivity: The Language of Sexism," in *Views on Language,* ed. by Reza Ordoubadian and Wilburga Von Raffler Engel (Murfreesboro, Tenn.: Inter-University Publishing, 1975).

71. Cited in Kraditor, *Up from the Pedestal,* p. 196.

72. Sylvia Plath, *The Bell Jar* (New York: Bantam, 1971), p. 55.

73. See Helen Caldicott, *Missile Envy* (New York: William Morrow, 1984).

74. Norman O. Brown, *Love's Body* (New York: Vintage Books, 1968), p. 134.

75. Penelope, "Prescribed Passivity," in *Views on Language.*

76. Monique Wittig, "Author's Note," *The Lesbian Body,* trans. by David Le Vay (New York: William Morrow, 1975), pp. 10–11.

77. Cited in de Beauvoir, *The Second Sex,* p. 246.

78. Diana Beguine, personal communication, Feb. 2, 1986.

79. Alice Walker, *The Color Purple* (New York: Harcourt Brace Jovanovich, 1982), p. 168.

80. D. H. Lawrence, *Women in Love* (New York: Viking Press, 1960), p. 337.

81. For further information, see Kathleen Barry, *Female Sexual Slavery* (Englewood Cliffs, N.J.: Prentice-Hall, Inc., 1979), pp. 73–102.

82. For information concerning F. Scott Fitzgerald's pillaging of the creativity of his wife Zelda Sayre, see Nancy Milford, *Zelda* (New York: Harper and Row, 1970). See also Phyllis Chesler, *Women and Madness* (Garden City, N.Y.: Doubleday & Co., Inc., 1972), pp. 5–9.

83. Karl Menninger, with the collaboration of Jeanetta Lyle Menninger, *Love Against Hate* (New York: Harcourt, Brace & Company, 1942), pp. 117–18.

84. For information on Harlow's re-search, see Richard Ryder, "Experiments on Animals" in *Animals, Men and Morals: An Enquiry into the Maltreatment of Non-Humans,* ed. by Stanley and Roslind Godlovitch and John Harris (New York: Taplinger, 1972). See also Peter Singer, *Animal Liberation: A New Ethics for Our Treatment of Animals* (New York: Avon Books, 1975), pp. 41–44.

85. Pete Seeger, "Turn, Turn," on *The Bitter and the Sweet,* Columbia, CL1916, 1962. The words of this song were adapted from Eccles. 3:1–8.

86. "Tehran Using Force to Cover up Women," *Boston Globe,* June 7, 1986, p. 4.

87. See *New York Times,* Feb. 15, 1984, p. A26 (editorial page).

88. See Erik Eckholm, "Will There Be Enough Chimps for Research?" *New York Times,* Nov. 19, 1985, p. C1. Eckholm writes: "With the nation's future supply of research chimpanzees in jeopardy, Federal authorities plan to create a special population of 350 pampered animals that would be exempted from medical duties. . . ."

89. A marine sergeant, describing a gang rape in Vietnam, concluded his narrative with the following statement: "But at any rate, they raped the girl, and then the last man to make love to her shot her in the head." Cited in Susan Brownmiller, *Against Our Will: Men, Women, and Rape* (New York: Simon and Schuster, 1975), p. 110.

90. "Literary Garbage," anon. review, *Saturday Review,* 33 (Jan. 27, 1862), p. 109, cited in Angeline Goreau, *Reconstructing Aphra: A Social Biography of Aphra Behn* (New York: The Dial Press, 1980), p. 14.

91. Granville Hicks, *The Great Tradition* (New York: Macmillan, 1933), p. 104.

92. This word was Dis-covered by Janice G. Raymond in *The Transsexual Empire: The Making of the She-Male* (Boston: Beacon Press, 1979), pp. xv–xvi. Raymond credits Emily Culpepper for the language of this definition.

93. James L. Franklin, "An Influential Voice at Synod," *Boston Globe,* Dec. 5, 1985, p. 22.

94. Alfred, lord Tennyson, "Locksley Hall," cited in *Bartlett's* [all too familiar] *Quotations,* p. 647b.

95. Cited in "Know Your Enemy: A Sampling of Sexist Quotes," in Morgan, *Sisterhood Is Powerful,* p. 33.

96. This word was suggested by Diana Beguine (Conversation, January 1986).

97. Rudyard Kipling, "The White Man's Burden" (1899), cited in *Bartlett's Familiar Quotations,* p. 875b.

98. Alice Walker, "Only Justice Can Stop a Curse," in *In Search of Our Mothers' Gardens* (New York: Harcourt Brace Jovanovich, Harvest Books, 1983), p. 341.

99. Anne Cameron, *Daughters of Copper Woman* (Vancouver, British Columbia: Press Gang Publishers), 1981, p. 12.

100. Abigail Adams, cited in *Domestick Beings,* selected by June Sprigg (New York: Alfred A. Knopf, 1984), p. 23.

101. This word was Dis-covered by Nancy Kelly (Conversation, Newton, Mass., November 1986).

102. Cameron, *Daughters of Copper Woman,* p. 32.

103. saint Jerome, PL 26, 570. *Comm. in epist. ad Ephes.,* III, 5.

104. Brownmiller, *Against Our Will,* pp. 14–15.

105. Louky Bersianik, *The Euguélionne,* a triptych novel, trans. by Gerry Denis, Alison Hewitt, Donna Murray, and Martha O'Brien (Victoria, British Columbia: Press Porcépic, 1981), pp. 131–32.

106. Marabel Morgan, *The Total Woman* (New York: Pocket Books, 1975), p. 96. See also p. 60.

107. Ruth Carter Stapleton, *The Gift of Inner Healing* (Waco, Tex.: Word Books, Publisher, 1976), p. 32.

108. Cited in Jan Zimmerman, "Technology and the Future of Women: Haven't We Met Somewhere Before?" *Women's Studies International Quarterly,* vol. 4, no. 3 (1981), pp. 355–67.

109. Sylvia Plath, "Daddy," in *The Norton Anthology of Literature by Women: The Tradition in English,* ed. by Sandra M. Gilbert and Susan Gubar (New York: W. W. Norton, 1985), p. 2209.

110. Erich Neumann has pointed out that "the magical caldron or pot is always [in early imagery] in the hand of the female mana figure, the priestess, or, later, the witch." Erich Neumann, *The Great Mother: An Analysis of the Archetype,* trans. by Ralph Manheim, Bollingen Series XLVII (Princeton, N.J.: Princeton University Press, 1972), p. 288.

111. Song cited in Morgan, *Sisterhood Is Powerful,* p. 554.

112. Cited in Barasch, *The Little Black Book of Atomic War,* p. 58.

113. Solanas, *Scum Manifesto,* p. 4.

114. From Martin Luther, *The Table Talk,* trans. and ed. by T. G. Tappert, in *Luther's Works,* vol. LIV (Philadelphia: Fortress Press, 1967), p. 8.

APPENDICULAR WEB ONE

Exposing elementary terms and phrases: mummies, dummies, anti-biotics, and reversals

1. See Manly P. Hall, *The Mystical and Medical Philosophy of Paracelsus* (Los Angeles: The Philosophical Research Society, Inc., 1964), p. 54.

2. Richard N. Ostling, "At the Synod, 'Variety in Unity,'" *Time*, Dec. 16, 1985, p. 59.

3. Anne Cameron, *Daughters of Copper Woman* (Vancouver, British Columbia: Press Gang Publishers, 1981), p. 12.

4. Robert Jastrow, "How to Make Nuclear War Obsolete," Part One, *Science Digest*, June 1984, p. 40.

5. *McGraw-Hill Dictionary of Scientific and Technical Terms* (New York: McGraw-Hill, 1974, 1981).

6. John Packs, *A Glossary of Arms Control Terms* (Washington, D.C.: Arms Control Association, 1979), n.p.

7. Ibid.

8. "Third-generation" nuclear technology is different from "first-generation" (the atom bomb) and "second-generation" (the hydrogen bomb) in that it posits devices such as X-ray lasers, directed microwave weapons, and others still undisclosed. See William J. Broad, "The Young Physicists: Atoms and Patriotism Amid the Coke Bottles," *New York Times*, Jan. 31, 1984, pp. C1, C5.

9. *The Random House Dictionary of New Information Technology*, ed. by A. J. Meadows, M. Gordon, and A. Singleton (New York: Vintage Books, 1982).

10. George Orwell, *1984* (1949; New York: New American Library, Signet Classics, 1961), p. 48.

11. The word *anti-biotic* was suggested by Krystina Colburn (personal communication, Jan. 13, 1985).

12. See Robert C. Aldridge, *The Counterforce Syndrome: A Guide to U.S. Nuclear Weapons and Strategic Doctrine* (Washington, D.C.: Institute for Policy Studies, 1978), p. 83.

13. Ibid., p. 81.

14. Packs, *A Glossary of Arms Control Terms*.

15. This term was used by General Bernard Rogers, in an interview reported by William Beecher in his article "General Outlines Plan to Avert Nuclear War," *Boston Globe*, Dec. 29, 1984.

16. See Fred Landis, "CIA Psychological Warfare Operations: Case Studies in Chile, Jamaica, and Nicaragua," *Science for the People*, January/February 1982, pp. 6–37.

17. On Nov. 3, 1984, Ronald Reagan denied that references to "neutralizing" Nicaraguan officials in a C.I.A. manual had anything to do with assassination. He said that this reference meant removing them from office. See Joel Brinkley, "C.I.A. Said to Urge Disciplinary Plan for Latin Manual," *New York Times*, Nov. 10, 1984, p. 1.

18. The word *man-akin* was invented by Mary Ellen McCarthy (personal communication, Jan. 13, 1985).

19. *Quick Thrust* was explained in "25 U.S. Warships in Caribbean, in Easy Reach of Nicaragua," *New York Times*, Nov. 9, 1984, p. 6.

20. See James Edward Oberg, *New Earths: Restructuring Earth and Other Planets* (New York: New American Library, 1981), p. 16.

21. See Orwell, *1984*, pp. 32–33. Orwell, the obvious source of *Webster's* defini-

tion, develops the concept at some length, explaining that it means "to forget, whatever it was necessary to forget, then to draw it back into memory again at the moment when it was needed, and then promptly to forget it again, and above all, to apply the same process to the process itself—that was the ultimate subtlety: consciously to induce unconsciousness and then, once again, to become unconscious of the act of hypnosis you had just performed. Even to understand the word 'doublethink' involved the use of doublethink."

22. This passage is from *Psychologie comparée de l'homme et de la femme* (1898) and is cited in Edmund Bergler, *Fashion and the Unconscious* (New York: Robert Brunner, 1953), p. 39.

23. Valerie Solanas, *SCUM Manifesto* (1967, 1968; London: The Matriarchy Study Group, 1983), pp. 3–4. Copies can be obtained from The Matriarchy Study Group, c/o 190 Upper St., London N.1.

24. Jerry Ackerman, "Do Mice Hold Too Much Power Over Us?" *Boston Globe*, Dec. 16, 1985, p. 49.

25. Lisa Belkin, "For Thriving Furriers, Protesters Pose Threats," *New York Times*, Dec. 17, 1985, pp. D1, D5.

26. See *off our backs: a women's newsjournal*, vol. 15, no. 6 (June 1985). This issue has several important articles about the conflict over pornography. See also *off our backs: a women's newsjournal*, vol. 15, no. 8 (August–September 1985) for "An Open Letter on Pornography: A Critical Response to the FACT Brief," pp. 28–29.

27. See Adriane J. Fugh-Berman, "Right-to-Life Convention," *off our backs: a women's newsjournal*, vol. 15, no. 8 (August–September 1985), p. 7.

28. Ibid.

29. Pierre Teilhard de Chardin, *The Future of Man*, trans. by Norman Denny (New York: Harper and Row, 1964), p. 146.

30. Johannes Kepler, "Letter to Herwart von Hohenburg," Feb. 10, 1605, trans. and quoted in Gerald Holton, "Johannes Kepler's Universe: Its Physics and Metaphysics," in *Thematic Origins of Scientific Thought: Kepler to Einstein* (Cambridge, Mass.: Harvard University Press, 1973), p. 72.

31. René Descartes, *Discourse on Method*, Part V.

32. For a discussion of the limitations of male womb envy theories see Daly, *Gyn/Ecology*, pp. 57–64. These limitations are evident in Philip E. Slater, *The Glory of Hera: Greek Mythology and the Greek Family* (Boston: Beacon Press, 1968).

33. Any Nag, noting the male propensity for penis measurement—from the locker room to the symbolic realms of the nuclear arms race—is aware of the phenomenon of penis envy/missile envy. The message is conveyed nicely in the title of Helen Caldicott's book *Missile Envy: The Arms Race and Nuclear War* (New York: William Morrow, 1984).

34. Millions of women have been and still are physically castrated. Millions are genitally mutilated in Africa, by clitoridectomy and/or infibulation. (See Daly, *Gyn/Ecology*, Chapter Five.) With the rise of the profession of gynecology in the United States and Europe in the nineteenth century, clitoridectomies and unnecessary oophorectomies became legitimate medical practices, for the purpose of taming women. (See *Gyn/Ecology*, Chapter Seven.) It is essential also to consider that one definition of *castration* is "to deprive of vigor or vitality (*intelligence* is castrated—John Dewey)" (*Webster's*). The psychic/intellectual/emotional castration of women is ubiquitous under patriarchy. (For an analysis of common dictionary definitions of *castration*, as these relate to women, see Daly, *Pure Lust*, pp. 166–70.)

35. See Barbara Ehrenreich and Deirdre English, *Witches, Midwives and Nurses: A History of Women Healers*, 2nd ed. (Old Westbury, N.Y.: Feminist Press, 1973).

36. Gena Corea, *The Hidden Malpractice: How American Medicine Mistreats*

Women, updated edition (1977; New York: Harper Colophon, 1985), pp. 247–48. See also Gena Corea, *The Mother Machine: Reproductive Technologies from Artificial Insemination to Artificial Wombs* (New York: Harper and Row, 1985).

37. See G. J. Barker-Benfield, *The Horrors of the Half-Known Life: Male Attitudes Toward Women and Sexuality in Nineteenth-Century America* (New York: Harper and Row, 1976).

38. See Daly, *Gyn/Ecology*, pp. 13–14, 57–64, 69–72. See also Daly, *Pure Lust*, pp. 41, 44, 82–83.

39. Broad, "The Young Physicists," pp. C1, C5.

40. For a thorough and scholarly analysis of this phenomenon, see Janice G. Raymond, *The Transsexual Empire: The Making of the She-Male* (Boston: Beacon Press, 1979). It is important to note that *transsexual* is itself an elementary term requiring myriad reversals to sustain its pseudoreality.

41. Neil Malamuth, Seymour Feshbach, and Yoram Jaffe, "Sexual Arousal and Aggression: Recent Experiments and Theoretical Issues," *The Journal of Social Issues*, vol. 33, no. 2 (1977), p. 129.

42. Virginia Woolf, *Three Guineas* (New York: Harcourt, Brace & World, 1938; Harbinger Books, 1966), p. 52.

43. Ibid., especially pp. 18–21.

APPENDICULAR WEB TWO

Be-Laughing: Nixing, Hexing, and X-ing

1. Information concerning the etymological connection between *follis* and *phallos* is not given in *Webster's* at *fool*, but is clearly revealed in the etymological history at *blow*. Only persistent Searchers will uncover this stunning connection.

2. Modern examples of such authority-legitimating fools are Bob Hope, Johnny Carson, Eddie Murphy, Carroll O'Connor as Archie Bunker (*All in the Family*).

3. In recent years the faces of somber snools and "funny" fools have shown a tendency to merge—to display publicly their heretofore hidden identity. The image of Ronald Reagan is an illustrious example of the blatant blending of the two roles. One of the most ominous indications of psychic numbing in the United States in the 1980s is the fact that Reagan's flagrant foolishness was flaunted before the public for years before being noticed by the majority. Indeed, for a considerable period of time the increase of his popularity appeared to keep pace with the mounting evidence of his ineffable foolishness.

4. Anton C. Zijderveld, *Reality in a Looking-Glass: Rationality Through an Analysis of Traditional Folly* (Boston: Routledge & Kegan Paul, 1982), p. 33.

5. Ibid., p. 33.

6. See Daly, *Pure Lust*, pp. 243–53.

7. See Virginia Woolf, *Three Guineas* (New York: Harcourt, Brace & World, 1938; Harbinger Books, 1966), p. 52. The need for what Woolf Named "freedom from unreal loyalties" has been known by women all over the world. One scholar describes the problem that this poses for ethnographers: "Ethnographers report that women cannot be reached so easily as men: they giggle when young, snort when old, reject the question, laugh at the topic, and the like. The male members of a society frequently see the ethnographer's difficulties as simply a caricature of their own daily case." See Edwin Ardener, "Belief and the Problem of Women," in *The Interpretation of Ritual: Essays in Honour of A. I. Richards*, ed. by Jean Sibyl La Fontaine (London: Tavistock Publications, 1972), p. 137.

8. Hans Peter Duerr, *Dreamtime: Concerning the Boundary Between Wilderness and Civilization,* trans. by Felicitas Goodman (New York: Basil Blackwell, Inc., 1985), p. 46.

9. Ibid., p. 47.

10. Barbara Walker points out that in folk tradition, to open the door of a fairy hill, one must walk around it three times widdershins. See Barbara G. Walker, *The Woman's Encyclopedia of Myths and Secrets* (San Francisco: Harper and Row, 1983), p. 1076. See also Rossell Hope Robbins, *The Encyclopedia of Witchcraft and Demonology* (1959; New York: Bonanza Books, 1981), pp. 421–22.

11. Cited in Duerr, *Dreamtime,* p. 248, n. 29. See also Margaret A. Murray, *The Witch-Cult in Western Europe* (New York: Oxford University Press, 1921), pp. 124, 135.

12. At a seminar held by feminists in Washington, D.C., in 1969, a "futurist" who presented himself as an affiliate of a think tank authorized by President Nixon addressed the group. He told the group that, by the most "optimistic" calculations, the "X-factor" might survive in human society for another twenty years. By "X-factor," he said, he meant something like what is commonly called "free will" and/or "spirit." As this book goes to press, eighteen years have elapsed since the "optimistic" futurist's prediction.

13. Connections between convergence and divergence are discussed in Daly, *Beyond God the Father,* pp. 190–93.

14. In ancient Greece, statues of Hecate, Goddess of Witches, were built at the crossing of three roads with faces turned in three directions. In the Middle Ages, crossroads, specifically the places where three roads converged, were believed to be loci of preternatural visions and happenings. *Trivia,* derived from the latin *trivium* (crossroads) was one of the names of the Triple Goddess.

APPENDICULAR WEB THREE

Spinning Beyond the Compass: Regaining the Sense of Direction

1. Virginia Woolf, *Moments of Being: Unpublished Autobiographical Writings,* ed. and with an introduction and notes by Jeanne Schulkind (New York: Harcourt Brace Jovanovich, 1976), p. 93.

2. See Woolf, *Moments of Being.* She writes: "In certain favorable moods, memories—what one has forgotten—come to the top. . . . I see it—the past—as an avenue lying behind; a long ribbon of scenes, emotions."

3. The "estimative power" was considered to be one of the four "interior senses." When referring to animals, Aquinas called this the "estimative power," but in attributing it to "man" he called it the "cogitative power." He wrote: "But the animal needs to seek or to avoid certain things, not only because they are pleasing or otherwise to the senses, but also on account of other advantages and uses, or disadvantages: just as the sheep runs away when it sees a wolf, not on account of its color or shape, but as a natural enemy: and again a bird gathers together straws, not because they are pleasant to the sense but because they are useful for building its nest. Animals, therefore, need to perceive such intentions, which the exterior sense does not perceive. (See *Summa theologiae,* I, 78, 4c.)

4. Sonia Johnson discusses the power of morphic resonance in her book *Going Out of Our Minds* (Trumansburg, N.Y.: The Crossing Press, 1987), Chapter Seven.

Jumping Off the doomsday clock: Eleven, Twelve . . . Thirteen

1. A brief history of the "doomsday clock" is presented in an editorial entitled "Three Minutes to Midnight," in *Bulletin of the Atomic Scientists,* January 1984, p. 2.

2. The Lies of the media whiteout during the aftermath of Chernobyl precisely illustrate the mystifying manner in which mental and physical contamination—conjoined in deadly wedlock/deadlock—process endlessly together. One stunning example of the American media's coverage/hiding of the effects of Chernobyl was a *Boston Globe* report (published in its "Sci-Tech" section), July 14, 1986, pp. 37, 39. The article states: "Countries outside the Soviet Union received so little radioactive fallout from the Chernobyl nuclear disaster that any potential health risk is too small to calculate, says the head of a US government committee assessing health effects from the accident." The article goes on to discuss the statements of radiation biologist Marvin Goldman, head of a scientific panel assembled by the Department of Energy: "Goldman, who is based at the University of California at Davis, said Europe 'lucked out' because of weather conditions at the time of the disaster. . . . 'There was lots of dispersion, and what came down was washed out by rain' in many areas." Hags who have been in Touch with women in such countries as Sweden, Norway, Germany, Switzerland, Italy, and other parts of Europe are aware of just how "lucky" these women feel to have been trapped in Europe after Chernobyl. Whereas some European newspapers, particularly those published in West Germany, exposed some of the horror, the American media functioned smoothly as "organs" of deception and propaganda concerning this and other nuclear atrocities, whose lethal effects, such as contamination of the food chain, keep spreading.

3. Robert Jay Lifton, "Chernobyl, Three Mile Island, Hiroshima," *New York Times,* May 18, 1986, Section 4, p. 25.

4. A *baxter,* of course, originally meant a female baker. See *The Oxford English Dictionary.*

5. Northern peoples said the cosmic doomsday-wolf Fenrir was fettered by a heavenly chain to the north pole and would be released by the Norns to devour the heavenly father at the end of the world. See Barbara G. Walker, *The Woman's Encyclopedia of Myths and Secrets* (San Francisco: Harper and Row, 1983), pp. 243, 307.

6. Barbara G. Walker, *The Crone: Woman of Age, Wisdom, and Power* (San Francisco: Harper and Row, 1985), pp. 175–76.

7. Ibid., pp. 177–78.